Exploring
the
Philosophy
of
Religion

Exploring the Philosophy of Religion

DAVID STEWART

Department of Philosophy
Ohio University

Prentice-Hall, Inc., Englewood Cliffs, N.J. 07632

Library of Congress Cataloging in Publication Data

Main entry under title:
Exploring the philosophy of religion.

  Includes bibliographies and index.
  1. Religion—Philosophy—Addresses, essays, lectures.
I. Stewart, David,
BL51.E96   200′1   79-18903
ISBN 0-13-297366-9

PRENTICE-HALL INTERNATIONAL, INC., *London*
PRENTICE-HALL OF AUSTRALIA PTY. LIMITED, *Sydney*
PRENTICE-HALL OF CANADA, LTD., *Toronto*
PRENTICE-HALL OF INDIA PRIVATE LIMITED, *New Delhi*
PRENTICE-HALL OF JAPAN, INC., *Tokyo*
PRENTICE-HALL OF SOUTHEAST ASIA PTE. LTD., *Singapore*
WHITEHALL BOOKS LIMITED, *Wellington, New Zealand*

Contents

Preface

The best definition of philosophy I have come across lately is that of Alvin Plantinga, who suggests that philosophical reflection is not much different from just thinking hard.[1] Even if you have never studied philosophy before but are willing to think hard about religion, then this book is for you. It presupposes no philosophical background and asks only that you be willing to work through the topics with care and diligence.

The topics presented here were chosen because they have a permanent place in the philosophy of religion, but the book does not presume that you have to read each chapter in order. You can begin with whatever topic interests you the most. Some books on philosophy of religion offer only a group of selections from famous philosophers. If you have never studied philosophy before, this can be rather bewildering. Other books tell you a lot about philosophy but never confront you firsthand with selections of philosophical writing from significant philosophers. This book gives you both readings and a discussion of the issues. It contains extensive commentary and analysis of the issues followed by selections from philosophers themselves. Some of these philosophers are famous, others are not. I have attempted to avoid including material just because it has become a classic in the field, and I have also attempted to avoid technical jargon as much as possible. When technical terms are used,

[1] Alvin C. Plantinga, *God, Freedom, and Evil* (Grand Rapids: William B. Eerdmans Publishing Company, 1977), p. 1.

every effort has been made to define them clearly, and a glossary of terms has been included in the back of the book as an additional help. I have tried to include selections that are clear and readable, but this is not a promise that they will all be easy.

Many persons who pick up a book on the philosophy of religion expect to find a discussion that compares and contrasts different religions, both Eastern and Western. You will not find that in this book. In fact, the topics covered here are pretty much restricted to the main concerns raised by the Judaeo-Christian tradition. There are two reasons for this. First, a book that attempts to cover philosophical issues in both Eastern and Western religions will probably not do justice to either. Second, I presume that the religious tradition of most readers of this book will be either Judaism or Christianity, and you should understand your own religious tradition before exploring a different one. Also, since the Judaeo-Christian worldview has dominated the Western world for the last two millennia, the philosophical issues raised by this tradition have cultural as well as philosophical value.

This book does not discuss every important philosophical issue in religion, and there are important questions and thinkers who have been omitted. In these days of spiraling book costs, a comprehensive treatment is neither possible nor desirable. As the title suggests, this book is an exploration of issues in the philosophy of religion. Like all explorations, it leaves some territory uncharted, but the issues presented are central ones, and mastery of them is essential to further philosophical study of religion.

Acknowledgments should also be included here: to Professor Tom L. Beauchamp for his helpful suggestions, and to my colleagues Donald M. Borchert and Stanley Grean for their valuable critiques. Inadequacies and errors, however, are strictly my fault, not theirs. Thanks also to Lisa Bibbee who carefully typed the manuscript, and to my students who worked their way through this material with me in class.

DAVID STEWART
Ohio University

part one

RELIGIOUS EXPERIENCE

Philosophy and Religion

Both philosophy and religion are common terms, although precisely defining them is difficult due to the diversity of meanings each has acquired. The word *religion* derives from a Latin term that referred to the bond between man and the gods, and in the view of most persons religion implies a belief in some kind of supernatural being or beings. This is the definition of religion usually offered by dictionaries, but such an understanding of religion would exclude some religious traditions; for example, in Confucianism the question of the existence of supernatural beings never arises. The term religion has even been extended to such secular movements as communism or various nationalisms which, even while denying the existence of God, demand a total, "religious" commitment from their adherents.

Further complicating the problem of arriving at a satisfactory definition of religion is the wide diversity of religious traditions. Every culture has a religious tradition of some sort, and these are as varied as the cultures that gave them birth. Many religious traditions are thoroughly bound up with cultic and ritual practices, but others are not. Some religions are tied to a priesthood, but this is not true of all. Divine revelation plays an important role in some traditions, but the relative importance of revelation in contrast with what can be known by reason alone is itself often a matter of disagreement.

In the study of religion, one response to this diversity of meanings is to adopt a neutral, descriptive approach. That is, one simply investigates a religion in its various cultural manifestations, describing religious phenomena whatever they may be. Such descriptive study concentrates on comparing or contrasting the various modes of religious awareness which are encountered, and perhaps deriving from this descriptive analysis certain conclusions about the nature of the religion under study. Whatever the merits of this approach may be, it cannot be considered a philosophical study of religion, for philosophy is the *critical* examination of human life and thought.

The study of religion, like the study of any other organized human activity, can be approached from a variety of standpoints. The historian, sociologist and psychologist each approach religion with a unique concern. The historian will be interested in the development over time of a religious tradition, its similarities to other traditions, and the influence that a religion has on the economic, political, and social affairs of a particular society. The sociologist is concerned with discovering what societal values are expressed in a religious tradition, how the religious beliefs of a group provide cohesiveness in a society, and how stratifications within the society are affected by its religious traditions. The psychologist will focus on belief structures themselves as indicative of a particular kind of self-understanding. Of course, the concerns of historians, sociologists, and psychologists will overlap, for the border-line between disciplines is not always sharply defined.

Besides the differences among the interests of the various academic disciplines, there is also the difference between being a student *of* a religion and being a believer *in* that religion. A student might investigate Islam and try to understand what Moslems believe, how those beliefs are incorporated into ritual and cultic practices, what the various Islamic sects are, and how the beliefs of Islam relate to other religions in the Near East—all without accepting as true the tenets of Islam. A believer, on the other hand, may adopt the neutral stance of a student of religion, but the believer's attitude toward a religion will inevitably be influenced by personal religious commitments, particularly if the religion under scrutiny is the believer's own. The believer's attitude is a much more existential one, since the religion under scrutiny is not just a subject for academic study but a matter of personal commitment. The principal difficulty encountered by studying their own religious tradition is in adopting an objective viewpoint (insofar as any objectivity is possible in religious study).

The philosophical study of religion, by virtue of the critical task of philosophy, demands detachment from personal beliefs in order to be able to examine critically the fundamental questions raised by religion. This detachment is a necessary first step if one is to conduct a truly philosophical study of religion. This does not mean that an individual committed to a particular religious tradition cannot philosophize about that tradition; that would imply that a person could not believe religiously what had been discovered philosophically: a strange state of affairs indeed. The point is that the philosophical study of religion demands a degree of detachment from personal religious beliefs. In turn, a philosophical approach to religion may well produce fresh understanding and increased clarity, upon which an even deeper commitment can be based. In a philosophical analysis of a religion, the student will be enriched by contact with the work of historians, sociologists, psychologists, and scholars of comparative religion. But encounters with these disciplines merely prepare the student for the philosophical task, which is to analyze critically the fundamental issues raised by religion, and to subject these issues to rigorous scrutiny.

If, however, as we have seen, even the task of discovering an essential nature of religion seems impossible, how can the philosopher begin? One answer to this question is to recognize that there is no such thing as religion, only religions. Religions can be grouped into various traditions, and within these traditions certain fundamental and common questions will emerge. This means that, for example, a philosopher analyzing a family of Eastern religions, would discover a different set of questions than would emerge from the study of an ancient animistic religion. In other words, each religion raises its own set of questions, and part of the philosopher's job is to ferret out these fundamental issues and submit them to as thorough an examination as possible.

The religious tradition that most readers of this book know best is that of Judaism and Christianity. That these two distinct religions constitute a single tradition is seen in the fact that Christianity has its roots in Judaism, and also in the similarity of the problems which have historically been of concern to both religions. Before we attempt a philosophical study of completely different religion, it would be well for us to examine philosophically the principal issues raised by our own religious tradition. But there is another reason for beginning with the Judaeo-Christian tradition. Even though both Judaism and Christianity developed in the ancient Near East, they have come to represent virtually the total religious tradition of the Western world. Similarly, our concept of the nature of philosophy, though born in Greece, has become identified with a particularly Western way of thinking. Both Western philosophy and Western religion have placed great emphasis on the human faculty of rationality and the role played by reason and argument in discovering truth. This is in sharp contrast, for example, to a Zen master who might refuse to answer questions, much less take part in a syllogistic argument. Western philosophy, in a very real sense, began with Zeno, the pre-Socratic Greek philosopher, who was credited with being the first to reason dialectically. That is, he juxtaposed conflicting viewpoints and attempted to reason to a conclusion that would result in the acceptance of one viewpoint and the rejection of the other. Since reason and argument are central in the Western attitude toward philosophy, a Western philosopher studying a Western religion will immediately want to know the relationship between faith and reason. He might ask, "Is faith rational? Can the claims of the Judaeo-Christian tradition about God be proved? If not, can we understand rationally what we accept by faith?"

In general, we can say with the contemporary philosopher John Hick that philosophy of religion is philosophical thinking about religion. But we must understand this not as philosophical thinking about religion in general, but about the *problems* raised by a particular religious tradition—in our case, the Judaeo-Christian tradition. To quote Hick, philosophy of religion "seeks to analyze concepts such as God, holy, salvation, worship, creation, sacrifice, eternal life, etc., and to determine the nature of religious utterances in comparison with those of everyday life, scientific discovery, morality, and the imaginative expressions of the arts."[1] We must emphasize, however, that these concepts, while central to the Judaeo-Christian tradition, are not universal to all religions. When we look at what phi-

[1]John Hick, *Philosophy of Religion,* 2nd ed., Foundations of Philosophy Series (Englewood Cliffs, N.J.: Prentice-Hall, Inc, 1973), p. 2.

losophers in both the Jewish and Christian traditions have pointed to as central concerns, we find a cluster of problems—the nature and existence of God, the problem of evil, the relation between faith and reason, the nature of religious language, the meaning of death, the relationship between morality and religion, and the question of human destiny. It is to these concepts, therefore, that we will seek to apply the rigors of philosophical analysis.

THE RELATION OF PHILOSOPHY AND RELIGION

The philosophy of religion, in the sense defined above, can be a useful tool in understanding religion, but the two are distinct. As has already been mentioned, philosophy can concern itself with varied religions—the religions of the East, ancient religions, contemporary religions, religions of the Middle Ages, and so forth. In each case the philosopher's task is to determine the central issues, and analyze them through careful scrutiny and investigation. In this sense, philosophy of religion is analogous to similar philosophical efforts aimed at other human disciplines. There can be philosophy of science, philosophy of education, philosophy of law, philosophy of art, philosophy of culture, and philosophy of psychology, just to name a few possibilities. In each case, the philosophical study of the discipline is distinct from the discipline itself. A philosophical study of law would raise such fundamental notions as the nature of justice, the meaning of *rights,* equality, and the status of law itself. The philosopher dealing with science would probe beneath the methods of scientists and question the meaning of *proof* and the assumptions made by scientists as their belief in the uniformity and regularity of nature, the dependability of inductive reasoning, and the meaning of such fundamental concepts as cause and effect. In both cases, the philosopher is not practicing law or doing science; instead he is forcing to the forefront the fundamental questions raised by these activities. Lawyers may talk a lot about justice, but what do they mean by it? Scientists may believe that the present law of physics will hold true in the future, but on what basis do they accept the conviction?

Similarly, philosophy of religion is different from the practice of religion. Philosophy of religion is not a systematic statement of religious beliefs (which would be theology, or dogmatics) but a second-order activity focused on the fundamental issues of a given religion. Christians, for example, talk a lot about God, but what is the evidence that God exists? If God's existence can be proved, how does one go about it? And if God exists, how can one account for the presence of evil in the world? Such questions are philosophical in nature, and the philosopher will not be content to let such questions go unexamined. The task of philosophy, at least as it is conceived of in the West, is to submit claims such as those made by religions to a thoroughgoing rational investigation.

There are philosophers, however, who question Western philosophy's focus on rational analysis. They point out that this emphasis on rationality is one-sided, for human beings are not just creatures of reason but function through a complex unity of reason, emotion, will, appetites, and feelings. Religion, they insist, makes an appeal not just to human reason but to emotion and feelings as well; therefore, any philosophical investigation of religion must include its nonrational as well as rational aspects. Indeed, though religion has rational elements, it appeals as well to the heart. Are people religious because they have felt the force of a powerful rational argument? Probably not. There are grounds for saying that religion seems to arise not so much from rational insight as from a powerful nonrational experience of something ultimate which demands allegiance and loyalty. How such experience arises and how it can be accounted for is the concern of the first group of readings.

MYSTICAL EXPERIENCE

Religious experience can mean so many different things that before going on it would be well to state explicitly the sense in which it is used in the following selections. Ambiguity likewise surrounds the term *mysticism,* which has been used to mean anything from a profound emotional experience encountered as a result of religious devotion, to any experience slightly out of the ordinary. In a popularized, and extremely loose, sense of the term, anything religious is thought to be mystical; this is an inaccurate use of the term, however, which renders it valueless by obliterating any distinctions among the various types of religious experience.

Not every kind of religious experience is mystical. In its precise sense, mysticism refers to an experience characterized by a sense of unity and oneness with the divine, an experience that is indescribable in ordinary language, if at all. Obviously, mystical experience is a rare occurrence, and it is not looked upon in the same way by all religious traditions. Some of the Eastern religions, such as Hinduism, place a great deal of value on mystical experience, whereas the Western religions, notably Judaism and Christianity, have tended to view mysticism with a fair degree of suspicion. During the Middle Ages Judaism developed a mystical minority movement in the form of Cabalism. Medieval Christianity likewise had its mystics, such as St. Bonaventure and St. John of the Cross. But for both Judaism and Christianity, mysticism has always remained on the margins of ordinary religious life. This has especially been the case with Christianity, which frequently found that mystics had uncomfortably close associations with heretical views.

Mysticism is a claim to a certain type of religious experience that is not confined to any particular religious tradition. No single set of doctrines is associated with it, and not all mystics are even in agreement as to what precisely constitutes a mystical experience. Some mystics have found the experience to be a spontaneous and unexpected joy; others have found the experience only after a long and tortuous ascetic life. Aldous Huxley, in his book *The Doors of Perception,* claims to have undergone heightened experiences not unlike those of the mystics through the use of hallucinogenic drugs.

Whatever their differences, mystics usually claim to have experienced an overwhelming sense of unity and oneness, but here a further distinction must be made between what is known as *introvertive* (inward-looking) and *extrovertive* (outward-looking) mysticism. Extrovertive forms of mysticism seem to result in the experience of a sense of unity with nature in which all distinctions between the self and nature seem to disappear and a feeling of overwhelming totality and oneness occurs. Introvertive mysticism, in contrast, offers an experience of complete withdrawal from the world and a union with the Absolute, characterized variously as the One, as God, or paradoxically, as the Abyss or as sheer Nothing. For both types of mystical experience, the sense of union with the ineffable is paramount. Mystics almost uniformly claim to have risen above the limitations of space and time and to have experienced a loss of individuality in union with something greater than themselves. A mystical experience is intensely private, beyond words, beyond reason, and essentially indescribable.

The readings that follow exclude any account of mystical experience and focus instead on a kind of religious experience that arises within ordinary life. There are two reasons for omitting from this book any lengthy treatment of mysticism. The first has already been referred to: mysticism has not been a central concern of either Judaism or Christianity, but has remained a minor element within both religions. A second reason for not including readings from mystics in this section is that the mystical experience, even among those who cultivate it, remains an unusual and intensely private experience, certainly one that is remote from the religious background of most of the users of this book. There are many excellent studies of mysticism, including a section in William James's *The Varieties of Religious Experience,* and Evelyn Underhill's *Mysticism,* which contains a lengthy bibliography on the topic. (See the "Additional Reading Suggestions" at the end of Part I for bibliographic details.) The thinkers whose views are presented in the following selections have taken great pains to distinguish their accounts of religious experience from mysticism. Their writings should be understood as describing nonmystical experiences that give rise to the religious dimension of life.

PAUL TILLICH

The Experience
of
Ultimate Concern

The first reading in this section is from Paul Tillich, one of the most influential theologians in the twentieth century. A central theme in Tillich's writing is the significance of faith as *ultimate concern,* a phrase so perceptive that it has entered the theological vocabulary of our time. Religious faith, for Tillich, grows out of those experiences which we invest with ultimate value and to which we give our ultimate allegiance. Behind Tillich's assertion that religious faith is ultimate concern lie two assumptions. The first assumption is that ultimate concern is common to all religions. No matter what their differences, a "religious" experience is precisely that which makes an ultimate claim on our loyalties. The second assumption is that no one is without some kind of "faith" in the sense of an ultimate concern.

There are several suggestive implications in Tillich's view. It enables us to understand the intensity of viewpoints that we would perhaps not ordinarily classify as religious; it also allows us to speak of "gods" of various sorts—power, wealth, ideologies and "isms" of different kinds. A dedicated Marxist is committed to a philosophical view which rejects any belief in God, yet the Marxist's commitment may be as intense as that of a traditional religious zealot. We can speak of an individual consumed with the desire for monetary gain, another person with an almost fanatical desire for power or fame, still another totally consumed with the goal of national liberation or the overthrow of the current political regime. All have in common an intense desire for the success of the cause which claims their ultimate allegiance. To use Tillich's phrase, their "faith" is their ultimate concern, and like all faiths it makes a total demand of the individual committed to it.

A study of the history of religions reveals that there is such a wide variety of

9

objects to which human beings have attached religious importance at some time or another that virtually nothing has not in some culture been considered worthy of veneration and worship. But as humanity's collective consciousness evolved, it became obvious that stones, trees, and animals were not worthy of ultimate concern. An anthropologist studying this diversity of religious commitments with a value-free method of inquiry, would not want to make any normative judgments. Tillich, however, does offer a way of judging rival faith commitments by distinguishing between *true* and *false ultimacy*. That which demands our ultimate concern must indeed be ultimate if it is worthy of our commitment. If the object of faith is not itself ultimate, then such a faith is idolatrous and can give rise to the demonic. The term *demonic* is one Tillich frequently uses to describe an ultimate commitment to that which is not ultimate, as when an individual submits to the demand of a totalitarian state for total allegiance. The demonic events unleashed on the world by the Nazis are an example of how an ideology can claim ultimacy only to produce the most savage kind of human activity.

It should also be obvious that a person's real "faith" (in the sense of ultimate concern) may not be the same as the religion to which lip service is given. A professing Christian's real "faith" (that is, ultimate concern) may be something quite different than the Christian religion. When we give our ultimate allegiance to something which is not ultimate, we take the risk of being disappointed, perhaps even destroyed, by the failure of our "faith." It is only when we commit ourselves ultimately to what is truly ultimate that faith can be said to be genuine.

FAITH AS CENTERED ACT

Not only is it the case for Tillich that every act of faith is an act of ultimate concern; it is also apparent in his view that faith provides unity and focus to the human personality. A corollary to this is that without some sort of faith, one would be without any core of meaning to provide coherence to one's personality. Camus' absurd hero is a literary example of this sort of breakdown of human purpose. In Camus' novel *The Stranger,* Mersault is precisely the sort of individual without authentic faith commitments of any kind who is caught up in an existential vacuum from which there is no escape. It is important to note, however, that Tillich does not view faith as a purely rational response, but rather a response of the whole person, which includes feelings as well as reason.

FAITH AS ECSTATIC

We commonly speak of ecstasy as an intense and positive emotional experience. Certainly Tillich does not rule out the emotional element in religion, for as a response of the whole person, faith contains an emotional element. To speak of faith as ecstatic implies that faith leads the individual beyond the limitations of one aspect of the human personality. The term *ecstasy* literally means standing outside. An ecstatic experience is one that leads beyond the immediacy of the moment or, to use a parallel term, an experience that transcends the selfish tendencies of our nature.

A good example of the experience of ecstasy would be that of the person in love. Like faith, love has an emotional element but is more than an emotion; indeed it embraces the totality of the human personality. To experience the ecstasy of love means that an individual is led by the love-experience to be directed toward something other than selfish concerns, namely, the beloved. The ecstasy of love calls the lover beyond the immediacy of self-centeredness to a someone who demands loyalty and allegiance and to whom such dedication is gladly given.

FAITH AS UNITY OF OBJECTIVE AND SUBJECTIVE

This is one of the most difficult of all the notions which Tillich discusses, but using the example just given of being in love will show how ecstasy is closely related to overcoming the distinction between the objective and the subjective. The ecstasy of being "in love" means that the individual has gone beyond self to a sense of unity with and belonging to another person. The lover's entire being takes on a new significance when in the presence of the beloved, so much so that the absence of the beloved leads to feelings of incompleteness on the lover's part. Such feelings are perhaps best expressed in poetry, and love poetry frequently speaks of the emptiness of the self when the beloved is absent. No longer does the lover feel like an independent subject distinct from an object. Indeed, the lover's whole being is encompassed by the relationship with another person; in a sense the lover is swallowed up in love and in the person loved. Being "in love," in the truest sense, is an act of commitment, though it cannot be an ultimate commitment in Tillich's sense without becoming idolatrous.

In an analogous way an individual can be swallowed up in an ideology, a nationalistic movement, desire for success, or some other finite goal, and treat this commitment with all the ultimacy that faith implies. But if the object of one's faith is not ultimate, the ultimacy attached to it not only risks becoming demonic, but will finally fail and be a disappointment. By being caught up in the ultimacy of the cause, or whatever one's ultimate concern is directed to, the individual feels at one with that to which ultimate concern is given. Like love, faith—even in its perverted form—erases the distinction between the subject and the object of faith.

FAITH AS EMBRACING THE NONRATIONAL

The Western philosophical and religious traditions have emphasized the rational aspects of our nature to such an extent that reason, argument, and logic are considered by many to be the only guarantee of truth. We tend to identify rationality as the hallmark of our humanness, and coupled with this is a parallel tendency to downplay the nonrational aspects of our nature as unable to provide any useful information about the world. To be sure, we would agree that there is a place for the emotional and noncognitive, but it is thought by many to be a small place, especially if we are concerned with defending our commitments by appealing to logical proofs. Perhaps part of our distrust of the nonrational aspects of our nature stems from our feeling that we are on much less firm ground when we leave the security of logical argument. Freud opened the pathway for psychology to explore the nonrational aspects of our psyche, but we do not have to wander in the labyrinths of the unconscious to be convinced that there is more to our humanness than merely our ability to construct logical arguments or rational proofs.

To underscore this point we should distinguish between the terms *rational, irrational,* and *nonrational.* The rational refers to that aspect of our nature which reasons according to logical principles and which provides insight into the nature of things by means of intellectual insight. Armed with data provided by the senses, we can produce proof for many of the conclusions we reach about the world, and the startling advances in our ability to understand—and master—the physical world speak forcibly of the power of reason to enlarge our intellectual grasp of things. So confident have we become about reason's power to distinguish truth from error that to show how an action or viewpoint is contrary to reason is to discredit it completely. We accept as a truism that it is irrational to persist in a point of view against which reason has been successful in constructing proofs. If a person says that it is possible to fly merely by flapping one's arms while jumping off a cliff, we would conclude that the individual is thinking irrationally, for there is solid evidence from physics as well as from past experience that this type of behavior will produce a bad fall. Most of us would agree that when there is rational guidance for our actions and beliefs, we should follow it. Tillich raises the possibility, however, that not everything within human experience can be neatly divided into the categories of rationality and irrationality.

Let's return to the example of falling in love. To say that love is not just a matter of the head but of the heart as well is to say that being in love is not just an intellectual activity but a response of the whole person to another individual. It is not irrational to fall in love, but neither is it a rational act. Love deals with something other than reason: the nonrational. Similarly, our response to great paintings and music, dance, or any of the arts is not totally rational but involves as well other aspects of our nature—our feelings, an intuitive sense, perhaps even a response that we who are experiencing it cannot fully understand. All this points to the nonrational aspect of our nature; it is not contrary to reason, just different. To treat all experience with the categories of rationality not only mistakenly reduces all to the power of reason; it also may even debase experiences which do not make their appeal to our intellectual capacities.

The story is told of a great French mathematician and physicist who attended a ballet and afterward responded, when asked his opinion of it, "What does it prove?" We pity a person so dependent on the rational that he cannot even see meaning in an activity that makes its appeal to something other than reason. We will return to these themes in the section dealing with the question of the relation between faith and reason. At this point, though, we should note that Tillich is suggesting that to respond in faith is to commit the whole person, and this includes the nonrational aspects of our nature as well as the rational. He denies "that man's essential nature is identical with the rational character of his mind." There is a power of the self which goes beyond reason in the commitment of faith, and Tillich defines this as "a total and centered act of the personal self, the act of unconditional, infinite and ultimate concern." Only if we open ourselves up to the nonrational aspects of our humanness can we understand the meaning of faith as an essential aspect of religious experience.

In summary, Tillich's point is that within human experience there arises something that calls for an act of ultimate commitment. In this sense, then, religious experience for Tillich is not some mystical vision of God but an experience within the ordinary world of something that elicits our ultimate concern, something to which the individual is devoted with passionate intensity and which, in turn, provides a center and focus to the individual's existence. This is an experience that everyone has, but whether one's ultimate concern is directed toward that which is really ultimate or to something which is not ultimate but falsely claims ultimacy determines whether this faith is genuine or idolatrous.

What Faith Is*

FAITH AS ULTIMATE CONCERN

Faith is the state of being ultimately concerned: the dynamics of faith are the dynamics of man's ultimate concern. Man, like every living being, is concerned about many things, above all about those which condition his very existence, such as food and shelter. But man, in contrast to other living beings, has spiritual concerns—cognitive, aesthetic, social, political. Some of them are urgent, often extremely urgent, and each of them as well as the vital concerns can claim ultimacy for a human life or the life of a social group. If it claims ultimacy it demands the total surrender of him who accepts this claim, and it promises total fulfillment even if all other claims have to be subjected to it or rejected in its name. If a national group makes the life and growth of the nation its ultimate concern, it demands that all other concerns, economic well-being, health and life, family, aesthetic and cognitive truth, justice and humanity, be sacrificed. The extreme nationalisms of our century are laboratories for the study of what ultimate concern means in all aspects of human existence, including the smallest concern of one's daily life. Everything is centered in the only god, the nation—a god who certainly proves to be a demon, but who shows clearly the unconditional character of an ultimate concern.

But it is not only the unconditional demand made by that which is

*Source: Abridged from pp. 1-12 in *Dynamics of Faith* by Paul Tillich. Volume 10 of the World Perspective Series. Edited by Ruth Nanda Anshen. Copyright © 1957 by Paul Tillich. Reprinted by permission of Harper & Row, Publishers, Inc.

one's ultimate concern, it is also the promise of ultimate fulfillment which is accepted in the act of faith. The content of this promise is not necessarily defined. It can be expressed in indefinite symbols or in concrete symbols which cannot be taken literally, like the "greatness" of one's nation in which one participates even if one has died for it, or the conquest of mankind by the "saving race," etc. In each of these cases it is "ultimate fulfillment" that is promised, and it is exclusion from such fulfillment which is threatened if the unconditional demand is not obeyed.

An example—and more than an example—is the faith manifest in the religion of the Old Testament. It also has the character of ultimate concern in demand, threat and promise. The content of this concern is not the nation—although Jewish nationalism has sometimes tried to distort it into that—but the content is the God of justice, who, because he represents justice for everybody and every nation, is called the universal God, the God of the universe. He is the ultimate concern of every pious Jew, and therefore in his name the great commandment is given: "You shall love the Lord your God with all your heart, and with all your soul, and with all your might" (Deut 6:5). This is what ultimate concern means and from these words the term "ultimate concern" is derived. They state unambiguously the character of genuine faith, the demand of total surrender to the subject of ultimate concern. The Old Testament is full of commands which make the nature of this surrender concrete, and it is full of promises and threats in relation to it. Here also are the promises of symbolic indefiniteness, although they center around fulfillment of the national and individual life, and the threat is the exclusion from such fulfillment through national extinction and individual catastrophe. Faith, for the men of the Old Testament, is the state of being ultimately and unconditionally concerned about Jahweh and about what he represents in demand, threat and promise.

Another example—almost a counter-example, yet nevertheless equally revealing—is the ultimate concern with "success" and with social standing and economic power. It is the god of many people in the highly competitive Western culture and it does what every ultimate concern must do: it demands unconditional surrender to its laws even if the price is the sacrifice of genuine human relations, personal conviction, and creative *eros*. Its threat is social and economic defeat, and its promise—indefinite as all such promises—the fulfillment of one's being. It is the breakdown of this kind of faith which characterizes and makes religiously important most contemporary literature. Not false calculations but a misplaced faith is revealed in novels like *Point of No Return*. When fulfilled, the promise of this faith proves to be empty.

Faith is the state of being ultimately concerned. The content matters infinitely for the life of the believer, but it does not matter for the formal definition of faith. And this is the first step we have to make in order to understand the dynamics of faith.

FAITH AS A CENTERED ACT

Faith as ultimate concern is an act of the total personality. It happens in the center of the personal life and includes all its elements. Faith is the most centered act of the human mind. It is not a movement of a special section or a special function of man's total being. They all are united in the act of faith. But faith is not the sum total of their impacts. It transcends every special impact as well as the totality of them and it has itself a decisive impact on each of them.

Since faith is an act of the personality as a whole, it participates in the dynamics of personal life. These dynamics have been described in many ways, especially in the recent developments of analytic psychology. Thinking in polarities, their tensions and their possible conflicts, is a common characteristic of most of them. This makes the psychology of personality highly dynamic and requires a dynamic theory of faith as the most personal of all personal acts. The first and decisive polarity in analytic psychology is that between the so-called unconscious and the conscious. Faith as an act of the total personality is not imaginable without the participation of the unconscious elements in the personality structure. They are always present and decide largely about the content of faith. But, on the other hand, faith is a conscious act and the unconscious elements participate in the creation of faith only if they are taken into the personal center which transcends each of them. If this does not happen, if unconscious forces determine the mental status without a centered act, faith does not occur, and compulsions take its place. For faith is a matter of freedom. Freedom is nothing more than the possibility of centered personal acts. The frequent discussion in which faith and freedom are contrasted could be helped by the insight that faith is a free, namely, centered act of the personality. In this respect freedom and faith are identical. . . .

This leads to the question of how faith as a personal, centered act is related to the rational structure of man's personality which is manifest in his meaningful language, in his ability to know the true and to do the good, in his sense of beauty and justice. All this, and not only his possibility to analyze, to calculate and to argue, makes him a rational being. But in spite of this larger concept of reason we must deny that man's essential nature is identical with the rational character of his mind. Man is able to decide for or against reason, he is able to create beyond reason or to destroy below reason. This power is the power of his self, the center of self-relatedness in which all elements of his being are united. Faith is not an act of any of his rational functions, as it is not an act of the unconscious, but it is an act in which both the rational and the nonrational elements of his being are transcended.

Faith as the embracing and centered act of the personality is "ecstatic." It transcends both the drives of the nonrational unconscious and the structures of the rational conscious. It transcends them, but it does not destroy them. The ecstatic character of faith does not exclude its rational character although it is not identical with it, and it includes nonrational strivings without being identical with them. In the ecstasy of faith there is an awareness of truth and of ethical value; there are also past loves and hates, conflicts and reunions, individual and collective influences. "Ecstasy" means "standing outside of oneself"—without ceasing to be oneself—with all the elements which are united in the personal center.

A further polarity in these elements, relevant for the understanding of faith, is the tension between the cognitive function of man's personal life, on the one hand, and emotion and will, on the other hand. In a later discussion I will try to show that many distortions of the meaning of faith are rooted in the attempt to subsume faith to the one or the other of these functions. At this point it must be stated as sharply and insistently as possible that in every act of faith there is cognitive affirmation, not as the result of an independent process of inquiry but as an inseparable element in a total act of acceptance and surrender. This also excludes the idea that faith is the result of an independent act of "will to believe." There is certainly affirmation by the will of what conerns one ultimately, but faith is not a creation of the will. In the ecstasy of faith the will to accept and to surrender is an element, but not the cause. And this is true also of feeling. Faith is not an emotional outburst: this is not the meaning of ecstasy. Certainly, emotion is in it, as in every act of man's spiritual life. But emotion does not produce faith. Faith has a cognitive content and is an act of the will. It is the unity of every element in the centered self. Of course, the unity of all elements in the act of faith does not prevent one or the other element from dominating in a special form of faith. It dominates the character of faith but it does not create the act of faith.

This also answers the question of a possible psychology of faith. Everything that happens in man's personal being can become an object of psychology. And it is rather important for both the philosopher of religion and the practical minister to know how the act of faith is embedded in the totality of psychological processes. But in contrast to this justified and desirable form of a psychology of faith there is another one which tries to derive faith from something that is not faith but is most frequently fear. The presupposition of this method is that fear or something else from which faith is derived is more original and basic than faith. But this presupposition cannot be proved. On the contrary, one can prove that in the scientific method which leads to such consequences faith is already effective. Faith precedes all attempts to derive it from something else, because these attempts are themselves based on faith.

THE SOURCE OF FAITH

We have described the act of faith and its relation to the dynamics of personality. Faith is a total and centered act of the personal self, the act of unconditional, infinite and ultimate concern. The question now arises: what is the source of this all-embracing and all-transcending concern? The word "concern" points to two sides of a relationship, the relation between the one who is concerned and his concern. In both respects we have to imagine man's situation in itself and in his world. The reality of man's ultimate concern reveals something about his being, namely, that he is able to transcend the flux of relative and transitory experiences of his ordinary life. Man's experiences, feelings, thoughts are conditioned and finite. They not only come and go, but their content is of finite and conditional concern—unless they are elevated to unconditional validity. But this presupposes the general possibility of doing so; it presupposes the element of infinity in man. Man is able to understand in an immediate personal and central act the meaning of the ultimate, the unconditional, the absolute, the infinite. This alone makes faith a human potentiality.

Human potentialities are powers that drive toward actualization. Man is driven toward faith by his awareness of the infinite to which he belongs, but which he does not own like a possession. This is in abstract terms what concretely appears as the "restlessness of the heart" within the flux of life.

The unconditional concern which is faith is the concern about the unconditional. The infinite passion, as faith has been described, is the passion for the infinite. Or, to use our first term, the ultimate concern is concern about what is experienced as ultimate. In this way we have turned from the subjective meaning of faith as a centered act of the personality to its objective meaning, to what is meant in the act of faith. It would not help at this point of our analysis to call that which is meant in the act of faith "God" or "a god." For at this step we ask: What in the idea of God constitutes divinity? The answer is: It is the element of the unconditional and of ultimacy. This carries the quality of divinity. If this is seen, one can understand why almost everything "in heaven and on earth" has received ultimacy in the history of human religion. But we also can understand that a critical principle was and is at work in man's religious consciousness, namely, that which is really ultimate over against what claims to be ultimate but is only preliminary, transitory, finite.

The term "ultimate concern" unites the subjective and the objective side of the act of faith—the *fides qua creditur* (the faith through which one believes) and the *fides quae creditur* (the faith which is believed). The first is the classical term for the centered act of the personality, the ultimate concern. The second is the classical term for that toward which this act is directed, the ultimate itself, expressed in symbols of the divine. This distinction is very important, but not ultimately so, for the one side cannot be without the other. There is no faith without a content toward which it is directed. There is always something meant in the act of faith. And there is no way of having the content of faith except in the act of faith. All speaking about divine matters which is not done in the state of ultimate concern is meaningless. Because that which is meant in the act of faith cannot be approached in any other way than through an act of faith.

In terms like ultimate, unconditional, infinite, absolute, the difference between subjectivity and objectivity is overcome. The ultimate of the act of faith and the ultimate that is meant in the act of faith are one and the same. This is symbolically expressed by the mystics when they say that their knowledge of God is the knowledge God has of himself; and it is expressed by Paul when he says (I Cor. 13) that he will know as he is known, namely, by God. God never can be object without being at the same time subject. Even a successful prayer is, according to Paul (Rom. 8), not possible without God as Spirit praying within us. The same experience expressed in abstract language is the disappearance of the ordinary subject-object scheme in the experience of the ultimate, the unconditional. In the act of faith that which is the source of this act is present beyond the cleavage of subject and object. It is present as both and beyond both.

This character of faith gives an additional criterion for distinguishing true and false ultimacy. The finite which claims infinity without having it (as, e.g., a nation or success) is not able to transcend the subject-object scheme. It remains an object which the believer looks at as a subject. He can approach it with ordinary knowledge and subject it to ordinary handling. There are, of course, many degrees in the endless realm of false ultimacies. The nation is nearer to true ultimacy than is success. Nationalistic ecstasy can produce a state in which the subject is almost swallowed by the object. But after a period the subject emerges again, disappointed radically and totally, and by looking at the nation in a skeptical and calculating way does injustice even to its justified claims. The more idolatrous a faith the less it is able to overcome the cleavage between subject and object. For that is the difference between true and idolatrous faith. In true faith the ultimate concern is a concern about the truly ultimate; while in idolatrous faith preliminary, finite realities are elevated to the rank of ultimacy. The inescapable consequence of idolatrous faith is "existential disappointment," a disappointment which penetrates into the very existence of man! This is the dynamics of idolatrous faith: that it is faith, and as such, the centered act of a personality; that the centering point is something which is more or less on the periphery; and that, therefore, the act of faith leads to a loss of the center and to a disruption of the personality. The ecstatic character of even an idolatrous faith can hide this consequence only for a certain time. But finally it breaks into the open.

DISCUSSION QUESTIONS

1. In identifying faith with a person's ultimate concern, Tillich seems to be saying that everyone has a faith of some kind. Do you find this way of defining faith so broadly that everyone has it a good thing or not? Give reasons for your answer.

2. Do you agree that without the centering act that faith is thought to be that one's personality will have no focus and will be in danger of collapse in the face of trial and hardship? What are your reasons?

3. On the basis of Tillich's analysis, would you agree that human beings have a basic need for religion? If your answer is yes, how is one to distinguish between good and bad religious commitments?

4. Is the distinction between the nonrational and the irrational justifiable? Why or why not?

5. Given Tillich's analysis, do you find that the term "idolatry" can be useful in understanding the appeal that many secular movements seem to have? If not, why not? If your answer is yes, can you give some examples?

6. If you were to apply Tillich's analysis to your own experience, what would you say it is that has a specifically religious meaning for you?

RUDOLF OTTO

The Experience
of
the Holy

The selection from Paul Tillich emphasized the importance of including the nonrational element in any account of religious experience. Even though there is a place for the rational and the cognitive in religion, many philosophers have protested against the somewhat one-sided emphasis, at least in Christian thought, on the rational arguments for elements of religious beliefs.

One of the most eloquent spokesmen for the significance of the nonrational in religion was Friedrich Schleiermacher, who in the eighteenth century proposed an alternative way of viewing the sources of religion. The eighteenth century mechanistic worldview left little room for God. Advances in physics, mathematics, astronomy, and the geological sciences all posed threats to the traditional arguments for the existence of God and the truth of the Christian religion. In response to these attacks, Schleiermacher proposed in a book written in 1799 to explore the nonrational aspect of religion. This book, *On Religion: Speeches to its Cultured Despisers,* suggested that religion arises not in our intellectual faculties but in the feelings of utter dependence that a finite creature experiences when faced with its own finitude and contingency. Although influential in his own day, Schleiermacher was rediscovered in the twentieth century, which witnessed some of the same attitudes toward religion that had been prevalent in Schleiermacher's century. In a 1926 reprint of the first edition of Schleiermacher's book, the German theologian Rudolf Otto made the following assessment of the importance of Schleiermacher's work:

> He wished to show that man is not wholly confined to knowledge and action, that the relationship of men to their environment—the world, being, mankind,

events—is not exhausted in the mere perception or shaping of it. He sought to prove that if one experienced the environing world in a state of deep emotion, as intuition and feeling, and that if one were deeply affected by a sense of its eternal and abiding essence to the point where one was moved to feelings of devotion, awe, and reverence—then such an affective state was worth more than knowledge and action put together. And this was what the cultured had to learn from the beginning.[1]

There was, however, a major flaw in Schleiermacher's proposal. It was an entirely subjective account of religion. Religion arises in feelings, but feelings of what? When Schleiermacher described these feelings, he did so solely in terms of the subjectivity of these feelings—utter dependence, devotion, awe, and so forth. As the selection from Tillich pointed out, there can be no feelings worthy of the name faith without a content. What indeed was the content of the feelings of "creature consciousness" to which Schleiermacher pointed?

It was, in part, to answer this question that Rudolf Otto proposed to describe that to which the feelings of dependence and devotion are directed. He used the term "holy" (Das Héilige in German) and offered a synonym for the word holy in the term numinous. Like Schleiermacher, Otto rejected the excessive emphasis on rational approaches to religion which he thought had dominated theological thought, and constituted a bias against discovering the origins of religion in feelings not unlike those which Schleiermacher had described a century and a half earlier. But unlike Schleiermacher, Otto was more interested in the content of this experience than in the subjective side of the experience itself. By using the term "holy" to describe this experience, Otto was aware that he was open to misunderstanding, for "holy" has taken on the meaning of moral perfection and ethical purity. This was not its original meaning, however; it first signified that which was separate and unapproachable, set apart and distinct from man. When the ancient Hebrews spoke of the holiness of God, they were thinking not only of God's moral perfection but of God's distinct otherness as a being completely different and separate from sinful mankind.

Since the term holy had taken on these moral connotations, Otto coined a new term, numinous, from the Latin numen, signifying divine power or divine will. The experience of the numinous is difficult to describe, yet Otto insisted that it is an experience basic to all religions. Being a student of world religions, Otto was convinced that religion arises not from rational argumentation but from a profound experience of divine power which can take many forms, although there are common features in all its manifestations. As Otto describes this experience,

> The feeling of it may at times come sweeping like a gentle tide, pervading the mind with a tranquil mood of deepest worship. It may pass over into a more set and lasting attitude of the soul, continuing, as it were, thrillingly vibrant and resonant, until at last it dies away and the soul resumes its "profane," nonreligious mood of everyday experience. It may burst in sudden eruptions up from the depths of the soul with spasms and convulsions, or lead to the strangest excitements, to intoxicated frenzy, to transport, and to ecstacy. It has its wild and

[1]Rudolf Otto, "Introduction" to Friedrich Schleiermacher, On Religion: Speeches to its Cultured Despisers, trans. John Oman (New York: Harper & Row, 1958), p. xix.

demonic forms and can sink to an almost grisly horror and shuddering. It has its crude barbaric antecedents and early manifestations, and again it may be developed into something beautiful and pure and glorious. It may become hushed, trembling, and speechless humility of the creature in the presence of—whom or what? In the presence of that which is a *mystery* inexpressible and above all creatures.[2]

As you read through the selection from Otto, notice that he uses various descriptive phrases for the experience of the numinous. These differing descriptions should not be taken as different experiences, but as various aspects of the same experience of the numinous. The descriptions must vary because the experience itself may be articulated differently depending on whether the religious consciousness undergoing the experience is primitive or well developed. A central descriptive phrase Otto used to describe the experience of the numinous is *mysterium tremendum. Tremendum,* as its English derivative *tremendous* suggests, involves the notions of power and might. Otto further analyzed the sense of *Tremendum* as involving elements of awefulness, overpoweringness, and energy. Corresponding to these qualities (or *quale*) are the subjective responses of dread, insignificance, and impotence. All these feelings are reflected in the description given by the Hebrew prophet Isaiah of an experience that qualifies in every way as an experience of the holy.

And the foundations of the thresholds shook at the voice of him who called, and the house was filled with smoke. And I said: "Woe is me! For I am lost; for I am a man of unclean lips, and I dwell in the midst of a people of unclean lips; for my eyes have seen the King, the Lord of hosts" (Isaiah 6:4-5, RSV).

If all this is difficult to understand, this should only be expected, for as the adjective *mysterium* suggests, there is something "wholly other" about the numinous, something which reason with its limited powers can never grasp. Twentieth-century, scientifically-educated people do not like mystery; they think more in terms of problems and difficulties that can be dispelled by an increase in human knowledge. A mystery, as Otto points out, is entirely different from a problem. There is within a mystery something which will forever elude attempts to comprehend it. "The truly 'mysterious' object," Otto says, "is beyond our apprehension and comprehension, not only because in it we come upon something inherently 'wholly other.' . . ."

If Otto's description of the experience of the numinous still seems remote and difficult, perhaps C. S. Lewis's description of an analogous experience will help.

Suppose you were told there was a tiger in the next room; you would know that you were in danger and would probably feel fear. But if you were told "There is a ghost in the next room," and believed it, you would feel, indeed, what is often called fear, but of a different kind. It would not be based on that knowledge of danger, for no one is primarily afraid of what a ghost may do to him, but of the mere fact that it is a ghost. It is "uncanny" rather than dangerous, and with the special kind of fear it excites may be called Dread. With the Uncanny one has reached the fringes of the Numinous. Now suppose that you were told simply, "There is a mighty spirit in the room," and believed it. Your feelings would then be

[2]Rudolf Otto, *The Idea of the Holy,* 2nd ed., trans. John W. Harvey (London: Oxford University Press, 1950), pp. 12–13.

even less like the mere fear of danger: but the disturbance would be profound. You would feel wonder and a certain shrinking—a sense of inadequacy to cope with such a visitant and of prostration before it—an emotion which might be expressed in Shakespeare's words "Under it my genius is rebuked." This feeling may be described as awe, and the object which excites it as the *Numinous*.[3]

Lewis's analogy also points up the other aspect of the experience of the numinous as Otto describes it: the feeling of fascination and attraction. Who has not had an experience of being around a camp fire swapping ghost stories? Each person attempts to outdo the other in piling horrible detail upon grisly fact. While all this should be repelling, there is something fascinating and compelling about tales of the preternatural. And so it is with the numinous. While there is within the experience of the numinous that which repels, the awefulness, power, and urgency of the numinous also fascinate and attract and give rise to feelings that in their more developed forms are the basis of religion. Experiencing the presence of God in a thirteenth-century cathedral may be a far cry from the more robust forms that the experience of the numinous has taken, but however the numinous is experienced, it defies conceptual analysis and will forever elude attempts to understand it completely.

[3]C. S. Lewis, *The Problem of Pain* (London: Geoffrey Bles, 1956), p. 5.

The Idea of the Holy*

"NUMEN" AND THE "NUMINOUS"

"Holiness"—"the holy"—is a category of interpretation and valuation peculiar to the sphere of religion. It is, indeed, applied by transference to another sphere—that of ethics—but it is not itself derived from this. While it is complex, it contains a quite specific element or "moment," which sets it apart from "the rational" in the meaning we gave to that word above, and which remains inexpressible—an αρρητον or *ineffabile*—in the sense that it completely eludes apprehension in terms of concepts. The same thing is true (to take a quite different region of experience) of the category of the beautiful.

Now these statements would be untrue from the outset if "the holy" were merely what is meant by the word, not only in common parlance, but in philosophical, and generally even in theological usage. The fact is we have come to use the words "holy," "sacred" (*heilig*) in an entirely derivative sense, quite different from that which they originally bore. We generally take "holy" as meaning "completely good"; it is the absolute moral

*Source: From *The Idea of the Holy* by Rudolf Otto, trans. by John W. Harvey 2nd ed. 1950 pp. 5–7, 12–14, 19–29, 57–60. Reprinted by permission of Oxford University Press.

attribute, denoting the consummation of moral goodness. In this sense Kant calls the will which remains unwaveringly obedient to the moral law from the motive of duty a "holy" will; here clearly we have simply the *perfectly moral* will. In the same way we may speak of the holiness or sanctity of duty or law, meaning merely that they are imperative upon conduct and universally obligatory.

But this common usage of the term is inaccurate. It is true that all this moral significance is contained in the word "holy," but it included in addition—as even we cannot but feel—a clear overplus of meaning, and this it is now our task to isolate. Nor is this merely a later or acquired meaning; rather, "holy," or at least the equivalent words in Latin and Greek, in Semitic and other ancient languages, denoted first and foremost *only* this overplus: if the ethical element was present at all, at any rate it was not original and never constituted the whole meaning of the word. Any one who uses it to-day does undoubtedly always feel "the morally good" to be implied in "holy"; and accordingly in our inquiry into that element which is separate and peculiar to the idea of the holy it will be useful, at least for the temporary purpose of the investigation, to invent a special term to stand for "the holy" *minus* its moral factor or "moment," and, as we can now add, minus its "rational" aspect altogether. . . .

Accordingly, it is worth while, as we have said, to find a word to stand for this element in isolation, this "extra" in the meaning of "holy" above and beyond the meaning of goodness. By means of a special term we shall the better be able, first, to keep the meaning clearly apart and distinct, and second, to apprehend and classify connectedly whatever subordinate forms or stages of development it may show. For this purpose I adopt a word coined from the Latin *numen. Omen* has given us "ominous," and there is no reason why from *numen* we should not similarly form a word "numinous." I shall speak, then, of a unique "numinous" category of value and of a definitely "numinous" state of mind, which is always found wherever the category is applied. This mental state is perfectly *sui generis* and irreducible to any other; and therefore, like every absolutely primary and elementary datum, while it admits of being discussed, it cannot be strictly defined. There is only one way to help another to an understanding of it. He must be guided and led on by consideration and discussion of the matter through the ways of his own mind, until he reach the point at which "the numinous" in him perforce begins to stir, to start into life and into consciousness. We can co-operate in this process by bringing before his notice all that can be found in other regions of the mind, already known and familiar, to resemble, or again to afford some special contrast to, the particular experience we wish to elucidate. Then we must add: "This X of ours is not precisely *this* experience, but akin to this one and the opposite of that other. Cannot you now realize for yourself what it is?" In other words our X cannot, strictly speaking, be taught, it can only be evoked, awakened in the mind; as everything that comes "of the spirit" must be awakened.

"MYSTERIUM TREMENDUM"

The Analysis of "Tremendum"

We said above that the nature of the numinous can only be suggested by means of the special way in which it is reflected in the mind in terms of feeling. "Its nature is such that it grips or stirs the human mind with this and that determinate affective state." We have now to attempt to give a further indication of these determinate states. We must once again endeavour, by adducing feelings akin to them for the purpose of analogy or contrast, and by the use of metaphor and symbolic expressions, to make the states of mind we are investigating ring out, as it were, of themselves.

Let us consider the deepest and most fundamental element in all strong and sincerely felt religious emotion. Faith unto salvation, trust, love—all these are there. But over and above these is an element which may also on occasion, quite apart from them, profoundly affect us and occupy the mind with a wellnigh bewildering strength. Let us follow it up with every effort of sympathy and imaginative intuition wherever it is to be found, in the lives of those around us, in sudden, strong ebullitions of personal piety and the frames of mind such ebullitions evince, in the fixed and ordered solemnities of rites and liturgies, and again in the atmosphere that clings to old religious monuments and buildings, to temples and to churches. If we do so we shall find we are dealing with something for which there is only one appropriate expression, *"mysterium tremendum."* The feeling of it may at times come sweeping like a gentle tide, pervading the mind with a tranquil mood of deepest worship. It may pass over into a more set and lasting attitude of the soul, continuing, as it were, thrillingly vibrant and resonant, until at last it dies away and the soul resumes its "profane," non-religious mood of everyday experience. It may burst in sudden eruption up from the depths of the soul with spasms and convulsions, or lead to the strangest excitements, to intoxicated frenzy, to transport, and to ecstasy. It has its wild and demonic forms and can sink to an almost grisly horror and shuddering. It has its crude, barbaric antecedents and early manifestations, and again it may be developed into something beautiful and pure and glorious. It may become the hushed, trembling, and speechless humility of the creature in the presence of—whom or what? In the presence of that which is a *mystery* inexpressible and above all creatures.

It is again evident at once that here too our attempted formulation by means of a concept is once more a merely negative one. Conceptually *mysterium* denotes merely that which is hidden and esoteric, that which is beyond conception of understanding, extraordinary and unfamiliar. The term does not define the object more positively in its qualitative character. But though what is enunciated in the word is negative, what is meant is something absolutely and intensely positive. This pure positive we can experience in feelings, feelings which our discussion can help to make clear to us, in so far as it arouses them actually in our hearts.

The Element of Awefulness

To get light upon the positive *"quale"* of the object of these feelings, we must analyse more closely our phrase *mysterium tremendum,* and we will begin first with the adjective.

Tremor is in itself merely the perfectly familiar and "natural" emotion of *fear.* But here the term is taken, aptly enough but still only by analogy, to denote a quite specific kind of emotional response, wholly distinct from that of being afraid, though it so far resembles it that the analogy of fear may be used to throw light upon its nature. There are in some languages special expressions which denote, either exclusively or in the first instance, this "fear" that is more than fear proper. The Hebrew *hiqdīsh* (hallow) is an example. To "keep a thing holy in the heart" means to mark it off by a feeling of peculiar dread, not to be mistaken for any ordinary dread, that is, to appraise it by the category of the numinous. But the Old Testament throughout is rich in parallel expressions for this feeling. Specially noticeable is the *'emāh* of Yahweh ("fear of God"), which Yahweh can pour forth, dispatching almost like a daemon, and which seizes upon a man with paralysing effect. It is closely related to the δεῖμα πανικόν of the Greeks. Compare Exod. xxiii. 27: "I will send my fear before thee, and will destroy all the people to whom thou shalt come . . ."; also Job ix. 34; xiii. 21 ("let not his fear terrify me"; "let not thy dread make me afraid"). Here we have a terror fraught with an inward shuddering such as not even the most menacing and overpowering created thing can instil. It has something spectral in it. . . .

The Element of "Overpoweringness" ("majestas")

We have been attempting to unfold the implications of that aspect of the *mysterium tremendum* indicated by the adjective, and the result so far may be summarized in two words, constituting, as before, what may be called an "ideogram," rather than a concept proper, viz. "absolute unapproachability."

It will be felt at once that there is yet a further element which must be added, that, namely, of "might," "power," "absolute overpoweringness." We will take to represent this the term *majestas*, majesty—the more readily because anyone with a feeling for language must detect a last faint trace of the numinous still clinging to the word. The *tremendum* may then be rendered more adequately *tremenda majestas*, or "aweful majesty." This second element of majesty may continue to be vividly preserved, where the first, that of unapproachability, recedes and dies away, as may be seen, for example, in mysticism. It is especially in relation to this element of majesty or absolute overpoweringness that the creature-consciousness, of which we have already spoken, comes upon the scene, as a sort of shadow or subjective reflection of it. Thus, in contrast to "the overpowering" of which we are conscious as an object over against the self, there is the feeling of one's own submergence, of being but "dust and ashes" and nothingness. And this forms the numinous raw material for the feeling of religious humility.[1] . . .

The Element of "Energy" or Urgency

There is, finally, a third element comprised in those of *tremendum* and *majestas*, awefulness and majesty, and this I venture to call the "urgency" or "energy" of the numinous object. It is particularly vividly perceptible in the οργή or "wrath"; and it everywhere clothes itself in symbolical expressions—vitality, passion, emotional temper, will, force, movement,[2] excitement, activity, impetus. These features are typical and recur again and again from the daemonic level up to the idea of the "living" God. We have here the factor that has everywhere more than any other prompted the fiercest opposition to the "philosophic" God of mere rational speculation, who can be put into a definition. And for their part the philosophers have condemned these expressions of the energy of the numen, whenever they are brought on to the scene, as sheer anthropomorphism. In so far as their opponents have for the most part themselves failed to recognize that the terms they have borrowed from the sphere of human conative and affective life have merely value as analogies, the philosophers are right to condemn them. But they are wrong, in so far as, this error notwithstanding, these terms stood for a genuine aspect of the divine nature—its non-rational aspect—a due consciousness of which served to protect religion itself from being "rationalized" away.

For wherever men have been contending for the "living" God or for

---

[1]Cf. R. R. Marett, "The Birth of Humility," in *The Threshold of Religion*, 2nd ed., 1914. [Tr.]

[2]The "mobilitas Dei" of Lactantius.

voluntarism, there, we may be sure, have been non-rationalists fighting rationalists and rationalism. It was so with Luther in his controversy with Erasmus; and Luther's *omnipotentia Dei* in his *De Servo Arbitrio* is nothing but the union of "majesty"—in the sense of absolute supremacy—with this "energy," in the sense of a force that knows not stint nor stay, which is urgent, active, compelling, and alive. In mysticism, too, this element of "energy" is a very living and vigorous factor, at any rate in the "voluntaristic" mysticism, the mysticism of love, where it is very forcibly seen in that "consuming fire" of love whose burning strength the mystic can hardly bear, but begs that the heat that has scorched him may be mitigated, lest he be himself destroyed by it. And in this urgency and pressure the mystic's "love" claims a perceptible kinship with the οργή itself, the scorching and consuming wrath of God; it is the same "energy," only differently directed. "Love," says one of the mystics, "is nothing else than quenched wrath."

The element of "energy" reappears in Fichte's speculations on the Absolute as the gigantic, never-resting, active world-stress, and in Schopenhauer's daemonic "Will." At the same time both these writers are guilty of the same error that is already found in myth; they transfer "natural" attributes, which ought only to be used as "ideograms" for what is itself properly beyond utterance, to the non-rational as real qualifications of it, and they mistake symbolic expressions of feelings for adequate concepts upon which a "scientific" structure of knowledge may be based.

In Goethe, as we shall see later, the same element of energy is emphasized in a quite unique way in his strange descriptions of the experience he calls "daemonic."

THE ANALYSIS OF "MYSTERIUM"

> *Ein begriffener Gott ist kein Gott.*
> "A God comprehended is no God."
> TERSTEEGEN.

We gave to the object to which the numinous consciousness is directed the name *mysterium tremendum,* and we then set ourselves first to determine the meaning of the adjective *tremendum*—which we found to be itself only justified by analogy—because it is more easily analyzed than the substantive idea *mysterium.* We have now to turn to this, and try, as best we may, by hint and suggestion, to get to a clearer apprehension of what it implies.

The "Wholly Other"

It might be thought that the adjective itself gives an explanation of the substantive; but this is not so. It is not merely analytical; it is a synthetic

attribute to it; i.e. *tremendum* adds something not necessarily inherent in
mysterium. It is true that the reactions in consciousness that correspond to
the one readily and spontaneously overflow into those that correspond to
the other; in fact, anyone sensitive to the use of words would commonly
feel that the idea of "mystery" (*mysterium*) is so closely bound up with its
synthetic qualifying attribute "aweful" (*tremendum*) that one can hardly say
the former without catching an echo of the latter, "mystery" almost of
itself becoming "aweful mystery" to us. But the passage from the one idea
to the other need not by any means be always so easy. The elements of
meaning implied in "awefulness" and "mysteriousness" are in themselves
definitely different. The latter may so far preponderate in the religious
consciousness, may stand out so vividly, that in comparison with it the
former almost sinks out of sight; a case which again could be clearly
exemplified from some forms of mysticism. Occasionally, on the other
hand, the reverse happens, and the *tremendum* may in turn occupy the
mind without the *mysterium*.

This latter, then, needs special consideration on its own account. We
need an expression for the mental reaction peculiar to it; and here, too,
only one word seems appropriate, though, as it is strictly applicable only to
a "natural" state of mind, it has here meaning only by analogy: it is the
word "stupor." *Stupor* is plainly a different thing from *tremor;* it signifies
blank wonder, an astonishment that strikes us dumb, amazement absolute.[3] Taken, indeed, in its purely natural sense, *mysterium* would first
mean merely a secret or a mystery in the sense of that which is alien to us,
uncomprehended and unexplained; and so far *mysterium* is itself merely
an ideogram, an analogical notion taken from the natural sphere, illustrating, but incapable of exhaustively rendering, our real meaning.
Taken in the religious sense, that which is "mysterious" is—to give it
perhaps the most striking expression—the "wholly other" ($\theta\acute{\alpha}\tau\epsilon\rho\text{ον}$, *any-
ad, alienum*), that which is quite beyond the sphere of the usual, the
intelligible, and the familiar, which therefore falls quite outside the limits
of the "canny," and is contrasted with it, filling the mind with blank
wonder and astonishment. . . .

In accordance with laws of which we shall have to speak again later,
this feeling or consciousness of the "wholly other" will attach itself to, or

[3]Compare also *obstupefacere*. Still more exact equivalents are the Greek $\theta\acute{\alpha}\mu\beta\text{ος}$ and
$\theta\alpha\mu\beta\epsilon\acute{\iota}\nu$. The sound $\theta\ \alpha\ \mu\ \beta$ *(thamb)* excellently depicts this state of mind of blank,
staring wonder. And the difference between the moments of *stupor* and *tremor* is very
finely suggested by the passage, Mark x. 32 (cf. *infra*, p. 158). On the other hand, what
was said above of the facility and rapidity with which the two moments merge and
blend is also markedly true of $\theta\acute{\alpha}\mu\beta\text{ος}$, which then becomes a classical term for the
(ennobled) awe of the numinous in general. So Mark xvi. 5 is rightly translated by
Luther "und sie entsetzten sich," and by the English Authorized Version "and they
were affrighted."

sometimes be indirectly aroused by means of, objects which are already puzzling upon the "natural" plane, or are of a surprising or astounding character; such as extraordinary phenomena or astonishing occurrences or things in inanimate nature, in the animal world, or among men. But here once more we are dealing with a case of association between things specifically different—the "numinous" and the "natural" moments of consciousness—and not merely with the gradual enhancement of one of them—the "natural"—till it becomes the other. As in the case of "natural fear" and "daemonic dread" already considered, so here the transition from natural to daemonic amazement is not a mere matter of degree. But it is only with the latter that the complementary expression *mysterium* perfectly harmonizes, as will be felt perhaps more clearly in the case of the adjectival form "mysterious." No one says, strictly and in earnest, of a piece of clockwork that is beyond his grasp, or of a science that he cannot understand: "That is 'mysterious' to me."

It might be objected that the mysterious is something which is and remains absolutely and invariably beyond our understanding, whereas that which merely eludes our understanding for a time but is perfectly intelligible in principle should be called, not a "mystery," but merely a "problem." But this is by no means an adequate account of the matter. The truly "mysterious" object is beyond our apprehension and comprehension, not only because our knowledge has certain irremovable limits, but because in it we come upon something inherently "wholly other," whose kind and character are incommensurable with our own, and before which we therefore recoil in a wonder that strikes us chill and numb.[4]

This may be made still clearer by a consideration of that degraded offshoot and travesty of the genuine "numinous" dread or awe, the fear of ghosts. Let us try to analyse this experience. We have already specified the peculiar feeling-element of "dread" aroused by the ghost as that of "grue," grisly horror.[5] Now this "grue" obviously contributes something to the attraction which ghost-stories exercise, in so far, namely, as the relaxation of tension ensuing upon our release from it relieves the mind

----

[4]In *Confessions*, ii. 9. 1, Augustine very strikingly suggests this stiffening, benumbing element of the "wholly other" and its contrast to the rational aspect of the numen; the *dissimile* and the *simile:*

"Quid est illud, quod interlucet mihi et percutit cor meum sine laesione? Et inhorresco et inardesco. *Inhorresco,* in quantum *dissimilis* ei sum. Inardesco, in quantum similis ei sum."

("What is that which gleams through me and smites my heart without wounding it? I am both a-shudder and a-glow. A-shudder, in so far as I am unlike it, a-glow in so far as I am like it.")

[5]*gruseln, gräsen.*

in a pleasant and agreeable way. So far, however, it is not really the ghost itself that gives us pleasure, but the fact that we are rid of it. But obviously this is quite insufficient to explain the ensnaring attraction of the ghost-story. The ghost's real attraction rather consists in this, that of itself and in an uncommon degree it entices the imagination, awakening strong interest and curiosity; it is the weird thing itself that allures the fancy. But it does this, not because it is "something long and white" (as someone once defined a ghost), nor yet through any of the positive and conceptual attributes which fancies about ghosts have invented, but because it is a thing that "doesn't really exist at all," the "wholly other," something which has no place in our scheme of reality but belongs to an absolutely different one, and which at the same time arouses an irrepressible interest in the mind.

But that which is perceptibly true in the fear of ghosts, which is, after all, only a caricature of the genuine thing, is in a far stronger sense true of the "daemonic" experience itself, of which the fear of ghosts is a mere off-shoot. And while, following this main line of development, this element in the numinous consciousness, the feeling of the "wholly other," is heightened and clarified, its higher modes of manifestation come into being, which set the numinous object in contrast not only to everything wonted and familiar (i.e. in the end, to nature in general), thereby turning it into the "supernatural," but finally to the world itself, and thereby exalt it to the "supramundane," that which is above the whole worldorder. . . .

Let us look back once more from the point we have reached over the course our inquiry has so far taken. As the sub-title of this book suggests, we were to investigate the non-rational element in the idea of the divine. The words "non-rational" and "irrational" are to-day used almost at random. The nonrational is sought over the most widely different regions, and writers generally shirk the trouble of putting down precisely what they intend by the term, giving it often the most multifarious meanings or applying it with such vague generality that it admits of the most diverse interpretations. Pure fact in contrast to law, the empirical in contrast to reason, the contingent in contrast to the necessary, the psychological in contrast to transcendental fact, that which is known *a posteriori* in contrast to that which is determinable *a priori;* power, will, and arbitrary choice in contrast to reason, knowledge, and determination by value; impulse, instinct, and the obscure forces of the subconscious in contrast to insight, reflection, and intelligible plan; mystical depths and stirrings in the soul, surmise, presentiment, intuition, prophecy, and finally the "occult" powers also; or, in general, the uneasy stress and universal fermentation of the time, with its groping after the thing never yet heard or seen in poetry or the plastic arts—all these and more may claim the names "non-rational," "irrational," and according to circumstances are extolled or condemned as modern "irrationalism." Whoever makes use of the word "non-rational" to-day ought to say what he actually means by it. This we did in our introductory chapter. We began with the "rational" in the idea of God and the divine, meaning by the term that in it which is clearly to be grasped by our power of conceiving, and enters the domain of familiar and definable conceptions. We went on to maintain that beneath this sphere of clarity and lucidity lies a hidden depth, inaccessible to our conceptual thought, which we in so far call the "non-rational."

The meaning of the two contrasted terms may be made plainer by an illustration. A deep joy may fill our minds without any clear realization upon our part of its source and the object to which it refers, though some such objective reference there must always be. But as attention is directed to it the obscure object becomes clearly identified in precise conceptual terms. Such an object cannot, then, be called, in our sense of the word, "non-rational." But it is quite otherwise with religious "bliss" and its essentially numinous aspect, the *fascinans*. Not the most concentrated attention can elucidate the object to which this state of mind refers, bringing it out of the impenetrable obscurity of feeling into the domain of the conceptual understanding. It remains purely a felt experience, only to be indicated symbolically by "ideograms." That is what we mean by saying it is non-rational.

And the same is true of all the moments of the numinous experience. The consciousness of a "wholly other" evades precise formulation in words, and we have to employ symbolic phrases which seem sometimes sheer paradox, that is, *ir*rational, not merely non-rational, in import. So with religious awe and reverence. In ordinary fear and in moral reverence I can indicate in conceptual terms what it is that I fear or revere; injury, e.g., or ruin in the one case, heroism or strength of character in the other. But the object of *religious* awe or reverence—the *tremendum* and *augustum*, cannot be fully determined conceptually: it is non-rational, as is the beauty of a musical composition, which no less eludes complete conceptual analysis.

DISCUSSION QUESTIONS

1. Do you agree with Schleiermacher's claim that religion arises out of the experience of a feeling of utter dependence, awe, and finitude? Why or why not?
2. Do you think it makes sense to speak of the experience of the numinous as nonmystical? Give reasons for your answer.
3. Is the term numinous a good substitution for what Otto wants to describe as the "holy"? Can you think of a better term?

4. Have you ever had an experience of the numinous? If so, can you describe it?
5. What aspects of the numinous does Otto try to capture in the terms *mysterium tremendum, majestas,* and "urgency"?
6. What is the relation between an experience of the numinous and one's ultimate concern as Tillich describes it?
7. What is the relationship between mystery and the Wholly Other? That is, can the Wholly Other be experienced and present itself in a nonmysterious way? And how would you relate mystery and the nonrational element in religion?

MARTIN BUBER

The Experience
of
the Eternal You

Thus far we have examined two kinds of human experience in which the religious dimension emerges. Tillich described the sense of ultimate concern that is at the heart of our humanness. Our ultimate concern, whatever it may be, gives focus and unity to our personality, and when the content of this concern is truly ultimate, then religious faith in the proper sense of the term arises. Rudolf Otto gave more attention to the content of such a faith when he focused on the experience of the numinous, the divine experienced as wholly other, majestic, and powerful. Although Otto undoubtedly pinpointed an important phenomenon in religion, the numinous may not be a part of the experience of most persons reading this book. To be sure, there are many experiences that have a numinous quality to them, but to build a satisfying analysis of religion based on the analysis of the *mysterium tremendum, majestas,* and *fascinans* may seem remote to those for whom religion is a much more inward affair of the heart.

It is to such persons that another German philosopher, Martin Buber, may appeal. Buber, whose own religious tradition was that of Judaism, emphasizes a side of religious experience that is faithful both to the Jewish and Christian religions, namely, that without meaningful relations to other persons, no one can have a meaningful relation to God. Because he underscored the interpersonal aspect of religion, Buber has frequently been classified with the existentialist theologians who, among other things, are known for their emphasis on personal encounter. For existentialists, the point of departure for philosophy is the question of what it means to be an existing, human being, and central to this question is our relationship to other persons. Although one does not find in Buber the usual vocabulary of existential philosophy, the central emphases of his work are certainly compatible with existentialism. It is with the central question of the meaning of humanness that Buber begins.

Before turning to the selection from Buber, a word or two of background on the terms he uses is required. The citation is from his book originally published in German under the title *Ich und Du,* which in its English translation can be rendered either *I and Thou* or *I and You.* The fact that either English translation is possible is due to the lack in English of a distinction between formal and informal pronouns. German, as well as French, has two forms for the personal pronoun which are collapsed into the single English pronoun *you.* In German, the formal pronoun is *Sie;* in French *vous.* One always uses the formal pronoun when addressing casual acquaintances or in formal settings. The informal pronouns, *du* in German and *tu* in French, are reserved for intimate friends, members of one's family, small children, and animals.

At one time, speakers of English were able to make a similar distinction. The pronoun *you* was used in situations requiring formal language; the familiar pronoun *thou* was used only in situations of the most intimate familiarity. Through the passage of time this distinction has been lost, and if anything the word *thou* has taken on a formal significance by its use almost exclusively in liturgical language. This was probably a result of the continued widespread use of the King James Version of the Bible in which *thee, thine* and *thou,* as well as the verb forms that went with them *(art, hast* and *wilt)* were used throughout. In 1611, the year in which the King James Version appeared, the distinction between formal and familiar pronouns was still recognized. It is significant to note that the translators of that day chose the familiar pronouns for the language of Scripture. As mentioned, *thee, thou,* etc., have since taken on a formal meaning. In fact, when the translators of the 1946 Revised Standard Version of the Bible omitted the archaic pronouns, many persons actually considered it an act of irreverence. The original Greek of the New Testament knows of no such distinctions, and the current use of the pronouns, *you, yours,* etc., is in keeping with the meanings of *thee* and *thou* when they were current in the seventeenth century.

Today, however, English does not allow a distinction between the formal and familiar second-person pronouns the way German does, so one must choose between *I and Thou* and *I and You* as a translation for the German *Ich und Du.* Which translation is used matters little so long as one knows that Buber's use of the familiar pronoun is intended to signify a relationship based on the most intimate kind of personal relationship. The translation of the selections used in this book is from Walter Kaufmann, who chose *I and You* (which, in view of current English usage, is probably preferable to the archaic *I and Thou).*

Buber begins by suggesting that there are two basic *word-pairs:* "I-You" and "I-It." By calling these the two *primary* or *basic* word-pairs, Buber emphasizes that there are two ways of becoming a self or an "I," for there are two primary ways of relating. In short, the terms I-You, and I-It denote two modes of human existence. Although the vocabulary Buber uses is unique, the ideas are not, for it was an insight of the ancient Greek philosophers that human beings are indisputably social creatures. Aristotle observed that a person who had no need of human society was either a beast or a god, not a human being. The Greek language also gives us the term *idiot* from the Greek word *idios,* meaning one's own or personal. A person who avoids human society and shuns personal relationships by insisting on being alone is truly "idiotic" in the Greek way of thinking. This is echoed by Buber, who sees two modes of human existence, characterized by the pair of terms I-You and I-It. A person only becomes human in relationships, and these paired terms describe two possible ways of relating.

The I-You relationship is one of intimacy, mutuality, sharing and trust. The I-it relationship is one of having, using, exploiting. To put it in different terms, the I-It relationship is one-way, from subject to object, from I to thing. The I-You relationship is a two-way form of relating in which the I gives to and receives from the You. Examples of these two types of relationships are easy to find. Anyone who has ever dealt with a large bureaucracy, a huge organization, or perhaps even registered for college courses, knows what it is like to be treated as a thing. When one is treated as an "it," there is no mutuality; the one so treating you has only an interest in getting something from you and is totally unconcerned about relating to you as a person.

When we relate to another person as a You, we do not treat that person as a thing or an object. This is what Buber means when he says, "When I confront a human being as my You and speak the basic word I-You to him, then he is no thing among things nor does he consist of things." There is nothing wrong with the I-It relationship per se as long as it is limited to things, to objects. But to treat a person as a thing, as an It, is to debase not only the other person but to sacrifice one's own humanity as well. Buber's point is that we become human only through genuinely human relationships, I-You relationships, and when we treat a You as an It, we lose something of our own humanness. This can be applied to many situations: in the master-slave relationship, the master treats the slave as an It, and the master is dehumanized just as surely as the slave. We should not possess another person or exploit another person. Our vocabulary, if we follow Buber's lead, would have to be changed. We could speak of having a car, having a house, or having a dog, for all these are in the sphere of the I-It, and we do relate ourselves to objects in the sphere of having. It would, however, debase the relationship between husband and wife or parent and child to say that we *have* a wife, or *have* children. It would be better to say that we are married (a relationship) and are parents (a relationship).

This might seem highly abstract until we realize that Buber has pointed out an extremely important issue. The I-You relationship is one involving our whole being which calls for a response of the whole being of the other. If we establish an I-You relationship with another person, we will not be able to hate that person, for hate can arise only in an I-It relationship. We see this vividly in wartime when the powerful forces of public propaganda are brought to bear against the "enemy," whom we are taught to hate. We devise a whole arsenal of epithets to depersonalize the "enemy": wartime propaganda speaks of the reds, gooks, nips, huns, krauts, and so forth. We can hate an abstract "enemy" but not a person to whom we are related in an I-You way.

It is easy to misread Buber and think that the I-You relationship can only be between persons. Buber suggests, however, that it is possible to sustain an I-You relationship with animals, trees, flowers, and even inanimate objects. A logger surveying a stand of timber and calculating the number of board feet that will result when the trees are harvested has only an I-It relationship with the forest. The logger is concerned only with exploiting the resources of the forest and marketing the lumber successfully to make the largest possible profit. This is not the only way to relate to a tree or to a forest. Basking in the shade of a tree, contemplating it, writing a poem about it, marveling at its wonder and complexity—all these signal an I-You relationship. And who has not experienced an I-You relationship with a family pet whose whole life is focused on the relationship with the family?

Again this might sound like the abstract meditations of a philosopher until one realizes that it meshes perfectly with the current ecological emphasis on the symbiotic relationship we must establish with nature. We have come to, or are at least rapidly approaching, the end of the era when we can look at nature as an unlimited source of material to be exploited at our whim. The biosphere is a fragile thing, and only if we can place ourselves in a relationship in which we see our interdependence—us on nature, nature on us—can we hope to avoid ecological disaster.

When we think of God, a word which Buber says is "the most burdened of all human words," it is possible to have either an I-It or an I-Thou relationship with God. For many persons God is an abstraction to be argued about, proved by rational argument, or discussed with the same intensity one devotes to an examination of the current state of the weather. The philosopher who attempts to prove the existence of God, according to Buber, is relating to God in an I-It way. To treat God as a problem to be solved by rationalistic exercises is to relate to God as an object, a thing, an it. The only satisfying relationship with God is one of mutuality and inward intensity in an I-You relationship. We relate to God not only as a You but as the Eternal You. But where, we might ask, is such a relationship to be discovered?

Buber's answer is that God, the Eternal You, is ever present. God is present in every genuine I-You relationship, and each genuine I-You relationship whets the appetite for a relationship with God as the Eternal You. Buber would demur at Otto's insistence that God is the Wholly Other. God is that, to be sure, but Buber insists that God is also the Wholly Present. The proper relationship to God is not one of argumentation and debate over his existence and attributes, but one based on prayer and sacrifice. It is for this reason that the most widely used analogy in terms of which we speak of God is as a person. This way of referring to God is an attempt to capture the sense of God as the Eternal You while recognizing that the analogy of God as person cannot exhaust the nature and essence of God.

As was the case with Otto, reading Buber is less like analyzing a traditional philosophical argument than it is like reading a poem. The comparison is proper, for Buber is something of a philosophical poet. He is not so much attempting to prove something to you as he is calling to your attention aspects of human experience that might otherwise be overlooked. Like all great poets, he sometimes creates his own vocabulary, but in this creation lies the richness of his thought.

I and Thou*

The world is twofold for man in accordance with his twofold attitude.

The attitude of man is twofold in accordance with the two basic words he can speak.

The basic words are not single words but word pairs.

One basic word is the word pair I-You.

The other basic word is the word pair I-It; but this basic word is not changed when He or She takes the place of It.

Thus the I of man is also twofold.

For the I of the basic word I-You is different from that in the basic word I-It.[1]

Basic words do not state something that might exist outside them; by being spoken they establish a mode of existence.[2]

Basic words are spoken with one's being.[3]

When one says You, the I of the word pair I-You is said, too.

When one says It, the I of the word pair I-It is said, too.

The basic word I-You can only be spoken with one's whole being.

The basic word I-It can never be spoken with one's whole being.

There is no I as such but only the I of the basic word I-You and the I of the basic word I-It.

When a man says I, he means one or the other. The I he means is present when he says I. And when he says You or It, the I of one or the other basic word is also present.

Being I and saying I are the same. Saying I and saying one of the two basic words are the same.

Whoever speaks one of the basic words enters into the word and stands in it.

The life of a human being does not exist merely in the sphere of goal-directed verbs. It does not consist merely of activities that have something for their object.

*Source: Selections from *I and Thou* by Martin Buber are used with the permission of Charles Scribner's Sons. Copyright © 1970 Charles Scribner's Sons.

[1]In the first edition the next section began: "Basic words do not signify things but relations." This sentence was omitted by Buber in 1957 and in all subsequent editions.

[2]*stiften sie einen Bestand.* The locution is most unusual, and *Bestand* in any applicable sense is very rare. Buber intends a contrast with "that might exist" (*was . . . bestünde*).

[3]*Wesen.*

I perceive something. I feel something. I imagine something. I want something. I sense something. I think something. The life of a human being does not consist merely of all this and its like.

All this and its like is the basis of the realm of It.

But the realm of You has another basis.

Whoever says You does not have something for his object. For wherever there is something there is also another something; every It borders on other Its; It is only by virtue of bordering on others. But where You is said there is no something. You has no borders.

Whoever says You does not have something; he has nothing. But he stands in relation. . . .

When I confront a human being as my You and speak the basic word I-You to him, then he is no thing among things nor does he consist of things.

He is no longer He or She, limited by other Hes and Shes, a dot in the world grid of space and time, nor a condition that can be experienced and described, a loose bundle of named qualities. Neighborless and seamless, he is You and fills the firmament. Not as if there were nothing but he; but everything else lives in *his* light.

Even as a melody is not composed of tones, nor a verse of words, nor a statue of lines—one must pull and tear to turn a unity into a multiplicity—so it is with the human being to whom I say You. I can abstract from him the color of his hair or the color of his speech or the color of his graciousness; I have to do this again and again; but immediately he is no longer You.

And even as prayer is not in time but time in prayer, the sacrifice not in space but space in the sacrifice—and whoever reverses the relation annuls the reality—I do not find the human being to whom I say You in any Sometime and Somewhere. I can place him there and have to do this again and again, but immediately he becomes a He or a She, an It, and no longer remains my You.

As long as the firmament of the You is spread over me, the tempests of causality cower at my heels, and the whirl of doom[4] congeals.

The human being to whom I say You I do not experience. But I stand in relation to him, in the sacred basic word. Only when I step out of this do I experience him again. Experience is remoteness from You.

The relation can obtain even if the human being to whom I say You does not hear it in his experience. For You is more than It knows. You does more, and more happens to it, than It knows. No deception reaches this far: here is the cradle of actual life. . . .

---

[4]*Verhängnis* means, and has been consistently translated as, doom; *Schicksal*, as fate.

The You encounters me by grace—it cannot be found by seeking. But that I speak the basic word to it is a deed of my whole being, is my essential deed.

The You encounters me. But I enter into a direct relationship to it. Thus the relationship is election and electing, passive and active at once. An action of the whole being must approach passivity, for it does away with all partial actions and thus with any sense of action, which always depends on limited exertions.

The basic word I-You can be spoken only with one's whole being. The concentration and fusion into a whole being can never be accomplished by me, can never be accomplished without me. I require a You to become; becoming I, I say You.

All actual life is encounter. . . .

Extended, the lines of relationships intersect in the eternal You.

Every single You is a glimpse of that. Through every single You the basic word addresses the eternal You. The mediatorship of the You of all beings accounts for the fullness of our relationships to them—and for the lack of fulfillment. The innate You is actualized each time without ever being perfected. It attains perfection solely in the immediate relationship to the You that in accordance with its nature cannot become an It.

Men have addressed their eternal You by many names. When they sang of what they had thus named, they still meant You: the first myths were hymns of praise. Then the names entered into the It-language; men felt impelled more and more to think of and to talk about their eternal You as an It. But all names of God remain hallowed—because they have been used not only to speak *of* God but also to speak *to* him.

Some would deny any legitimate use of the word God because it has been misused so much. Certainly it is the most burdened of all human words. Precisely for that reason it is the most imperishable and unavoidable.[5] And how much weight has all erroneous talk about God's nature and works (although there never has been nor can be any such talk that is not erroneous) compared with the one truth that all men who have addressed God really meant him? For whoever pronounces the word God and really means You, addresses, no matter what his delusion, the true You of his life that cannot be restricted by any other and to whom he stands in a relationship that includes all others.

But whoever abhors the name and fancies[6] that he is godless—when he addresses with his whole devoted being the You of his life that cannot be restricted by any other, he addresses God. . . .

[5]*das unvergänglichste und unumgänglichste.*
[6]*wähnt.* Until 1957: *glaubt* (believes).

Every actual relationship to another being[7] in the world is exclusive. Its You is freed and steps forth to confront us in its uniqueness. It fills the firmament—not as if there were nothing else, but everything else lives in *its* light. As long as the presence of the relationship endures, this world-wideness cannot be infringed. But as soon as a You becomes an It, the world-wideness of the relationship appears as an injustice against the world, and its exclusiveness as an exclusion of the universe.

In the relation to God, unconditional exclusiveness and unconditional inclusiveness are one. For those who enter into the absolute relationship, nothing particular retains any importance—neither things nor beings, neither earth nor heaven—but everything is included in the relationship. For entering into the pure relationship does not involve ignoring everything but seeing everything in the You, not renouncing the world but placing it upon its proper ground. Looking away from the world is no help toward God; staring at the world is no help either; but whoever beholds the world in him stands in his presence. "World here, God there"—that is It-talk; and "God in the world"—that, too, is It-talk; but leaving out nothing, leaving nothing behind, to comprehend all—all the world—in comprehending the You, giving the world its due and truth, to have nothing besides God but to grasp everything in him, that is the perfect relationship.

One does not find God if one remains in the world; one does not find God if one leaves the world. Whoever goes forth to his You with his whole being and carries to it all the being of the world, finds him whom one cannot seek.

Of course, God is "the wholly other"; but he is also the wholly same: the wholly present. Of course, he is the *mysterium tremendum* that appears and overwhelms; but he is also the mystery of the obvious that is closer to me than my own I.[8]

When you fathom the life of things and of conditionality, you reach the indissoluble; when you dispute the life of things and of conditionality, you wind up before the nothing; when you consecrate life you encounter the living God. . . .

By its very nature the eternal You cannot become an It; because by its very nature it cannot be placed within measure and limit, not even within the measure of the immeasurable and the limit of the unlimited; because by its very nature it cannot be grasped as a sum of qualities, not

---

[7] *zu enem Wesen oder einer Wesenheit:* in English the single word "being" must serve for both terms.

[8] Rudolf Otto had argued in *Das Heilige* (1917; translated as *The Idea of the Holy,* 1923) that God is "the wholly other" and experienced as a *mysterium tremendum.*

even as an infinite sum of qualities that have been raised to transcendence; because it is not to be found either in or outside the world, because it cannot be experienced; because it cannot be thought; because we transgress against it, against that which has being, if we say: "I believe that he is"—even "he" is still a metaphor, while "you" is not.

And yet we reduce the eternal You ever again to an It, to something, turning God into a thing, in accordance with our nature. Not capriciously. The history of God as a thing, the way of the God-thing through religion and its marginal forms,[9] through its illuminations and eclipses, the times when it heightened and when it destroyed life, the way from the living God and back to him again, the metamorphoses of the present, of embedment in forms,[10] of objectification, of conceptualization, dissolution, and renewal are one way, are *the* way. . . .

The encounter with God does not come to man in order that he may henceforth attend to God[11] but in order that he may prove its meaning in action in the world. All revelation is a calling and a mission. But again and again man shuns actualization and bends back toward the revealer: he would rather attend to God than to the world. Now that he has bent back, however, he is no longer confronted by a You; he can do nothing but place a divine It in the realm of things, believe that he knows about God as an It, and talk about him. Even as the egomaniac does not live anything directly, whether it be a perception or an affection, but reflects on his perceiving or affectionate I and thus misses the truth of the process, thus the theomaniac (who, incidentally, can get along very well with the egomaniac in the very same soul) will not let the gift take full effect but reflects instead on that which gives, and misses both.

When you are sent forth, God remains presence for you; whoever walks in his mission always has God before him: the more faithful the fulfillment, the stronger and more constant the nearness. Of course, he cannot attend to God but he can converse with him. Bending back, on the other hand, turns God into an object. It appears to be a turning toward the primal ground, but belongs in truth to the world movement of turning away, even as the apparent turning away of those who fulfill their mission belongs in truth to the world movement of turning toward. . . .

How—people ask—can the eternal You be at the same time exclusive and inclusive? How is it possible for man's You-relationship to God, which requires our unconditional turning toward God, without any distraction, nevertheless to embrace all the other I-You relationships of this man and to bring them, as it were, to God?

[9]Buber in March 1937 suggested: "and through the products" and "fringe?" But "its marginal forms" is closer to *ihre Randgebilde*.

[10]*Eingestaltung:* a coinage.

[11]*sich mit Gott befasse.*

Note that the question is not about God but only about our relationship to him. And yet in order to be able to answer, I have to speak of him. For our relationship to him is as supra-contradictory as it is because he is as supra-contradictory as he is.

Of course, we shall speak only of what God is in his relationship to a human being. And even that can be said only in a paradox; or more precisely, by using a concept paradoxically; or still more precisely, by means of a paradoxical combination of a nominal concept with an adjective that contradicts the familiar content of the concept. The insistence on this contradiction must give way to the insight that thus, and only thus, the indispensable designation of this object by this concept can be justified. The content of the concept undergoes a revolutionary transformation and expansion, but that is true of every concept that, impelled by the actuality of faith, we take from the realm of immanence and apply to transcendence.

The designation of God as a person is indispensable for all who, like myself, do not mean a principle when they say "God," although mystics like Eckhart occasionally equate "Being" with him, and who, like myself, do not mean an idea when they say "God," although philosophers like Plato could at times take him for one—all who, like myself, mean by "God" him that, whatever else he may be in addition, enters into a direct relationship to us human beings through creative, revelatory, and redemptive acts, and thus makes it possible for us to enter into a direct relationship to him. This ground and meaning of our existence establishes each time a mutuality of the kind that can obtain only between persons. The concept of personhood is, of course, utterly incapable of describing the nature of God; but it is permitted and necessary to say that God is *also* a person. If for once I were to translate what I mean into the language of a philosopher, Spinoza, I should have to say that of God's infinitely many attributes we human beings know not two, as Spinoza thought, but three: in addition to spiritlikeness—the source of what we call spirit—and naturelikeness exemplified by what we know as nature, also thirdly the attribute of personlikeness.[12] From this last attribute I should then derive my own and all men's being persons, even as I should derive from the first two my own and all men's being spirit and being nature. And only this third attribute, personlikeness, could then be said to be known directly in its quality as an attribute.

But now the contradiction appears, appealing to the familiar content of the concept of a person. A person, it says, is by definition an independent individual and yet also relativized by the plurality of other independent individuals; and this, of course, could not be said of God.

[12]*Geisthaftigkeit . . . Naturhaftigkeit . . . Personhaftigkeit.* These three coinages are highly abstract and elusive.

This contradiction is met by the paradoxical designation of God as the absolute person, that is one that cannot be relativized. It is as the absolute person that God enters into the direct relationship to us. The contradiction must give way to this higher insight.

Now we may say that God carries his absoluteness into his relationship with man. Hence the man who turns toward him need not turn his back on any other I-You relationship: quite legitimately he brings them all to God and allows them to become transfigured "in the countenance of God."

One should beware altogether of understanding the conversation with God—the conversation of which I had to speak in this book and in almost all of my later books—as something that occurs merely apart from or above the everyday. God's address to man penetrates the events in all our lives and all the events in the world around us, everything biographical and everything historical, and turns it into instruction,[13] into demands for you and me. Event upon event, situation upon situation is enabled and empowered by this personal language to call upon the human person to endure and decide. Often we think that there is nothing to be heard as if we had not long ago plugged wax into our own ears.

The existence of mutuality between God and man cannot be proved any more than the existence of God. Anyone who dares nevertheless to speak of it bears witness and invokes the witness of those whom he addresses—present or future witness.

DISCUSSION QUESTIONS

1. Whereas Otto suggests that we view God as Wholly Other, Buber urges that we understand God as both Wholly Other and wholly same. Do you think this is a contradiction? Give reasons for your answer.
2. Does the phrase I-Thou or I-You best capture the sense of intimacy that Buber intended?
3. What would be the practical difference in establishing an I-Thou relationship with God rather than an I-It relationship with God?
4. Do you agree with the implication of Buber's view that we encounter God in every meaningful I-Thou relationship with other persons? If so, what does this do to attempt to prove that God exists by means of rational arguments and proofs?
5. "All life is encounter," Buber says. In what sort of encounter does the religious dimension of life arise?

[13]*Weisung* is Buber's translation of *Torah*. He entitled his version of the Pentateuch: *Die Fünf Bücher der Weisung*. But *ein Wegweiser* is a signpost that, literally, points the way. *Weisung* could also be rendered as "direction."

PETER BERGER

The Experience
of
Signals of Transcendence

While reading Otto and Buber, perhaps you were thinking that their descriptions of religious experience are somewhat removed from the world of everyday experience. Certainly Buber's suggestion that we can experience the Eternal You through meaningful encounters with other persons is clear enough, but it may prove more difficult to relate this to the experience Otto describes of the Wholly Other. For those who have never experienced the numinous, Otto's account may sound like the geography of a strange, never-visited land. If you feel this way, don't give up on religious experience yet, for the last reading in this section is from a contemporary author who attempts to describe a type of religious experience that arises within the realm of ordinary life. Peter Berger is a sociologist whose writings show a thorough knowledge of philosophical issues and whose arguments evidence a philosophical frame of mind. His keen insights into religion as a social phenomenon are provocative for theologians and philosophers alike.

Like Buber and Otto, Berger speaks of a transcendent order, that is, a realm of being that lies beyond and hence transcends the natural world of ordinary experience. Certainly a transcendent order is presupposed by both Christian theology and Judaism, for God as a transcendent being is basic to both religious traditions. Yet there is perhaps something arcane about speaking of the numinous breaking in on our everyday life or the Eternal You being glimpsed in every genuine I-You relationship.

In fact, there may be a more troubling doubt lurking in your mind at this point. To be sure, we can admit that we have moods that might be described as producing numinous feelings, and we are doubtless moved by genuine personal relationships that make us long for something like the Eternal You; but how can we be sure that there genuinely is a Something, or a Someone, who can satisfy these longings? What if it all is just a giant exercise in wishful thinking, a projection of our own fears, incapacities, and inadequacies into a longed-for Being of supernatural dimensions. This is not a new objection to religious experience, but it has perhaps been restated more forcefully by the work of Freud who saw in the figure of a Father God an infantile projection of mankind's own weakness. The nineteenth century theologian Ludwig Feuerbach, in his book *The Essence of Christianity* went so far as to suggest that religion is entirely a matter of our projection of the ideal images of humanity. Feuerbach in effect reversed the traditional theological claim that God made man in his own image by suggesting that man makes God in man's own image.

Berger discusses this question within the context of sociology, and his pene-trating criticisms of some of the directions of contemporary sociological analyses are well worth reading for their own sake; a discussion of them here, however, would lead us away from the topic at hand. The central point of Berger's analysis of religion is to meet the challenge head-on. Let us admit that religion, as well as the other belief structures that mankind has produced, is a construction or a projection of human ideals. Where does that leave us? Berger's answer is that this admission leaves us with a fresh starting point for theology, a starting point beginning with man. This may not be such a bad place to start after all, for if there is a transcendent reality that lies beyond the world of ordinary experience, one might reasonably propose that there are indications of such a reality within our normal, everyday experience. Berger calls these indications "signals of transcendence," and describes them as "phenomena that are to be found within the domain of our 'natural' reality but that appear to point beyond that reality."[1]

There are echoes in Berger of older philosophical views; those of Hegel, of Plato, and a student of philosophy will immediately recognize them. Like Plato, Berger is faced within his own discipline with the claims (also current in Plato's day) that all of our alleged "knowledge" is merely a human product and that all truth is relative. A corollary of this view is that there is no way to decide among alternative truth claims, since they are all nothing but unprovable human opinions or, to use current language, human projections. This view is inherently unsatisfactory, as both Plato and Aristotle recognized, for the claim that there is no truth implies that it cannot itself be true. In other words, if we accept this relativizing tendency we are left with no more reason to accept the claim that "everything is relative" than the claim of someone else offering us some different "truth."

There is still another consideration that provides plausible reasoning for rejecting this relativizing tendency. It may be easy, even tempting, to relativize religion, ethics, and social "reality," but there is little support for relativizing the physical sciences. If any belief characterizes our twentieth-century mode of thought, it is that the physical sciences deal with reality, whereas philosophy and the other human sciences deal only with human opinions. There are, of course, disagree-ments among scientists; there may be heated debate among astrophysicists whether the big bang theory or the steady state theory about the origin of the universe is true, but there is scarcely any doubt that *some* theory is true. The history

---

[1]Peter Berger, *A Rumor of Angels* (Garden City: Doubleday & Co., Inc., 1969), p. 66.

of science is a continuous story of the proposing of hypotheses, which are subsequently abandoned for more adequate explanations, with each discarded theory viewed as a step closer to the discovery of the truth about physical nature. It would be something of a scientific heresy for a scientist to suggest that there is no truth about the origin of the universe, and it would be even less plausible for a scientist to suggest that any view in physics is just as good as any other since they are all only human opinions (philosophers may be able to get away with saying things like that, but physicists cannot).

The question of proof in the natural sciences is complex, and many renowned philosophers of science have devoted considerable effort to understanding it. But central to any proof theory is the notion of induction, which is the type of reasoning that proceeds step-by-step from specific experiences to general principles. Newton may not have been hit on the head by an apple as the myth has it, but he did generalize from specific observations to a group of formulas that describe physical motion. Not all mathematicians have been so rewarded, but some mathematical "projections" have adequately described physical reality. If the work of mathematicians is a construction, or a projection, why should we dismiss the "projections" of religious thinkers any more summarily than we would the "projections" of mathematicians? Earlier in the book from which the selection is taken, Berger makes the following observation:

> If there is any intellectual enterprise that appears to be a pure projection of human consciousness it is mathematics. A mathematician can be totally isolated from any contact with nature and still go on about his business of constructing mathematical universes, which spring from his mind as pure creations of human intellect. Yet the most astounding result of modern natural science is that the reiterated discovery (quite apart from this or that mathematical formulation of natural processes) that nature, too, is in its essence a fabric of mathematical relations. Put crudely, the mathematics that man projects out of his own consciousness somehow corresponds to a mathematical reality that is external to him, and which indeed his consciousness appears to reflect. How is this possible? It is possible, of course, because man himself is part of the same over-all reality, so that there is a fundamental affinity between the structures of his consciousness and the structures of the empirical world. Projection and reflection are movements within the same encompassing reality.[2]

The presupposition behind the approach that Berger pursues is that even if we admit that religion is a projection of human consciousness, that in itself is no reason to discard religion as not revealing anything about a reality that lies beyond the natural world of empirical life, for the one who projects is also a part of the total order of reality. As Berger explains in the following selection, his procedure is to suggest the outlines of what he calls an "inductive" faith. Whereas deductive faith would begin with certain truth claims about a transcendent order and deduce others from them, an inductive faith begins with human experience and proceeds to an interpretation of a possible realm that lies beyond human experience.

Berger's writing is straightforward and clear, and his discussion of the five "signals of transcendence" needs no further comment here. It is important to notice,

[2] *Ibid.,* pp. 58–59.

however, that with Berger we have moved from the pure descriptions of types of religious experience given by Tillich, Otto, and Buber, to a more argumentative form of exposition. Berger does offer incisive descriptions of the experiences that he refers to as signals of transcendence, but behind the description lies an inductive form of argument. The inductive faith that Berger proposes is not intended to lead to a set of dogmas about the nature of transcendence, even less to an organized religion. But it does point to a method of approach that may be more compatible with the beliefs of the Judaeo-Christian tradition than are other contemporary views of world.

In order to set Berger's analysis in a wider context, it is helpful to contrast his views with those of humanism and naturalism. Naturalism can be generally defined as the philosophical view that nature, or physical reality, can be explained on its own terms without recourse to any transcendent or "supernatural" reality. A humanist who shares naturalistic presuppositions would argue that human reality is the highest form of reality of which we have knowledge, and therefore human values demand our highest allegiances. Berger is certainly not a naturalist, but he could be described as a humanist; but here humanism takes on a different sense. Berger's humanism implies that human reality is the starting point for theology, but signals of transcendence lead beyond human reality, and even natural reality (considered as the empirical world of common life), to a transcendent reality which we can sometimes glimpse in the ordinary pursuits of life. In short, Berger's humanism suggests that human experience should be the focal point of theology because it leads to something more ultimate than our human existence. If there is such a transcendent realm, it is certainly religion's concern to examine it.

Starting With Man*

Throughout most of human history men have believed that the created order of society, in one way or another, corresponds to an underlying order of the universe, a divine order that supports and justifies all human attempts at ordering. . . . This faith is experienced not only in the history of societies and civilizations, but in the life of each individual—indeed, child psychologists tell us there can be no maturation without the presence of this faith at the outset of the socialization process. Man's propensity for order is grounded in a faith or trust that, ultimately, reality is "in order," "all right," "as it should be." Needless to say, there is no empirical method by which this faith can be tested. To assert it is itself

---

*Source: Selections from *A Rumor of Angels* by Peter L. Berger. Copyright © 1969 by Peter L. Berger. Reprinted by permission of Doubleday & Company, Inc.

an act of faith. But it is possible to proceed from the faith that is rooted in experience to the act of faith that transcends the empirical sphere, a procedure that could be called the *argument from ordering.*

In this fundamental sense, every ordering gesture is a signal of transcendence. This is certainly the case with the great ordering gestures that the historian of religion Mircea Eliade called "nomizations"—such as the archaic ceremonies in which a certain territory was solemnly incorporated into a society, or the celebration, in our own culture as in older ones, of the setting up of a new household through the marriage of two individuals. But it is equally true of more everyday occurrences. Consider the most ordinary, and probably most fundamental, of all—the ordering gesture by which a mother reassures her anxious child.

A child wakes up in the night, perhaps from a bad dream, and finds himself surrounded by darkness, alone, beset by nameless threats. At such a moment the contours of trusted reality are blurred or invisible, and in the terror of incipient chaos the child cries out for his mother. It is hardly an exaggeration to say that, at this moment, the mother is being invoked as a high priestess of protective order. It is she (and, in many cases, she alone) who has the power to banish the chaos and to restore the benign shape of the world. And, of course, any good mother will do just that. She will take the child and cradle him in the timeless gesture of the Magna Mater who became our Madonna. She will turn on a lamp, perhaps, which will encircle the scene with a warm glow of reassuring light. She will speak or sing to the child, and the content of this communication will invariably be the same—"Don't be afraid—everything is in order, everything is all right." If all goes well, the child will be reassured, his trust in reality recovered, and in this trust he will return to sleep.

All this, of course, belongs to the most routine experiences of life and does not depend upon any religious preconceptions. Yet this common scene raises a far from ordinary question, which immediately introduces a religious dimension: *Is the mother lying to the child?* The answer, in the most profound sense, can be "no" only if there is some truth in the religious interpretation of human existence. Conversely, if the "natural" is the only reality there is, the mother is lying to the child—lying out of love, to be sure, and obviously *not* lying to the extent that her reassurance is grounded in the fact of this love—but, in the final analysis, lying all the same. Why? *Because the reassurance, transcending the immediately present two individuals and their situation, implies a statement about reality as such. . . .*

If reality is coextensive with the "natural" reality that our empirical reason can grasp, then the experience *is* an illusion and the role that embodies it *is* a lie. For then it is perfectly obvious that everything is *not* in order, is *not* all right. The world that the child is being told to trust is the same world in which he will eventually die. If there is no other world, then the ultimate truth about this one is that eventually it will kill the child as it will kill his mother. This would not, to be sure, detract from the real presence of love and its very real comforts; it would even give this love a quality of tragic heroism. Nevertheless, the final truth would be not love but terror, not light but darkness. The nightmare of chaos, not the transitory safety of order, would be the final reality of the human situation. For, in the end, we must all find ourselves in darkness, alone with the night that will swallow us up. The face of reassuring love, bending over our terror, will then be nothing except an image of merciful illusion. In that case the last word about religion is Freud's. Religion is the childish fantasy that our parents run the universe for our benefit, a fantasy from which the mature individual must free himself in order to attain whatever measure of stoic resignation he is capable of.

It goes without saying that the preceding argument is not a moral one. It does not condemn the mother for this charade of world-building, if it be a charade. It does not dispute the right of atheists to be parents (though it is not without interest that there have been atheists who have rejected parenthood for exactly these reasons). The argument from ordering is metaphysical rather than ethical. To restate it: In the observable human propensity to order reality there is an intrinsic impulse to give cosmic scope to this order, an impulse that implies not only that human order in some way corresponds to an order that transcends it, but that this transcendent order is of such a character that man can trust himself and his destiny to it. There is a variety of human roles that represent this conception of order, but the most fundamental is the parental role. Every parent (or, at any rate, every parent who loves his child) takes upon himself the representation of a universe that is ultimately in order and ultimately trustworthy. This representation can be justified only within a religious (strictly speaking a supernatural) frame of reference. In this frame of reference the natural world within which we are born, love, and die is not the only world, but only the foreground of another world in which love is not annihilated in death, and in which, therefore, the trust in the power of love to banish chaos is justified. Thus man's ordering propensity implies a transcendent order, and each ordering gesture is a signal of this transcendence. The parental role is not based on a loving lie. On the contrary, it is a witness to the ultimate truth of man's situation in reality. In that case, it is perfectly possible (even, if one is so inclined, in Freudian terms) to analyze religion as a cosmic projection of the child's experience of the protective order of parental love. What is projected is, however, itself a reflection, an imitation, of ultimate reality. Religion, then, is not only (from the point of view of empirical reason) a projection of human order, but (from the point of view of what might be called *inductive faith*) the ultimately true vindication of human order.

Since the term "inductive faith" will appear a number of times, its meaning should be clarified. I use induction to mean any process of thought that begins with experience. Deduction is the reverse process; it begins with ideas that precede experience. By "inductive faith," then, I mean a religious process of thought that begins with facts of human experience; conversely, "deductive faith" begins with certain assumptions (notably assumptions about divine revelation) that cannot be tested by experience. Put simply, inductive faith moves from human experience to statements about God, deductive faith from statements about God to interpretations of human experience.

Closely related to, though still distinct from, the foregoing considerations is what I will call the *argument from play*. Once more, as the Dutch historian Johan Huizinga has shown, we are dealing with a basic experience of man.[1] Ludic, or playful, elements can be found in just about any sector of human culture, to the point where it can be argued that culture as such would be impossible without this dimension. One aspect of play that Huizinga analyzes in some detail is the fact that play sets up a separate universe of discourse, with its own rules, which suspends, "for the duration," the rules and general assumptions of the "serious" world. One of the most important assumptions thus suspended is the time structure of ordinary social life. When one is playing, one is on a different time, no longer measured by the standard units of the larger society, but rather by the peculiar ones of the game in question. In the "serious" world it may be 11 A.M., on such and such a day, month, and year. But in the universe in which one is playing it may be the third round, the fourth act, the *allegro* movement, or the second kiss. In playing, one steps out of one time into another.[2]

This is true of all play. Play always constructs an enclave within the "serious" world of everyday social life, and an enclave within the latter's chronology as well. This is also true of all play that creates pain rather than joy. It may be 11 A.M., say, but in the universe of the torturer it will be thumbscrews again. Nevertheless one of the most pervasive features of play is that it is usually a joyful activity. Indeed, when it ceases to be joyful and becomes misery or even indifferent routine, we tend to think of this as a perversion of its intrinsic character. Joy is play's intention. When this intention is actually realized, in joyful play, the time structure of the playful universe takes on a very specific quality—namely, *it becomes eternity*. This is probably true of all experiences of intense joy, even when they are not enveloped in the separate reality of play. This is the final insight of

---

[1]Cf. Johan Huizinga, *Homo Ludens—A Study of the Play Element in Culture* (Boston, Beacon Press, 1955).

[2]On this cf. Alfred Schutz, *Collected Papers* (The Hague, Nijhoff, 1962), vol. I.

Nietzsche's Zarathustra in the midnight song: "All joy wills eternity—wills deep, deep eternity!"[3] This intention is, however, particularly patent in the joy experienced in play, precisely because the playful universe has a temporal dimension that is more than momentary and that can be perceived as a distinct structure. In other words, in joyful play it appears as if one were stepping not only from one chronology into another, but from time into eternity. Even as one remains conscious of the poignant reality of that other, "serious" time in which one is moving toward death, one apprehends joy as being, in some barely conceivable way, a joy forever. Joyful play appears to suspend, or bracket, the reality of our "living towards death" (as Heidegger aptly described our "serious" condition). . . .

The logic of the argument from play is very similar to that of the argument from order. The experience of joyful play is not something that must be sought on some mystical margin of existence. It can be readily found in the reality of ordinary life. Yet within this experienced reality it constitutes a signal of transcendence, because its intrinsic intention points beyond itself and beyond man's "nature" to a "supernatural" justification. Again, it will be perfectly clear that this justification cannot be empirically proved. Indeed, the experience can be plausibly interpreted as a merciful illusion, a regression to childish magic (along the lines, say, of the Freudian theory of wishful fantasy). The religious justification of the experience can be achieved only in an act of faith. The point, however, is that this faith is inductive—it does not rest on a mysterious revelation, but rather on what we experience in our common, ordinary lives. All men have experienced the deathlessness of childhood and we may assume that, even if only once or twice, all men have experienced transcendent joy in adulthood. Under the aspect of inductive faith, religion is the final vindication of childhood and of joy, and of all gestures that replicate these.

Another essential element of the human situation is hope, and there is an *argument from hope* within the same logic of inductive faith. . . .

Human existence is always oriented toward the future. Man exists by constantly extending his being into the future, both in his consciousness and in his activity. Put differently, man realizes himself in projects. An essential dimension of this "futurity" of man is hope. It is through hope that men overcome the difficulties of any given here and now. And it is through hope that men find meaning in the face of extreme suffering. A key ingredient of most (but not all) theodicies is hope. The specific content of such hope varies. In earlier periods of human history, when the concept of the individual and his unique worth was not as yet so sharply defined, this hope was commonly invested in the future of the group. The

---

[3] *"Alle Lust will Ewigkeit—will tiefe, tiefe Ewigkeit!"*—Friedrich Nietzsche, *Also sprach Zarathustra* (Leipzig, Kroener, 1917), p. 333.

individual might suffer and die, be defeated in his most important projects, but the group (clan, or tribe, or people) would live on and eventually triumph. Often, of course, theodicies were based on the hope of an individual afterlife, in which the sufferings of this earthly life would be vindicated and left behind. Through most of human history, both collective and individual theodicies of hope were legitimated in religious terms. Under the impact of secularization, ideologies of this-worldly hope have come to the fore as theodicies (the Marxist one being the most important of late). In any case, human hope has always asserted itself most intensely in the face of experiences that seemed to spell utter defeat, most intensely of all in the face of the final defeat of death. Thus the profoundest manifestations of hope are to be found in gestures of courage undertaken in defiance of death.

Courage, of course, can be exhibited by individuals committed to every kind of cause—good, bad, or indifferent. A cause is not justified by the courage of its proponents. After all, there were some very courageous Nazis. The kind of courage I am interested in here is linked to hopes for human creation, justice, or compassion; that is, linked to other gestures of *humanitas*—the artist who, against all odds and even in failing health, strives to finish his creative act; the man who risks his life to defend or save innocent victims of oppression; the man who sacrifices his own interests and comfort to come to the aid of afflicted fellow men. There is no need to belabor the point with examples. Suffice it to say that it is this kind of courage and hope that I have in mind in this argument.

We confront here once more, then, observable phenomena of the human situation whose intrinsic intention appears to be a depreciation or even denial of the reality of death. Once more, under the aspect of inductive faith, these phenomena are signals of transcendence, pointers toward a religious interpretation of the human situation. . . . There seems to be a death-refusing hope at the very core of our *humanitas*. While empirical reason indicates that this hope is an illusion, there is something in us that, however shamefacedly in an age of triumphant rationality, goes on saying "no!" and even says "no!" to the ever so plausible explanations of empirical reason.

In a world where man is surrounded by death on all sides, he continues to be a being who says "no!" to death—and through this "no!" is brought to faith in another world, the reality of which would validate his hope as something other than illusion. It is tempting to think here of a kind of Cartesian reduction, in which one finally arrives at a root fact of consciousness that says "no!" to death and "yes!" to hope. In any case, the argument from hope follows the logical direction of induction from what is empirically given. It starts from experience but takes seriously those implications or intentions within experience that transcend it—and takes them, once again, as signals of a transcendent reality.

Inductive faith acknowledges the omnipresence of death (and thus of the futility of hope) in "nature," but it also takes into account the intentions within our "natural" experience of hope that point toward a "supernatural" fulfillment. This reinterpretation of our experience encompasses rather than contradicts the various explanations of empirical reason (be they psychological, sociological, or what-have-you). . . .

A somewhat different sort of reasoning is involved in what I will call the *argument from damnation*. This refers to experiences in which our sense of what is humanly permissible is so fundamentally outraged that the only adequate response to the offense as well as to the offender seems to be a curse of supernatural dimensions. I advisedly choose this negative form of reasoning, as against what may at first appear to be a more obvious argument from a positive sense of justice. The latter argument would, of course, lead into the territory of "natural law" theories, where I am reluctant to go at this point. As is well known, these theories have been particularly challenged by the relativizing insights of both the historian and the social scientist, and while I suspect that these challenges can be met, this is not the place to negotiate the question. The negative form of the argument makes the intrinsic intention of the human sense of justice stand out much more sharply as a signal of transcendence over and beyond socio-historical relativities.

The ethical and legal discussion that surrounded, and still surrounds, the trials of Nazi war criminals has given every thinking person, at least in Western countries, an unhappy opportunity to reflect upon these matters. I will not discuss here either the agonizing question "How can such things have been done by human beings?" or the practical question of how the institution of the law is to deal with evil of this scope. In America both questions have been debated very fruitfully in the wake of the publication of Hannah Arendt's *Eichmann in Jerusalem,* and I do not wish to contribute to the debate here. What concerns me at the moment is not how Eichmann is to be explained or how Eichmann should have been dealt with, but rather *the character and intention of our condemnation* of Eichmann. For here is a case (as Arendt revealed, especially in the last pages of her book) in which condemnation can be posited as an absolute and compelling necessity, irrespective of how the case is explained or of what practical consequences one may wish to draw from it. Indeed, a refusal to condemn in absolute terms would appear to offer prima facie evidence not only of a profound failure in the understanding of justice, but more profoundly of a fatal impairment of *humanitas*.

There are certain deeds that cry out to heaven. These deeds are not only an outrage to our moral sense, they seem to violate a fundamental awareness of the constitution of our humanity. In this way, these deeds are not only evil, but *monstrously evil*. And it is this monstrosity that seems to compel even people normally or professionally given to such perspectives to suspend relativizations. It is one thing to say that moralities are socio-historical products, which are relative in time and space. It is quite another thing to say that *therefore* the deeds of an Eichmann can be viewed with scientific detachment as simply an instance of one such morality—and thus, ultimately, can be considered a matter of taste. Of course, it is possible, and for certain purposes may be very useful, to attempt a dispassionate analysis of the case, but it seems impossible to let the matter rest there. It also seems impossible to say something like, "Well, we may not like this at all, we may be outraged or appalled, but that is only because we come from a certain background and have been socialized into certain values—we would react quite differently if we had been socialized [or, for that matter, resocialized, as Eichmann presumably was] in a different way." To be sure, *within a scientific frame of reference,* such a statement may be quite admissible. The crucial point, though, is that this whole relativizing frame of reference appears woefully inadequate to the phenomenon if it is taken as the last word on the matter. Not only are we constrained to condemn, and to condemn absolutely, but, if we should be in a position to do so, we would feel constrained to take action on the basis of this certainty. The imperative to save a child from murder, even at the cost of killing the putative murderer, appears to be curiously immune to relativizing analysis. It seems impossible to deny it even when, because of cowardice or calculation, it is not obeyed.

The signal of transcendence is to be found in a clarification of this "impossibility." Clearly, the murder of children is both practically and theoretically "possible." It can be done, and has been done in innumerable massacres of the innocent stretching back to the dawn of history. It can also be justified by those who do it, however abhorrent their justifications may seem to others. And it can be explained in a variety of ways by an outside observer. None of these "possibilities," however, touch upon the fundamental "impossibility" that, when everything that can be said about it has been said, still impresses us as the fundamental truth. The transcendent element manifests itself in two steps. First, our condemnation is absolute and certain. It does not permit modification or doubt, and it is made in the conviction that it applies to all times and to all men as well as to the perpetrator or putative perpetrator of the particular deed. In other words, we give the condemnation the status of a necessary and universal truth. But, as sociological analysis shows more clearly than any other, this truth, while empirically given in our situation as men, cannot be empirically demonstrated to be either necessary or universal. We are, then, faced with a quite simple alternative: Either we deny that there is here anything that can be called truth—a choice that would make us deny what we experience most profoundly as our own being; or we must look beyond the realm of our "natural" experience for a validation of our certainty. Second, the condemnation does not seem to exhaust its intrinsic intention in terms of this world alone. Deeds that cry out to heaven also cry out for hell. This is the point that was brought out very clearly in the debate over Eichmann's execution. Without going into the question of either the legality or the wisdom of the execution, it is safe to say that there was a very general feeling that "hanging is not enough" in this case. But what would have been "enough"? If Eichmann, instead of being hanged, had been tortured to death in the most lengthy and cruel manner imaginable, would this have been "enough"? A negative answer seems inevitable. No human punishment is "enough" in the case of deeds as monstrous as these. These are deeds that demand not only condemnation, but *damnation* in the full religious meaning of the word—that is, the doer not only puts himself outside the community of men; he also separates himself in a final way from a moral order that transcends the human community, and thus invokes a retribution that is more than human. . . .

Finally, there is an *argument from humor*.[4] A good deal has been written about the phenomenon of humor, much of it in a very humorless vein. In recent thought, the two most influential theories on the subject have probably been those of Freud and Bergson.[5] Both interpret humor as the apprehension of a fundamental discrepancy—in Freud's theory, the discrepancy between the demands of superego and libido; in Bergson's, between a living organism and the mechanical world. I have strong reservations about either theory, but I readily concede one common proposition—that the comic (which is the object of any humorous perception) is fundamentally discrepancy, incongruity, incommensurability. This leads to a question, which Freud does not raise because of his psychological perspective and which Bergson, I think, answers incorrectly, as to the nature of the two realities that are discrepant or incongruous with respect to each other.

I agree with Bergson's description: "A situation is invariably comic when it belongs simultaneously to two altogether independent series of events and is capable of being interpreted in two entirely different meanings at the same time."[6] But I insist upon adding that this comic quality always refers to *human* situations, not to encounters between organisms and the non-organic. The biological as such is not comic. Animals become

---

[4]An earlier version of this argument may be found in my *Precarious Vision*, pp. 209ff. I have not changed my mind about this and what I say here is substantially a repetition.

[5]Sigmund Freud, "Wit and Its Relation to the Unconscious," in A. A. Brill (ed.), *The Basic Writings of Sigmund Freud* (New York, Modern Library, 1938): Henri Bergson, "Laughter," in W. Sypher (ed.), *Comedy* (Garden City, N.Y., Doubleday-Anchor, 1956).

[6]Bergson, op. cit., p. 123.

comic only when we view them anthropomorphically, that is, when we imbue them with human characteristics. Within the human sphere, just about any discrepancy can strike us as funny. Discrepancy is the stuff of which jokes are made, and frequently it is the punch line that reveals the "entirely different meaning." The little Jew meets the big Negro. The mouse wants to sleep with the elephant. The great philosopher loses his pants. But I would go further than this and suggest that there is one fundamental discrepancy from which all other comic discrepancies are derived—the discrepancy between man and universe. It is *this* discrepancy that makes the comic an essentially human phenomenon and humor an intrinsically human trait. *The comic reflects the imprisonment of the human spirit in the world.* This is why, as has been pointed out over and over since classical antiquity, comedy and tragedy are at root closely related. Both are commentaries on man's finitude—if one wants to put it in existentialist terms, on his condition of "thrown-ness." If this is so, then the comic is an objective dimension of man's reality, not just a subjective or psychological reaction to that reality. One of the most moving testimonies to this is that made by the French writer David Rousset, commenting on his time spent in a Nazi concentration camp. He writes that one of the few lasting lessons he took with him from this period was the recognition that the comic was an objective fact that was *there* and could be perceived as such, no matter how great the inner terror and anguish of the mind perceiving it.

There is an additional point to be made. Humor not only recognizes the comic discrepancy in the human condition, it also relativizes it, and thereby suggests that the tragic perspective on the discrepancies of the human condition can also be relativized. At least for the duration of the comic perception, the tragedy of man is bracketed. By laughing at the imprisonment of the human spirit, humor implies that this imprisonment is not final but will be overcome, and by this implication provides yet another signal of transcendence—in this instance in the form of an intimation of redemption. I would thus argue that humor, like childhood and play, can be seen as an ultimately religious vindication of joy. . . .

This is by no means an exhaustive or exclusive list of human gestures that may be seen as signals of transcendence. . . . My choice of examples may not be convincing to everyone and, in any case, is fairly arbitrary. I could have chosen other examples, though I would contend that the ones just discussed are particularly useful because they all refer to very basic human experiences. I have deliberately omitted any discussion of claims to direct religious experience (in the sense of experience of the supernatural). This is by no means intended to depreciate efforts to study and understand such phenomena; it merely follows from my earlier expressed belief that theological thought would do well to turn from the projections to the projector, and thus to empirical data about man. It is fairly clear that mysticism, or any other alleged experience of supernatural realities, is not accessible to everyone. Almost by definition, it partakes of the quality of the esoteric. My aim has been to explore theological possibilities that take as their starting point what is generally accessible to all men. . . .

DISCUSSION QUESTIONS

1. Discuss the significance of the term "inductive faith." What would be a "deductive faith"?

2. Which of the five "signals of transcendence" suggested by Berger can you relate to most directly in terms of your own experience? Be specific in your answer.

3. Basing your attempt on Berger's analysis, can you suggest other "signals of transcendence" that point beyond merely natural existence to a transcendent dimension of reality?

4. Would you agree that Berger's view could be characterized as humanistic? If so, in what ways would his views differ from those of a naturalistic humanist?

5. How does Berger's analysis offer a response to those who allege that religion is just a matter of wishful thinking?

Retrospective

We have examined four types of human experience from which the religious impulse emerges. Tillich claims that religious faith, in the sense of ultimate concern, is an essential part of human existence. The question for him is not whether we do or do not have faith, but rather the kind of faith we have. We have included Tillich's essay within the section on religious experience because he suggests that there arise within our ordinary experience certain commitments which can properly be labeled religious. If the content of our faith is truly ultimate, then we can say that our faith is legitimate; if our ultimate commitment is directed toward that which is not ultimate, then idolatry results or, worse, the demonic emerges.

Further exploring the nonrational aspect of religion, Otto describes the sense of the numinous that can press upon us in many and varied ways: it may be a gentle feeling of overpowering presence, or the awe-striken emotion aroused by feelings of an ultimate reality which we can only characterize as the Wholly Other. Buber's emphasis on the Eternal You as the Wholly Same is not ultimately in conflict with Otto, but rather emphasizes another aspect of the experience of the divine. In every genuine I-You relationship we both catch a glimpse of the Eternal You and have our desire for such a Someone whetted. Berger attempts to bring the experience of transcendence down to the level of ordinary life in his discussion of the five signals of transcendence which confront us with the possibility of a transcendent realm within the normal "work-a-day" world. His arguments from ordering, play, and hope are all ways of saying that we are creatures who recognize another dimension to our *humanitas* which breaks into the world of ordinary human experience. Berger's argument from damnation may be less satisfying inasmuch as it raises serious moral questions, but it does indicate the possibility of a moral evaluation of human conduct which transcends the varying cultural and individual opinions regarding the morality of human actions. His argument from humor likewise suggests that we can step out of the context of our ordinary experience and see ourselves from a detached perspective.

All of this provides an interesting account of one aspect of the human situation, the nonrational element in our consciousness which we tend to ignore but which nevertheless provides a vital element in religion. A philosophical study of religion, however, cannot be content to dwell on the nonrational alone; philosophy's concern must also be to question, to analyze, to argue, and to explore the cognitive claims made by religion. Questions such as the existence and nature of God, the problem of evil, and the nature of religious language are concerns which raise serious philosophical issues. Accordingly, subsequent sections of this book will emphasize the cognitive elements in religion and the logical implications of certain religious claims. The first of these issues to be considered is the question of the existence of God, whether or not God's existence can be proved by rational argument, and the investigation of the limits of rational investigation. This moves us from the nonrational world squarely into the rational, from experience and feelings into argument and logical analysis.

ADDITIONAL READING SUGGESTIONS
FOR PART ONE

Anyone interested in knowing more about mysticism should consult Evelyn Underhill, *Mysticism* (New York: Dutton, 1915, reprinted 1961), which is a classic on the subject. For an excellent survey of the various kinds of mysticism, see the article by Ronald Hepburn, "Mysticism, Nature and Assessment of," in *The Encyclopedia of Philosophy* (1967), 5, 429–34. Reading Paul Tillich can at times be difficult, and if you are not familiar with his work a good place to begin is the book edited by D. Mackenzie Brown, *Ultimate Concern: Tillich in Dialogue* (New York: Harper & Row, 1965); this book is a record of a seminar with Tillich in the spring of 1963 at the University of California, Santa Barbara. Additional insight into the philosophy of Buber is found in the book by Maurice Friedman, *Martin Buber: The Life of Dialogue,* 3rd ed. (Chicago: The University of Chicago Press, 1976). The methodology employed by Peter Berger is more thoroughly explained in his *Invitation to Sociology* (Garden City: Doubleday-Anchor, 1963). For an overall study of religious experience, the classic source is William James, *Varieties of Religious Experience* (New York: Longmans, Green and Co., 1902; reprinted ed. New York: New American Library, 1974), which is available in numerous editions.

part two

ARGUMENTS
FOR
GOD'S EXISTENCE

The Existence
of
God

Probably no single issue in religion has received more philosophical attention than the question of God's existence. For both Judaism and Christianity, the existence of God is the fundamental fact of life, and the reality of the living God is the basic presupposition of these religions. Yet surprising as it is to those who have never encountered it, neither the Old Testament nor the New Testament contain any arguments for God's existence. Arguing for God's existence would be as foreign to biblical writers as arguing for the air we breathe would be to us. The writer of Psalm 19 could say "The heavens are telling the glory of God; and the firmament proclaims his handiwork," but this is not an *argument;* it is less concerned with proclaiming God's existence than describing how the created order reflects God's glory and majesty. The closest references to the religious problem of atheism are found in the Hebrew psalms, notably in Psalm 14:1 (also Psalms 10:4 and 51:13) which says, "The fool says in his heart, 'There is no God.'" But the concern here is with what might be called practical atheism: the person who lives without taking God into account. What we might call intellectual atheism, a denial that there is a reality called God, was hardly considered a possibility, even for the "fool."

There are several reasons for the absence of arguments for God's existence in the Bible. One of the most obvious is that the religious problem facing ancient Israel was not atheism but polytheism. The first of the Ten Commandments consequently forbids polytheism: "You shall have no other gods before me" (Exodus 20:3). And the Hebrew confession of faith, the Shema, affirms: "Hear, O Israel, the Lord our God is one Lord" (Deuteronomy 6:4). For the New Testament writers, who were steeped in the faith of Israel, there was likewise no question that God exists;

63

they saw their task not as arguing for the existence of God, but proclaiming a unique activity of God in human history in the person of Jesus of Nazareth.

A second reason for the absence of arguments for God's existence in the Bible is that its authors were not attracted to argumentative modes of thought. We owe our dependence upon logic, reason, dialectical disputation, and the power of argument to the Greeks, and even in Greece the importance of logic was not appreciated until around the fourth century B.C. If Christianity had its roots in the soil of Judaism, it was nurtured in a world in which the Greek language and Greek culture prevailed (the New Testament, for example, was written in Greek). It was only a matter of time until Christian writers, armed with the deductive powers of Greek philosophy, would attempt to express Christian doctrines in Greek philosophical categories and to argue for the basic doctrines of the Christian faith. Origen, Augustine, Anselm, and Thomas Aquinas were but a few of the more notable Christian writers whose approach to Christian doctrine shows the influence of Greek philosophical thought.

A third reason for the lack of argument in the Old Testament is that Judaism was not an especially evangelical religion; Jews were not concerned with convincing non-Jews of the truth of their faith, and therefore developed no apologetic approach (that is, a defense of the truth of their religious convictions). But Christianity *was* evangelistic, and as it engaged upon its ever-expanding missionary enterprise, it found it necessary to be able to present arguments for its beliefs and reasons for its claims, especially when confronted with the task of convincing someone completely unacquainted with the Christian scriptures of the truth of the Christian faith. Much of the impetus behind the systematic exposition of the Christian faith by Thomas Aquinas was to provide a point of approach to those who would accept the dictates of reason but not the writings of the prophets and apostles.

NATURAL AND REVEALED THEOLOGY

Before going any further, we must clarify some terminology. Within the Christian tradition there have existed two views of how we acquire knowledge of God. The one view insists that we can know about God only through his own self-disclosure, that is through *revelation*. The second view is that an alternative route to knowledge of God is provided by what has come to be called *natural theology;* a claim that reason, unaided by divine revelation, can discover truths about God.

Revelation is just what the name implies—a divine self-disclosure through such means as visions, dreams, oracles, or as was the case with the faith of Israel, through God's mighty actions within human history. Claims to mystical experience could also be considered revelation, but since they are usually intensely private and, in the view of mystics, beyond articulation, mystical experiences cannot provide a basis for doctrines about the nature of God in the same way as, say, the prophetic tradition of ancient Israel. For the Hebrews, God's self-revelation was principally in terms of the significant events in the life of Israel—the call of Abraham, the Exodus, the giving of the Law on Mt. Sinai. Christians likewise interpreted revelation principally in terms of God's self-disclosure in Jesus of Nazareth. The scriptures are records of this divine self-disclosure and, in a secondary sense, are referred to as revelation themselves. To be strictly accurate, one should follow the distinctions made by the twentieth-century theologian Karl Barth and say that the scriptures contain the revelation of God, that is, they bear witness to God's redemptive actions on mankind's behalf. There is, of course, a significant difference between bearing witness of God's actions and arguing for God's existence. An argument for the existence of God does not presuppose the claims of scripture, but attempts to discover truths about God solely through the use of reason apart from any divine self-disclosure.

Natural theology, however, is "natural" in two senses. In the first sense the claim is made that nature itself gives evidence not only of God's existence but of God's nature as well. In a second sense such an approach to theology is natural in that human reason, unaided by revelation, is able to achieve knowledge of God, since it is within the nature of reason itself to aspire to such knowledge. Perhaps the most forceful advocate of the power of natural theology was the thirteenth-century thinker Thomas Aquinas, whose confidence in the power of human reason to ascend to knowledge of God was virtually unlimited. Thomas argued that there can be no conflict between natural and revealed theology since both aim at knowledge, and knowledge gained in one way cannot disagree with knowledge gained in another way. This twofold path, as he referred to it, was necessary because some people do not accept scripture, and for them rational arguments are necessary. We will say more about this in section three.

There is a further distinction to be made within natural theology itself, for arguments have taken one of two forms. Arguments *a priori* are attempts to determine knowledge of God solely by means of intellectual insight, independent of the senses. *A posteriori* arguments are based on observations about the world which lead to a claim that God is the logical result of reasoning about these facts. We will return later to a more detailed examination of *a priori* and *a posteriori* arguments, but perhaps brief examples may clarify the differences between the two approaches. The classic *a priori* argument for God's existence was formulated by St. Anselm, who attempted to prove that God exists on the basis of nothing other than the idea of God itself. More precisely, Anselm attempted to argue on the basis of the concept of God's *being;* hence the argument is called the ontological argument (from the Greek *ontos,* which means "being"). Here no appeal is made to facts derived from human experience; the argument centers solely on an analysis of the concept of God. The *a posteriori* approach begins with knowledge derived from sense experience and argues on this basis to the claim that God is the only adequate explanation for these experiences. One such argument is based on the perception of order in the world. According to this argument, only a supreme intelligence could be capable of instilling order and purpose in the universe; therefore God must exist. The Greeks referred to the universe as a *cosmos,* an ordered system, and such arguments are called cosmological. Teleological arguments (from the Greek *telos,* "purpose") are a form of cosmological argument emphasizing one type of order, namely, the purposive quality that the cosmos seems to exhibit. Similar arguments have been based on the human experience of moral obligation. All *a posteriori* arguments begin with some fact of human experience and attempt to argue on the basis of this experience to God as its source.

The philosopher's task is to evaluate the strength of such arguments, and to attempt to spot their weaknesses and their strengths. It is for this reason that natural theology is sometimes referred to as philosophical theology. Philosophers have directed attention to the idea of revelation or to some specific claim of revelation, but here their concern is with the concept of revelation itself and the problems it poses, such as the difficulty of validating the genuineness of an alleged revelation and verifying its truth claims. The specific content of a revelation, whatever it may happen to be, is probably not in itself of philosophical concern; the study of the content of revelation takes one into the realm of what has usually been referred to as dogmatic or systematic theology.

Since our attention will primarily be directed to natural theology, the following diagram may prove helpful in sorting out the distinctions just made.

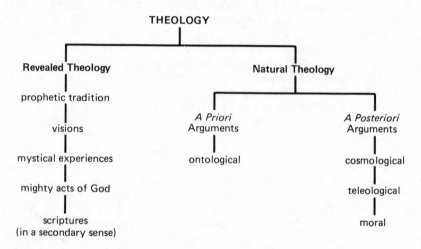

THEOLOGY

It should now be apparent that the approach to an awareness of God offered by the writers in the last section was within the sphere of natural theology. Otto specifically excluded mystical experience from his consideration and focused instead on the awareness of the numinous that one can have apart from any specific claim to a revelatory experience. Buber likewise called attention to a facet of human experience that provided a glimpse of the Eternal You. Berger, perhaps more explicitly than the other writers, put forward inductive arguments (and these would be arguments *a posteriori),* the purpose of which was to point to experiences that signal a transcendent order. All this shows that it is only a short step from the analysis of certain kinds of religious experience to a consideration of the formal arguments for God's existence.

We will begin with what is perhaps the most difficult of all arguments for the existence of God: the ontological argument. Reading the ontological argument is much like looking at an "optical illusion" which seems to show a flight of stairs running upwards that soon appear to change their direction and run downwards. At times the ontological argument seems to make perfectly good sense (although even then it may be unconvincing), but at other times the very form of argument itself seems totally elusive. Perhaps this is one of the reasons the ontological argument has attracted so much philosophical attention. Even those who are convinced that the argument is invalid may not be able to agree on the reasons for its invalidity, and there are also defenders of the argument who think that it offers a significant way of thinking about God. With these considerations in mind, we will look at the form of the argument proposed by the seventeenth-century philosopher René Descartes.

RENÉ DESCARTES

The Ontological Argument

As was mentioned in the introduction to this section, the name for the ontological argument is derived from the Greek word for "being" *(ontos);* the argument takes as its point of departure only the concept of the being of God. Its classic formulation was by the eleventh-century archbishop of Canterbury, St. Anselm, though the argument has since been restated by other philosophers.

There are several reasons for the emergence of an argument based solely on the idea of God's being, but two predominated in the thinking of the eleventh century. The first was that Plato's philosophical view provided a virtually unchallenged metaphysical framework for Christian thought in Anselm's time. At the heart of Plato's metaphysics is the notion of a great chain of being, in terms of which one can rank objects according to their degree of reality. Images and reflections are at the lowest end of the chain, and above these (that is, having more reality) are physical objects, then mathematical objects, and finally pure Forms which are eternal and unchanging. Topping off this heirarchy is the idea of the Good, which was itself the Form of all Forms. Drawing on this metaphysical system, the medievals developed the view that God was to be conceived of as highest in the order of Being as well as first in the order of Truth and Goodness. To refer to God as the Supreme Being—that is, the greatest reality—was very much in line with this medieval metaphysics, and consequently an argument based only on an analysis of the idea of God's being would suggest itself.

A second reason for the importance of the ontological argument in medieval thought was a passage of scripture, Exodus 3:13. This text is part of the story of Moses and the burning bush. According to the story, Moses witnesses a *theophany,* a manifestation of God, in the bush which burned but was not consumed. A voice spoke to Moses out of the bush and commissioned him to be the deliverer of Israel from Egyptian slavery. It is interesting to note that Moses' reaction was typical of the response to the numinous that Otto describes, but more surprising was Moses' reluctance. He made excuses—he was a nobody, he could not speak well—and finally he asked for the voice from the bush to identify itself. In effect he said, "If I go to the people of Israel, they will ask me the name of the God who sends me. What shall I say to them?" The voice replied that Moses should tell the people that I AM sent him. This term in Hebrew is a tenseless form of the verb *to be* which could be translated either I AM WHAT I AM or I WILL BE WHAT I WILL BE. In point of fact, subsequent Jewish interpreters took I AM to be the name of God, and they treated it with virtual superstitious reverence, refusing even to pronounce it. I AM is written with four Hebrew consonants (Hebrew has no vowels) and is transliterated into English as YHWH. Called the *tetragrammaton,* the word was probably pronounced as either Yahweh or Jahweh. Most English translations of the Old Testament substitute the term *The Lord* for the tetragrammaton, which follows the ancient Hebrew practice of substituting *adonai* (The Lord) for the sacred name of God whenever they encountered it in public reading. Medieval interpreters interpreted Exodus 3:13 to mean that God revealed to Moses that God's name was *being.* Consequently an analysis of the concept of God's being would fit in well both with Platonic metaphysics and with the view that "being" was God's name.

We can, however, consider the ontological argument quite apart from this historical background which forms the cultural context in which the argument was first formulated. The argument begins with the idea of the being of God, and Anselm defined the term *God* as "a being than which nothing greater can be conceived." There is really nothing surreptitious about this definition of the term God, for it is what Judaism and Christianity have always meant by the term. Given this definition of the name of God, the argument is based on the claim that it is greater for something to exist in reality than it is for something to exist only in human understanding. Anselm gives as an example the painter who has an idea or concept of a possible painting. At this stage the idea of the painting is not as great as it could be, for when the painter has committed this idea to canvas, the completed painting is greater than the mere idea of it, since it exists both in the painter's understanding *and* in reality.

In a similar way, Anselm argues that when a person claims to understand what the term God means but also says that God does not exist, such a person cannot really be thinking of that "being than which nothing greater can be conceived." For a being that existed in reality as well as in a person's understanding would be greater than a being that existed only as an idea in someone's mind. In short, that being than which nothing greater can be conceived could not exist in the understanding alone but would have to exist in reality as well, for it is greater to exist both in the understanding *and* in reality than it is to exist in the understanding alone.

One of the difficulties in Anselm's ontological argument is what he meant by *greater*. He says that a being which exists in reality *and* in the understanding is greater than a being which exists only in the understanding. This use of *greater* is usually taken to mean "more perfect"; that which exists in reality is more perfect than that which is merely an idea in the understanding. Anselm's example is that the idea of a painting in the painter's mind is not as perfect (since it does not exist in reality) as the actually existing reality of the painting after it has been committed to canvas.

The reformulation of the ontological argument by the seventeenth-century

French philosopher René Descartes faces this issue squarely. Although there is no evidence that Descartes was familiar with Anselm's argument, he offers a version of the argument that is similar to Anselm's, with the exception that Descartes explicitly states that existence is a perfection. In his development of the argument Descartes writes with all the precision of a mathematician; in fact, it was he who first developed coordinate geometry. Descartes' being a mathematician is important for two reasons. He was struck by the clarity and precision of mathematical reasoning, and impressed with the certainty that mathematical reasoning could attain. When one develops geometrical proofs, they are both precise and certain. Other mathematicians will agree with them if they do not contain errors, and if they are erroneous the source of the difficulty can be discovered. Descartes hoped to bring the same kind of precision and certainty to philosophy that he had achieved in mathematics. In fact, Descartes was obsessed with a desire for certainty in everything, and he succesfully argued that natural science must be based on certainty rather than on the mere calculation of probabilities, which was the prevailing view of his contemporaries.

Without going into detail concerning Descartes' system, a few comments in summary will help to situate his version of the ontological argument in his philosophy. Descartes devoted considerable attention to an attempt to arrive at something absolutely certain upon which philosophy could be based, and in previous sections of the work from which the selection is taken, he had advanced arguments to prove that we can be certain of our own existence. His famous statement *cogito ergo sum,* "I think, therefore I am," was taken by him to be irrefutable. But if we can be certain of our own existence as a thinking being, what else can we be certain of? We cannot trust our senses totally, for they frequently deceive us, but we can trust the mathematical constructions of our reason. Geometry, in fact, is a science of mathematical relations, and the interesting thing about geometry is that the mathematician is not concerned with the actual existence of the objects of mathematics. A geometrician can prove the nature of a triangle, for example, without ever seeing a real triangle, and the statements that geometry can prove about a triangle are true and certain irrespective of whether there are or are not actually existing triangles. We can prove that the interior angles of a triangle equal two right angles, that the square of the hypotenuse of a right triangle is equal to the sum of the square of the other two sides (the Pythagorean theorem), and so forth, without ever observing or measuring an existing triangle. When we are dealing with triangles, however, the issue is somewhat clouded, since we *have* in fact seen triangles and can draw them at will on a chalkboard. But geometry can also deal with figures that we have not seen—a hundred-sided figure, for example, or a figure with a thousand sides—with the same precision and clarity brought to bear on the geometry of triangles.

All this was extremely impressive to Descartes, and he began his ontological argument with the observation that the idea of geometry forms a model for his subsequent argument. Geometry shows that "from my mere ability to elicit the idea of some objects from my consciousness, that all the properties that I clearly and distinctly perceive the object to have do really belong to it. . . ." When Descartes uses the world *perceive* here, he does not mean sense perception but a kind of purely mental insight. Quite apart from whether or not the objects of geometry exist, we can discover certain things about them purely by the use of reason unaided by the senses. In other words, Descartes is making the claim that geometry is an *a priori* science.

Can the same approach be used in developing a proof of God's existence? A troubling problem emerges at this point: it is quite clear that geometry can devise concepts of many figures which in fact have no real existence outside the mind of the person who conceives of them. Descartes underscores this point by distinguishing between *essence* and *existence*. Geometry is concerned with the essence, the "whatness" of the objects with which it deals; it is unconcerned with the existence of the objects and in fact cannot prove (or disprove) their existence from a mere consideration of their essense. To be sure, we can form the idea of a figure with a thousand sides, but this does not prove that a thousand-sided figure anywhere exists. In the same way, if I form the idea of God in my mind, this does not prove that God exists in reality.

Descartes, however, saw a way around this problem. When we form in our minds the idea of God, it is an idea of a most perfect being, a being who is all-wise, all-knowing, all-powerful, completely good—in short, a being perfect in every respect. But if God is truly perfect in every respect, then existence must be a part of God's essence, that is, one of the perfections God enjoys. Perhaps this point can be made clearer by going back to the distinction between existence and essence. Whenever we investigate the essence of something, we list all the qualities without which the thing would not be what it is. For example, we can describe the essence of a triangle in the following way:

Triangle
three sides
three angles
the three angles equal two right angles
etc.

We do not have to list "existence" as part of the essence of triangle, since we have already admitted that mathematical objects do not have to exist in order to be the concern of geometry. Now, let us try the same thing with the idea of God's essence. As we do this, remember that we are going to list all the qualities that form a part of our idea of God's being.

God
All-wise
All-knowing
All-powerful
All-good
Existence

Descartes argues that in the case of God, existence is one of the qualities that necessarily forms part of the idea of God (unlike a triangle which cannot claim existence as a part of its essence).

This point is so important for Descartes' argument that he repeats it in several ways. We certainly can form ideas of nonexisting things—winged horses, centaurs, golden mountains, etc.—and our ability to form ideas in no way proves the existence of the objects of which we are thinking. But some qualities are so necessarily a part of the idea of a thing that we cannot think of that thing without including these qualities. Descartes gives the example of the idea of mountain and valley. These two ideas are inseparable. One cannot think of a mountain that has no valley or a valley not formed by a mountain. The mere thought of the idea mountain/valley does not, of course, prove that there are mountains and valleys but only that if we think of mountain, we must also think of valley as a part of the idea. To have an idea of a Pegasus does not prove that a Pegasus exists, but if we think of a Pegasus, we must think of a winged horse. The idea of a triangle does not prove that triangles exist but only that when we think of a triangle we are thinking of a three-sided figure. It is not necessary that we ever think about triangles, mountains and valleys, or any other thing; but when we think of them, we must include in our idea the qualities that form the essence of the thing. Neither is there any necessity for us to think about God, but when we do think of God, if we are truly thinking of the Supreme Being, then we must think of him as possessing all perfections. Descartes then claims, "This necessity clearly ensures that, when later on I observe that existence is a perfection, I am justified in concluding that the First and Supreme Being exists." Nonexistence attributed to our idea of God would be just as absurd as four-sidedness as a part of our idea of a triangle. The concept of a nonexisting Supreme Being would be as self-contradictory as the idea of a square circle.

Descartes, like other defenders of the ontological argument, insists that the argument works only in the case of God, for God alone is that being in whom existence and essence are conjoined. Descartes argues that it is necessary to include existence as part of the essence of God, for existence is a perfection without which God would not be the most perfect Being. We can summarize Descartes' argument in the following way:

> Existence is a perfection
>
> God is the most perfect being (that is, God shares in all perfections)
>
> Therefore, God exists (since existence is a perfection)

Descartes also claims that he cannot conceive of two or more such Gods, and that God must have existed from all eternity and will exist to all eternity. Descartes does not give arguments for these views, but they were well known to philosophers in his day and he perhaps assumed that his readers were familiar with them. There cannot be two Gods, since they would mutually limit each other. If God is truly supreme in power, God cannot be limited by any other being; therefore there cannot be two beings completely unlimited in power. Similar arguments can be used to prove the eternality of God: God cannot have been brought into being, for a greater being would be required to bring God into being (a greater being cannot proceed from a lesser being). Similarly, God cannot cease to exist, for this would require a being greater in power to destroy God; but this is impossible since God is the greatest being. Hence, God is eternal. This is only a sketch of the type of arguments Descartes undoubtedly had in mind, but since they are not essential to a consideration of Descartes' ontological argument, it would carry us too far afield to consider them in more detail here.

The Most Perfect Being*

The most important point, I think, is that I find within myself innumerable ideas of a kind of objects that, even if perhaps they have no existence anywhere outside me, cannot be called nonentities; my thinking of them *(a me cogitentur)* is in a way arbitrary, but they are no figments of mine; they have their own genuine and unchangeable natures. For example, when I imagine a triangle, it may be that no such figure exists anywhere outside my consciousness *(cogitationem)*, or never has existed; but there certainly exists its determinate nature (its essence, its form), which is unchangeable and eternal. This is no figment of mine, and does not depend on my mind, as is clear from the following: various properties can be proved of this triangle, e.g. that its three angles are together equal to two right angles, that its greatest side subtends its greatest angle, and so on; willy-nilly, I now clearly see them, even if I have not thought of them *(cogitaverim)* in any way when I have previously imagined a triangle; they cannot, then, be figments of mine.

It would be irrelevant for me to say that perhaps this idea of a triangle came to me from external objects by way of the sense-organs (since I have sometimes seen bodies of triangular shape); for I can mentally form countless other figures, as to which there can be no suspicion that they ever came my way through the senses, and yet I can prove various properties of them, just as I can of the triangle. All these properties are true, since I perceive them clearly; and so they are something, not mere nothingness; for it is obvious that whatever is true is something; and I have already proved abundantly that whatever I clearly perceive is true. Even apart from that proof, my mind is assuredly so constituted that I cannot but assent to them, at least at the time of clearly perceiving them; moreover, I remember that even previously at a time when I was utterly immersed in the objects of sensation, I regarded this kind of truths as the most certain of all—namely, those that I recognised as evident in regard to figures, and numbers, and other matters of arithmetic, or of geometry, or in general of pure abstract mathematics.

Now if it follows, from my mere ability to elicit the idea of some object from my consciousness *(cogitatione)*, that all the properties that I clearly and distinctly perceive the object to have do really belong to it; could not this give rise to an argument by which the existence of God might be proved? I assuredly find in myself the idea of God—of a

*Source: From Descartes; *Philosophical Writings,* edited by Elizabeth Anscombe and Peter Thomas Geach, copyright ©1971 by the Bobbs-Merrill Co., Inc., reprinted by permission.

supremely perfect being—no less than the idea of a figure or a number; and I clearly and distinctly understand that everlasting existence belongs to his nature, no less than I can see that what I prove of some figure, or number, belongs to the nature of that figure, or number. So, even if my meditations on previous days were not entirely true, yet I ought to hold the existence of God with at least the same degree of certainty as I have so far held mathematical truths.

At first sight, indeed, this is not quite clear; it bears a certain appearance of being a fallacy. For, since I am accustomed to the distinction of existence and essence in all other objects, I am readily convinced that existence can be disjoined even from the divine essence, and that thus God can be conceived *(cogitari)* as non-existent. But on more careful consideration it becomes obvious that existence can no more be taken away from the divine essence than the magnitude of its three angles together (that is, their being equal to two right angles) can be taken away from the essence of a triangle; or than the idea of a valley can be taken away from the idea of a hill. So it is not less[1] absurd to think of God (that is, a supremely perfect being) lacking existence (that is, lacking a certain perfection), than to think of a hill without a valley.

"Perhaps I cannot think of *(cogitare)* God except as existing, just as I cannot think of a hill without a valley. But from my thinking of a hill with a valley, it does not follow that there is any hill in the world; similarly, it appears not to follow, from my thinking of God as existent, that God does exist. For my thought *(cogitatio)* imposes no necessity on things; and just as I can imagine a winged horse, although no horse has wings, so, it may be, I can feign the conjunction of God and existence even though no God should exist."

There is a lurking fallacy here. What follows from my inability to think of a mountain apart from a valley is not that a mountain and a valley exist somewhere, but only that mountain and valley, whether they exist or not, are mutually inseparable. But from my inability to think of God as non-existent, it follows that existence is inseparable from God and thus that he really does exist. It is not that my thought makes this so, or imposes any necessity on anything; on the contrary, the necessity of the fact itself, that is, of God's existence, is what determines me to think this way. I am not free to think of God apart from existence (that is, of a supremely perfect being apart from the supreme perfection) in the way that I can freely imagine a horse either with or without wings.

Moreover, I must not say at this point: "After supposing God to have all perfections, I must certainly suppose him to be existent, since existence

---

[1][The Latin word is *magis;* but the sense seems to require *minus.* So the French version: *moins de répugnance.*—Tr.]

is one among perfections; but the initial supposition was not necessary. In the same way, there is no necessity for me to think all quadrilaterals can be inscribed in a circle; but given that I do think so, I shall necessarily have to admit that a rhombus can be inscribed in a circle; this, however, is obviously false." For there is indeed no necessity for me ever to happen upon any thought of *(cogitationem de)* God; but whenever I choose to think of *(cogitare de)* the First and Supreme Being, and as it were bring out the idea of him from the treasury of my mind, I must necessarily ascribe to him all perfections, even if I do not at the moment enumerate them all, or attend to each. This necessity clearly ensures that, when later on I observe that existence is a perfection, I am justified in concluding that the First and Supreme Being exists. In the same way, it is not necessary that I should ever imagine any triangle; but whenever I choose to consider a rectilinear figure that has just three angles, I must ascribe to it properties from which it is rightly inferred that its three angles are not greater than two right angles; even if I do not notice this at the time. When, on the other hand, I examine what figures can be inscribed in circles, it is in no way necessary for me to think all quadrilaterals belong to this class; indeed, I cannot even imagine this, so long as I will admit only what I clearly and distinctly understand. Thus there is a great difference between such false suppositions and my genuine innate ideas, among which the first and chief is my idea of God. In many ways, I can see that this idea is no fiction depending on my way of thinking (*cogitatione*), but an image of a real and immutable nature. First, I can frame no other concept of anything to whose essence existence belongs, except God alone; again, I cannot conceive of two or more such Gods; and given that one God exists, I clearly see that necessarily he has existed from all eternity, and will exist to all eternity; and I perceive many other Divine attributes, which I can in no wise diminish or alter.

Whatever method of proof I use, it always comes back to this: I am not utterly convinced of anything but what I clearly and distinctly perceive. Of the things I thus perceive, some are obvious to anybody; others are discovered only by those who undertake closer inspection and more careful investigation, but, when once discovered, are regarded as no less certain than the others. It is not so readily apparent that the square on the base of a right-angled triangle is equal to the squares of the sides, as it is that the base subtends the greatest angle; but once it has been seen to be so, it is just as much believed. Now as regards God, assuredly there would be nothing that I perceived earlier or more readily, if it were not that I am overwhelmed by prejudices, and my consciousness (*cogitationem*) beset in every direction by images of sensible objects. For what is intrinsically more obvious than that the Supreme Being is; that God, to whose essence alone existence belongs, exists? And though it took careful consideration for

me to see this, yet now I am as certain of it as I am of anything else that appears most certain; not only that, but I can further see that the certainty of everything else depends on this, so that apart from this no perfect knowledge is ever possible. . . .

DISCUSSION QUESTIONS

1. What aspects of the Judaeo-Christian religious tradition make the ontological argument an especially significant way of thinking about God?

2. Explain what it means to say that the ontological argument is purely *a priori,* hence deductive.

3. Do you think the ontological argument would convince a nonbeliever? Why or why not? What does your answer to this question tell you about the nature of faith?

4. A common response to the ontological argument is to say that just because we can think of something does not prove that it exists. Is this an adequate refutation of the argument? What might Descartes have said to this objection?

5. Most defenders of the ontological argument claim that it works only in the case of God. Explain the basis for this claim.

RICHARD TAYLOR

The Cosmological Argument

The ontological argument is an attempt to argue for God's existence on purely *a priori* grounds, and what is distinctive about the argument is that it makes no appeal to sense experience or to alleged facts about the world. Since it begins with the definition of God and seeks to infer from this the necessity of God's existence, the *a priori* form of argument can be called deductive. The ontological argument attempts to deduce the existence of God solely from an examination of the concept of God's being.

If you were to stop the average person on the street and ask for an argument for God's existence, you would probably not get an answer in any way resembling the ontological argument. What you would probably get by way of response is something like the following: "Well, something had to create the world. It did not just happen, and I suppose that there must be a God in order to account for the order and beauty of the world." Whether or not our streetside observer would recognize it as such, this is a cosmological type of argument. The term cosmological has already been introduced in previous sections, but a little refinement of it is in order at this point.

The ancient Greeks were the first to refer to the world as a *cosmos,* an ordered system in contrast to a disordered, random *chaos.* The insight that the world is orderly, that it functions according to rational principles, was a brilliant leap forward in the history of thought, an advance absolutely essential to the development of modern physical science. We take the regularity and uniformity of nature so much for granted that we cease to be startled by the insight that nature is orderly, but it was this view, perhaps more than any other, that gave rise to the creative impulses of ancient Greek philosophical and scientific thought. The Greeks also questioned how the universe came to be orderly. One prevailing view, advanced by atomists, was that through endless eons of random motion, a world just happened to form and that what is operative in the world is simply random order due to the chance motions of atoms. The alternative view, held by other Greek thinkers, was that the regularity and uniformity of nature is due to the activity of something more like a mind than anything else we can imagine. Behind the visible world is an Intelligence or Reason which imposes the order and structure upon nature which we can observe in the processes of the world. With various refinements, these two opposed views continue to be the two poles in ongoing debate about the nature of nature.

It is not surprising that believers would identify God with the world Reason or Intelligence that the Greeks first glimpsed as standing behind the world process. All similar arguments that move from the existence of the world, or certain facts about the world, to God as the best explanation for these facts are called cosmological arguments. Whatever their differences may be, all cosmological arguments start from the basic premise that there are certain facts about the world which we must explain. From this point of departure, the arguments proceed to propose God, or at least an absolute mind, as the best explanation of these facts about nature. Any argument which argues inductively from the world to God is cosmological. Such arguments presume that the universe is a cosmos, not a chaos, and seek to understand the principle by which the order of the universe can be explained. (As an interesting aside, the Greek word *cosmos* has another English derivative— cosmetics—which provide a way of bringing order out of what would otherwise perhaps be a chaotic situation.) Because they begin with alleged facts about the world known through sense experience, all arguments of the cosmological type are arguments *a posteriori*.

We will consider three principal *a posteriori* arguments, since most of the variations which cosmological arguments have undergone through the years can be reduced to one of these three types. The first argument is the *argument from contingency,* and its most frequent formulation is in terms of an argument from causation. The second type of *a posteriori* argument is the *design argument,* which takes as its point of departure the order and apparent purposiveness in the world. Sometimes this argument is referred to as the teleological proof (from the Greek *telos,* meaning purpose or end). The third type of *a posteriori* argument is the moral argument, which proceeds from the claim that human beings have an awareness of moral obligation, and this can only be adequately accounted for by the existence of a supreme mind. Sometimes writers reserve the term cosomological for only the first type—arguments from contingency or causation. And, as has already been mentioned, since cosmological arguments begin with observed facts and argue from them to God as the most plausible explanation for these facts, all cosmological arguments are inductive in their form of reasoning.

The classic formulation of cosmological arguments was by St. Thomas Aquinas, a thirteenth-century Dominican monk who without question was one of the greatest intellectuals of the Middle Ages. Thomas offered five proofs, the first three of which can be reduced to the argument from contingency. The fifth argument was essentially a design argument. The fourth argument presupposes a Platonic metaphysics which assumes that there are degrees of reality—a view that has been briefly discussed in the introduction. Because of the Platonic view it presupposes, the fourth argument is not generally discussed as a convincing argument in contemporary circles. Thomas claimed no originality for his proofs, deriving their general outline from similar proofs worked out by the Greek philosopher Aristotle. Because Thomas's treatment of the arguments is brief and presumes a familiarity with Aristotelian terminology, we will mainly concentrate on the more recent formulations of the arguments, an approach that has the added benefit of demonstrating that cosmological arguments are still taken seriously by philosophers. As background material, however, we will look at relevant features of the Thomistic arguments when discussing the cosmological proofs in their contemporary forms.

Basic to the cosmological type of argument is the notion of *contingency,* a term which essentially means dependence. Something which is contingent can be dependent upon something else in many senses, and in his first two arguments Thomas Aquinas pinpointed two indications of dependency: the fact that every change in the world is the result of some source of change, and in the plausible view that every effect results from a prior cause. There is really nothing mystifying about this; they are facts about the world that seem to be confirmed by all our experience. Everything that changes presupposes some previous source of the change. Things do not simply change by themselves, but as a result of something acting upon them. The term "change" here can include the almost bewildering variety of processes in nature. Trees grow and die; human beings are born, mature, and grow old; mountains erode away; rivers alter their courses. So widespread is the fact of change in nature that it would appear that change is a fundamental fact of world. But how are we to account for this universal flux of things if nothing changes by itself? The obvious answer is that something else acts upon an object to cause change. In other words, to change is to be changed. But the cause of a given change is itself the result of some previous source of change, and so on. Following out this line of argument, Thomas concluded that we are led ultimately to a source of change which is itself unchanged, and this is what we mean by God.

Generalizing somewhat from this line of reasoning, Thomas suggested in his second argument that causation is also a fact about the world. Everything that happens has a cause. That cause itself is the effect of some prior cause, and so forth, until we ultimately reach an uncaused cause, which is God. Perhaps a crude metaphor will help. Imagine a train proceeding down a railroad track. If someone asked you what makes the last car in the train move, you could reply that the car in front of it imparts motion to the car. If your questioner then asked what makes that car move, you could also reply that its motion is imparted by the car in front of it, and so on. If your questioner had a particularly stubborn sort of mind, these questions would continue until at last you reached the engine which you would describe as the source of motion for the entire train, the engine being the source of motion which is itself unmoved by any other car on the train.

There is, however, one major flaw with this metaphor. It is easy to imagine the train itself as analogous to a series of causes in time. This would make the cosmological argument saying, in effect, that what happens at the present moment is dependent on what happened in the moment prior to it; that in turn is the result of some past cause, until we finally reach God who at some distant moment in time created the world and set the world process in motion. Most modern interpreters of the cosmological argument reject this interpretation, although it was popular in the eighteenth century. They rather see the cosmological argument as saying that at any point in time there is a series of relationships of dependence which lead to God as the source of all change and all causation. In other words, at this present moment God is the source of all change in an ultimate sense and the cause of there being something rather than nothing.

Perhaps this last point will be clarified by a further examination of the notion of contingency. In fact, Thomas's third argument was based squarely on the notion of the contingency of the world since, to a great extent, the arguments from change and causation presuppose it. To say that something is contingent means, among other things, that a contingent thing is merely possible; that is, it does not have to exist. In the world everything is contingent, or merely possible. If all things were merely possible, then at some time they would not have existed, since among the possibilities of a contingent being is the possibility of nonexistence. But should nothing exist, there would not be anything in existence now (since things do not come into being out of nothing). This, however, is absurd because there are existing things now. This leads to the conclusion that there is a Being which is not merely contingent but necessary, a Being which does not depend upon anything else for its existence. All other, merely contingent things depend upon it. And this necessary Being is what we mean by God.

In this form, which is essentially the way Thomas Aquinas presented the argument, the argument from contingency is implied but is not as forcibly presented as in the following selection from the contemporary philosopher Richard Taylor. Taylor is a clear and straightforward writer, and not much in the way of exposition and commentary is required. But it is important to underscore the importance of the *principle of sufficient reason*. This principle flows directly out of the analysis of the notion of contingency, and claims that it is a basic pattern of thought to expect that there is a reason for everything that exists. Things do not happen without a cause or without some reason sufficient to explain their happening. We might not know what this reason is, but basic to our human modes of thought is the conviction that things do not happen for no reason at all. This consideration points up the fact that Thomas Aquinas' arguments from change and causation are merely variants of the principle of sufficient reason.

There is a world. That much is obvious to us. But how can we explain its existence? The principle of sufficient reason demands that there be an explanation, for it would be rationally intolerable to say that there is no sufficient reason for the world's existence. Taylor devotes considerable attention to arguing that we demand a similar explanation for the existence of anything. Where can we find a sufficient reason for the world's existence? We can scarcely find this reason within the world itself, for everything in the world is contingent. We must, therefore, seek the sufficient reason for the existence of the world in a Being that is purely necessary, and this being is God.

Two important admissions need to be made here. The first is that we cannot prove that the principle of sufficient reason is true; yet without assuming this principle we could prove nothing else. A scientist attempting to find a cure for cancer does not know what the cause of cancer is but nonetheless believes that there is a cause, for this is the basic presupposition of all scientific research. Or go back to the metaphor of the train. Your inquirer would find you exceedingly tiresome were you to keep answering the question about the motion of the train cars by attributing the motion of each car to that of the car in front. At some point your friend would say, "But what makes the whole train move?" You could then logically, but perhaps not very plausibly, reply that the explanation you are giving is perfectly correct. The motion of any given car is provided by the car in front of it, since there is no self-moving engine but rather an infinity of railroad cars. We would reject such a response as absurd, since it amounts in effect to saying that there is no sufficient reason for the motion of the train. In short, to say that there is no sufficient reason is to say that there is no explanation at all, and this we would find implausible because it violates an assumption underlying all rational thought. We could reply that the world is just what it is and there is no logical necessity for an unmoved mover or uncaused cause of the world; everything in the world is caused by some prior cause in an infinity of causes. While perhaps not illogical, such an explanation, at least in Taylor's view, is implausible.

The second admission is that there is nothing in the argument from contingency to prove that the world had a beginning in time. In fact Thomas Aquinas thought there was no argument to prove that the world had a beginning and that this was an item to be accepted by faith. Taylor subjects the argument from contingency to considerable scrutiny and shows, however, that there is no contradiction in maintaining that the world is both contingent and without beginning in time. Strange as it may at first appear, the argument from contingency is not the least damaged by the view that the world is eternal, for it can be eternal—that is, have had no beginning in time—and yet still be dependent upon God.

A final thrust of Taylor's analysis is to scrutinize the notion of God as self-caused. An obvious question, which frequently occurs even to children, is "Who caused God?" Obviously nothing could have caused God, for that would make of this cause a being greater than God, which is contradictory. The only logical response to the question is that God is his own principle of sufficient reason; that is, God is self-caused. God is not dependent upon anything. God had no beginning and will have no end. This characteristic is referred to as *aseity,* which is the idea of a being without beginning or end and without dependence upon anything else for its existence. To speak of God as first cause is therefore to speak of a Being which is its own sufficient reason, a Being that is necessary and eternal. Although the ontological argument and the cosmological arguments begin with different premises, they conclude at the same point by affirming the existence of a necessary Being who is the cause (in the sense of sufficient reason) of everything else.

The Argument from Contingency*

THE PRINCIPLE OF SUFFICIENT REASON

Suppose you were strolling in the woods and, in addition to the sticks, stones, and other accustomed litter of the forest floor, you one day came upon some quite unaccustomed object, something not quite like

*Source: Richard Taylor, *Metaphysics,* 2nd edition, © 1974, pp. 103–112. Reprinted by permission of Prentice-Hall, Inc.

what you had ever seen before and would never expect to find in such a place. Suppose, for example, that it is a large ball, about your own height, perfectly smooth and translucent. You would deem this puzzling and mysterious, certainly, but if one considers the matter, it is no more inherently mysterious that such a thing should exist than that anything else should exist. If you were quite accustomed to finding such objects of various sizes around you most of the time, but had never seen an ordinary rock, then upon finding a large rock in the woods one day you would be just as puzzled and mystified. This illustrates the fact that something that is mysterious ceases to seem so simply by its accustomed presence. It is strange indeed, for example, that a world such as ours should exist; yet few men are very often struck by this strangeness, but simply take it for granted.

Suppose, then, that you have found this translucent ball and are mystified by it. Now whatever else you might wonder about it, there is one thing you would hardly question; namely, that it did not appear there all by itself, that it owes its existence to something. You might not have the remotest idea whence and how it came to be there, but you would hardly doubt that there was an explanation. The idea that it might have come from nothing at all, that it might exist without there being any explanation of its existence, is one that few people would consider worthy of entertaining.

This illustrates a metaphysical belief that seems to be almost a part of reason itself, even though few men ever think upon it; the belief, namely, that there is some explanation for the existence of anything whatever, some reason why it should exist rather than not. The sheer nonexistence of anything, which is not to be confused with the passing out of existence of something, never requires a reason; but existence does. That there should never have been any such ball in the forest does not require any explanation or reason, but that there should ever be such a ball does. If one were to look upon a barren plain and ask why there is not and never has been any large translucent ball there, the natural response would be to ask why there should be; but if one finds such a ball, and wonders why it is there, it is not quite so natural to ask why it should *not* be, as though existence should simply be taken for granted. That anything should not exist, then, and that, for instance, no such ball should exist in the forest, or that there should be no forest for it to occupy, or no continent containing a forest, or no earth, nor any world at all, do not seem to be things for which there needs to be any explanation or reason; but that such things should be, does seem to require a reason.

The principle involved here has been called the principle of sufficient reason. Actually, it is a very general principle, and is best expressed by saying that, in the case of any positive truth, there is some sufficient reason for it, something which, in this sense, makes it true—in short, that there is some sort of explanation, known or unknown, for everything.

Now some truths depend on something else, and are accordingly called *contingent,* while others depend only upon themselves, that is, are true by their very natures and are accordingly called *necessary.* There is, for example, a reason why the stone on my window sill is warm; namely, that the sun is shining upon it. This happens to be true, but not by its very nature. Hence, it is contingent, and depends upon something other than itself. It is also true that all the points of a circle are equidistant from the center, but this truth depends upon nothing but itself. No matter what happens, nothing can make it false. Similarly, it is a truth, and a necessary one, that if the stone on my window sill is a body, as it is, then it has a form, because this fact depends upon nothing but itself for its confirmation. Untruths are also, of course, either contingent or necessary, it being contingently false, for example, that the stone on my window sill is cold, and necessarily false that it is both a body and formless, because this is by its very nature impossible.

The principle of sufficient reason can be illustrated in various ways, as we have done, and if one thinks about it, he is apt to find that he presupposes it in his thinking about reality, but it cannot be proved. It does not appear to be itself a necessary truth, and at the same time it would be most odd to say it is contingent. If one were to try proving it, he would sooner or later have to appeal to considerations that are less plausible than the principle itself. Indeed, it is hard to see how one could even make an argument for it, without already assuming it. For this reason it might properly be called a presupposition of reason itself. One can deny that it is true, without embarrassment or fear of refutation, but one is then apt to find that what he is denying is not really what the principle asserts. We shall, then, treat it here as a datum—not something that is provably true, but as something which all men, whether they ever reflect upon it or not, seem more or less to presuppose.

THE EXISTENCE OF A WORLD

It happens to be true that something exists, that there is, for example, a world, and although no one ever seriously supposes that this might not be so, that there might exist nothing at all, there still seems to be nothing the least necessary in this, considering it just by itself. That no world should ever exist at all is perfectly comprehensible and seems to express not the slightest absurdity. Considering any particular item in the world it seems not at all necessary in itself that it should ever have existed, nor does it appear any more necessary that the totality of these things, or any totality of things, should ever exist.

From the principle of sufficient reason it follows, of course, that there must be a reason, not only for the existence of everything in the world but for the world itself, meaning by "the world" simply everything that ever does exist, except God, in case there is a god. This principle does not imply that there must be some purpose or goal for everything, or for the totality of all things; for explanations need not, and in fact seldom are, teleological or purposeful. All the principle requires is that there be some sort of reason for everything. And it would certainly be odd to maintain that everything in the world owes its existence to something, that nothing in the world is either purely accidental, or such that it just bestows its own being upon itself, and then to deny this of the world itself. One can indeed *say* that the world is in some sense a pure accident, that there simply is no reason at all why this or any world should exist, and one can equally say that the world exists by its very nature, or is an inherently necessary being. But it is at least very odd and arbitrary to deny of this existing world the need for any sufficient reason, whether independent of itself or not, while presupposing that there is a reason for every other thing that ever exists.

Consider again the strange ball that we imagine has been found in the forest. Now we can hardly doubt that there must be an explanation for the existence of such a thing, though we may have no notion what that explanation is. It is not, moreover, the fact of its having been found in the forest rather than elsewhere that renders an explanation necessary. It matters not in the least where it happens to be, for our question is not how it happens to be *there* but how it happens to exist at all. If we in our imagination annihilate the forest, leaving only this ball in an open field, our conviction that it is a contingent thing and owes its existence to something other than itself is not reduced in the least. If we now imagine the field to be annihilated, and in fact everything else as well to vanish into nothingness, leaving only this ball to constitute the entire physical universe, then we cannot for a moment suppose that its existence has thereby been explained, or the need of any explanation eliminated, or that its existence is suddenly rendered self-explanatory. If we now carry this thought one step further and suppose that no other reality ever has existed or ever will exist, that this ball forever constitutes the entire physical universe, then we must still insist on there being some reason independent of itself why it should exist rather than not. If there must be a reason for the existence of any particular thing, then the necessity of such a reason is not eliminated by the mere supposition that certain other things do *not* exist. And again, it matters not at all what the thing in question is, whether it be large and complex, such as the world we actually find ourselves in, or whether it be something small, simple and insignificant, such as a ball, a bacterium, or the merest grain of sand. We do not avoid the necessity of a reason for the existence of something merely by describing it in this way or that. And it would, in any event, seem quite plainly absurd to say that if the world were comprised entirely of a single ball about six feet in diameter, or of a single grain of sand, then it would be contingent and there would have to be some explanation other than itself why such a thing exists, but that, since the actual world is vastly more complex than this, there is no need for an explanation of its existence, independent of itself.

BEGINNINGLESS EXISTENCE

It should now be noted that it is no answer to the question, why a thing exists, to state *how long* it has existed. A geologist does not suppose that he has explained why there should be rivers and mountains merely by pointing out that they are old. Similarly, if one were to ask, concerning the ball of which we have spoken, for some sufficient reason for its being, he would not receive any answer upon being told that it had been there since yesterday. Nor would it be any better answer to say that it had existed since before anyone could remember, or even that it had existed; for the question was not one concerning its age but its existence. If, to be sure, one were to ask where a given thing came from, or how it came into being, then upon learning that it had always existed he would learn that it never really *came* into being at all; but he could still reasonably wonder why it should exist at all. If, accordingly, the world—that is, the totality of all things excepting God, in case there is a god—had really no beginning at all, but has always existed in some form or other, then there is clearly no answer to the question, where it came from and when; it did not, on this supposition, *come* from anything at all, at any time. But still, it can be asked why there is a world, why indeed there is a beginningless world, why there should have perhaps always been something rather than nothing. And, if the principle of sufficient reason is a good principle, there must be an answer to that question, an answer that is by no means supplied by giving the world an age, or even an infinite age.

CREATION

This brings out an important point with respect to the concept of creation that is often misunderstood, particularly by those whose thinking has been influenced by Christian ideas. People tend to think that creation—for example, the creation of the world by God—*means* creation *in time,* from which it of course logically follows that if the world had no beginning in time, then it cannot be the creation of God. This, however, is erroneous, for creation means essentially *dependence,* even in Christian theology. If one thing is the creation of another, then it depends for its existence on that other, and this is perfectly consistent with saying that both are eternal, that neither ever came into being, and hence, that neither was ever created at any point of time. Perhaps an analogy will help convey this point. Consider, then, a flame that is casting beams of light. Now there seems to be a clear sense in which the beams of light are dependent for their existence upon the flame, which is their source, while the flame, on the other hand, is not similarly dependent for its existence upon them. The beams of light arise from the flame, but the flame does not arise from them. In this sense, they are the creation of the flame; they derive their existence from it. And none of this has any reference to time; the relationship of dependence in such a case would not be altered in the slightest if we supposed that the flame, and with it the beams of light, had always existed, that neither had ever *come* into being.

Now if the world is the creation of God, its relationship to God should be thought of in this fashion; namely, that the world depends for its existence upon God, and could not exist independently of God. If God is eternal, as those who believe in God generally assume, then the world may (though it need not) be eternal too, without that altering in the least its dependence upon God for its existence, and hence without altering its being the creation of God. The supposition of God's eternality, on the other hand, does not by itself imply that the world is eternal too; for there is not the least reason why something of finite duration might not depend for its existence upon something of infinite duration—though the reverse is, of course, impossible.

GOD

If we think of God as "the creator of heaven and earth," and if we consider heaven and earth to include everything that exists except God, then we appear to have, in the foregoing considerations, fairly strong reasons for asserting that God, as so conceived, exists. Now of course most people have much more in mind than this when they think of God, for religions have ascribed to God ever so many attributes that are not at all implied by describing him merely as the creator of the world; but that is not relevant here. Most religious persons do, in any case, think of God as being at least the creator, as that being upon which everything ultimately depends, no matter what else they may say about him in addition. It is, in fact, the first item in the creeds of Christianity that God is the "creator of heaven and earth." And, it seems, there are good metaphysical reasons, as distinguished from the persuasions of faith, for thinking that such a creative being exists.

If, as seems clearly implied by the principle of sufficient reason, there must be a reason for the existence of heaven and earth—i.e., for the world—then that reason must be found either in the world itself, or outside it, in something that is literally supranatural, or outside heaven and earth. Now if we suppose that the world—i.e., the totality of all things except God—contains within itself the reason for its existence, we are supposing that it exists by its very nature, that is, that it is a necessary being. In that case there would, of course, be no reason for saying that it must depend upon God or anything else for its existence; for if it exists by its very nature, then it depends upon nothing but itself, much as the sun depends upon nothing but itself for its heat. This, however, is implausible, for we find nothing about the world or anything in it to suggest that it exists by its own nature, and we do find, on the contrary, ever so many things to suggest that it does not. For in the first place, anything that exists by its very nature must necessarily be eternal and indestructible. It would be a self-contradiction to say of anything that it exists by its own nature, or is a necessarily existing thing, and at the same time to say that it comes into being or passes away, or that it ever could come into being or pass away. Nothing about the world seems at all like this, for concerning anything in the world, we can perfectly easily think of it as being annihilated, or as never having existed in the first place, without there being the slightest hint of any absurdity in such a supposition. Some of the things in the universe are, to be sure, very old; the moon, for example, or the stars and the planets. It is even possible to imagine that they have always existed. Yet it seems quite impossible to suppose that they owe their existence to nothing but themselves, that they bestow existence upon themselves by their very natures, or that they are in themselves things of such nature that it would be impossible for them not to exist. Even if we suppose that something, such as the sun, for instance, has existed forever, and will never cease, still we cannot conclude just from this that it exists by its own nature. If, as is of course very doubtful, the sun has existed forever and will never cease, then it is possible that its heat and light have also existed forever and will never cease; but that would not show that the heat and light of the sun exist by their own natures. They are obviously contingent and depend on the sun for their existence, whether they are beginningless and everlasting or not.

There seems to be nothing in the world, then, concerning which it is at all plausible to suppose that it exists by its own nature, or contains within itself the reason for its existence. In fact, everything in the world appears to be quite plainly the opposite, namely, something that not only need not exist, but at some time or other, past or future or both, does not in fact exist. Everything in the world seems to have a finite duration, whether long or short. Most things, such as ourselves, exist only for a short while;

they come into being, then soon cease. Other things, like the heavenly bodies, last longer, but they are still corruptible, and from all that we can gather about them, they too seem destined eventually to perish. We arrive at the conclusion, then, that although the world may contain some things that have always existed and are destined never to perish, it is nevertheless doubtful that it contains any such thing and, in any case, everything in the world is capable of perishing, and nothing in it, however long it may already have existed and however long it may yet remain, exists by its own nature, but depends instead upon something else.

Although this might be true of everything in the world, is it necessarily true of the world itself? That is, if we grant, as we seem forced to, that nothing in the world exists by its own nature, that everything in the world is contingent and perishable, must we also say that the world itself, or the totality of all these perishable things, is also contingent and perishable? Logically, we are not forced to, for it is logically possible that the totality of all perishable things might itself be imperishable, and hence, that the world might exist by its own nature, even though it is comprised exclusviely of things that are contingent. It is not logically necessary that a totality should share the defects of its members. For example, even though every man is mortal, it does not follow from this that the human race, or the totality of all men, is also mortal; for it is possible that there will always be human beings, even though there are no human beings who will always exist. Similarly, it is possible that the world is in itself a necessary thing, even though it is comprised entirely of things that are contingent.

This is logically possible, but it is not plausible. For we find nothing whatever about the world, any more than in its parts, to suggest that it exists by its own nature. Concerning anything in the world, we have not the slightest difficulty in supposing that it should perish, or even that it should never have existed in the first place. We have almost as little difficulty in supposing this of the world itself. It might be somewhat hard to think of everything as utterly perishing and leaving no trace whatever of its ever having been, but there seems to be not the slightest difficulty in imagining that the world should never have existed in the first place. We can, for instance, perfectly easily suppose that nothing in the world had ever existed except, let us suppose, a single grain of sand, and we can thus suppose that this grain of sand has forever constituted the whole universe. Now if we consider just this grain of sand, it is quite impossible for us to suppose that it exists by its very nature, and could never have failed to exist. It clearly depends for its existence upon something other than itself, if it depends on anything at all. The same will be true if we consider the world to consist, not of one grain of sand, but of two, or of a million, or, as we in fact find, of a vast number of stars and planets and all their minuter parts.

It would seem, then, that the world, in case it happens to exist at all—and this is quite beyond doubt—is contingent and thus dependent upon something other than itself for its existence, if it depends upon anything at all. And it must depend upon something, for otherwise there could be no reason why it exists in the first place. Now that upon which the world depends must be something that either exists by its own nature or does not. If it does not exist by its own nature, then it, in turn, depends for its existence upon something else, and so on. Now then, we can say either of two things; namely, (1) that the world depends for its existence upon something else, which in turn depends on still another thing, this depending upon still another, *ad infinitum;* or (2) that the world derives its existence from something that exists by its own nature and that is accordingly eternal and imperishable, and is the creator of heaven and earth. The first of these alternatives, however, is impossible, for it does not render a sufficient reason why anything should exist in the first place. Instead of supplying a reason why any world should exist, it repeatedly begs off giving a reason. It explains what is dependent and perishable in terms of what is itself dependent and perishable, leaving us still without a reason why perishable things should exist at all, which is what we are seeking. Ultimately, then, it would seem that the world, or the totality of contingent or perishable things, in case it exists at all, must depend upon something that is necessary and imperishable, and that accordingly exists, not in dependence upon something else, but by its own nature.

"SELF-CAUSED"

What has been said thus far gives some intimation of what meaning should be attached to the concept of a self-caused being, a concept that is quite generally misunderstood, sometimes even by scholars. To say that something—God, for example—is self-caused, or is the cause of its own existence, does not mean that this being brings itself into existence, which is a perfectly absurd idea. Nothing can *bring* itself into existence. To say that something is self-caused (*causa sui*) means only that it exists, not contingently or in dependence upon something else, but by its own nature, which is only to say that it is a being which is such that it can neither come into being nor perish. Now whether such a being in fact exists or not, there is in any case no absurdity in the idea. We have found, in fact, that the principle of sufficient reason seems to point to the existence of such a being, as that upon which the world, with everything in it, must ultimately depend for its existence.

"NECESSARY BEING"

A being that depends for its existence upon nothing but itself, and is in this sense self-caused, can equally be described as a necessary being; that is to say, a being that is not contingent, and hence not perishable. For in the case of anything that exists by its own nature and is dependent upon nothing else, it is impossible that it should not exist, which is equivalent to saying that it is necessary. Many persons have professed to find the gravest difficulties in this concept, too, but that is partly because it has been confused with other notions. If it makes sense to speak of anything as an *impossible* being, or something that by its very nature does not exist, then it is hard to see why the idea of a necessary being, or something that in its very nature exists, should not be just as comprehensible. And of course, we have not the slightest difficulty in speaking of something, such as a square circle or a formless body, as an impossible being. And if it makes sense to speak of something as being perishable, contingent, and dependent upon something other than itself for its existence, as it surely does, then there seems to be no difficulty in thinking of something as imperishable and dependent upon nothing other than itself for its existence.

"FIRST CAUSE"

From these considerations we can see also what is properly meant by a first cause, an appellative that has often been applied to God by theologians, and that many persons have deemed an absurdity. It is a common criticism of this notion to say that there need not be any first cause, because the series of causes and effects that constitute the history of the universe might be infinite or beginningless and must, in fact, be infinite in case the universe itself had no beginning in time. This criticism, however, reflects a total misconception of what is meant by a first cause. *First* here does not mean first in time, and when God is spoken of as a first cause, he is not being described as a being which, at some time in the remote past, *started* everything. To describe God as a first cause is only to say that he is literally a *primary* rather than a secondary cause, an *ultimate* rather than a derived cause, or a being upon which all other things, heaven and earth, ultimately depend for their existence. It is, in short, only to say that God is the creator, in the sense of creation explained above. Now this, of course, is perfectly consistent with saying that the world is eternal or beginningless. As we have seen, one gives no reason for the existence of a world merely by giving it an age, even if it is supposed to have an infinite age. To use a helpful analogy, we can say that the sun is the first cause of daylight and, for that matter, of the moonlight of the night as well, which means only that daylight and moonlight ultimately depend upon the sun for their existence. The moon, on the other hand, is only a secondary or derivative cause of its light. This light would be no less dependent upon the sun if we affirmed that it had no beginning, for an ageless and beginningless light requires a source no less than an ephemeral one. If we supposed that the sun has always existed, and with it its light, then we would have to say that the sun has always been the first—i.e., the primary or ultimate—cause of its light. Such is precisely the manner in which God should be thought of, and is by theologians often thought of, as the first cause of heaven and earth.

DISCUSSION QUESTIONS

1. Show how the notion of the contingency of the world is a basic presupposition of the cosmological argument.
2. Taylor admits that the principle of sufficient reason is not a necessary truth and that it cannot be proved; yet he insists that it is a basic presupposition of thinking. Do you agree? Why or why not?
3. Some thinkers have argued that the notion of a noncontingent being, that is, a necessary being, is a meaningless juxtaposition of words. What would be your response to this?
4. Do you agree with Taylor that it is not contradictory to hold that the world has always existed yet is contingent? Give reasons for your answer.
5. What would be your answer to the question "Who caused God?"
6. In what sense does the cosmological argument point to God as "first cause"? In what sense does it not point to God as "first cause"?

A. C. EWING

The Design Argument

The argument from design, or teleological argument, begins with the alleged fact that the world exhibits order and regularity. Indeed, one may even go so far as to claim that the natural order appears to exhibit purpose in that all aspects of nature are intricately interdependent in such a way as to produce intelligent life. The design argument was extremely popular in the eighteenth century and, as was mentioned previously, a form of it appeared in the thirteenth century as Thomas Aquinas' fifth argument. Its classic formulation was by William Paley whose book, *Natural Theology,* written in 1802, lays out in great detail the considerations for the teleological argument and also answers many possible objections to it.

Paley begins with a parable. Suppose that you are walking along a meadow and there discover a watch lying on the ground. Paley suggests that your attitude toward the watch would be vastly different from your attitude toward a nearby stone. You would immediately conclude that the watch, unlike the stone, was not placed there by the forces of wind and weather but was the product of an intelligent designer. This supposition would hold even if you did not know what the contrivance was or had never seen a watch before or knew nothing about how watches were made. The very intricacy and detail of the mechanism would alone be sufficient to establish that it was the product of a conscious intelligence, that is, a watchmaker. Even if the watch did not keep perfect time, or even if parts of it were badly made, you would still conclude that the mechanism did not come into existence accidentally or by chance but was the deliberate result of the work of a watchmaker.

Paley explicitly admitted that the argument was based on analogy. Anyone who has taken a College Board Exam knows about analogies, where one is asked: A is to B as C is to what? In this case, the analogy is: watch is to watchmaker as world is to God. Paley was much impressed by the intricacy of human and animal bodies, and found the human eye to be a particularly notable example of an intricate and marvelous machine. By so squarely posing his argument as one of analogy, Paley opened himself up to the counterattacks leveled at the argument by David Hume in his *Dialogues Concerning Natural Religion.* Hume's basic attack was on the analogy itself. We have no right, Hume insisted, to claim that the analogy of the world as a machine is a proper one. Other analogies might work equally well—for example, the world as a kind of animal or vegetable; why all this preoccupation with mechanical contrivances? Hume also accused Paley of assuming too much. After all, we do not know what kind of forces are necessary to bring a world into being; besides, we have no basis for assuming that in the business of world-making anything like human intelligence is the operative principle. Because of our innate egotism, we assume that human intelligence is the highest principle in nature, but according to Hume, this is an unproven assumption.

An additional shortcoming of Paley's presentation of the design argument is that it was formulated before the publication of Darwin's *Origin of Species,* although we can scarcely blame Paley for that. In Paley's day, the only counter response to a design argument was that the universe came into being purely by chance through the random forces of nature over an incredibly lengthy period of time, and all the diversity in nature and the intricacy of animal forms is due purely to chance. Today, the theory of evolution is generally taken to provide an explanation for the biological diversity in nature, and since Paley's examples of design were virtually all biological in nature, this has seriously weakened the impact of his argument.

The selection that follows from A. C. Ewing avoids Paley's pitfall by denying that the design argument is based on an analogy at all. Ewing thinks the argument works perfectly well without likening the world to a machine or any other analogue; the mere fact of complexity in nature must be explained (remember the principle of sufficient reason), and Ewing argues that God is the most plausible explanation for the apparent design in nature. Ewing also faces the force of the theory of evolution but argues that the theory, by itself, cannot account for biological diversity. Evolution may explain the process of change in animal forms, but it cannot account for the existence of the process itself. In short, Ewing observes that there is nothing in the theory of evolution to discount the impact of the design argument, since evolution can be viewed as the process of God's creative activity.

Neither is an appeal to an "unconscious purpose" adequate to account for the intricacy of the world in Ewing's view. The term is vague, perhaps even contradictory, but whatever else it might mean it certainly includes the notion of a purposive intelligence. Ewing observes that, as far as our own experience goes, we know of purposes only as occurring in mind. Whatever else we might say about the purpose behind the universe, we at least must say that it has the characteristics of mind.

There have been objections raised against the cosmological type of argument. Kant rejected all arguments of the cosmological type because they assume that we can apply the notion of cause and effect to the world as a totality. Kant held that causality was a perfectly valid principle, indeed one that is essential to rational thought. But he insisted that we can legitimately apply it only to things which can be experienced by the senses. Obviously no one has an experience of the world as a whole, so we therefore have no grounds for assuming that the principle of causality has any validity as an explanatory principle outside the realm of experience. David Hume went even further and questioned the defensibility of the principle of causality itself. We do, to be sure, attribute cause and effect to the events we experience, but Hume argued that this is only a convenient fiction, a customary way of thinking, that we impose on experience. The principle of cause and effect, he argued, has no experiential validation, for we never experience a necessary connection between events, but only events following one another in time. Given the repeated succession of events, we think of them as causally connected, but this is something we can never prove.

Obviously such an attack on the principle of causality, if accepted, undermines the force of the cosmological form of argument. Even for Kant, who argued that causality is a legitimate principle of human reason, the principle has no application beyond the realm of empirical experience and therefore cannot be used to prove that there is a cause of the world. Allied with this is a second Kantian objection to the cosmological argument. To prove the God of traditional Jewish and Christian belief, the cosmological argument must point to the existence of a necessary being. But Kant did not think that such a notion was acceptable. Of all the arguments for God's existence covered thus far, Kant thought the design argument the best, but he pointed out that the most it can do is point to the possible existence of a mighty being who created the world out of existing materials. This being would be a kind of artificer who imposed a certain degree of order on the world (though not perfect order), but such a being is hardly the God of traditional theistic belief.

Kant's own approach to the question was to argue for grounds for belief in God based on human moral awareness. Kant's own formulation of these moral grounds for belief presupposes a rather thorough understanding of his moral philosophy, a consideration of which would lead us somewhat away from our central concern. Consequently, the moral argument that is offered in the next section does not presuppose an understanding of Kant's ethics and, like the previous two selections, is from a contemporary writer and shows the continued vitality of the moral argument.

Like the argument based on the principle of sufficient reason considered previously, the design argument cannot claim to offer logical proof for God's existence. It is rather an appeal to the plausibility that the order of the world is due to intelligent design, not randomness and chance. It is more plausible, according to Ewing, to attribute the world to a conscious designer than to accident and caprice. There is, to be sure, much disorder in the world, and the existence of evil is itself a challenge to the design argument; the world does not exhibit perfect order, and it could be better. Any argument for God's existence, however, must come to terms with the problem of evil, so the problem of evil does not strike at the design argument alone. Ewing argues that the fact that there is some disorder in the world does not negate the degree of order that the world does exhibit, and he further suggests that what may appear as disorder to us might even be expressive of a higher order of things. Even though the world may not be perfect, it does exhibit some degree of order and it is to the explanation of this empirical fact that the design argument addresses itself.

The Argument from Design*

The *teleological argument* or the *argument from design* is the argument from the adaptation of the living bodies of organisms to their ends and the ends of their species. This is certainly very wonderful: there are thousands of millions of cells in our brain knit together in a system which works; twenty or thirty different muscles are involved even in such a simple act as a sneeze; directly a wound is inflicted or germs enter an animal's body all sorts of protective mechanisms are set up, different cells are so cunningly arranged that, if we cut off the tail of one of the lower animals, a new one is grown, and the very same cells can develop according to what is needed into a tail or into a leg. Such intricate arrangements seem to require an intelligent purposing mind to explain them. It may be objected that, even if such an argument shows wisdom in God, it does not show goodness and is therefore of little value. The reply may be made that it is incredible that a mind who is so much superior to us in intelligence as to have designed the whole universe should not be at least as good as the best men and should not, to put it at its lowest, care for his offspring at least as well as a decent human father and much more wisely because of his superior knowledge and intellect. Still it must be admitted that the argument could not at its best establish all that the theist would ordinarily wish to establish. It might show that the designer was very powerful, but it could not show him to be omnipotent or even to have created the world as opposed to manufacturing it out of given material; it might make it probable that he was good, but it could not possibly prove him perfect. And of course the more unpleasant features of the struggle for existence in nature are far from supporting the hypothesis for a good God.

But does the argument justify any conclusion at all? It has been objected that it does not on the following ground. It is an argument from analogy, it is said, to this effect: animal bodies are like machines, a machine has a designer, therefore animal bodies have a designer. But the strength of an argument from analogy depends on the likeness between what is compared. Now animal bodies are really not very like machines, and God is certainly not very like a man. Therefore the argument from analogy based on our experience of men designing machines has not enough strength to give much probability to its conclusion. This criticism, I think, would be valid if the argument from design were really in the

*Source: A. C. Ewing, *The Fundamental Questions of Philosophy* (London: Routledge & Kegan Paul, 1951), pp. 225–31. Used by permission of the publishers.

main an argument from analogy,[1] but I do not think it is. The force of the argument lies not in the analogy, but in the extraordinary intricacy with which the details of a living body are adapted to serve its own interests, an intricacy far too great to be regarded as merely a coincidence. Suppose we saw pebbles on the shore arranged in such a way as to make an elaborate machine. It is theoretically possible that they might have come to occupy such positions by mere chance, but it is fantastically unlikely, and we should feel no hesitation in jumping to the conclusion that they had been thus deposited not by the tide but by some intelligent agent. Yet the body of the simplest living creature is a more complex machine than the most complex ever devised by a human engineer.

Before the theory of evolution was accepted the only reply to this argument was to say that in an infinite time there is room for an infinite number of possible combinations, and therefore it is not, even apart from a designing mind, improbable that there should be worlds or stages in the development of worlds which display great apparent purposiveness. If a monkey played with a typewriter at random, it is most unlikely that it would produce an intelligible book; but granted a sufficient number of billions of years to live and keep playing, the creature would probably eventually produce quite by accident a great number. For the number of possible combinations of twenty-six letters in successions of words is finite, though enormously large, and therefore given a sufficiently long time it is actually probable that any particular one would be reached. This may easily be applied to the occurrence of adaptations in nature. Out of all the possible combinations of things very few would display marked adaptation; but if the number of ingredients of the universe is finite the number of their combinations is also finite, and therefore it is only probable that, given an infinite time, some worlds or some stages in a world process should appear highly purposeful, though they are only the result of a chance combination of atoms. The plausibility of this reply is diminished when we reflect what our attitude would be to somebody who, when playing bridge, had thirteen spades in his hand several times running— according to the laws of probability an enormously less improbable coincidence than would be an unpurposed universe with so much design unaccounted for—and then used such an argument to meet the charge of cheating. Our attitude to his reply would surely hardly be changed even if we believed that people had been playing bridge for an infinite time. If only we were satisfied that matter had existed and gone on changing for ever, would we conclude that the existence of leaves or pebbles on the ground in such positions as to make an intelligible book no longer pro-

---

[1]Hume's criticisms of it in the famous *Dialogues Concerning Natural Religion* depend mainly on the assumption that it is such an argument.

vided evidence making it probable that somebody had deliberately arranged them? Surely not. And, if not, why should the supposition that matter had gone on changing for ever really upset the argument from design? Of course the appearance of design *may be* fortuitous; the argument from design never claims to give certainty but only probability. But, granted the universe as we have it, is it not a much less improbable hypothesis that it should really have been designed than that it should constitute one of the fantastically rare stages which showed design in an infinite series of chance universes? Further, that matter has been changing for an infinite time is a gratuitous assumption and one not favoured by modern science.[2]

But now the theory of evolution claims to give an alternative explanation of the adaptation of organisms that removes the improbability of which we have complained. Once granted the existence of some organisms their offspring would not all be exactly similar. Some would necessarily be somewhat better equipped than others for surviving and producing offspring in their turn, and their characteristics would therefore tend to be more widely transmitted. When we take vast numbers into account, this will mean that a larger and larger proportion of the species will have had relatively favourable variations transmitted to them by their parents, while unfavourable variations will tend to die out. Thus from small beginnings accumulated all the extraordinarily elaborate mechanism which now serves the purpose of living creatures.

There can be no question for a properly informed person of denying the evolution theory, but only of considering whether it is adequate by itself to explain the striking appearance of design. If it is not, it may perfectly well be combined with the metaphysical hypothesis that a mind has designed and controls the universe. Evolution will then be just the way in which God's design works out. Now in reply to the purely evolutionary explanation it has been said that for evolution to get started at all some organisms must have already appeared. Otherwise the production of offspring and their survival or death in the struggle for existence would not have come into question at all. But even the simplest living organism is a machine very much more complex than a motor car. Therefore, if it would be absurd to suppose inorganic matter coming together fortuitously of itself to form a motor car, it would be even more absurd to

[2]Strictly speaking, what is required by those who put forward the objection in question to the argument from design is not necessarily that matter should have been changing for an infinite time but only for a sufficiently long, though finite, time. But the length of time allowed by modern science for the development of the earth and indeed for that of the whole universe does not in the faintest degree approach what would be needed to make the appearance of organized beings as a result of mere random combinations of atoms anything less than monstrously improbable.

suppose it thus coming together to form an organism, so without design the evolutionary process would never get started at all. Nor, even granting that this miracle had occurred, could the evolutionists claim that they had been altogether successful in removing the antecedent improbability of such an extensive adaptation as is in fact shown by experience. It has been urged that, since we may go wrong in a vast number of ways for one in which we may go right, the probability of favourable variations is very much less than that of unfavourable; that in order to produce the effect on survival required a variation would have to be large, but if it were large it would usually lessen rather than increase the chance of survival, unless balanced by other variations the occurrence of which simultaneously with the first would be much more improbable still; and that the odds are very great against either a large number of animals in a species having the variations together by chance or their spreading from a single animal through the species by natural selection. The arguments suggest that, so to speak, to weight the chances we require a purpose, which we should not need, however, to think of as intervening at odd moments but as controlling the whole process. The establishment of the evolution theory no doubt lessens the great improbability of the adaptations having occurred without this, but the original improbability is so vast as to be able to survive a great deal of lessening, and it does not remove it.

Some thinkers would regard it as adequate to postulate an unconscious purpose to explain design, but it is extraordinarily difficult to see what such a thing as an unconscious purpose could be. In one sense indeed I can understand such a phrase. "Unconscious" might mean "unintrospected" or "unintrospectible," and then the purpose would be one which occurred in a mind that did think on the matter but did not self-consciously notice its thinking. But this sense will not do here, for it already presupposes a mind. To talk of a purpose which is not present in any mind at all seems to me as unintelligible as it would be to talk of rectangles which had no extension. The argument from design has therefore to my mind considerable, though not, by itself at least, conclusive force. It is also strange that there should be so much beauty in the world, that there should have resulted from an unconscious unintelligent world beings who could form the theory that the world was due to chance or frame moral ideals in the light of which they could condemn it. It might be suggested that a mind designed the organic without designing the inorganic, but the connection between organic and inorganic and the unity of the world in general are too close to make this a plausible view.

The counter argument from evil is of course formidable, but I shall defer discussion of it to a later stage in the chapter, as it is rather an argument against theism in general than a specific objection to the argument from design. I must, however, make two remarks here. First, it is almost a commonplace that the very large amount of apparent waste in nature is a strong prima facie argument against the world having been designed by a good and wise being. But is there really much "wasted"? A herring may produce hundreds of thousands or millions of eggs for one fish that arrives at maturity, but most of the eggs which come to grief serve as food for other animals. We do not look on the eggs we eat at breakfast, when we can get them, as "wasted", though the hen might well do so. It is certainly very strange that a good God should have designed a world in which the living beings can only maintain their life by devouring each other, but this is part of the general problem of evil and not a specific problem of waste in nature. Secondly, the occurrence of elaborate adaptations to ends is a very much stronger argument for the presence of an intelligence than its apparent absence in a good many instances is against it. A dog would see no purpose whatever in my present activity, but he would not therefore have adequate grounds for concluding that I had no intelligence. If there is a God, it is only to be expected *a priori* that in regard to a great deal of his work we should be in the same position as the dog is in regard to ours, and therefore the fact that we are in this position is no argument that there is no God. The occurrence of events requiring intelligence to explain them is positive evidence for the presence of intelligence, but the absence of results we think worth while in particular cases is very slight evidence indeed on the other side where we are debating the existence of a being whose intelligence, if he exists, we must in any case assume to be as much above ours as the maker of the whole world would have to be. The existence of positive evil of course presents a greater difficulty to the theist.

DISCUSSION QUESTIONS

1. What features of the natural order are presupposed by the teleological argument? Do you think these presuppositions are defensible? Give reasons for your answer.

2. In your view, does the evolutionary view of biological development enhance or detract from the design argument? Why?

3. What are some of the major attacks on the design argument? Which of these, if any, do you think provides a satisfactory refutation of the argument?

4. Is the design argument destroyed by the obvious fact that there are also disorder and imperfection exhibited by the natural order? Why or why not?

5. Of all the arguments thus far considered, which do you think would be most appealing to a physicist? A mathematician? An engineer? A poet?

C. S. LEWIS

The Moral
Argument

The previous arguments for the existence of God that we have investigated have attempted to demonstrate God's existence using as their point of departure either the concept of God alone (the ontological argument) or certain facts about the world (the arguments from contingency and design). The moral argument takes as its point of departure a different kind of fact—a fact about human nature—namely, the human experience of moral obligation. Since this recognition of the sense of moral obligation is put forward as an empirical fact, the moral argument belongs squarely in the realm of *a posteriori* arguments.

Few philosophers would deny that human beings possess a sense of moral obligation, but there is wide disagreement as to the source of moral awareness. In the history of philosophy, there have been thinkers who denied that there are moral values or, for that matter, that there is any truth in any subject. This skeptical position is generally recognized by philosophers as a blind alley, which produces strange logical results. If the skeptic says there is no truth in ethical matters, then the claim cannot be advanced that this skeptical position is true. If we can know nothing about ethical principles, then we cannot know that the skeptic's ethical principle is true either. The skeptic can doggedly persist in skepticism, just like those who stubbornly insist that the world is flat, contrary evidence notwithstanding. Aristotle dismissed such individuals with a most unphilosophic remark: he said they were no better than vegetables. A skeptic would, to be sure, reject the moral argument for God's existence, but the skeptic would reject any argument on any subject. There is no refuge for the skeptic.

Basic to the moral argument is the conviction that there are objective principles in ethics; that is, the conviction that an ethical statement can be either true or false. How to determine whether an ethical injunction such as "murder is wrong" is true or false may be the subject of vigorous philosophical debate, but the objectivist in ethics is committed to the view that it is possible to discover truth in ethics just as it can be discovered in physics, history, or any of the human sciences.

An alternative view of ethics is that of subjectivism. The subjectivist in ethics denies that ethical statements can have a truth value since they originate from our own subjective preferences. In its most extreme form, subjectivism would say that when I utter the statement, "murder is wrong," all I am doing is stating my own preference. To the subjectivist, this has the same meaning as, "I don't approve of murder." This would be on a par with saying, "liver and onions are awful." That is a subjective preference, and the statement means, "I do not like liver and onions." The subjectivist would claim that ethical statements are logically equivalent to statements about likes and dislikes in matters of food and drink. There are many varieties of subjectivism in ethics, but we do not need to go into them at this point; what is important is to recognize that if one chooses the subjectivist view in ethics at the outset, the moral argument ceases to have any appeal as evidence for the existence of God.

The moral argument, therefore, takes as its basic presupposition that there are objective principles in ethics. Given this view, the argument then seeks to demonstrate that God is the best explanation for human moral awareness. Since this is a book about religion and not ethics, we will avoid going into many details about these opposing views; because objectivism is so central to the moral argument, however, a few misconceptions about it should be cleared up at this point.

It is a common misunderstanding to think that objectivists say that every human being has an innate moral sense that provides a guide to action. Some advocates of the objectivist position have argued for something like this, but it is not necessary to the objectivist view. C. S. Lewis, the author from whom the following selection is taken, argues elsewhere that ethical principles have to be learned just as one learns any other item of human knowledge. Neither are objectivists committed to the view that all persons naturally (and easily) know what sort of conduct is right and what is wrong any more than a person knows naturally (and easily) the multiplication tables or the method for solving a quadratic equation. All the objectivist is committed to is the view that some ethical statements are right and others are wrong, even though we may not know the truth about a given ethical matter. A person can hold that there are objective principles or norms in ethics without necessarily being able to demonstrate what these norms are.

Perhaps the most frequently advanced objection to objectivism in ethics is the alleged variety of moral standards existing among the different peoples and cultures of the world. The subjectivist in ethics would point to these variations as proof that ethics is merely a matter of subjective preference. For example, in one culture action A is morally acceptable and action B is morally reprehensible, whereas in a different society the reverse is true. One objectivist response is to point out that the alleged differences in morality among different cultures is probably greatly exaggerated. A truly different moral system would be one in which, for example, murder is approved and cowardice considered a virtue, where honesty is considered vile and loyalty is looked upon as stupid. But suppose we should really find a society in which these topsy turvy morals were accepted. Objectivists would say that such a society was morally inferior, for they are committed to a view that allows value judgments to be made about different ethical systems. Objectivists would also argue that individuals and societies can make progress in ethics. We can compare individuals and societies and conclude that some have made more progress in ethics, and that the moral principles of some individuals and some cultures are better than those of others. Subjectivists could not and would not make such value judgments; they would conclude that, since ethical matters are merely expressions of subjective preferences, there is no way to say that the ethics of a particular society are better than those of any other.

This lends to a dilemma of sorts, for subjectivists cannot really argue for the truth of their ethical views. The subjectivist can try to persuade an opponent to accept a certain ethical view but cannot logically condemn the opponent's view as false, since the subjectivist position does not acknowledge the possibility of truth or falsity of ethical statements. Few subjectivists would try to present their view in such an extreme manner. Instead, they would argue that there could be no human society if all persons did merely what they wanted to. Subjectivists would maintain that there must be laws, rules, and standards if anything like an organized human society is to exist, but that any particular set of moral rules is simply the prevailing standards of a society elevated to the status of morality. Lewis's rejoinder to this is to point out that the subjectivist cannot say that it is *better* to think of the good of society than to ignore it; if you talk about the good of society, this automatically assumes some norm or standard by which you are doing the judging. This standard is what Lewis calls the Law of Nature or the Law of Decent Behavior.

It is important to recognize that the term *law* here does not mean the same thing as it does in physics. A physical law is a description of how inanimate objects behave, that is, how they are affected by the forces that impinge upon them. The moral law, in contrast, is a description not of how human beings behave but of how they *ought* to behave. Moral law does not describe human behavior, but prescribes principles to regulate human behavior; it tells us how we ought to behave. This sense of ought is basic to the objectivist view for—as far as we know—human beings are the only creatures who feel this sense of moral obligation, an obligation to obey a moral law which they did not originate but nonetheless ought to obey. From this point it is a short step for Lewis to suggest that the most adequate account for the source of this moral law is something like a mind that stands behind the universe and has implanted within mankind the ability to recognize and feel bound by a higher standard of behavior.

Like the cosmological arguments previously considered, the moral argument attempts to proceed inductively from a fact about the world—human moral experience—to God as the most plausible explanation for this fact. And like all proofs of an *a posteriori* type, the most obvious way to fault the argument is by rejecting the premise on which it is based, the premise in this case being that there is a sense of obligation which must be explained. Immanuel Kant felt that the realization of one's duty is the highest action to which we can attain, and he further believed that eliciting principles of ethics was a task of reason. There are, for Kant, two roles for reason: one is to discover truth about the world, the second is to provide moral legislation for human actions. There are two things, Kant said, that fill us with wonder: the starry sky above, and the moral law within. Kant was careful not to claim that the "moral law within" provided a proof for God's existence, but he did think that it provided the best basis for belief in God.

The Argument from Morality*

THE REALITY OF THE LAW

I now go back to what I said at the end of the first chapter, that there were two odd things about the human race. First, that they were haunted by the idea of a sort of behaviour they ought to practise, what you might call fair play, or decency, or morality, or the Law of Nature. Second, that they did not in fact do so. Now some of you may wonder why I called this odd. It may seem to you the most natural thing in the world. In particular, you may have thought I was rather hard on the human race. After all, you may say, what I call breaking the Law of Right and Wrong or of Nature, only means that people are not perfect. And why on earth should I expect them to be? That would be a good answer if what I was trying to do was to fix the exact amount of blame which is due to us for not behaving as we expect others to behave. But that is not my job at all. I am not concerned at present with blame; I am trying to find out truth. And from that point of view the very idea of something being imperfect, of its not being what it ought to be, has certain consequences.

If you take a thing like a stone or a tree, it is what it is and there seems no sense in saying it ought to have been otherwise. Of course you may say a stone is "the wrong shape" if you want to use it for a rockery, or that a tree is a bad tree because it does not give you as much shade as you expected. But all you mean is that the stone or tree does not happen to be convenient for some purpose of your own. You are not, except as a joke, blaming them for that. You really know, that, given the weather and the soil, the tree could not have been any different. What we, from our point of view, call a "bad" tree is obeying the laws of its nature just as much as a "good" one.

Now have you noticed what follows? It follows that what we usually call the laws of nature—the way weather works on a tree for example—may not really be *laws* in the strict sense, but only in a manner of speaking. When you say that falling stones always obey the law of gravitation, is not

*Source: C. S. Lewis, *Mere Christianity* (London: Geoffrey Bles, 1952), pp. 13–21. Used by permission.

this much the same as saying that the law only means "what stones always do"? You do not really think that when a stone is let go, it suddenly remembers that it is under orders to fall to the ground. You only mean that, in fact, it does fall. In other words, you cannot be sure that there is anything over and above the facts themselves, any law about what ought to happen, as distinct from what does happen. The laws of nature, as applied to stones or trees, may only mean "what Nature, in fact, does." But if you turn to the Law of Human Nature, the Law of Decent Behaviour, it is a different matter. That law certainly does not mean "what human beings, in fact, do"; for as I said before, many of them do not obey this law at all, and none of them obey it completely. The law of gravity tells you what stones do if you drop them; but the Law of Human Nature tells you what human beings ought to do and do not. In other words, when you are dealing with humans, something else comes in above and beyond the actual facts. You have the facts (how men do behave) and you also have something else (how they ought to behave). In the rest of the universe there need not be anything but the facts. . . .

Some people say that though decent conduct does not mean what pays each particular person at a particular moment, still, it means what pays the human race as a whole; and that consequently there is no mystery about it. Human beings, after all, have some sense; they see that you cannot have real safety or happiness except in a society where every one plays fair, and it is because they see this that they try to behave decently. Now, of course, it is perfectly true that safety and happiness can only come from individuals, classes, and nations being honest and fair and kind to each other. It is one of the most important truths in the world. But as an explanation of why we feel as we do about Right and Wrong it just misses the point. If we ask: "Why ought I to be unselfish?" and you reply "Because it is good for society," we may then ask, "Why should I care what's good for society except when it happens to pay *me* personally?" and then you will have to say, "Because you ought to be unselfish"—which simply brings us back to where we started. You are saying what is true, but you are not getting any further. If a man asked what was the point of playing football, it would not be much good saying "in order to score goals," for trying to score goals is the game itself, not the reason for the game, and you would really only be saying that football was football— which is true, but not worth saying. In the same way, if a man asks what is the point of behaving decently, it is no good replying, "in order to benefit society," for trying to benefit society, in other words being unselfish (for "society" after all only means "other people"), is one of the things decent behaviour consists in; all you are really saying is that decent behaviour is decent behaviour. You would have said just as much if you had stopped at the statement, "Men ought to be unselfish."

And that is where I do stop. Men ought to be unselfish, ought to be
fair. Not that men are unselfish, nor that they like being unselfish, but that
they ought to be. The Moral Law, or Law of Human Nature, is not simply
a fact about human behaviour in the same way as the Law of Gravitation is,
or may be, simply a fact about how heavy objects behave. On the other
hand, it is not a mere fancy, for we cannot get rid of the idea, and most of
the things we say and think about men would be reduced to nonsense if we
did. And it is not simply a statement about how we should like men to
behave for our own convenience; for the behaviour we call bad or unfair is
not exactly the same as the behaviour we find inconvenient, and may even
be the opposite. Consequently, this Rule of Right and Wrong, or Law of
Human Nature, or whatever you call it, must somehow or other be a real
thing—a thing that is really there, not made up by ourselves. And yet it is
not a fact in the ordinary sense, in the same way as our actual behaviour is
a fact. It begins to look as if we shall have to admit that there is more than
one kind of reality; that, in this particular case, there is something above
and beyond the ordinary facts of men's behaviour, and yet quite definitely
real—a real law, which none of us made, but which we find pressing on us.

WHAT LIES BEHIND THE LAW

. . . I now want to consider what this tells us about the universe we
live in. Ever since men were able to think, they have been wondering what
this universe really is and how it came to be there. And, very roughly, two
views have been held. First, there is what is called the materialist view.
People who take that view think that matter and space just happen to exist,
and always have existed, nobody knows why; and that the matter, behaving in certain fixed ways, has just happened, by a sort of fluke, to produce
creatures like ourselves who are able to think. By one chance in a
thousand something hit our sun and made it produce the planets; and by
another thousandth chance the chemicals necessary for life, and the right
temperature, occurred on one of these planets, and so some of the matter
on this earth came alive; and then, by a very long series of chances, the
living creatures developed into things like us. The other view is the
religious view.* According to it, what is behind the universe is more like a
mind than it is like anything else we know. That is to say, it is conscious,
and has purposes, and prefers one thing to another. And on this view it
made the universe, partly for purposes we do not know, but partly, at any
rate, in order to produce creatures like itself—I mean, like itself to the

---

*See Note at the end.

extent of having minds. Please do not think that one of these views was held a long time ago and that the other has gradually taken its place. Wherever there have been thinking men both views turn up. And note this too. You cannot find out which view is the right one by science in the ordinary sense. Science works by experiments. It watches how things behave. Every scientific statement in the long run, however complicated it looks, really means something like, "I pointed the telescope to such and such a part of the sky at 2:20 A.M. on January 15th and saw so-and-so," or, "I put some of this stuff in a pot and heated it to such-and-such a temperature and it did so-and-so." Do not think I am saying anything against science: I am only saying what its job is. And the more scientific a man is, the more (I believe) he would agree with me that this is the job of science—and a very useful and necessary job it is too. But why anything comes to be there at all, and whether there is anything behind the things science observes—something of a different kind—this is not a scientific question. If there is "Something Behind," then either it will have to remain altogether unknown to men or else make itself known in some different way. The statement that there is any such thing, and the statement that there is no such thing, are neither of them statements that science can make. And real scientists do not usually make them. It is usually the journalists and popular novelists who have picked up a few odds and ends of half-baked science from textbooks who go in for them. After all, it is really a matter of common sense. Supposing science ever became complete so that it knew every single thing in the whole universe. Is it not plain that the questions, "Why is there a universe?" "Why does it go on as it does?" "Has it any meaning?" would remain just as they were?

Now the position would be quite hopeless but for this. There is one thing, and only one, in the whole universe which we know more about than we could learn from external observation. That one thing is Man. We do not merely observe men, we *are* men. In this case we have, so to speak, inside information; we are in the know. And because of that, we know that men find themselves under a moral law, which they did not make, and cannot quite forget even when they try, and which they know they ought to obey. Notice the following point. Anyone studying Man from the outside as we study electricity or cabbages, not knowing our language and consequently not able to get any inside knowledge from us, but merely observing what we did, would never get the slightest evidence that we had this moral law. How could he? for his observations would only show what we did, and the moral law is about what we ought to do. In the same way, if there were anything above or behind the observed facts in the case of stones or the weather, we, by studying them from outside, could never hope to discover it.

The position of the question, then, is like this. We want to know whether the universe simply happens to be what it is for no reason or whether there is a power behind it that makes it what it is. Since that power, if it exists, would not be one of the observed facts but a reality which makes them, no mere observation of the facts can find it. There is only one case in which we can know whether there is anything more, namely our own case. And in that one case we find there is. Or put it the other way round. If there was a controlling power outside the universe, it could not show itself to us as one of the facts inside the universe—no more than the architect of a house could actually be a wall or staircase or fireplace in that house. The only way in which we could expect it to show itself would be inside ourselves as an influence or a command trying to get us to behave in a certain way. And that is just what we do find inside ourselves. Surely this ought to arouse our suspicions? In the only case where you can expect to get an answer, the answer turns out to be Yes; and in the other cases, where you do not get an answer, you see why you do not. Suppose someone asked me, when I see a man in a blue uniform going down the street leaving little paper packets at each house, why I suppose that they contain letters? I should reply, "Because whenever he leaves a similar little packet for me I find it does contain a letter." And if he then objected, "But you've never seen all these letters which you think the other people are getting," I should say, "Of course not, and I shouldn't expect to, because they're not addressed to me. I'm explaining the packets I'm not allowed to open by the ones I am allowed to open." It is the same about this question. The only packet I am allowed to open is Man. When I do, especially when I open that particular man called Myself, I find that I do not exist on my own, that I am under a law; that somebody or something wants me to behave in a certain way. I do not, of course, think that if I could get inside a stone or a tree I should find exactly the same thing, just as I do not think all the other people in the street get the same letters as I do. I should expect, for instance, to find that the stone had to obey the law of gravity—that whereas the sender of the letters merely tells me to obey the law of my human nature, He compels the stone to obey the laws of its stony nature. But I should expect to find that there was, so to speak, a sender of letters in both cases, a Power behind the facts, a Director, a Guide.

Do not think I am going faster than I really am. I am not yet within a hundred miles of the God of Christian theology. All I have got to is a Something which is directing the universe, and which appears in me as a law urging me to do right and making me feel responsible and uncomfortable when I do wrong. I think we have to assume it is more like a mind than it is like anything else we know—because after all the only other thing we know is matter and you hardly imagine a bit of matter giving instructions. . . .

NOTE.—In order to keep this section short enough when it was given on the air, I mentioned only the Materialist view and the Religious view. But to be complete I ought to mention the In-between view called Life-Force philosophy, or Creative Evolution, or Emergent Evolution. The wittiest expositions of it come in the works of Bernard Shaw, but the most profound ones in those of Bergson. People who hold this view say that the small variations by which life on this planet "evolved" from the lowest forms to Man were not due to chance but to the "striving" or "purposiveness" of a Life-Force. When people say this we must ask them whether by Life-Force they mean something with a mind or not. If they do, then "a mind bringing life into existence and leading it to perfection" is really a God, and their view is thus identical with the Religious. If they do not, then what is the sense in saying that something without a mind "strives" or has "purposes"? This seems to me fatal to their view. One reason why many people find Creative Evolution so attractive is that it gives one much of the emotional comfort of believing in God and none of the less pleasant consequences. When you are feeling fit and the sun is shining and you do not want to believe that the whole universe is a mere mechanical dance of atoms, it is nice to be able to think of this great mysterious Force rolling on through the centuries and carrying you on its crest. If, on the other hand, you want to do something rather shabby, the Life-Force, being only a blind force, with no morals and no mind, will never interfere with you like that troublesome God we learned about when we were children. The Life-Force is a sort of tame God. You can switch it on when you want, but it will not bother you. All the thrills of religion and none of the cost. Is the Life-Force the greatest achievement of wishful thinking the world has yet seen?

DISCUSSION QUESTIONS

1. Show how the moral argument presupposes an objectivist view of ethics.
2. What consideration does Lewis advance that supports his apparent belief in the superiority of the moral argument to cosmological type arguments? Do you find his position convincing? Why or why not?
3. Discuss the evidence that can be used in support of an objectivist view in ethics. Do you think this evidence is adequate? Give reasons for your answer.
4. Is there a difference in speaking of a moral law and in speaking of natural law? Explain.
5. Do you see any resemblance between the moral argument and Berger's "signals of transcendence"? Give reasons for your answer.
6. Do you find the moral argument a convincing approach to the question of proving God's existence? Why or why not?

Retrospective

What is the final force of the arguments for God's existence? For each argument there seems to be a counterargument, and we have to admit that all the arguments for God's existence—ontological, cosmological, moral—fail to provide a logically irrefutable proof. The debate among philosophers over the relative merits and demerits of these arguments has been going on for a long time and will likely continue, at least as long as there are philosophers around to continue them.

There are, however, several positive outcomes of the debate about the existence of God despite its seeming inconclusiveness. First, a review of the material just covered should dispel the notion that only naive persons believe in God or the view that only stupid people are atheists. Serious philosophical issues divide persons of good will on both sides of the controversy. A second positive effect of the dialogue generated by a discussion of the arguments is that it does clarify some of the options: either there is an ultimate Principle behind the visible universe, call it God, or else the universe is just a brute fact for which no explanation is possible. The arguments also focus our attention upon aspects of the world that evoke a sense of wonder and mystery, and that cannot fully be accounted for except on the theistic hypothesis. The order and regularity of the world, as well as human moral awareness, point to God as a possible explanation. But the arguments—all of them—only point; they do not coerce.

The theistic arguments are nonetheless significant. The ontological argument, in particular, is useful because it clarifies some of the logical implications of the concept of God. This is especially important in view of the suggestions made recently by Erich Von Däniken, who has written of the view that ancient humans were visited by a race of nonterrestrial "supermen" who, because of their extreme might and power, were looked upon as gods by our primitive ancestors. Von Däniken speaks of the "chariots" of the gods as spaceships and the "gods" as beings from another planet, although the evidence offered to support his view is open to dispute. Of course, it is possible that earth has been visited by nonterrestrial beings—in the sense that such a claim is not logically contradictory; and had such visitations occurred, it is possible that ancient peoples would attribute divinity to beings who exhibited extraordinary power. What our consideration of the ontological argument shows, however, is that there can be no confusing of the concept of God as it is articulated by the Judaeo-Christian religious tradition with the idea of spacemen from another planet. God is not the greatest being ever encountered by humans; God is not even the greatest being of which human thinking has formed the idea. God is a being than which nothing greater *can be* conceived. God is a being eternal and necessary, omnipotent and unlimited in knowledge. This is a vastly different concept than that of superhuman beings armed with advanced technology visiting earth in spaceships.

But would any of the arguments we have just investigated convince an atheist that God exists? Probably not. Even if a person agreed that the reasoning of one of the arguments is sound, the argument alone would probably not lead an unbeliever to embrace belief in God. As the discussion of the last section showed, there is more to religion than rational argument, and the dynamics of faith certainly involve more than logical debate. This points to one of the most important contributions of the existence of God debate. If someone were to construct an absolutely undeniable proof of the existence of God, a proof so strong that it could not be refuted, or a proof against which there are no cogent counterarguments, this would not be a good thing for religion, at least for the Judaeo-Christian tradition. For basic to this tradition is the view that religion is a matter of faith, not of demonstrable proof. "We walk by faith and not by sight," a New Testament writer states. What this means is that faith is only possible where there is also room for doubt. That the arguments for the existence of God, and the counter arguments against them, remain inconclusive leaves open the possibility of faith. But this brings up another area for philosophical investigation—the relationship between faith and reason. And that is the topic of the next section.

ADDITIONAL READING SUGGESTIONS
FOR PART TWO

During the last twenty years a great deal has been written about the onotological argument. Two excellent collections of representative essays dealing with the topic are the following: Alvin Plantinga, *The Ontological Argument* (Garden City: Doubleday-Anchor, 1965) and John Hick and Arthur C. McGill, eds., *The Many-Faced Argument* (New York: The Macmillan Company, 1967). *The Encyclopedia of Philosophy* has articles on each of the arguments discussed in this section, and other arguments are discussed in the article by G. C. Nerlick, "Popular Arguments for the Existence of God," *The Encyclopedia of Philosophy* (1967), 6, 407–11. All the articles in this valuable encyclopedia also contain helpful bibliographies. An overall discussion and analysis of theistic arguments is found in the work by John Hick, *Arguments for the Existence of God* (London: Macmillan, 1970).

part three

FAITH
AND
REASON

Opinion, Belief, and Knowledge

The relationship between faith and reason has been a background concern in our readings from the very first. In one sense it was raised by the questioning of a purely rational approach to religion in the writings of Otto and Buber. If there is a nonrational aspect to religion, as both Otto and Buber insist, then one should not look to rational argument and analysis alone for a thorough understanding of religion. Most philosophers, however, have concluded that there is a place for rational inquiry in religion, and the various arguments for God's existence that we have examined are attempts to provide rational arguments to support belief in God. Even though these arguments do not offer an absolute proof for God's existence, they offer some rational support for belief in God. They do not, however, give conclusive evidence; were the evidence for God's existence conclusive and not subject to doubt, faith would be impossible. Faith is not knowledge, and because we do not have absolutely certain knowledge of God's existence, there is room for faith.

The quest for knowledge, and the desire for certainty, are two of the concerns most characteristic of Western philosophy. This attitude toward the goal of philosophy was perhaps given its clearest expression by Descartes when he set forth as one of his five rules for the direction of the mind to refuse to believe anything which is subject to doubt. Descartes, as was shown in Part two, thought that his version of the ontological argument offered proof for God's existence, and he accordingly accepted God as one of the proven principles of philosophy. It is clear to us, though perhaps it was not obvious to Descartes, that all such arguments for God's existence are less than absolutely convincing; at least we have to admit that they are not completely coercive in their effect. If we cannot have rational certainty of the existence of God, are we to conclude that the only philosophically defensible attitude is to doubt that God exists? Some philosophers have argued for this view, based on the principle that we have no right to extend belief beyond the available evidence. Other thinkers have argued that we are justified in believing in God even though we cannot claim absolute certainty for these beliefs.

Two questions emerge in the continuing dialogue between faith and reason: (1) Do we have what can legitimately be called *knowledge* of God based on rational proofs? and (2) Even without such a proof, is it rational to *believe* in God? Since there are two ways of approaching the question of God, either through faith or through reason, and since there are two attitudes toward each of these, we can begin to see the issues in this debate taking shape. Some philosophers have thought that we can relate to God through both faith and reason. Others have denied that we can have rationally justified knowledge of God, and have also rejected faith as a defensible attitude. Still others, though agreeing that we cannot have knowledge of God, have pointed to faith as the only way of having access to a relationship with God. Perhaps the following table of possibilities will illustrate the different attitudes possible toward the relation between faith and reason. "Reason" includes what we can claim to *know;* "faith" means what we are entitled to believe. In short, can we claim knowledge of God, or can we legitimately defend faith in him, or neither?

Faith	Reason	
Yes	Yes	St. Thomas Aquinas
No	No	Antony Flew
Yes	No	Søren Kierkegaard

The above tabulation is a little too pat in that it ignores the subtleties of the positions of these philosophers, but it does provide a general idea of their respective attitudes toward the relation of faith and reason in the selections included in this section.

As we flesh out these viewpoints you will see that there are many other issues raised by the readings, but our attention in this section is focused on the relation between faith and reason. The question is basically: Are we justified in claiming to have knowledge of God? If not, is it defensible to have faith in what we cannot prove with complete certainty? St. Thomas Aquinas is the most optimistic on these questions, claiming both that we can have knowledge of God and that faith is defensible. Antony Flew does not think we can claim to have knowledge of God, and further thinks that our claims to faith are equally indefensible. If you accept the claim that we are never justified in believing what we are unable to prove with absolute certainty, then ask yourself if you are willing to apply this same criterion to other areas of life. Quite apart from the question of religious faith, are we *ever* justified in accepting something, and acting on it, even though we cannot be certain about it? This is the issue raised by the selection from William James, who argues that we can—and must—act on principles for which we do not have empirical evidence and of which we cannot be certain.

Before turning to the readings themselves, we should clarify for ourselves the difference between belief and knowledge. Here Immanuel Kant can once again be our guide, for one of his ongoing concerns was to discover the basic structures of human knowledge. Kant thought that in every rational judgment there is a subjective factor and an objective factor. We might say that the subjective factor is the degree of certainty we ourselves have about something, whereas the objective factor is the demonstrable evidence we can elicit to support this certainty. Sometimes we are quite convinced of the truth of something even though the evidence is not very strong to support the conviction. At other times our subjective conviction may not be very strong even though the objective evidence is sufficient. Using these distinctions, Kant defined three modes of awareness: opinion, belief, and knowledge.

The following example illustrates the application of Kant's analysis. Suppose you are having an argument with a friend about the population of the greater Paris area. You are sure that the population is eight million persons. Your friend disagrees and is equally sure that it is at least nine million or more. Here you both are experiencing a high degree of what Kant called subjective sufficiency for your views; that is, you both are persuaded that your judgment about the population of the Paris metropolitan area is correct. Obviously the only way to resolve the dispute is to consult a current atlas or almanac for a report based on objective data. Let's suppose that the current almanac reports that the population of the greater Paris area is nine and one-quarter million persons. Your friend could reply, "I was certain that I was right, but here is the evidence to support my certainty." Your friend would then have objective sufficiency for his claim for which he previously only had subjective sufficiency. If you are a particularly stubborn sort of person, you could reply, "I don't care what the almanac says, I still am not convinced." Here you cannot claim objective sufficiency for your viewpoint, even though you still experience subjective sufficiency for it.

To summarize, Kant thought that every judgment has both a subjective and objective pole. Each of these, in turn, can either be sufficient or insufficient. This gives us four possibilities which can be viewed as producing four different levels of awareness.[1]

| | | SUBJECTIVELY | |
		Insufficient	Sufficient
	Insufficient	Opinion	Belief
OBJECTIVELY			
	Sufficient		Knowledge

Kant does not give a name to the type of judgment which is subjectively insufficient but objectively sufficient. We might want to call it some form of disbelief, since the evidence is objectively sufficient, yet the person still remains unpersuaded.

Now, let's apply this to the matter of religious belief, or faith. If we could have objectively sufficient evidence that God exists, then we could claim that we also have subjective sufficiency for the view that there is a God, and the resulting judgment could be called knowledge. We have already seen in our examination of the arguments for God's existence that no such objectively sufficient evidence is available, so it would be inaccurate to say that we can claim to know that God exists. If the evidence for God's existence is objectively insufficient, then we must look to the types of judgment resulting from evidence that is objectively insufficient. If we are

[1]Immanuel Kant, *Critique of Pure Reason,* A820; B848.

not persuaded that there is a God (or that there is not a God), then our subjective state can only be called opinion. But if we are strongly persuaded of the existence of God even in the face of inadequate evidence, the state of our subjective awareness can be called belief. When we get to the selection from Kierkegaard we will see that he defended faith in precisely this sense—subjective commitment to that which is objectively uncertain. We will return to these distinctions later.

No readings from St. Thomas Aquinas are included in this section, but a brief summary of his views will indicate his optimistic and positive attitude toward the relation between faith and reason. The most interesting thing about Thomas's view is that he was convinced we can have knowledge of God and that faith was only required to lead us to those truths reason alone was incapable of discovering. Not only did Thomas think we can have knowledge of God, he thought that there are two sources for such knowledge. One of these is reason itself. Thomas believed that God has implanted within us the capacity to learn of his existence and nature through the power of reason. His massive *Summa Theologica* was an attempt to give reasoned arguments in support of the truth of Christian doctrine. Another path to knowledge of God, Thomas believed, was provided by sacred scriptures, namely the Old and New Testaments. If we reason correctly, and if we interpret scripture correctly, we have two sources for knowledge of God; indeed, if there is ever a conflict between what we can know about God through the power of reason and what scripture tell us, either we are reasoning incorrectly or are not understanding scripture properly. Reason (natural theology) and the scriptures (revelation) constitute a twofold path to knowledge of God.

The existence of a twofold path to knowledge of God raised two interesting questions. The first is: If we can discover truths about God by the power of reason unaided by revelation, why do we have scripture? Thomas thought there were several answers to this. Without God's self-revelation, few people would possess knowledge of God. Some persons simply do not have the natural disposition to arrive at knowledge of God through the strenuous exercise of reason; not everybody is cut out to be a philosopher. Others are too busy with such matters as earning a living and just don't have the time to think speculatively about divine matters. Still others are just too lazy to think their way to knowledge of God. Besides all this, a trained intellect is not easily attained. It takes time to learn to reason philosophically, and until one's intellect was thoroughly trained, that individual would not have an adequate knowledge of God. And without revelation, young people would be at a disadvantage in spiritual matters, since their minds are on other things. A final reason for the necessity of revelation is that our minds are limited and prone to error, and we can inadvertently fall into falsehood in our thinking. Revelation provides a corrective to errors in our reasoning. So much for the need for revelation.

The second issue is the converse of the first: Why do we need to bother ourselves about natural theology and speculative philosophy if revelation is a sufficient source of truth about God? Thomas answered that since not everybody accepts the authority of the scriptures, the power of reason is required to convince them of the truth of Christian doctrine. Specifically Thomas had in mind two types of people: the pagans, who do not accept the authority of scripture, and the heretics, those who incorrectly understand scripture. In refuting heretics it is necessary to provide rational support for religious doctrine since heretics also use scripture to support their views, although they use it incorrectly. The pagans have to be convinced of the truth of scripture through the power of reason before they will accept it.

Even though scripture and reason give us a twofold path to knowledge of God, there are some truths about God that are too lofty for human reason alone to discover, and here we need to accept the truth of revelation by faith. The Christian doctrine of the trinity is an example of something that must be accepted on faith, as are other claims about the divine nature. Here is how Thomas put it:

> It is also necessary that such truth be proposed to men for belief so that they may have a truer knowledge of God. For then only do we know God truly when we believe Him to be above everything that it is possible for man to think about Him; for, as we have shown, the divine substance surpasses the natural knowledge of which man is capable. Hence, by the fact that some things about God are proposed to man that surpass his reason, there is strengthened in man the view that God is something above what he can think.[2]

In short, faith adds to what we can claim as genuine knowledge about God, and faith is necessary if we are to have the highest awareness of God's nature. Nonetheless, Thomas was convinced that we can gain knowledge of God sufficient for salvation through the power of reason alone unaided by divine revelation.

Few philosophers today would speak quite so easily of the possibility of arriving at knowledge of God. Indeed the debate today centers not on the question of whether we can have knowledge of God, but on the issue of the legitimacy of believing in God. Returning to the distinctions made earlier, a belief is a view which, though subjectively sufficient, is based on objectively insufficient grounds. But just how insufficient can these grounds be? Will we at some point have such objective insufficiency that we are no longer entitled to our belief? If objective sufficiency is not possible for belief, how then are we to distinguish between legitimate beliefs and illegitimate ones? When are we entitled to hold a belief, and when must we abandon it as indefensible? These are the questions raised by the first reading in this section.

---

[2]Thomas Aquinas, *On the Truth of the Catholic Faith: Summa Contra Gentiles,* trans. Anton C. Pegis (Garden City: Doubleday-Image, 1955), p. 70; Book I, 5, 3.

ANTONY FLEW

Belief
and
Falsification

One of the characteristics of religious belief is that it rests on evidence that is less than absolutely certain. As the discussion in the introduction indicated, the distinction between what can legitimately be called *knowledge* and what must be viewed as a matter of *belief* is the objective sufficiency of the evidence for the assertion. If we cannot prove that a religious belief is true, that is, if we cannot verify it, perhaps we can show under what conditions it would be false. If we can neither verify a statement of religious belief nor admit any conditions that would falsify it, then in what sense is a statement of religious belief an assertion?

These are the questions raised in the following article by Antony Flew, and central to his attack on the legitimacy of religious belief is his analysis of the conditions under which a sentence or an utterance can be properly viewed as an assertion. An assertion is a particular kind of speech act in which we make a claim that a certain state of affairs is true, or that it is false. When you say, "It is raining outside," you are making an assertion. If you go outside and discover that rain is falling, you have verified the truth of your assertion. But if, on going outside, you discover that the day is bright and sunny and that no rain is falling, you have falsified your assertion. You might think that most of our utterances are assertions, but if you kept track of all the things you say for just an hour you might be surprised to discover that many of the things you say are not assertions but other kinds of speech acts. For example, the sentence, "Close the door," is not an assertion but a command. To say, "Congratulations on passing the course" is not to make an assertion but to perform the speech act of congratulating. There are dozens, perhaps hundreds, of speech acts which are not assertions, but since we are dealing here with the question of belief and not the nature of language, let's focus our attention on assertions.[1]

Flew claims that statements of religious beliefs are not genuine assertions. To see how he argues for this view, we must examine more closely the nature of an assertion. To be an assertion, a statement must make a claim which has a truth value; that is, the assertion is either true or false. Philosophers of language call this its *propositional content*. An assertion, in other words, refers to something and makes some sort of claim about it. In the sentence, "God loves us," the reference is to God, and the claim is that of loving us. The religious believer accepts this statement as true. But how are we to know that it is true? If we could verify its truth, the statement would no longer be a matter of belief but a matter of knowing. So it seems to be a peculiar quality of statements of religious belief that they cannot, in principle, be *proved* to be true; otherwise they would cease to be beliefs. Flew has no quarrel with this but brings up another interesting question: What kind of evidence would be required to convince a person who holds a religious belief to be true that in fact it was false? Or as Flew puts this question, what would it take to *falsify* the assertion? Even if there is not sufficient evidence to show that the statement is false, we must be prepared to admit that some kind of evidence would be sufficient to falsify the statement. If, however, we insist that there is no evidence whatsoever sufficient to make us give up our belief, then in what sense is it a genuine assertion?

To illustrate how the principle of falsification is applied, Flew borrows the parable of the invisible gardener. Two explorers come upon a clearing in the woods, and one of them attributes it to the work of an invisible gardener. They set up elaborate tests to detect the presence of the gardener, and there is no evidence that such an invisible gardener exists. One of the explorers stubbornly refuses to abandon belief in the unseen gardener, so he begins to qualify his belief: the gardener is invisible, undetectable, and leaves no traces of his nocturnal visits. With each qualification something of the original belief is lost; the assertion "dies the death of a thousand qualifications." At some point a reasonable person would abandon belief in an unseen gardener, realizing the legitimacy of the question asked by the skeptic: "Just how does what you call an invisible, intangible, eternally elusive gardener differ from an imaginary gardener or even from no gardener at all?" In short, a reasonable person would recognize that the statement that there is an unseen gardener is not a legitimate assertion.

Flew's analysis raises a number of important questions. We can see how it relates to the question of the nature of religious language. It also raises the thorny difficulty for religious belief posed by the problem of evil. But basically it deals with the question of faith versus reason. At what point, Flew asks, does reason demand that we abandon a belief in the face of evidence that seems to weigh against the belief? How much should one allow to count against a religious belief before it is abandoned as indefensible? Can religious assertions really "die the death of a thousand qualifications" as Flew claims?

Flew's article originally appeared in a periodical called *University* and was

---

[1] John Searle gives a partial list of different speech acts and cites J. L. Austin's claim that there are more than one thousand different speech acts in the English language. See John Searle, *Speech Acts* (Cambridge: At the University Press, 1969), p. 23.

followed by a written discussion. Two of the responses, with Flew's summation, are included in the readings.

In the first of these responses, R. M. Hare admits that, in a sense, Flew is correct. People do hold certain views so tenaciously that no evidence seems to be sufficient to cause them to abandon these views. But the interesting claim made by Hare is that such beliefs are not uncommon at all, nor are they restricted to matters of religious belief. We all have deeply held convictions which are not verifiable and which likewise do not seem to be falsifiable, which he calls *bliks*. A *blik* is an unverifiable, unfalsifiable presupposition or set of presuppositions in terms of which people orient themselves to the world. It is in the very nature of a *blik* that it also determines what evidence counts against it; and what makes a *blik* a *blik* is that nothing is sufficient to dislodge it. For example, some people have a *blik* about airplanes. They refuse to believe that ariplanes are a safe mode of transportation. Others may complete hundreds of airplane trips safely, but persons with a *blik* about airplanes are convinced that the moment they board an aircraft it will be doomed to crash. One could point out statistics that show the probability of safely completing a journey on a scheduled U.S. airline are 99.99992%, but this evidence would have no effect. Let an aircraft crash, however, and persons with a *blik* about airplanes immediately feel that this is evidence in support of their belief about air travel, and their resolve never to take an airplane trip is fortified.

If Hare is correct in saying that all of us have *bliks*, then the position of the religious believer does not seem so strange. But Hare admits that some *bliks* are abnormal; indeed he suggests that there are sane as well as insane *bliks*, though he does not offer a clear principle for distinguishing between them. The example he offers of an insane *blik* is a college undergraduate who thinks that every professor is a homicidal maniac. His example of a sane *blik* is the confidence most of us have in the reliability of the mechanical linkages of an automobile. There is, of course, evidence that automobiles can experience mechanical difficulty, and that some people die in auto crashes caused by mechanical malfunction. But most of us have a *blik* about the safety of automobiles and continue to take auto trips. Hare seems to assume that the difference between a sane or "right" *blik* and an insane or "wrong" *blik* is primarily in the number of persons who hold them. A wrong *blik* is one that is clearly a minority viewpoint.

If this is the distinction Hare is making between sane and insane *bliks*, it is hardly a sufficient one, for the question raised by Flew is about the cumulative weight of evidence. If it turned out that most automobiles fell apart in transit, and most airplanes crashed while in flight, the reasonable conclusion would be that neither is a safe mode of transportation. In other words, the weight of the evidence, to use a lawyer's term, is an important consideration. This points up a weakness in Flew's original parable. In the case of the explorers and the unseen gardener, all the evidence seems to point against the existence of an invisible gardener who secretly cares for the garden. But let's change the parable somewhat. Suppose that even though the explorers are unsuccessful in detecting the presence of the gardener through their various contrivances—the bloodhounds still smell nothing, they hear no shrieks from someone being injured on the electrified barbed-wire fence—there is still evidence that something unusual is happening. Each morning some of the weeds have been pulled. Fresh flowers have been planted. The shrubs have been trimmed, the trees fertilized. The explorers in that case would no doubt be led to mystification, but could hardly be faulted for concluding that something, or someone, was the cause of the strange phenomena, even though they could detect nothing with their elaborate devices.

This is the point made by Basil Mitchell in the second response to Flew by his parable of the partisans and the mysterious stranger. One of the members of an underground guerrilla band meets a stranger who assures him that he is on the side of the partisans, but warns that there will be times when he will seem to be working for the enemy. The partisan is warned not to be deceived on these occasions, but to believe that the stranger is indeed on the side of the guerrillas. At times there is evidence that the stranger is helping the partisans. At other times the evidence seems to be that the stranger is in the service of their enemy. Although the evidence is ambiguous, so strong was the effect of the stranger on the partisan that he continues to believe that the stranger is on their side even in the face of contradictory evidence. Unlike Hare's example of the *blik,* against which no evidence really counts, there is evidence which the partisan admits counts against the sincerity of the stranger; yet the partisan continues to trust the stranger.

Now, is the case of the religious believer more like that of the stubborn explorer, the person with a *blik,* or the trusting partisan? This is the question with which you will have to wrestle. Most religious thinkers would admit that there is some evidence that counts against the existence of a loving God—the problem of evil, for example. But there is also evidence, though perhaps not conclusive, for the existence of a loving God. The evidence is ambiguous, and it is precisely this ambiguity that makes religious faith possible.

Before turning to the readings, it should be noted that Flew has not had the last word on the principle of falsification as a way of distinguishing between genuine assertions and spurious ones. Flew seems to claim that every assertion, to be genuine, must either be verifiable or falsifiable. But this is not the case. Some assertions are, to be sure, both verifiable and falsifiable, such as the assertion "It is raining outside." There is another type of assertion, however, that has not been verified, yet does not seem falsifiable. Failure to verify an assertion of this type does not indicate that it is thereby falsified. John Hick gives as an example of this kind of assertion in the claim that "there are three successive sevens in the decimal determination of π." As is well known, the Greek letter pi is used as the symbol for the ratio of the circumference of a circle to its diameter. Although the value of pi has been computed to several thousand places, and thus far three successive sevens have not occurred, the possibility remains that in some further calculation three successive sevens will occur. Hick observes that "the proposition may one day be verified if it is true, but can never be falsified if it is false."[2] Although Flew's test for the genuineness of assertions is appropriate for some types of assertions, the debate over the principle of falsification as an appropriate test for the acceptability of *all* assertions continues. And disagreement continues to be lively over whether all assertions of religious belief must in principle be falsifiable in order to be accepted as genuine. These are the issues raised by the following readings, and you will have to be the judge of which side presents the most convincing arguments.

[2]John Hick, *Faith and Knowledge,* 2nd ed. (Ithaca: Cornell University Press, 1966), p. 175.

The Falsification Debate*

ANTONY FLEW

Let us begin with a parable. It is a parable developed from a tale told
by John Wisdom in his haunting and revelatory article 'Gods.'[1] Once
upon a time two explorers came upon a clearing in the jungle. In the
clearing were growing many flowers and many weeds. One explorer says,
"Some gardener must tend this plot." The other disagrees, "There is no
gardener." So they pitch their tents and set a watch. No gardener is ever
seen. "But perhaps he is an invisible gardener." So they set up a barbed-
wire fence. They electrify it. They patrol with bloodhounds. (For they
remember how H. G. Wells's *The Invisible Man* could be both smelt and
touched though he could not be seen.) But no shrieks ever suggest that
some intruder has received a shock. No movements of the wire ever
betray an invisible climber. The bloodhounds never give cry. Yet still the
Believer is not convinced. "But there is a gardener, invisible, intangible,
insensible to electric shocks, a gardener who has no scent and makes no
sound, a gardener who comes secretly to look after the garden which he
loves." At last the Sceptic despairs, "But what remains of your original
assertion? Just how does what you call an invisible, intangible, eternally
elusive gardener differ from an imaginary gardener or even from no
gardener at all?"

In this parable we can see how what starts as an assertion, that
something exists or that there is some analogy between certain complexes
of phenomena, may be reduced step by step to an altogether different
status, to an expression perhaps of a "picture preference."[2] The Sceptic
says there is no gardener. The Believer says there is a gardener (but
invisible, etc.). One man talks about sexual behaviour. Another man
prefers to talk of Aphrodite (but knows that there is not really a superhuman person additional to, and somehow responsible for, all sexual

---

*Source: Antony Flew, R. M. Hare and Basil Mitchell, "Theology and Falsification,"
in *New Essays in Philosophical Theology*, ed. Antony Flew and Alasdair MacIntyre,
London: SCM Press 1955, pp. 96-108. © 1953 by SCM Press Ltd. Used by Permission. Published in the United States by Macmillan Publishing Co., and reprinted with
permission of Macmillan Publishing Co., Inc.

[1] *P.A.S.*, 1944-5, reprinted as Ch. X of *Logic and Language*, Vol. I (Blackwell, 1951),
and in his *Philosophy and Psychoanalysis* (Blackwell, 1953).

[2] Cf. J. Wisdom, "Other Minds," *Mind*, 1940; reprinted in his *Other Minds* (Blackwell,
1952).

phenomena).[3] The process of qualification may be checked at any point before the original assertion is completely withdrawn and something of that first assertion will remain (Tautology). Mr. Wells's invisible man could not, admittedly, be seen, but in all other respects he was a man like the rest of us. But though the process of qualification may be, and of course usually is, checked in time, it is not always judiciously so halted. Someone may dissipate his assertion completely without noticing that he has done so. A fine brash hypothesis may thus be killed by inches, the death by a thousand qualifications.

And in this, it seems to me, lies the peculiar danger, the endemic evil, of theological utterance. Take such utterances as "God has a plan," "God created the world," "God loves us as a father loves his children." They look at first sight very much like assertions, vast cosmological assertions. Of course, this is no sure sign that they either are, or are intended to be, assertions. But let us confine ourselves to the cases where those who utter such sentences intend them to express assertions. (Merely remarking parenthetically that those who intend or interpret such utterances as crypto-commands, expressions of wishes, disguised ejaculations, concealed ethics, or as anything else but assertions, are unlikely to succeed in making them either properly orthodox or practically effective).

Now to assert that such and such is the case is necessarily equivalent to denying that such and such is not the case.[4] Suppose then that we are in doubt as to what someone who gives vent to an utterance is asserting, or suppose that, more radically, we are sceptical as to whether he is really asserting anything at all, one way of trying to understand (or perhaps it will be to expose) his utterance is to attempt to find what he would regard as counting against, or as being incompatible with, its truth. For if the utterance is indeed an assertion, it will necessarily be equivalent to a denial of the negation of that assertion. And anything which would count against the assertion, or which would induce the speaker to withdraw it and to admit that it had been mistaken, must be part of (or the whole of) the meaning of the negation of that assertion. And to know the meaning of the negation of an assertion, is as near as makes no matter, to know the

---

[3]Cf. Lucretius, *De Rerum Natura,* II, 655-60,
> Hic siquis mare Neptunum Cereremque vocare
> Constituet fruges et Bacchi nomine abuti
> Mavolat quam laticis proprium proferre vocamen
> Concedamus ut hic terrarum dictitet orbem
> Esse deum matrem dum vera re tamen ipse
> Religione animum turpi contingere parcat.

[4]For those who prefer symbolism: $p \equiv \sim \sim p$.

meaning of that assertion.[5] And if there is nothing which a putative assertion denies then there is nothing which it asserts either: and so it is not really an assertion. When the Sceptic in the parable asked the Believer, "Just how does what you call an invisible, intangible, eternally elusive gardener differ from an imaginary gardener or even from no gardener at all?" he was suggesting that the Believer's earlier statement had been eroded by qualification that it was no longer an assertion at all.

Now it often seems to people who are not religious as if there was no conceivable event or series of events the occurrence of which would be admitted by sophisticated religious people to be a sufficient reason for conceding "There wasn't a God after all" or "God does not really love us then." Someone tells us that God loves us as a father loves his children. We are reassured. But then we see a child dying of inoperable cancer of the throat. His earthly father is driven frantic in his efforts to help, but his Heavenly Father reveals no obvious sign of concern. Some qualification is made—God's love is "not a merely human love" or it is "an inscrutable love," perhaps—and we realize that such sufferings are quite compatible with the truth of the assertion that "God loves us as a father (but, of course, . . .)." We are reassured again. But then perhaps we ask: what is this assurance of God's (appropriately qualified) love worth, what is this apparent guarantee really a guarantee against? Just what would have to happen not merely (morally and wrongly) to tempt but also (logically and rightly) to entitle us to say "God does not love us" or even "God does not exist?" I therefore put to the succeeding symposiasts the simple central questions, "What would have to occur or to have occurred to constitute for you a disproof of the love of, or of the existence of, God?"

R. M. HARE[6]

I wish to make it clear that I shall not try to defend Christianity in particular, but religion in general—not because I do not believe in Christianity, but because you cannot understand what Christianity is, until you have understood what religion is.

I must begin by confessing that, on the ground marked out by Flew, he seems to me to be completely victorious. I therefore shift my ground by relating another parable. A certain lunatic is convinced that all dons want to murder him. His friends introduce him to all the mildest and most respectable dons that they can find, and after each of them has retired, they say, "You see, he doesn't really want to murder you; he spoke to you

[5]For by simply negating $\sim p$ we get p: $\sim \sim p \equiv p$.
[6]Some references to intervening discussion have been excised—Editors.

in a most cordial manner; surely you are convinced now?" But the lunatic replies "Yes, but that was only his diabolical cunning; he's really plotting against me the whole time, like the rest of them; I know it I tell you." However many kindly dons are produced, the reaction is still the same.

Now we say that such a person is deluded. But what is he deluded about? About the truth or falsity of an assertion? Let us apply Flew's test to him. There is no behaviour of dons that can be enacted which he will accept as counting against his theory; and therefore his theory, on this test, asserts nothing. But it does not follow that there is no difference between what he thinks about dons and what most of us think about them—otherwise we should not call him a lunatic and ourselves sane, and dons would have no reason to feel uneasy about his presence in Oxford.

Let us call that in which we differ from this lunatic, our respective *bliks*. He has an insane *blik* about dons; we have a sane one. It is important to realize that we have a sane one, not no *blik* at all; for there must be two sides to any argument—if he has a wrong *blik*, then those who are right about dons must have a right one. Flew has shown that a *blik* does not consist in an assertion or system of them; but nevertheless it is very important to have the right *blik*.

Let us try to imagine what it would be like to have different *bliks* about other things than dons. When I am driving my car, it sometimes occurs to me to wonder whether my movements of the steering-wheel will always continue to be followed by corresponding alterations in the direction of the car. I have never had a steering failure, though I have had skids, which must be similar. Moreover, I know enough about how the steering of my car is made, to know the sort of thing that would have to go wrong for the steering to fail—steel joints would have to part, or steel rods break, or something—but how do I know that this won't happen? The truth is, I don't know; I just have a *blik* about steel and its properties, so that normally I trust the steering of my car; but I find it not at all difficult to imagine what it would be like to lose this *blik* and acquire the opposite one. People would say I was silly about steel; but there would be no mistaking the reality of the difference between our respective *bliks*—for example, I should never go in a motor-car. Yet I should hesitate to say that the difference between us was the difference between contradictory assertions. No amount of safe arrivals or bench-tests will remove my *blik* and restore the normal one: for my *blik* is compatible with any finite number of such tests.

It was Hume who taught us that our whole commerce with the world depends upon our *blik* about the world; and that differences between *bliks* about the world cannot be settled by observation of what happens in the world. That was why, having performed the interesting experiment of doubting the ordinary man's *blik* about the world, and showing that no proof could be given to make us adopt one *blik* rather than another, he turned to backgammon to take his mind off the problem. It seems, indeed, to be impossible even to formulate as an assertion the normal *blik* about the world which makes me put my confidence in the future reliability of steel joints, in the continued ability of the road to support my car, and not gape beneath it revealing nothing below; in the general non-homicidal tendencies of dons; in my own continued well-being (in some sense of that word that I may not now fully understand) if I continue to do what is right according to my lights; in the general likelihood of people like Hitler coming to a bad end. But perhaps a formulation less inadequate than most is to be found in the Psalms: "The earth is weak and all the inhabiters thereof: I bear up the pillars of it."

The mistake of the position which Flew selects for attack is to regard this kind of talk as some sort of *explanation,* as scientists are accustomed to use the word. As such, it would obviously be ludicrous. We no longer believe in God as an Atlas—*nous n'avons pas besoin de cette hypothèse.* But it is nevertheless true to say that, as Hume saw, without a *blik* there can be no explanation; for it is by our *bliks* that we decide what is and what is not an explanation. Suppose we believed that everything that happened, happened by pure chance. This would not of course be an assertion; for it is compatible with anything happening or not happening, and so, incidentally, is its contradictory. But if we had this belief, we should not be able to explain or predict or plan anything. Thus, although we should not be *asserting* anything different from those of a more normal belief, there would be a great difference between us; and this is the sort of difference that there is between those who really believe in God and those who really disbelieve in him.

The word "really" is important, and may excite suspicion. I put it in, because when people have had a good Christian upbringing, as have most of those who now profess not to believe in any sort of religion, it is very hard to discover what they really believe. The reason why they find it so easy to think that they are not religious, is that they have never got into the frame of mind of one who suffers from the doubts to which religion is the answer. Not for them the terrors of the primitive jungle. Having abandoned some of the more picturesque fringes of religion, they think that they have abandoned the whole thing—whereas in fact they still have got, and could not live without, a religion of a comfortably substantial, albeit highly sophisticated, kind, which differs from that of many "religious people" in little more than this, that "religious people" like to sing Psalms about theirs—a very natural and proper thing to do. But nevertheless there may be a big difference lying behind—the difference between two people who, though side by side, are walking in different directions. I do not know in what direction Flew is walking; perhaps he does not know either. But we have had some examples recently of various ways in which one can walk away from Christianity, and there are any number of possibilities. After all, man has not changed biologically since primitive times; it is his religion that has changed, and it can easily change again. And if you do not think that such changes make a difference, get acquainted with some Sikhs and some Mussulmans of the same Punjabi stock; you will find them quite different sorts of people.

There is an important difference between Flew's parable and my own which we have not yet noticed. The explorers do not *mind* about their garden; they discuss it with interest, but not with concern. But my lunatic, poor fellow, minds about dons; and I mind about the steering of my car; it often has people in it that I care for. It is because I mind very much about what goes on in the garden in which I find myself, that I am unable to share the explorers' detachment.

BASIL MITCHELL

Flew's article is searching and perceptive, but there is, I think, something odd about his conduct of the theologian's case. The theologian surely would not deny that the fact of pain counts against the assertion that God loves men. This very incompatibility generates the most intractable of theological problems—the problem of evil. So the theologian *does* recognize the fact of pain as counting against Christian doctrine. But it is true that he will not allow it—or anything—to count decisively against it; for he is committed by his faith to trust in God. His attitude is not that of the detached observer, but of the believer.

Perhaps this can be brought out by yet another parable. In time of war in an occupied country, a member of the resistance meets one night a stranger who deeply impresses him. They spend that night together in conversation. The Stranger tells the partisan that he himself is on the side of the resistance—indeed that he is in command of it, and urges the partisan to have faith in him no matter what happens. The partisan is utterly convinced at that meeting of the Stranger's sincerity and constancy and undertakes to trust him.

They never meet in conditions of intimacy again. But sometimes the Stranger is seen helping members of the resistance, and the partisan is grateful and says to his friends, "He is on our side."

Sometimes he is seen in the uniform of the police handing over patriots to the occupying power. On these occasions his friends murmur against him: but the partisan still says, "He is on our side." He still believes that, in spite of appearances, the Stranger did not deceive him. Sometimes he asks the Stranger for help and receives it. He is then thankful. Sometimes he asks and does not receive it. Then he says, "The Stranger knows best." Sometimes his friends, in exasperation, say "Well, what *would* he have to do for you to admit that you were wrong and that he is not on our side?" But the partisan refuses to answer. He will not consent to put the Stranger to the test. And sometimes his friends complain, "Well, if *that's* what you mean by his being on our side, the sooner he goes over to the other side the better."

The partisan of the parable does not allow anything to count decisively against the proposition "The Stranger is on our side." This is because he has committed himself to trust the Stranger. But he of course recognizes that the Stranger's ambiguous behaviour *does* count against what he believes about him. It is precisely this situation which constitutes the trial of his faith.

When the partisan asks for help and doesn't get it, what can he do? He can *(a)* conclude that the stranger is not on our side or; *(b)* maintain that he is on our side, but that he has reasons for withholding help.

The first he will refuse to do. How long can he uphold the second position without its becoming just silly?

I don't think one can say in advance. It will depend on the nature of the impression created by the Stranger in the first place. It will depend, too, on the manner in which he takes the Stranger's behaviour. If he blandly dismisses it as of no consequence, as having no bearing upon his belief, it will be assumed that he is thoughtless or insane. And it quite obviously won't do for him to say easily, "Oh, when used of the Stranger the phrase 'is on our side' *means* ambiguous behavior of this sort." In that case he would like the religious man who says blandly of a terrible disaster "It is God's will." No, he will only be regarded as sane and reasonable in his belief, if he experiences in himself the full force of the conflict.

It is here that my parable differs from Hare's. The partisan admits that many things may and do count against his belief: whereas Hare's lunatic who has a *blik* about dons doesn't admit that anything counts against his *blik*. Nothing *can* count against *bliks*. Also the partisan has a reason for having in the first instance committed himself, viz. the character of the Stranger; whereas the lunatic has no reason for his *blik* about dons—because, of course, you can't have reasons for *bliks*.

This means that I agree with Flew that theological utterances must be assertions. The partisan is making an assertion when he says, "The Stranger is on our side."

Do I want to say that the partisan's belief about the Stranger is, in any sense, an explanation? I think I do. It explains and makes sense of the Stranger's behaviour: it helps to explain also the resistance movement in the context of which he appears. In each case it differs from the interpretation which the others put upon the same facts.

"God loves men" resembles "the Stranger is on our side" (and many other significant statements, e.g. historical ones) in not being conclusively falsifiable. They can both be treated in at least three different ways: (1) As provisional hypotheses to be discarded if experience tells against them; (2) As significant articles of faith; (3) As vacuous formulae (expressing, perhaps, a desire for reassurance) to which experience makes no difference and which make no difference to life.

The Christian, once he has committed himself, is precluded by his faith from taking up the first attitude: "Thou shalt not tempt the Lord thy God." He is in constant danger, as Flew has observed, of slipping into the third. But he need not; and, if he does, it is a failure in faith as well as in logic.

ANTONY FLEW

It has been a good discussion: and I am glad to have helped to provoke it. But now—at least in *University*—it must come to an end: and the Editors of *University* have asked me to make some concluding remarks. Since it is impossible to deal with all the issues raised or to comment separately upon each contribution, I will concentrate on Mitchell and Hare, as representative of two very different kinds of response to the challenge made in "Theology and Falsification."

The challenge, it will be remembered, ran like this. Some theological utterances seem to, and are intended to, provide explanations or express assertions. Now an assertion, to be an assertion at all, must claim that things stand thus and thus; *and not otherwise*. Similarly an explanation, to be an explanation at all, must explain why this particular thing occurs; *and not something else*. Those last clauses are crucial. And yet sophisticated religious people—or so it seemed to me—are apt to overlook this, and tend to refuse to allow, not merely that anything actually does occur, but that anything conceivably could occur, which would count against their theological assertions and explanations. But in so far as they do this their supposed explanations are actually bogus, and their seeming assertions are really vacuous.

Mitchell's response to this challenge is admirably direct, straightforward, and understanding. He agrees "that theological utterances must be assertions." He agrees that if they are to be assertions, there must be something that would count against their truth. He agrees, too, that believers are in constant danger of transforming their would-be assertions into "vacuous formulae." But he takes me to task for an oddity in my "conduct of the theologian's case. The theologian surely would not deny that the fact of pain counts against the assertion that God loves men.

This very incompatibility generates the most intractable of theological problems, the problem of evil." I think he is right. I should have made a distinction between two very different ways of dealing with what looks like evidence against the love of God: the way I stressed was the expedient of qualifying the original assertion; the way the theologian usually takes, at first, is to admit that it looks bad but to insist that there is—there must be—some explanation which will show that, in spite of appearances, there really is a God who loves us. His difficulty, it seems to me, is that he has given God attributes which rule out all possible saving explanations. In Mitchell's parable of the Stranger it is easy for the believer to find plausible excuses for ambiguous behaviour: for the Stranger is a man. But suppose the Stranger is God. We cannot say that he would like to help but cannot: God is omnipotent. We cannot say that he would help if he only knew: God is omniscient. We cannot say that he is not responsible for the wickedness of others: God creates those others. Indeed an omnipotent, omniscient God must be an accessory before (and during) the fact to every human misdeed; as well as being responsible for every non-moral defect in the universe. So, though I entirely concede that Mitchell was absolutely right to insist against me that the theologian's first move is to look for an *explanation,* I still think that in the end, if relentlessly pursued, he will have to resort to the avoiding action of *qualification.* And there lies the danger of that death by a thousand qualifications, which would, I agree, constitute "a failure in faith as well as in logic."

Hare's approach is fresh and bold. He confesses that "on the ground marked out by Flew, he seems to me to be completely victorious." He therefore introduces the concept of *blik.* But while I think that there is room for some such concept in philosophy, and that philosophers should be grateful to Hare for his invention, I nevertheless want to insist that any attempt to analyse Christian religious utterances as expressions or affirmations of a *blik* rather than as (at least would-be) assertions about the cosmos is fundamentally misguided. *First,* because thus interpreted they would be entirely unorthodox. If Hare's religion really is a *blik,* involving no cosmological assertions about the nature and activities of a supposed personal creator, then surely he is not a Christian at all? *Second,* because thus interpreted, they could scarcely do the job they do. If they were not even intended as assertions then many religious activities would become fraudulent, or merely silly. If "You ought *because* it is God's will" asserts no more than "You ought," then the person who prefers the former phraseology is not really giving a reason, but a fraudulent substitute for one, a dialectical dud cheque. If "My soul must be immortal *because* God loves his children, etc." asserts no more than "My soul must be immortal," then the man who reassures himself with theological arguments for immortality is being as silly as the man who tries to clear his overdraft by writing his bank a cheque on the same account. (Of course neither of these utterances would be distinctively Christian: but this discussion never pretended to be so confined.) Religious utterances may indeed express false or even bogus assertions: but I simply do not believe that they are not both intended and interpreted to be or at any rate to presuppose assertions, at least in the context of religious practice; whatever shifts may be demanded, in another context, by the exigencies of theological apologetic.

One final suggestion. The philosophers of religion might well draw upon George Orwell's last appalling nightmare *1984* for the concept of *doublethink.* "*Doublethink* means the power of holding two contradictory beliefs simultaneously, and accepting both of them. The party intellectual knows that he is playing tricks with reality, but by the exercise of *doublethink* he also satisfies himself that reality is not violated" (*1984,* p. 220). Perhaps religious intellectuals too are sometimes driven to doublethink in order to retain their faith in a loving God in face of the reality of a heartless and indifferent world. But of this more another time, perhaps.

DISCUSSION QUESTIONS

1. In your own words, describe the difference between knowledge, opinion, belief, and unbelief.
2. Do you think that the principle of falsification is an adequate criterion for the genuineness of assertions? Why or why not?
3. What distinction do you think Hare implicitly suggests between sane and insane bliks? Do you find this an adequate distinction? Give reasons for your answer.
4. In addition to the examples given in the readings, can you cite other examples of assertions that we would want to consider meaningful even though they do not appear to be falsifiable?
5. Do you find Hare's or Mitchell's response to Flew more adequate? In light of their critique, what is your own assessment of Flew's original proposal?

C. S. LEWIS

The Logic
of
Belief

The issues raised by the Flew-Hare-Mitchell discussion involved a number of interesting questions, but one of the principal themes of that discussion is the nature of religious belief, specifically its legitimacy in the face of less than certain evidence. This is the issue squarely faced by C. S. Lewis in the following article, which was originally given as a paper to the Socratic Club at Oxford. This was a club in only a loose sense, being principally a group of persons at Oxford University who met weekly over a period of several years to hear papers both defending and attacking the Christian faith. Though Lewis does not mention Flew's principle of falsification directly, he doubtless knew of Flew's work and may have had some of the issues raised by the falsification debate in mind when he wrote the following paper. In a letter to me, Professor Flew provided the following background information: "The pieces [on falsification] as originally printed in that long since defunct journal *University* were never in that form given as a paper anywhere. But the ideas contained, and some others, had been presented to a meeting of the Socratic Club. Indeed the editor and founder of that little journal *University,* D. L. Edwards, who has since risen through a Fellowship of All Souls to some prominence in the Church of England, once told me that his main purpose in founding the journal was to get these ideas and some others which he had heard discussed at the meetings of the Socratic Club discussed in print." Thus the following article is related to the discussion on falsification not only by commonality of themes but by historical connections as well.

Before turning to the Lewis article, let us go back to a suggestion made by Basil Mitchell in his response to Flew. He observes that statements of religious belief can be taken in at least three different ways: "(1) As provisional hypotheses to be discarded if experience tells against them; (2) As significant articles of faith; and (3) As vacuous formulae (expressing, perhaps, a desire for reassurance) to which experience makes no difference and which make no difference to life" (see p. 129). Mitchell concluded that religious beliefs must be of the second kind, and Lewis shows how taking religious belief in this second sense is a defensible attitude. Lewis also shows that "belief" taken in the sense of a provisional hypothesis is not what the religious believer has in mind when using the term, and is likewise to use the term "belief" in a vague sense.

Basic to Lewis's analysis is the distinction between what he calls the "logic of speculative thought" and "the logic of personal relations." Speculative thought here refers to the matter of apportioning belief to the evidence, the sort of task which the scientist is engaged in while doing research. But the term "belief" is ambiguous in ordinary usage. It can mean either a very weak degree of opinion, or it can refer to "assent to a proposition so overwhelmingly probable that there is a psychological exclusion of doubt, though not a logical exclusion of dispute." The former sense of the word "belief" is its usage in the "logic of speculative thought," and the latter sense is the meaning it has for the "logic of personal relations."

To clarify this distinction, consider how we sometimes use the term "belief" to refer to a weak degree of opinion . We may say, "I believe it is raining outside," but once we step out into the rain it is no longer a weakly held opinion but a matter of demonstrative certainty. It is in this sense of the term that "belief" refers to a scientific hypothesis. A hypothesis is not a belief in the proper sense of the term, but a presupposition about which a scientist organizes research, the purpose of the research being to prove or disprove the hypothesis. Lewis rejects the view that a hypothesis is a type of belief, for the purpose of scientific research is to move from opinon to knowledge. Though a scientist may express the belief that a certain result will emerge from an experiment, what this really means is that the scientist's working hypothesis is that a certain result from the experiment will prove the accuracy of the working hypothesis. We would hardly blame the scientist for abandoning a hypothesis when the evidence resulting from the experiment shows the hypothesis to be incorrect. The goal of scientific investigation is to move from a weakly held opinion, sometimes referred to as a "belief," to knowledge fortified by empirical evidence.

In short, the task of the scientist, as Lewis sees it, is to pass from opinion to knowledge. But even the scientist, as a human being, approaches personal relationships differently than a speculative problem in the laboratory. In personal relations, the scientist appeals to a different logic, the "logic of personal relations." If a close friend, perhaps a wife or husband, is accused of committing a crime but claims to be innocent, the scientist may believe the friend's word even though the evidence against the friend may be rather strong. No one would blame the scientist for defending a friend in spite of the evidence. In fact, we would probably think it strange sort of friendship if the scientist were to say, "Don't forget that I am a scientist, and to be consistent with my scientific methods I cannot accept your claims of innocence until all the evidence has been weighed. Then, depending on the weight of the evidence, I will inform you whether or not I believe that you are innocent." Such skepticism is hardly the stuff of which friendships are made.

We can underscore the difference between the two kinds of belief by distinguishing between believing *that* and believing *in*. The former is the kind of weak opinion that characterizes the uncertainty regarding speculative inquiries. But to believe *in* is to commit oneself to a point of view which one continues to hold even though there is evidence that seems to count against this belief. The scientist in the example above does not merely believe that the accused friend is innocent; the scientist, as a human being related in friendship to another human being, believes *in* the friend: "I know Joe; he just wouldn't do what he has been accused of doing." No one blames another person—even a scientist—for such obstinacy. In fact, we admire the sort of loyalty this stubborn refusal to abandon a friend in trouble represents.

Is faith in God more like the scientist attempting to prove a hypothesis in a laboratory, or is it more like a person's loyalty to a friend? Lewis argues that religious belief is like the latter; it is a matter of trust based on a commitment to a person. Lewis also argues that we must distinguish between (1) making such a commitment in the first place, and (2) maintaining this commitment even when the evidence against the commitment seems damaging. Commitments of this kind to other persons are not lightly made, and they are certainly not made without supporting evidence. Likewise, no one assents to the Christian faith—or to any other religious faith—without some sort of evidence. There are many kinds of evidence which lead people to faith in God—at least to faith in the God of the biblical faith. But Lewis's purpose in this article is not to analyze the basis for the original assent but to look at the stubbornness of the believer once such a faith commitment has been made. Lewis admits that there can be evidence which counts against continued loyalty to a faith commitment, just as in the example there was evidence against the friend's protestations of innocence. There could even be evidence of such a strong kind that the scientist would have to abandon trust in the friend's innocence in spite of an intense wish to continue to believe the friend's word. But no one blames a person for continued loyalty to a friend even when those who have no personal relationship with the accused have long since given up.

This matter of wish-fulfillment also requires further attention. A widely held objection to religious faith is that it is a kind of wish-projection; that is, people believe in God simply because they wish there were a God. As Voltaire said, *"Si Dieu n'existait pas, il faudrait l'inventer"* ("If God did not exist, it would be necessary to invent him"). But this matter of wishing, Lewis argues, cuts both ways. We wish for some things to be true; we wish for other things to be false. There are persons who wish that there is a God; and there are persons who wish for there not to be a God. In fact, if we take Freud's Oedipus complex seriously, the greatest suppressed wish of all mankind would be the desire to kill the Father-God figure. So if it counts against religious faith that some people wish there is a God, then it should count for religious faith that others wish there is no God. The two sorts of wishes cancel each other out—at least as far as any kind of argument is concerned.

So we are back to where we started. The very fact that our friend may be guilty makes it possible for us to trust in our friend's innocence. This trust may prove to be in vain, but we can scarcely be faulted for giving it and maintaining it when the evidence against our friend looks grim. There are other, completely nonreligious, examples of our placing trust in persons even though our natural inclination may be against doing what the person says. A drowning person has to fight against every instinct to follow the rescuer's instructions, "Just relax, quit struggling, and I will save you." Or when the rescuer says to the hapless mountain climber, "Let's go up higher, and then I can get you down." If you are in danger of losing your life, your response to a rescuer is hardly to appeal to the logic of speculative thought and carefully weigh the evidence. You don't ask the lifeguard to show you a Red Cross lifesaving certificate before trusting in the lifeguard to save you.

Lewis argues that we are always in a relation to God that is more like our relation to a rescuer than to a scientific hypothesis, and trust is only possible when the situation that calls for trust is ambiguous. If the situation were not ambiguous, trust could not even be given, for then it would be a matter of demonstrative truth. God being infinite, and man being finite, it should not strike us as strange that God's ways toward mankind sometimes appear baffling, and that the love of God seems at times ambiguous. But it is precisely this ambiguity that makes faith, in the sense of personal trust, possible.

To be sure, the presence of evil in the world is not to be dismissed lightly, for it certainly makes the possibility of continued trust in God more difficult. But the believer can scarcely be accused of ignoring the problem of evil. Just as continued trust in a friend is in spite of the damaging evidence that may have been assembled by those who are convinced of the person's guilt, so faith in God is in spite of the presence of evil in the world. We will come back to this question again, for the problem of evil is certainly one of the most formidable barriers to faith.

On Obstinacy in Belief*

Papers have more than once been read to the Socratic Club at Oxford in which a contrast was drawn between a supposedly Christian attitude and a supposedly scientific attitude to belief. We have been told that the scientist thinks it his duty to proportion the strength of his belief exactly to the evidence; to believe less as there is less evidence and to withdraw belief altogether when reliable adverse evidence turns up. We have been told that, on the contrary, the Christian regards it as positively praiseworthy to believe without evidence, or in excess of the evidence, or to maintain his belief unmodified in the teeth of steadily increasing evidence against it. Thus a "faith that has stood firm," which appears to mean a belief immune from all the assaults of reality, is commended.

*Source: C. S. Lewis, "On Obstinacy in Belief," in *They Asked for a Paper* (London: Geoffrey Bles, Ltd., 1962), pp. 183-96. © C. S. Lewis, 1962. Used by permission.

If this were a fair statement of the case, then the co-existence within the same species of such scientists and such Christians, would be a very staggering phenomenon. The fact that the two classes appear to overlap, as they do, would be quite inexplicable. Certainly all discussion between creatures so different would be hopeless. The purpose of this essay is to show that things are really not quite so bad as that. The sense in which scientists proportion their belief to the evidence and the sense in which Christians do not, both need to be defined more closely. My hope is that when this has been done, though disagreement between the two parties may remain, they will not be left staring at one another in wholly dumb and desperate incomprehension.

And first, a word about belief in general. I do not see that the state of "proportioning belief to evidence" is anything like so common in the scientific life as has been claimed. Scientists are mainly concerned not with believing things but with finding things out. And no one, to the best of my knowledge, uses the word "believe" about things he has found out. The doctor says he "believes" a man was poisoned before he has examined the body; after the examination, he says the man was poisoned. No one says that he believes the multiplication table. No one who catches a thief red-handed says he believes that man was stealing. The scientist, when at work, that is, when he is a scientist, is labouring to escape from belief and unbelief into knowledge. Of course he uses hypotheses or supposals. I do not think these are beliefs. We must look, then, for the scientist's behaviour about belief not to his scientific life but to his leisure hours.

In actual modern English usage the verb "believes," except for two special usages, generally expresses a very weak degree of opinion. "Where is Tom?" "Gone to London, I believe." The speaker would be only mildly surprised if Tom had not gone to London after all. "What was the date?" "430 B.C., I believe." The speaker means that he is far from sure. It is the same with the negative if it is put in the form "I believe not." ("Is Jones coming up this term?" "I believe not.") But if the negative is put in a different form it then becomes one of the special usages I mentioned a moment ago. This is of course the form "I don't believe it," or the still stronger "I don't believe you." "I don't believe it" is far stronger on the negative side than "I believe" is on the positive. "Where is Mrs. Jones?" "Eloped with the butler, I believe." "I don't believe it." This, especially if said with anger, may imply a conviction which in subjective certitude might be hard to distinguish from knowledge by experience. The other special usage is "I believe" as uttered by a Christian. There is no great difficulty in making the hardened materialist understand, however little he approves, the sort of mental attitude which this "I believe" expresses. The materialist need only picture himself replying, to some report of a miracle, "I don't believe it," and then imagine this same degree of conviction on the opposite side. He knows that he cannot, there and then, produce a refutation of the miracle which would have the certainty of mathematical demonstration; but the formal possibility that the miracle might after all have occurred does not really trouble him any more than a fear that water might not be H and O. Similarly, the Christian does not necessarily claim to have demonstrative proof; but the formal possibility that God might not exist is not necessarily present in the form of the least actual doubt. Of course there are Christians who hold that such demonstrative proof exists, just as there may be materialists who hold that there is demonstrative disproof. But then, whichever of them is right (if either is) while he retained the proof or disproof would be not believing or disbelieving but knowing. We are speaking of belief and disbelief in the strongest degree but not of knowledge. Belief, in this sense, seems to me to be assent to a proposition which we think so overwhelmingly probable that there is a psychological exclusion of doubt, though not a logical exclusion of dispute.

It may be asked whether belief (and of course disbelief) of this sort ever attaches to any but theological propositions. I think that many beliefs approximate to it; that is, many probabilities seem to us so strong that the absence of logical certainty does not induce in us the least shade of doubt. The scientific beliefs of those who are not themselves scientists often have this character, especially among the uneducated. Most of our beliefs about other people are of the same sort. The scientist himself, or he who was a scientist in the laboratory, has beliefs about his wife and friends which he holds, not indeed without evidence, but with more certitude than the evidence, if weighed in the laboratory manner, would justify. Most of my generation had a belief in the reality of the external world and of other people—if you prefer it, a disbelief in solipsism—far in excess of our strongest arguments. It may be true, as they now say, that the whole thing arose from category mistakes and was a pseudo-problem; but then we didn't know that in the twenties. Yet we managed to disbelieve in solipsism all the same.

There is, of course, no question so far of belief without evidence. We must beware of confusion between the way in which a Christian first assents to certain propositions and the way in which he afterwards adheres to them. These must be carefully distinguished. Of the second it is true, in a sense, to say that Christians do recommend a certain discounting of apparent contrary evidence, and I will later attempt to explain why. But so far as I know it is not expected that a man should assent to these propositions in the first place without evidence or in the teeth of the evidence. At any rate, if anyone expects that, I certainly do not. And in fact, the man who accepts Christianity always thinks he had good evidence; whether, like Dante, *fisici e metafisici argomenti,* or historical evidence, or the evidence of religious experience, or authority, or all these together. For of course authority, however we may value it in this or that particular instance, is a kind of evidence. All of our historical beliefs, most of our geographical beliefs, many of our beliefs about matters that concern us in daily life, are accepted on the authority of other human beings, whether we are Christians, Atheists, Scientists, or Men-in-the-Street.

It is not the purpose of this essay to weigh the evidence, of whatever kind, on which Christians base their belief. To do that would be to write a full-dress *apologia*. All that I need do here is to point out that, at the very worst, this evidence cannot be so weak as to warrant the view that all whom it convinces are indifferent to evidence. The history of thought seems to make this quite plain. We know, in fact, that believers are not cut off from unbelievers by any portentous inferiority of intelligence or any perverse refusal to think. Many of them have been people of powerful minds. Many of them have been scientists. We may suppose them to have been mistaken, but we must suppose that their error was at least plausible. We might indeed, conclude that it was, merely from the multitude and diversity of the arguments against it. For there is not one case against religion, but many. Some say, like Capaneus in Statius, that it is a projection of our primitive fears, *primus in orbe deos fecit timor:* others, with Euhemerus, that it is all a "plant" put up by wicked kings, priests, or capitalists; others, with Tylor, that it comes from dreams about the dead; others, with Frazer, that it is a by-product of agriculture; others, like Freud, that it is a complex; the moderns that it is a category mistake. I will never believe that an error against which so many and various defensive weapons have been found necessary was, from the outset, wholly lacking in plausibility. All this "post haste and rummage in the land" obviously implies a respectable enemy.

There are of course people in our own day to whom the whole situation seems altered by the doctrine of the concealed wish. They will admit that men, otherwise apparently rational, have been deceived by the arguments for religion. But they will say that they have been deceived first by their own desires and produced the arguments afterwards as a rationalisation: that these arguments have never been intrinsically even plausible, but have seemed so because they were secretly weighted by our wishes. Now I do not doubt that this sort of thing happens in thinking about religion as in thinking about other things: but as a general explanation of religious assent it seems to me quite useless. On that issue our wishes may favour either side or both. The assumption that every man would be pleased, and nothing but pleased, if only he could conclude that Christianity is true, appears to me to be simply preposterous. If Freud is right about the Oedipus complex, the universal pressure of the wish that God should not exist must be enormous, and atheism must be an admirable gratification to one of our strongest suppressed impulses. This argument, in fact, could be used on the theistic side. But I have no intention of so using it. It will not really help either party. It is fatally ambivalent. Men wish on both sides: and again, there is fear-fulfilment as well as wish-fulfilment, and hypochondriac temperaments will always tend to think true what they most wish to be false. Thus instead of the one predicament on which our opponents sometimes concentrate there are in fact four. A man may be a Christian because he wants Christianity to be true. He may be an atheist because he wants atheism to be true. He may be an atheist because he wants Christianity to be true. He may be a Christian because he wants atheism to be true. Surely these possibilities cancel one another out? They may be of some use in analysing a particular instance of belief or disbelief, where we know the case history, but as a general explanation of either they will not help us. I do not think they overthrow the view that there is evidence both for and against the Christian propositions which fully rational minds, working honestly, can assess differently.

I therefore ask you to substitute a different and less tidy picture for that with which we began. In it, you remember, two different kinds of men, scientists, who proportioned their belief to the evidence, and Christians, who did not, were left facing one another across a chasm. The picture I should prefer is like this. All men alike, on questions which interest them, escape from the region of belief into that of knowledge when they can, and if they succeed in knowing, they no longer say they believe. The questions in which mathematicians are interested admit of treatment by a particularly clear and strict technique. Those of the scientist have their own technique, which is not quite the same. Those of the historian and the judge are different again. The mathematician's proof (at least so we laymen suppose) is by reasoning, the scientist's by experiment, the historian's by documents, the judge's by concurring sworn testimony. But all these men, as men, on questions outside their own disciplines, have numerous beliefs to which they do not normally apply the methods of their own disciplines. It would indeed carry some suspicion of morbidity and even of insanity if they did. These beliefs vary in strength from weak opinion to complete subjective certitude. Specimens of such beliefs at their strongest are the Christian's "I believe" and the convinced atheist's "I don't believe a word of it." The particular subject-matter on which these two disagree does not, of course, necessarily involve such strength of belief and disbelief. There are some who moderately opine that there is, or is not, a God. But there are others whose belief or disbelief is free from doubt. And all these beliefs, weak or strong, are based on what appears to the holders to be evidence; but the strong believers or disbelievers of course think they have very strong evidence. There is no need to suppose stark unreason on either side. We need only suppose error. One side has estimated the evidence wrongly. And even so, the mistake cannot be supposed to be of a flagrant nature; otherwise the debate would not continue.

So much, then, for the way in which Christians come to assent to certain propositions. But we have now to consider something quite different; their adherence to their belief after it has once been formed. It is here that the charge of irrationality and resistance to evidence becomes really important. For it must be admitted at once that Christians do praise such an adherence as if it were meritorious; and even, in a sense, more meritorious the stronger the apparent evidence against their faith becomes. They even warn one another that such apparent contrary evidence—such "trials to faith" or "temptations to doubt"—may be expected to occur, and determine in advance to resist them. And this is certainly shockingly unlike the behaviour we all demand of the scientist or the historian in their own disciplines. There, to slur over or ignore the faintest evidence against a favourite hypothesis, is admittedly foolish and shameful. It must be exposed to every test; every doubt must be invited. But then I do not admit that a hypothesis is a belief. And if we consider the scientist not among his hypotheses in the laboratory but among the beliefs in his ordinary life, I think the contrast between him and the Christian would be weakened. If, for the first time, a doubt of his wife's fidelity crosses the scientist's mind, does he consider it his duty at once to entertain this doubt with complete impartiality, at once to evolve a series of experiments by which it can be tested, and to await the result with pure neutrality of mind? No doubt it may come to that in the end. There are unfaithful wives; there are experimental husbands. But is such a course what his brother scientists would recommend to him (all of them, I suppose, except one) as the first step he should take and the only one consistent with his honour as a scientist? Or would they, like us, blame him for a moral flaw rather than praise him for an intellectual virtue if he did so?

This is intended, however, merely as a precaution against exaggerating the difference between Christian obstinacy in belief and the behaviour of normal people about their non-theological beliefs. I am far from suggesting that the case I have supposed is exactly parallel to the Christian obstinacy. For of course evidence of the wife's infidelity might accumulate, and presently reach a point at which the scientist would be pitiably foolish to disbelieve it. But the Christians seem to praise an adherence to the original belief which holds out against any evidence whatever. I must now try to show why such praise is in fact a logical conclusion from the original belief itself.

This can be done best by thinking for a moment of situations in which the thing is reversed. In Christianity such faith is demanded of us; but there are situations in which we demand it of others. There are times when we can do all that a fellow creature needs if only he will trust us. In getting a dog out of a trap, in extracting a thorn from a child's finger, in teaching a boy to swim or rescuing one who can't, in getting a frightened beginner over a nasty place on a mountain, the one fatal obstacle may be their distrust. We are asking them to trust us in the teeth of their senses, their imagination, and their intelligence. We ask them to believe that what is painful will relieve their pain and that what looks dangerous is their only safety. We ask them to accept apparent impossibilities: that moving the paw farther back into the trap is the way to get it out—that hurting the finger very much more will stop the finger hurting—that water which is obviously permeable will resist and support the body—that holding on to the only support within reach is not the way to avoid sinking—that to go higher and on to a more exposed ledge is the way not to fall. To support all these *incredibilia* we can rely only on the other party's confidence in us—a confidence certainly not based on demonstration, admittedly shot through with emotion, and perhaps, if we are strangers, resting on nothing but such assurance as the look of our face and the tone of our voice can supply, or even, for the dog, on our smell. Sometimes, because of their unbelief, we can do no mighty works. But if we succeed, we do so because they have maintained their faith in us against apparently contrary evidence. No one blames us for demanding such faith. No one blames them for giving it. No one says afterwards what an unintelligent dog or child or boy that must have been to trust us. If the young mountaineer were a scientist, it would not be held against him, when he came up for a fellowship, that he had once departed from Clifford's rule of evidence by entertaining a belief with strength greater than the evidence logically obliged him to.

Now to accept the Christian propositions is *ipso facto* to believe that we are to God, always, as that dog or child or bather or mountain climber was to us, only very much more so. From this it is a strictly logical conclusion that the behaviour which was appropriate to them will be appropriate to us, only very much more so. Mark: I am not saying that the strength of our original belief must by psychological necessity produce such behaviour. I am saying that the content of our original belief by logical necessity entails the proposition that such behaviour is appropriate. If human life is in fact ordered by a beneficent being whose knowledge of our real needs and of the way in which they can be satisfied infinitely exceeds our own, we must expect *a priori* that His operations will often appear to us far from beneficent and far from wise, and that it will be our highest prudence to give Him our confidence in spite of this. This expectation is increased by the fact that when we accept Christianity we are warned that apparent evidence against it will occur—evidence strong enough "to deceive if possible the very elect." Our situation is rendered tolerable by two facts. One is that we seem to ourselves, besides the apparently contrary evidence, to receive favourable evidence. Some of it is in the form of external events: as when I go to see a man, moved by what I felt to be a whim, and find he has been praying that I should come to him that day. Some of it is more like the evidence on which the mountaineer or the dog might trust his rescuer—the rescuer's voice, look, and smell. For it seems to us (though you, on your premises, must believe us deluded) that we have something like a knowledge-by-acquaintance of the Person we believe in, however imperfect and intermittent it may be. We trust not because "a God" exists, but because *this* God exists. Or if we ourselves dare not claim to "know" Him, Christendom does, and we trust at least some of its representatives in the same way: because of the sort of people they are. The second fact is this. We think we can see already why, if our original belief is true, such trust beyond the evidence, against much apparent evidence, has to be demanded of us. For the question is not about being helped out of one trap or over one difficult place in a climb. We believe that His intention is to create a certain personal relation between Himself and us, a relation really *sui generis* but analogically describable in terms of filial or of erotic love. Complete trust is an ingredient in that relation— such trust as could have no room to grow except where there is also room for doubt. To love involves trusting the beloved beyond the evidence, even against much evidence. No man is our friend who believes in our good intentions only when they are proved. No man is our friend who will not be very slow to accept evidence against them. Such confidence, between one man and another, is in fact almost universally praised as a moral beauty, not blamed as a logical error. And the suspicious man is blamed for a meanness of character, not admired for the excellence of his logic.

There is, you see, no real parallel between Christian obstinacy in faith and the obstinacy of a bad scientist trying to preserve a hypothesis although the evidence has turned against it. Unbelievers very pardonably get the impression that an adherence to our faith is like that, because they meet Christianity, if at all, mainly in apologetic works. And there, of course, the existence and beneficence of God must appear as a speculative question like any other. Indeed, it is a speculative question as long as it is a question at all. But once it has been answered in the affirmative, you get quite a new situation. To believe that God—at least *this* God—exists is to believe that you as a person now stand in the presence of God as a Person. What would, a moment before, have been variations in opinion, now becomes variations in your personal attitude to a Person. You are no longer faced with an argument which demands your assent, but with a Person who demands your confidence. A faint analogy would be this. It is one thing to discuss *in vacuo* whether So-and-So will join us tonight, and another to discuss this when So-and-So's honour is pledged to come and some great matter depends on his coming. In the first case it would be merely reasonable, as the clock ticked on, to expect him less and less. In the second, a continued expectation far into the night would be due to our friend's character if we had found him reliable before. Which of us would not feel slightly ashamed if one moment after we had given him up he arrived with a full explanation of his delay? We should feel that we ought to have known him better.

Now of course we see, quite as clearly as you, how agonisingly two-edged all this is. A faith of this sort, if it happens to be true, is obviously what we need, and it is infinitely ruinous to lack it. But there can be faith of this sort where it is wholly ungrounded. The dog may lick the face of the man who comes to take it out of the trap; but the man may only mean to vivisect it in South Parks Road when he has done so. The ducks who come to the call "Dilly, dilly, come and be killed" have confidence in the farmer's wife, and she wrings their necks for their pains. There is that famous French story of the fire in the theatre, Panic was spreading, the spectators were just turning from an audience into a mob. At that moment a huge bearded man leaped through the orchestra on to the stage, raised his hand with a gesture full of nobility, and cried, *"Que chacun regagne sa place."* Such was the authority of his voice and bearing that everyone obeyed him. As a result they were all burned to death, while the bearded man walked quietly out through the wings to the stage door, took a cab which was waiting for someone else, and went home to bed.

That demand for our confidence which a true friend makes of us is exactly the same that a confidence trickster would make. That refusal to trust, which is sensible in reply to a confidence trickster, is ungenerous and ignoble to a friend, and deeply damaging to our relation with him. To be forewarned and therefore forearmed against apparently contrary appearance is eminently rational if our belief is true; but if our belief is a delusion, this same forewarning and forearming would obviously be the method whereby the delusion rendered itself incurable. And yet again, to be aware of these possibilities and still to reject them is clearly the precise mode, and the only mode, in which our personal response to God can establish itself. In that sense the ambiguity is not something that conflicts with faith so much as a condition which makes faith possible. When you are asked for trust you may give it or withhold it; it is senseless to say that you will trust if you are given demonstrative certainty. There would be no room for trust if demonstration were given. When demonstration is given what will be left will be simply the sort of relation which results from having trusted, or not having trusted, before it was given.

The saying "Blessed are those that have not seen and have believed" has nothing to do with our original assent to the Christian propositions. It was not addressed to a philosopher inquiring whether God exists. It was addressed to a man who already believed that, who already had long acquaintance with a particular Person, and evidence that that Person could do very odd things, and who then refused to believe one odd thing more, often predicted by that Person and vouched for by all his closest friends. It is a rebuke not to scepticism in the philosophic sense but to the psychological quality of being "suspicious." It says in effect, "You should have known me better." There are cases between man and man where we should all, in our different way, bless those who have not seen and have believed. Our relation to those who trusted us only after we were proved innocent in court cannot be the same as our relation to those who trusted us all through.

Our opponents, then, have a perfect right to dispute with us about the grounds of our original assent. But they must not accuse us of sheer insanity if, after the assent has been given, our adherence to it is no longer proportioned to every fluctuation of the apparent evidence. They cannot of course be expected to know on what our assurance feeds, and how it revives and is always rising from its ashes. They cannot be expected to see how the *quality* of the object which we think we are beginning to know by acquaintance drives us to the view that if this were a delusion then we should have to say that the universe had produced no real thing of comparable value and that all explanations of the delusion seemed somehow less important than the thing explained. That is knowledge we cannot communicate. But they can see how the assent, of necessity, moves us from the logic of speculative thought into what might perhaps be called the logic of personal relations. What would, up till then, have been variations simply of opinion become variations of conduct by a person to a Person. *Credere Deum esse* turns into *Credere in Deum*. And *Deum* here is this God, the increasingly knowable Lord.

DISCUSSION QUESTIONS

1. Do you agree that there is a viable distinction between the "logic of speculative thought" and "the logic of personal relations" as Lewis suggests? Give reasons for your answer.
2. Give additional examples from ordinary language illustrating the ambiguity of the term "belief."
3. Lewis claims that the obstinacy of a believer is in no way comparable to the stubbornness of a bad scientist refusing to abandon an indefensible hypothesis. Do you think that Lewis has made good his claim? Why or why not?
4. In addition to those given by Lewis, can you cite other nonreligious examples that illustrate a refusal to abandon a belief in the face of evidence which counts against the belief?

5. Do you accept the claim made by Lewis that religious beliefs should not be treated as hypotheses? Why or why not?

6. Lewis appeals to the area of personal relations in discussing the appropriate attitude one should take toward God. Do you see any similarities between this and Buber's approach to God? Explain.

7. Lewis argues that propositions for which there is a psychological exclusion of doubt may nonetheless not imply a logical exclusion of dispute. Do you accept this distinction? What are your reasons?

SØREN KIERKEGAARD

Truth
is
Subjectivity

Human reason gives us neat, logic-tight boxes in which to store our ideas. Philosophers construct beautiful speculative systems so complete that every aspect of reality can be accounted for. In such systems "truth" is a matter of finding an appropriate place within the system, and excluded from reason's domain is any place for emotion or the subjective aspects of our human existence. A place for everything, and everything in its place; every aspect of human knowledge completely accounted for, labeled, systematized, analyzed, criticized, and methodically evaluated. Such was reason's ideal in Kierkegaard's nineteenth century.

Those who fostered such systems were German philosophers in general and Kierkegaard's *bête noire* G. W. F. Hegel in particular. But Kierkegaard would have none of it. These elaborate philosophical systems may be beautiful to behold, he would have maintained, but they are good for little else. They certainly do not capture the meaning of the confused, ambiguous, messy experience we call human existence; in spite of their elaborateness, philosophical systems cannot do justice to the complexity of human existence. "Life is lived forward and understood backwards," Kierkegaard said. Don't expect to understand human existence completely by means of reason's philosophical analysis. The foolishness of philosophers is that when they have built their highly abstract systems they think they have actually done something significant. But what is really important to us as existing human beings? For Kierkegaard the important question was what it means to be an existing individual, and this is a concern that cannot be addressed by abstract analysis, for to be human is to exist. What does it mean to exist as a human being? It is first a matter of existing in time for a brief period. One is born, lives for a few years, and then dies, without ever having any choice in the matter. Seen from our limited perspective, life does not make much sense, and reason is of little help in guiding us through the tangle of human concerns that confront us as existing individuals.

It should be obvious how Kierkegaard would respond to the question of the relation between faith and reason. But before going any further, it should be noted that Kierkegaard was faced with something of a methodological problem. He was opposed to philosophical system-building and the distortion of human existence that all such types of philosophy entailed. But how does one attack system-building in philosophy? Certainly not systematically. It would be a curious contradiction to argue against argument or systematically to attack system-building. So Kierkegaard chose a form of indirect discourse. Many of his books were written under pseudonymns, and he used irony, analogy, veiled metaphors, and lyric description in an effort to get his readers to think about these important concerns facing each of us as existing individuals. The following selection, for example, is taken from a book entitled *Concluding Unscientific Postscript,* which has as its subtitle: *A Mimic-Pathetic-Dialectic Composition, An Existential Contribution*. Certainly no one today could get a book published with a title like that. But the real "joke" is that Kierkegaard had previously written a small book—93 pages in English translation—entitled *Philosophical Fragments,* though *Philosophical Scraps* would probably be a more appropriate translation. It is hard to imagine any other nineteenth-century philosopher, least of all Hegel, writing a book entitled *Philosophical Scraps,* but the very title itself showed something of Kierkegaard's disdain for the prevailing type of philosophy. To this book of fragments he added a sequel called not *Scientific Postscript* but *Unscientific Postscript,* and in English translation it is over 500 pages in length. The *Postscript,* in other words, is over five times as long as that to which it is the postscript. This must have amused Kierkegaard immensely.

Central to the theme of the *Postscript* is the distinction between the objective and the subjective thinker. This distinction is basically between reason and faith. The objective thinker is one who adopts an intellectual, detached, scientific attitude toward life. The holder of this attitude views life from the perspective of an observer, and the most ludicrous example of this kind of thinker for Kierkegaard is that of a professor who produces a "system" of philosophy with little thought to the fact that one who produces such a system is also an existing human being, who faces the same perplexities in life as the rest of us. The objective thinker feels no real commitment to the truth of what is under study, for to approach the question of truth in an objective fashion is to be uncommitted, free from passion, and principally directed toward the object under investigation. For us, the paradigm of objective thinking is probably the scientist in a laboratory. A scientific investigator approaches the question of truth in a detached manner, for the scientist is mainly concerned with confirming or disproving a scientific hypothesis. If the research being conducted confirms only one aspect of the hypothesis, then the rest of it is discarded and a new hypothesis formed which incorporates the truth inherent in the old one. By this *approximation-process,* to use Kierkegaard's term, the objective thinker gradually moves closer and closer to the truth, but it is a truth to which the scientist feels no intense attachment or passionate commitment.

The subjective thinker, in contrast, is passionately and intensely involved with truth. For the subjective thinker truth is not just a process of accumulating evidence to justify a viewpoint, but a matter of intense personal concern. Sometimes Kierkegaard calls the subjective thinker an existential thinker, for the questions of life and death, the meaning of human existence, and a person's ultimate destiny are issues in which the one who raises them is intensely involved. For the subjective thinker, the "approximation-process" of objective thinking is insufficient. The truth of what is under consideration matters enormously to the subjective thinker, and, a decision must be made, and made now.

There is certainly a place for objective thinking, and even though Kierkegaard's concern is primarily with the subjective thinker, he never denies that objective thinking has its place. He insists, however, that not all of life's concerns are open to objective analysis. One could even say, in the spirit of Kierkegaard, that life's most important questions are not open to objective analysis. Consider, for example, falling in love. Romantic love is essentially a relationship between two persons, and when love culminates in marriage an intensely felt relationship results, ideally a life-long relationship. We can easily see the difference between the way an objective and a subjective thinker would approach love and marriage relationships. The objective thinker would say, "Here I am thirty-five years old and unmarried. My social responsibilities demand that I be married. It is time that I fall in love." Being a systematic, rational sort of person, the objective thinker might compile a list of the ideal qualities to be found in a mate. *Mate* is an appropriate word here, since the concern for the objective thinker is not really of love or establishing a love-relationship, but of being married and producing progeny in order to satisfy the social demands of life. So the objective thinker begins to look around. Each potential marriage-partner is evaluated according to the list of ideal traits that a spouse should possess, and as each falls short of the ideal, the objective thinker continues to look for the one who most closely approximates the objective standards. Through this process of approximation, finally a person is discovered who nearly meets all the criteria. To this person the objective thinker says, "Congratulations. I have picked you as a life-long partner, for you most nearly meet all the criteria of an ideal mate. I love you. Will you marry me?"

All this sounds rather perverse. And it is for us, since the ideal in our society is to marry someone you also happen to love. We should remember, however, that it was not always the case that one married the person one loved, and in some societies today marriages are based on a contractual model and are often arranged by persons other than those who are to be married, most commonly by parents.

The subjective thinker, in contrast, "falls in love." There is not much rational thinking behind "falling in love." In fact, there is an irrational quality about love. A person in love is seized by an intense attachment to another individual. "I can't live without you," the subjective thinker says to the beloved. "My life will be meaningless without you. I can't bear to let you out of my sight. Will you marry me?" Here is inwardness and passion in the extreme. No rational calculation, no systematic elimination of less fit candidates for a marriage relationship, no approximation-process is ever considered by the lover. Being in love is an intense, inward experience, and the lover is not concerned with the objective analysis of the qualities of the other person but with establishing a relationship with another individual, and in the intensity of the moment no other relationship seems conceivable except one that will last, "until death us do part."

Given the high divorce rate in this country, one could argue that a little more objective thinking and a diminished amount of subjectivity in these matters might be appropriate. But enough of this, for this is a book about religion, not about marriage.

Religious faith, in the sense that Kierkegaard considered it, is not open to objective thinking, for it involves a relationship with God. The accent falls not on *what* is said, that is, on the content of religious doctrines, but *how* it is said, that is, on a relationship of a creature with the creator. Rational theology, or natural theology as we have been calling it, points to the existence of God but does not give us much on which to establish a relationship. "I contemplate the order of nature," Kierkegaard says, "in the hope of finding God, and I see omnipotence and wisdom; but I also see much else that disturbs my mind and excites anxiety. The sum of all this is objective uncertainty." We have already seen the inconclusiveness of "proofs" of the existence of God. We have observed that the debate between those who support the arguments and those who reject them seems endless, with each claiming to make a little further progress in the approximation-process that constitutes objective analysis and rational debate. While the debate rages on, life slips away, and we must make a decision. This decision is the "leap of faith." To be sure, such a leap is risky, but Kierkegaard observes that "without risk there is no faith."

Look back to the introduction to this section and review the analysis offered by Kant of the different modes of human awareness. If there is objective insufficiency, or objective uncertainty to use Kierkegaard's formula, then two modes of awareness can result, either opinion or belief. Opinion is appropriate to the objective thinker who views the existence of God as a problem to be rationally analyzed. The objective thinker views the question of whether there is or is not a God as a problem to be approached from a somewhat detached viewpoint, and since God's existence cannot be proved, the objective thinker is left only with an opinion on the question. For the subjective thinker, however, the question of God is not an intellectual problem but a matter of intense inwardness, and faith is this commitment to a relationship which defies objective analysis. An appeal to scripture, after the fashion of St. Thomas Aquinas, will not give us much help, for the content of Christian doctrine struck Kierkegaard as paradoxical in the extreme: that the eternal God was born as a human being, lived and died among men, and by this death brought salvation for all. No amount of objective analysis can make this rationally acceptable, and if we are to establish a relationship with the creator, it will have to be on faith.

The brief citation from Kierkegaard which follows highlights these themes, but it does not reflect the disdain Kierkegaard had for those for whom religious faith made little difference. And his disdain was directed not just toward unbelievers, but toward many of the "religious," church-going population of his native Denmark. He parodied the figure of the parson who perorates endlessly over a biblical text and is congratulated by the parishoners for preaching a "fine sermon," while in fact neither the preacher not the congregation felt the intensity of the experiences of an Abraham grappling with the demands of faith. Churches are filled with persons, Kierkegaard claimed, for whom the question of faith has never really arisen. Being a Christian is not merely a matter of accepting a few doctrines, going to church, and reciting the creeds. For Kierkegaard it is not even correct to say that one *is* a Christian; only that one is *becoming* a Christian, for establishing a relationship with the creator is a life-long task. All this was Kierkegaard's way of underscoring his central theme: that faith is a matter of intense commitment, a subjective relationship with God of the most passionate inwardness. What matters for the subjective thinker is not objective analysis but being in a true relationship, and this is equivalent to faith.

Objective and Subjective Reflection*

In an attempt to make clear the difference of way that exists between an objective and a subjective reflection, I shall now proceed to show how a subjective reflection makes its way inwardly in inwardness. Inwardness in an existing subject culminates in passion; corresponding to passion in the subject the truth becomes a paradox; and the fact that the truth becomes a paradox is rooted precisely in its having a relationship to an existing subject. Thus the one corresponds to the other. By forgetting that one is an existing subject, passion goes by the board and the truth is no longer a paradox; the knowing subject becomes a fantastic entity rather than a human being, and the truth becomes a fantastic object for the knowledge of this fantastic entity.

When the question of truth is raised in an objective manner, reflection is directed objectively to the truth, as an object to which the knower is related. Reflection is not focussed upon the relationship, however, but upon the question of whether it is the truth to which the knower is related. If only the object to which he is related is the truth, the subject is accounted to be in the truth. When the question of the truth is raised subjectively, reflection is directed subjectively to the nature of the individual's relationship; if only the mode of this relationship is in the truth, the individual is in the truth even if he should happen to be thus related to what is not true.[1] Let us take as an example the knowledge of God. Objectively, reflection is directed to the problem of whether this object is the true God; subjectively, reflection is directed to the question whether the individual is related to a something *in such a manner* that his relationship is in truth a God-relationship. On which side is the truth now to be found? Ah, may we not here resort to a mediation, and say: It is on neither side, but in the

---

*Source: Excerpts from Søren Kierkegaard, *Concluding Unscientific Postscript* trans. by David F. Swenson and Walter Lowrie (copyright 1941 © 1969 by Princeton University Press; Princeton Paperback, 1968): pp. 177-182. Reprinted by permission of Princeton University Press and the American Scandinavian Foundation.

[1] The reader will observe that the question here is about essential truth, or about the truth which is essentially related to existence, and that it is precisely for the sake of clarifying it as inwardness or as subjectivity that this contrast is drawn.

mediation of both? Excellently well said, provided we might have it explained how an existing individual manages to be in a state of mediation. For to be in a state of mediation is to be finished, while to exist is to become. Nor can an existing individual be in two places at the same time—he cannot be an identity of subject and object. When he is nearest to being in two places at the same time he is in passion; but passion is momentary, and passion is also the highest expression of subjectivity.

The existing individual who chooses to pursue the objective way enters upon the entire approximation-process by which it is proposed to bring God to light objectively. But this is in all eternity impossible, because God is a subject, and therefore exists only for subjectivity in inwardness. The existing individual who chooses the subjective way apprehends instantly the entire dialectical difficulty involved in having to use some time, perhaps a long time, in finding God objectively; and he feels this dialectical difficulty in all its painfulness, because every moment is wasted in which he does not have God.[2] That very instant he has God, not by virtue of any objective deliberation, but by virtue of the infinite passion of inwardness. The objective inquirer, on the other hand, is not embarrassed by such dialectical difficulties as are involved in devoting an entire period of investigation to finding God—since it is possible that the inquirer may die tomorrow; and if he lives he can scarcely regard God as something to be taken along if convenient, since God is precisely that which one takes *a tout prix,* which in the understanding of passion constitutes the true inward relationship to God.

It is at this point, so difficult dialectically, that the way swings off for everyone who knows what it means to think, and to think existentially; which is something very different from sitting at a desk and writing about what one has never done, something very different from writing *de omnibus dubitandum* and at the same time being as credulous existentially as the most sensuous of men. Here is where the way swings off, and the change is marked by the fact that while objective knowledge rambles comfortably on by way of the long road of approximation without being impelled by the urge of passion, subjective knowledge counts every delay a deadly peril, and the decision so infinitely important and so instantly pressing that it is as if the opportunity had already passed.

Now when the problem is to reckon up on which side there is most

[2]In this manner God certainly becomes a postulate, but not in the otiose manner in which this word is commonly understood. It becomes clear rather that the only way in which an existing individual comes into relation with God, is when the dialectical contradiction brings his passion to the point of despair, and helps him to embrace God with the "category of despair" (faith). Then the postulate is so far from being arbitrary that it is precisely a life necessity. It is then not so much that God is a postulate, as that the existing individual's postulation of God is a necessity.

truth, whether on the side of one who seeks the true God objectively, and pursues the approximate truth of the God-idea; or on the side of one who, driven by the infinite passion of his need of God, feels an infinite concern for his own relationship to God in truth (and to be at one and the same time on both sides equally, is as we have noted not possible for an existing individual, but is merely the happy delusion of an imaginary I-am-I): the answer cannot be in doubt for anyone who has not been demoralized with the aid of science. If one who lives in the midst of Christendom goes up to the house of God, the house of the true God, with the true conception of God in his knowledge, and prays, but prays in a false spirit; and one who lives in an idolatrous community prays with the entire passion of the infinite, although his eyes rest upon the image of an idol: where is there most truth? The one prays in truth to God though he worships an idol; the other prays falsely to the true God, and hence worships in fact an idol. . . .

The objective accent falls on WHAT is said, the subjective accent on HOW it is said. This distinction holds even in the aesthetic realm, and receives definite expression in the principle that what is in itself true may in the mouth of such and such a person become untrue. In these times this distinction is particularly worthy of notice, for if we wish to express in a single sentence the difference between ancient times and our own, we should doubtless have to say: "In ancient times only an individual here and there knew the truth; now all know it, except that the inwardness of its appropriation stands in an inverse relationship to the extent of its dissemination."[3] Aesthetically the contradiction that truth becomes untruth in this or that person's mouth, is best construed comically: In the ethico-religious sphere, accent is again on the "how." But this is not to be understood as referring to demeanor, expression, or the like; rather it refers to the relationship sustained by the existing individual, in his own

[3]*Stages on Life's Way,* Note on p. 426. Though ordinarily not wishing an expression of opinion on the part of reviewers, I might at this point almost desire it, provided such opinions, so far from flattering me, amounted to an assertion of the daring truth that what I say is something that everybody knows, even every child, and that the cultured know infinitely much better. If it only stands fast that everyone knows it, my standpoint is in order, and I shall doubtless make shift to manage with the unity of the comic and the tragic. If there were anyone who did not know it I might perhaps be in danger of being dislodged from my position of equilibrium by the thought that I might be in a position to communicate to someone the needful preliminary knowledge. It is just this which engages my interest so much, this that the cultured are accustomed to say: that everyone knows what the highest is. This was not the case in paganism, nor in Judaism, nor in the seventeen centuries of Christianity. Hail to the nineteenth century! Everyone knows it. What progress has been made since the time when only a few knew it. To make up for this, perhaps, we must assume that no one nowadays does it.

existence, to the content of his utterance. Objectively the interest is focussed merely on the thought-content, subjectively on the inwardness. At its maximum this inward "how" is the passion of the infinite, and the passion of the infinite is the truth. But the passion of the infinite is precisely subjectivity, and thus subjectivity becomes the truth. Objectively there is no infinite decisiveness, and hence it is objectively in order to annul the difference between good and evil; together with the principle of contradiction, and therewith also the infinite difference between the true and the false. Only in subjectivity is there decisiveness, to seek objectivity is to be in error. It is the passion of the infinite that is the decisive factor and not its content, for its content is precisely itself. In this manner subjectivity and the subjective "how" constitute the truth.

But the "how" which is thus subjectively accentuated precisely because the subject is an existing individual, is also subject to a dialectic with respect to time. In the passionate moment of decision, where the road swings away from objective knowledge, it seems as if the infinite decision were thereby realized. But in the same moment the existing individual finds himself in the temporal order, and the subjective "how" is transformed into a striving, a striving which receives indeed its impulse and a repeated renewal from the decisive passion of the infinite, but is nevertheless a striving.

When subjectivity is the truth, the conceptual determination of the truth must include an expression for the antithesis to objectivity, a memento of the fork in the road where the way swings off; this expression will at the same time serve as an indication of the tension of the subjective inwardness. Here is such a definition of truth: *An objective uncertainty held fast in an appropriation-process of the most passionate inwardness is the truth,* the highest truth attainable for an *existing* individual. At the point where the way swings off (and where this is cannot be specified objectively, since it is a matter of subjectivity), there objective knowledge is placed in abeyance. Thus the subject merely has, objectively, the uncertainty; but it is this which precisely increases the tension of that infinite passion which constitutes his inwardness. The truth is precisely the venture which chooses an objective uncertainty with the passion of the infinite. I contemplate the order of nature in the hope of finding God, and I see omnipotence and wisdom; but I also see much else that disturbs my mind and excites anxiety. The sum of all this is an objective uncertainty. But it is for this very reason that the inwardness becomes as intense as it is, for it embraces this objective uncertainty with the entire passion of the infinite. In the case of a mathematical proposition the objectivity is given, but for this reason the truth of such a proposition is also an indifferent truth.

But the above definition of truth is an equivalent expression for faith. Without risk there is no faith. Faith is precisely the contradiction between the infinite passion of the individual's inwardness and the objective uncertainty. If I am capable of grasping God objectively, I do not believe, but precisely because I cannot do this I must believe. If I wish to preserve myself in faith I must constantly be intent upon holding fast the objective uncertainty, so as to remain out upon the deep, over seventy thousand fathoms of water, still preserving my faith.

DISCUSSION QUESTIONS

1. What is the difference between the claim that truth is subjective and the claim that truth is subjectivity?
2. Can you cite nonreligious examples of the difference between objective and subjective thinking?
3. What is the relation between truth and faith as Kierkegaard understood those terms?
4. What is the significance of Kierkegaard's reference to God as an objective uncertainty? Do you consider this an adequate way of referring to God? Why or why not?
5. Explain what Kierkegaard meant by the following: "The objective accent falls on *what* is said, the subjective accent on *how* it is said."
6. Why did Kierkegaard think that the leap of faith was the only possible way to approach God? Do you agree? What are your reasons?

WILLIAM JAMES

Will
and
Belief

Can we really choose to believe whatever we want regardless of the evidence? Some people have understood Kierkegaard to be saying this. Often compared to Kierkegaard was the brilliant seventeenth-century mathematician and philosopher, Blaise Pascal, who argued that we can, and should, simply choose to believe in God. We have an intensely felt need for God, according to Pascal, yet reason is incapable of providing demonstrative certainty of his existence. "The heart has its reasons that reason does not know," Pascal said. So what are we to do in such a situation? Think of it as a wager, Pascal suggested, as a kind of gamble. As in any wager, there is first the matter of what we risk, and second what we stand to gain. In the case of religious belief, we risk very little—only the possiblity of being wrong. But we stand to gain an infinite reward—eternal happiness—if our wager for faith turns out to be true. All this sounds somewhat calculating, but let us not forget that Pascal was a mathematician. Suppose someone offered you a chance to participate in a lottery by buying a ticket which cost only ten cents, and the chances of winning the prize of five million dollars were "fifty-fifty." Who wouldn't take a chance like that?

Religious faith is precisely this kind of wager, Pascal thought. The terms of the wager are these: take the risk of believing in God, for the odds are roughly equal for and against the truth of God's existence. If you win your wager, you will receive infinite happiness, an eternal reward. If you lose your wager, you have suffered only a finite loss, and ultimately it will not make any difference anyway. Following through on the terms of your wager will involve going to Mass, receiving communion, taking holy water (Pascal was a devout Catholic), and participating in these activities will eventually stifle your doubts. And what is the loss of a few hours time each week in comparison to the possible infinite rewards that will accrue to you if your wager turns out to be true?

In the following selection, William James rejects all such deliberate calculations. To view religious belief in such terms seems in his opinion, to rob faith of its inner vitality. And who would attribute to God a willingness to accept such a calculating response? Besides, anybody could come along claiming to be the new savior and appeal to us on the basis of Pascal's wager. If we wanted to hedge our bets, we might even be forced into wagering on a multiplicity of such saviors, hoping that at least one of our bets would pay off. Not only is such a possibility insulting to our intelligence, it is simply not the case that we can believe whatever we choose to believe. But the matter is not so simple as this. Are there some issues concerning which "our will either helps or hinders our intellect in its perceptions of truth?" This is James's question, and he answers it in the affirmative. Where we have empirical evidence for a viewpoint, there is no rational alternative but to base our conclusions on it. But where empirical evidence is lacking, other factors besides reason enter into our decision procedure, and one of the important considerations is our will.

William James was a psychologist, but today he is known as widely for his philosophical inquiries as for his psychological studies. What is interesting about James is that he began his career as a scientist. He was appointed to teach physiology at Harvard when he was thirty. As his interests broadened, he became interested in physiological psychology, and in 1876 established one of the first psychological laboratories in the United States. He stood somewhat alone in the nineteenth century in arguing against the prevailing deterministic theories of human action, insisting instead on human freedom and its correlative moral responsibility. Consequently, many of James' philosophical writings deal with questions of freedom and morality, and with religion. One of his most famous philosophical works was *Varieties of Religious Experience* in which he analyzed and described the various forms of religious consciousness both as a psychologist and as a philosopher. In the selection that follows, James looks carefully at the nature of belief, and although the specific context is religious belief, the principles he outlines can be applied to other forms of belief as well.

In the background of the discussion is the opposition to religious belief known as agnosticism. Agnosticism was a term coined by Thomas Henry Huxley, grandfather of Aldous and Julian Huxley. Like Kierkegaard, Huxley reached the conclusion that there was no evidence sufficient to establish faith in God. But unlike Kierkegaard, Huxley did not conclude that faith was possible—even faith considered as a kind of leap in the dark. But Huxley did not advocate atheism, that is, the denial of God's existence, for this would also mean reaching a conclusion without adequate evidence. If neither faith in God nor denial of God's existence are rational choices, the only alternative according to Huxley is complete suspension of belief. Huxley justified this tactic by claiming that we not only do not know whether God exists, we cannot claim knowledge in this matter. How Huxley arrived at the term agnosticism to characterize this position he explains in the following way.

> When I reached intellecutal maturity and began to ask myself whether I was an atheist, a theist, or a pantheist; a materialist or an idealist; a Christian or a freethinker; I found that the more I learned and reflected, the less ready was the

answer; until, at last, I came to the conclusion that I had neither art nor part with any of these denominations, except the last. The one thing in which most of these good people were agreed was the one thing in which I differed from them. They were quite sure they had attained a certain "gnosis,"—had, more or less successfully, solved the problem of existence; while I was quite sure I had not, and had a pretty strong conviction that the problem was insoluble. . . . So I took thought, and invented what I conceived to be the appropriate title of "agnostic." It came into my head as suggestively antithetic to the "gnostic" of Church history, who professed to know so much about the very things of which I was ignorant.[1]

Huxley's position also reflected the view of one of his contemporaries, William Kingdon Clifford, who, in 1877, published a paper entitled "The Ethics of Belief." Clifford argued that not only was it illogical to believe in the face of insufficient evidence, it was positively immoral to do so. He gave an example of a shipowner sending a vessel to sea without knowing whether the ship is seaworthy. In Clifford's parable, the vessel founders, and all lives on board are lost. Could the owner avoid moral responsibility by saying that, since there was no evidence that the vessel would sink on that particular voyage, there was every justification for believing that the ship would successfully complete the trip? Not at all, Clifford says.

> It is admitted that he did sincerely believe in the soundness of his ship; but the sincerity of his conviction can in no wise help him, because *he had no right to believe on such evidence as was before him*. He had acquired his belief not by honestly earning it in patient investigation, but by stifling his doubts.[2]

The owner could have found out whether the ship was seaworthy; he could have had the vessel inspected to determine if confidence in its ability to make the voyage safely was warranted. Instead, the owner stifled his doubts, but to hold such a belief without sufficient evidence is immoral, and the owner was guilty of what we might call negligent homicide. A belief not supported by sufficient evidence is, to use Clifford's phrase, a "stolen belief."

Clifford's example is interesting, and doubtless most of us would agree that the shipowner's conduct is a perfect example of criminal negligence. After all, evidence of the vessel's condition could have been obtained. But is this example parallel to religious belief? Hardly, since belief in God cannot be based on sufficient evidence—as Kierkegaard pointed out—and we could equally well apply Clifford's principle to disbelief. What right have we to disbelieve in God when the evidence against there being a God is also insufficient?

These considerations led James to conclude that neither Huxley nor Clifford had really suspended belief at all; for them the issue was clear: there is no God. All their talk about suspending belief and "stolen beliefs" was simply a clever smoke-screen to hide their atheistic views. In short, James argues that there is no middle choice between belief and unbelief; agnosticism is a phony position. Where evidence is lacking, and we are forced to make a decision, we cannot ignore the function of will in the decision process. But we cannot will ourselves to believe

[1]Thomas Henry Huxley, "Agnosticism," in *Science and Christian Tradition* (New York: D. Appleton and Company, 1894), pp. 237-39.

[2]William Kingdon Clifford, "The Ethics of Belief," in *Lectures and Essays,* ed. Leslie Stephens and Sir Frederick Pollock (New York: The Macmillan Company, 1901), II, 164.

anything. The choice that confronts us must be between live hypotheses; by *hypotheses* James means things which are posed to us for belief, and a hypothesis can be, for us, either live or dead. There is nothing about hypotheses per se that determines whether they are live or dead; this depends on the individual. For a Christian living in Baltimore, belief in the *Mahdi* (the guided one, a title taken by Mohammed Ahmed, who captured Khartoum in 1885) is hardly a live hypothesis; for an Islamic Arab, however, this hypothesis may indeed be a live one. James calls decision between hypotheses an option, and he distinguishes several kinds of options:

> *Living Option:* both hypotheses are live
>
> *Dead Option:* neither hypothesis is live
>
> *Forced Option:* no alternative to the option exists
>
> *Avoidable Option:* there is an alternative to the option
>
> *Trivial Option:* nothing of consequence is at stake
>
> *Momentous Option:* The opportunity is *unique,* the issue *significant,* and the results *irreversible.*

James calls an option genuine when it is of the living, forced, momentous kind. The following diagram indicates the relationships among these various terms.

JAMES'S DECISION PROCEDURE

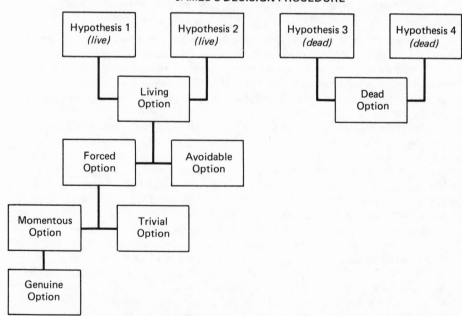

For the convenience of our discussion, we will refer to this as James's *decision procedure,* and to illustrate how it works, we will trace out several decisions, each time going a little further in the decision procedure. If at any point an option turns out to be dead, avoidable, or trivial, the decision procedure stops. The following examples will also illustrate that James's analysis can apply to matters other than religious belief, although religious belief is obviously his main concern in the essay.

The first example follows the decision procedure only to the first level and deals with a question dear to the hearts of most undergraduates: Where should I spend spring break?

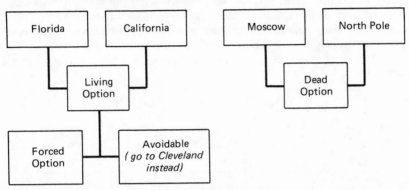

WHERE SHOULD I SPEND SPRING BREAK?

Note that the decision procedure terminated when we found that the living option which faces us is not forced; there is a third alternative. And to use James's language, this option was not genuine since it was not forced, nor was it momentous.

The next example goes one step further and gives us a forced option. Five minutes before closing time, on the last day of the spring sale, you discover a suit you would like to buy. The decision is forced since there is no more time left in the sale. You must decide, "to buy or not to buy"; that is the question.

Even though the option is forced, it does not qualify as a momentous decision, since it is not *unique* (there will be other sales), the issue is not *significant* (you do have other clothes to wear), and the decision is not *irreversible* (you can always find a suit like it). You might be tempted to conclude that in the above example the decision was not forced, for you could always walk out of the store and refuse to decide one way or the other. But it is clear that in this case, not to decide is to decide against buying the suit.

TO BUY OR NOT TO BUY?

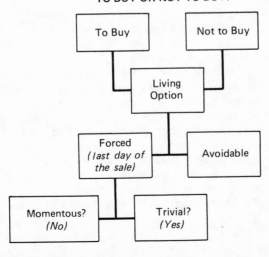

Now let us trace the decision procedure one step further by relating it to a life-and-death decision, the kind that frequently must be made by persons contemplating major surgery. Suppose that you are told by your physician that you probably have cancer of the spleen and that the malignant organ must be removed. The physician also informs you that the evidence is ambiguous, and it is not certain that your spleen is cancerous, but the only way to know is to operate. You are also told that it is a risky operation, and there is no certainty of success. Not only that, removal of the spleen is irreversible. You must decide now, since every day's delay would only allow the malignancy to spread. To postpone the choice is, in effect, to decide against the operation.

SHALL I HAVE THE OPERATION?

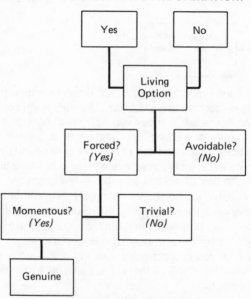

This decision qualifies as a genuine option on all three criteria. The opportunity is unique (it may be the only chance to prevent the spread of the malignancy), the issue is significant (the possible saving of your life), and the results are irreversible (once taken out, your spleen cannot be replaced).

Now let's apply the decision procedure to the question of faith in God. If the choice between belief and nonbelief in God is not a living option for you, then James has nothing more to say. Unlike Pascal, James did not think a person could believe anything at all merely through the force of will. But James disagreed with Clifford and Huxley concerning the possibility of suspending belief. Not to decide, in this case, is to decide, for there is no third possibility; the issue is not avoidable for those to whom the choice between belief and unbelief is a living option. The upshot of James's analysis is to show the defensibility of believing when the evidence is insufficient to provide grounds for a decision. A rule that says we cannot believe because of the risk of error is an illogical rule; not to believe is also to risk missing the

TO BELIEVE OR NOT TO BELIEVE?

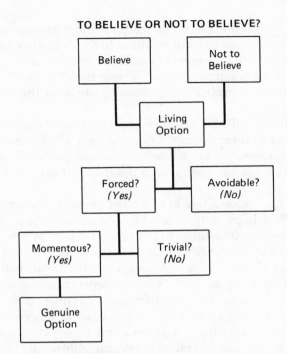

truth. As James puts it, "A rule of thinking which would absolutely prevent me from acknowledging certain kinds of truth if those kinds of truth were really there, would be an irrational rule."

The Will to Believe*

Let us give the name of *hypothesis* to anything that may be proposed to our belief; and just as the electricians speak of live and dead wires, let us speak of any hypothesis as either *live* or *dead*. A live hypothesis is one which appeals as a real possibility to him to whom it is proposed. If I ask you to believe in the Mahdi, the notion makes no electric connection with your nature,—it refuses to scintillate with any credibility at all. As an hypothesis it is completely dead. To an Arab, however (even if he be not one of the Mahdi's followers), the hypothesis is among the mind's pos-

*Source: From William James, "The Will to Believe," in *The Will to Believe and Other Essays in Popular Philosophy* (New York: Longmans, Green, and Co., 1910), pp. 2-11, 17-30

sibilities: it is alive. This shows that deadness and liveness in an hypothesis are not intrinsic properties, but relations to the individual thinker. They are measured by his willingness to act. The maximum of liveness in an hypothesis means willingness to act irrevocably. Practically, that means belief; but there is some believing tendency wherever there is willingness to act at all.

Next, let us call the decision between two hypotheses an *option*. Options may be of several kinds. They may be: (1) *living* or *dead;* (2) *forced* or *avoidable;* (3) *momentous* or *trivial;* and for our purposes we may call an option a *genuine* option when it is of the forced, living, and momentous kind.

1. A living option is one in which both hypotheses are live ones. If I say to you: "Be a theosophist or be a Mohammedan," it is probably a dead option, because for you neither hypothesis is likely to be alive. But if I say: "Be an agnostic or be a Christian," it is otherwise: trained as you are, each hypothesis makes some appeal, however small, to your belief.

2. Next, if I say to you: "Choose between going out with your umbrella or without it," I do not offer you a genuine option, for it is not forced. You can easily avoid it by not going out at all. Similarly, if I say, "Either love me or hate me," "Either call my theory true or call it false," your option is avoidable. You may remain indifferent to me, neither loving nor hating, and you may decline to offer any judgment as to my theory. But if I say, "Either accept this truth or go without it," I put on you a forced option, for there is no standing place outside of the alternative. Every dilemma based on a complete logical disjunction, with no possibility of not choosing, is an option of this forced kind.

3. Finally, if I were Dr. Nansen and proposed to you to join my North Pole expedition, your option would be momentous; for this would probably be your only similar opportunity, and your choice now would either exclude you from the North Pole sort of immortality altogether or put at least the chance of it into your hands. He who refuses to embrace a unique opportunity loses the prize as surely as if he tried and failed. *Per contra,* the option is trivial when the opportunity is not unique, when the stake is insignificant, or when the decision is reversible if it later prove unwise. Such trivial options abound in the scientific life. A chemist finds an hypothesis live enough to spend a year in its verification: he believes in it to that extent. But if his experiments prove inconclusive either way, he is quit for his loss of time, no vital harm being done.

It will facilitate our discussion if we keep all these distinctions well in mind.

The next matter to consider is the actual psychology of human opinion. When we look at certain facts, it seems as if our passional and volitional nature lay at the root of all our convictions. When we look at others, it seems as if they could do nothing when the intellect had once said its say. Let us take the latter facts up first.

Does it not seem preposterous on the very face of it to talk of our opinions being modifiable at will? Can our will either help or hinder our intellect in its perceptions of truth? Can we, by just willing it, believe that Abraham Lincoln's existence is a myth, and that the portraits of him in McClure's Magazine are all of some one else? Can we, by any effort of our will, or by any strength of wish that it were true, believe ourselves well and about when we are roaring with rheumatism in bed, or feel certain that the sum of the two one-dollar bills in our pocket must be a hundred dollars? We can *say* any of these things, but we are absolutely impotent to believe them; and of just such things is the whole fabric of the truths that we do believe in made up,—matters of fact, immediate or remote, as Hume said, and relations between ideas, which are either there or not there for us if we see them so, and which if not there cannot be put there by any action of our own.

In Pascal's Thoughts there is a celebrated passage known in litera-ture as Pascal's wager. In it he tries to force us into Christianity by reasoning as if our concern with truth resembled our concern with the stakes in a game of chance. Translated freely his words are these: You must either believe or not believe that God is—which will you do? Your human reason cannot say. A game is going on between you and the nature of things which at the day of judgment will bring out either heads or tails. Weigh what your gains and your losses would be if you should stake all you have on heads, or God's existence: if you win in such case, you gain eternal beatitude; if you lose, you lose nothing at all. If there were an infinity of chances, and only one for God in this wager, still you ought to stake your all on God; for though you surely risk a finite loss by this procedure, any finite loss is reasonable, even a certain one is reasonable, if there is but the possibility of infinite gain. Go, then, and take holy water, and have masses said; belief will come and stupefy your scruples,—*Cela vous fera croire et vous abêtira.* Why should you not? At bottom, what have you to lose?

You probably feel that when religious faith expresses itself thus, in the language of the gaming-table, it is put to its last trumps. Surely Pascal's own personal belief in masses and holy water had far other springs; and this celebrated page of his is but an argument for others, a last desperate snatch at a weapon against the hardness of the unbelieving heart. We feel that a faith in masses and holy water adopted wilfully after such a mechanical calculation would lack the inner soul of faith's reality; and if we were ourselves in the place of the Deity, we should probably take particular pleasure in cutting off believers of this pattern from their infinite reward. It is evident that unless there be some pre-existing tendency to believe in masses and holy water, the option offered to the will by Pascal is not a living option. Certainly no Turk ever took to masses and holy water on its account; and even to us Protestants these means of salvation seem such foregone impossibilities that Pascal's logic, invoked for them specifically, leaves us unmoved. As well might the Mahdi write to us, saying, "I am the Expected One whom God has created in his effulgence. You shall be infinitely happy if you confess me; otherwise you shall be cut off from the light of the sun. Weigh, then, your infinite gain if I am genuine against your finite sacrifice if I am not!" His logic would be that of Pascal; but he would vainly use it on us, for the hypothesis he offers us is dead. No tendency to act on it exists in us to any degree.

The talk of believing by our volition seems, then, from one point of view, simply silly. From another point of view it is worse than silly, it is vile. When one turns to the magnificent edifice of the physical sciences, and sees how it was reared; what thousands of disinterested moral lives of men lie buried in its mere foundations; what patience and postponement, what choking down of preference, what submission to the icy laws of outer fact are wrought into its very stones and mortar; how absolutely impersonal it stands in its vast augustness,—then how besotted and contemptible seems every little sentimentalist who comes blowing his voluntary smoke-wreaths, and pretending to decide things from out of his private dream! Can we wonder if those bred in the rugged and manly school of science should feel like spewing such subjectivism out of their mouths? The whole system of loyalties which grow up in the schools of science go dead against its toleration; so that it is only natural that those who have caught the scientific fever should pass over to the opposite extreme, and write sometimes as if the incorruptibly truthful intellect ought positively to prefer bitterness and unacceptableness to the heart in its cup.

> It fortifies my soul to know
> That, though I perish, Truth is so—

sings Clough, while Huxley exclaims: "My only consolation lies in the reflection that, however bad our posterity may become, so far as they hold by the plain rule of not pretending to believe what they have no reason to believe, because it may be to their advantage so to pretend [the word 'pretend' is surely here redundant], they will not have reached the lowest depth of immorality." And that delicious *enfant terrible* Clifford writes: "Belief is desecrated when given to unproved and unquestioned statements for the solace and private pleasure of the believer. . . . Whoso would deserve well of his fellows in this matter will guard the purity of his belief with a very fanaticism of jealous care, lest at any time it should rest on an unworthy object, and catch a stain which can never be wiped away.

. . . If [a] belief has been accepted on insufficient evidence [even though the belief be true, as Clifford on the same page explains] the pleasure is a stolen one. . . . It is sinful because it is stolen in defiance of our duty to mankind. That duty is to guard ourselves from such beliefs as from a pestilence which may shortly master our own body and then spread to the rest of the town. . . . It is wrong always, everywhere, and for every one, to believe anything upon insufficient evidence."

All this strikes one as healthy, even when expressed, as by Clifford, with somewhat too much of robustious pathos in the voice. Free-will and simple wishing do seem, in the matter of our credences, to be only fifth wheels to the coach. Yet if any one should thereupon assume that intellectual insight is what remains after wish and will and sentimental preference have taken wing, or that pure reason is what then settles our opinions, he would fly quite as directly in the teeth of the facts.

It is only our already dead hypotheses that our willing nature is unable to bring to life again. But what has made them dead for us is for the most part a previous action of our willing nature of an antagonistic kind. When I say "willing nature," I do not mean only such deliberate volitions as may have set up habits of belief that we cannot now escape from,—I mean all such factors of belief as fear and hope, prejudice and passion, imitation and partisanship, the circumpressure of our caste and set. As a matter of fact we find ourselves believing, we hardly know how or why. Mr. Balfour gives the name of "authority" to all those influences, born of the intellectual climate, that make hypotheses possible or impossible for us, alive or dead. Here in this room, we all of us believe in molecules and the conservation of energy, in democracy and necessary progress, in Protestant Christianity and the duty of fighting for "the doctrine of the immortal Monroe," all for no reasons worthy of the name. We see into these matters with no more inner clearness, and probably with much less, than any disbeliever in them might possess. His unconventionality would probably have some grounds to show for its conclusions; but for us, not insight, but the *prestige* of the opinions, is what makes the spark shoot from them and light up our sleeping magazines of faith. Our reason is quite satisfied, in nine hundred and ninety-nine cases out of every thousand of us, if it can find a few arguments that will do to recite in case our credulity is criticised by some one else. Our faith is faith in some one else's faith, and in the greatest matters this is most the case. Our belief in truth itself, for instance, that there is a truth, and that our minds and it are made for each other,—what is it but a passionate affirmation of desire, in which our social system backs us up? We want to have a truth; we want to believe that our experiments and studies and discussions must put us in a continually better and better position towards it; and on this line we agree to fight out our thinking lives. But if a pyrrhonistic sceptic asks us *how we know* all this, can our logic find a reply? No! certainly it cannot. It is just one volition against another,—we willing to go in for life upon a trust or assumption which he, for his part, does not care to make.[1]

As a rule we disbelieve all facts and theories for which we have no use. Clifford's cosmic emotions find no use for Christian feelings. Huxley belabors the bishops because there is no use for sacerdotalism in his scheme of life. Newman, on the contrary, goes over to Romanism, and finds all sorts of reasons good for staying there, because a priestly system is for him an organic need and delight. Why do so few "scientists" even look at the evidence for telepathy, so called? Because they think, as a leading biologist, now dead, once said to me, that even if such a thing were true, scientists ought to band together to keep it suppressed and concealed. It would undo the uniformity of Nature and all sorts of other things without which scientists cannot carry on their pursuits. But if this very man had been shown something which as a scientist he might *do* with telepathy, he might not only have examined the evidence, but even have found it good enough. This very law which the logicians would impose upon us—if I may give the name of logicians to those who would rule out our willing nature here—is based on nothing but their own natural wish to exclude all elements for which they, in their professional quality of logicians, can find no use.

Evidently, then, our non-intellectual nature does influence our convictions. There are passional tendencies and volitions which run before and others which come after belief, and it is only the latter that are too late for the fair; and they are not too late when the previous passional work has been already in their own direction. Pascal's argument, instead of being powerless, then seems a regular clincher, and is the last stroke needed to make our faith in masses and holy water complete. The state of things is evidently far from simple; and pure insight and logic, whatever they might do ideally, are not the only things that really do produce our creeds. . . .

One more point, small but important, and our preliminaries are done. There are two ways of looking at our duty in the matter of opinion,—ways entirely different, and yet ways about whose difference the theory of knowledge seems hitherto to have shown very little concern. *We must know the truth;* and *we must avoid error,*—these are our first and great commandents as would-be knowers; but they are not two ways of stating an identical commandment, they are two separable laws. Although

[1]Compare the admirable page 310 in S. H. Hodgson's "Time and Space," London, 1865.

it may indeed happen that when we believe the truth *A,* we escape as an incidental consequence from believing the falsehood *B,* it hardly ever happens that by merely disbelieving *B* we necessarily believe *A.* We may in escaping *B* fall into believing other falsehoods, *C* or *D,* just as bad as *B;* or we may escape *B* by not believing anything at all, not even *A.*

Believe truth! Shun error!—these, we see, are two materially different laws; and by choosing between them we may end by coloring differently our whole intellectual life. We may regard the chase for truth as paramount, and the avoidance of error as secondary; or we may, on the other hand, treat the avoidance of error as more imperative, and let truth take its chance. Clifford, in the instructive passage which I have quoted, exhorts us to the latter course. Believe nothing, he tells us, keep your mind in suspense forever, rather than by closing it on insufficient evidence incur the awful risk of believing lies. You, on the other hand, may think that the risk of being in error is a very small matter when compared with the blessings of real knowledge, and be ready to be duped many times in your investigation rather than postpone indefinitely the chance of guessing true. I myself find it impossible to go with Clifford. We must remember that these feelings of our duty about either truth or error are in any case only expressions of our passional life. Biologically considered, our minds are as ready to grind out falsehood as veracity, and he who says, "Better go without belief forever than believe a lie!" merely shows his own preponderant private horror of becoming a dupe. He may be critical of many of his desires and fears, but this fear he slavishly obeys. He cannot imagine any one questioning its binding force. For my own part, I have a horror of being duped; but I can believe that worse things than being duped may happen to a man in this world: so Clifford's exhortation has to my ears a thoroughly fantastic sound. . . . Whenever the option between losing truth and gaining it is not momentous, we can throw the chance of *gaining truth* away, and at any rate save ourselves from any chance of *believing falsehood,* by not making up our minds at all till objective evidence has come. In scientific questions, this is almost always the case; and even in human affairs in general, the need of acting is seldom so urgent that a false belief to act on is better than no belief at all. Law courts, indeed, have to decide on the best evidence attainable for the moment, because a judge's duty is to make law as well as to ascertain it, and (as a learned judge once said to me) few cases are worth spending much time over: the great thing is to have them decided on *any* acceptable principle, and got out of the way. But in our dealings with objective nature we obviously are recorders, not makers, of the truth. . . . The questions here are always trivial options, the hypotheses are hardly living (at any rate not living for us spectators), the choice between believing truth or falsehood is seldom forced. The attitude of sceptical balance is therefore the absolutely wise one if we would escape mistakes. What difference, indeed, does it make to most of us whether we have or have not a theory of the Röntgen rays, whether we believe or not in mind-stuff, or have a conviction about the causality of conscious states? It makes no difference. Such options are not forced on us. On every account it is better not to make them, but still keep weighing reasons *pro et contra* with an indifferent hand.

I speak, of course, here of the purely judging mind. For purposes of discovery such indifference is to be less highly recommended, and science would be far less advanced than she is if the passionate desires of individuals to get their own faiths confirmed had been kept out of the game. See for example the sagacity which Spencer and Weismann now display. On the other hand, if you want an absolute duffer in an investigation, you must, after all, take the man who has no interest whatever in its results: he is the warranted incapable, the positive fool. The most useful investigator, because the most sensitive observer, is always he whose eager interest in one side of the question is balanced by an equally keen nervousness lest he become deceived.[2] Science has organized this nervousness into a regular *technique,* her so-called method of verification; and she has fallen so deeply in love with the method that one may even say she has ceased to care for truth by itself at all. It is only truth as technically verified that interests her. The truth of truths might come in merely affirmative form, and she would decline to touch it. Such truth as that, she might repeat with Clifford, would be stolen in defiance of her duty of mankind. Human passions, however, are stronger than technical rules. "Le coeur a ses raisons," as Pascal says, "que la raison ne connaît pas;" and however indifferent to all but the bare rules of the game the umpire, the abstract intellect, may be, the concrete players who furnish him the materials to judge of are usually, each one of them, in love with some pet "live hypothesis" of his own. Let us agree, however, that wherever there is no forced option, the dispassionately judicial intellect with no pet hypothesis, saving us, as it does, from dupery at any rate, ought to be our ideal.

The question next arises: Are there not somewhere forced options in our speculative questions, and can we (as men who may be interested at least as much in positively gaining truth as in merely escaping dupery) always wait with impunity till the coercive evidence shall have arrived? It seems *a priori* improbable that the truth should be so nicely adjusted to our needs and powers as that. In the great boarding-house of nature, the cakes and the butter and the syrup seldom come out so even and leave the plates so clean. Indeed, we should view them with scientific suspicion if they did.

[2]Compare Wilfrid Ward's Essay, "The Wish to Believe," in his *Witnesses to the Unseen,* Macmillan & Co., 1893.

Moral questions immediately present themselves as questions whose solution cannot wait for sensible proof. A moral question is a question not of what sensibly exists, but of what is good, or would be good if it did exist. Science can tell us what exists; but to compare the *worths,* both of what exists and of what does not exist, we must consult not science, but what Pascal calls our heart. Science herself consults her heart when she lays it down that the infinite ascertainment of fact and correction of false belief are the supreme goods for man. Challenge the statement, and science can only repeat it oracularly, or else prove it by showing that such ascertainment and correction bring man all sorts of other goods which man's heart in turn declares. The question of having moral beliefs at all or not having them is decided by our will. Are our moral preferences true or false, or are they only odd biological phenomena, making things good or bad for *us,* but in themselves indifferent? How can your pure intellect decide? If your heart does not *want* a world of moral reality, your head will assuredly never make you believe in one. Mephistophelian scepticism, indeed, will satisfy the head's play-instincts much better than any rigorous idealism can. Some men (even at the student age) are so naturally cool-hearted that the moralistic hypothesis never has for them any pungent life, and in their supercilious presence the hot young moralist always feels strangely ill at ease. The appearance of knowingness is on their side, of *naïveté* and gullibility on his. Yet, in the inarticulate heart of him, he clings to it that he is not a dupe, and that there is a realm in which (as Emerson says) all their wit and intellectual superiority is no better than the cunning of a fox. Moral scepticism can no more be refuted or proved by logic than intellectual scepticism can. When we stick to it that there *is* truth (be it of either kind), we do so with our whole nature, and resolve to stand or fall by the results. The sceptic with his whole nature adopts the doubting attitude; but which of us is the wiser, Omniscience only knows.

Turn now from these wide questions of good to a certain class of questions of fact, questions concerning personal relations, states of mind between one man and another. *Do you like me or not?*—for example. Whether you do or not depends, in countless instances, on whether I meet you half-way, am willing to assume that you must like me, and show you trust and expectation. The previous faith on my part in your liking's existence is in such cases what makes your liking come. But if I stand aloof, and refuse to budge an inch until I have objective evidence, until you shall have done something apt, as the absolutists say, *ad extorquendum assensum meum,* ten to one your liking never comes. How many women's hearts are vanquished by the mere sanguine insistence of some man that they *must* love him! he will not consent to the hypothesis that they cannot. The desire for a certain kind of truth here brings about that special truth's existence; and so it is in innumerable cases of other sorts. Who gains promotions, boons, appointments, but the man in whose life they are seen to play the part of live hypotheses, who discounts them, sacrifices other things for their sake before they have come, and takes risks for them in advance? His faith acts on the powers above him as a claim, and creates its own verification.

A social organism of any sort whatever, large or small is what it is because each member proceeds to his own duty with a trust that the other members will simultaneously do theirs. Wherever a desired result is achieved by the co-operation of many independent persons, its existence as a fact is a pure consequence of the precursive faith in one another of those immediately concerned. A government, an army, a commercial system, a ship, a college, an athletic team, all exist on this condition, without which not only is nothing achieved, but nothing is even attempted. A whole train of passengers (individually brave enough) will be looted by a few highwaymen, simply because the latter can count on one another, while each passenger fears that if he makes a movement of resistance, he will be shot before any one else backs him up. If we believed that the whole car-full would rise at once with us, we should each severally rise, and train-robbing would never even be attempted. There are, then, cases where a fact cannot come at all unless a preliminary faith exists in its coming. *And where faith in a fact can help create the fact,* that would be an insane logic which should say that faith running ahead of scientific evidence is the "lowest kind of immorality" into which a thinking being can fall. Yet such is the logic by which our scientific absolutists pretend to regulate our lives!

In truths dependent on our personal action, then, faith based on desire is certainly a lawful and possibly an indispensable thing.

But now, it will be said, these are all childish human cases, and have nothing to do with great cosmical matters, like the question of religious faith. Let us then pass on to that. Religions differ so much in their accidents that in discussing the religious question we must make it very generic and broad. What then do we now mean by the religious hypothesis? Science says things are; morality says some things are better than other things; and religion says essentially two things.

First, she says that the best things are the more eternal things, the overlapping things, the things in the universe that throw the last stone, so to speak, and say the final word. "Perfection is eternal"—this phrase of Charles Secrétan seems a good way of putting this first affirmation of religion, an affirmation which obviously cannot yet be verified scientifically at all.

The second affirmation of religion is that we are better off now if we believe her first affirmation to be true.

Now, let us consider what the logical elements of this situation are *in case the religious hypothesis in both its branches be really true.* (Of course, we must admit that possibility at the outset. If we are to discuss the question at all, it must involve a living option. If for any of you religion be a hypothesis that cannot, by any living possibility be true, then you need go no farther. I speak to the "saving remnant" alone.) So proceeding, we see, first, that religion offers itself as a *momentous* option. We are supposed to gain, even now, by our belief, and to lose by our nonbelief, a certain vital good. Secondly, religion is a *forced* option, so far as that good goes. We cannot escape the issue by remaining sceptical and waiting for more light, because, although we do avoid error in that way *if religion be untrue,* we lose the good, *if it be true,* just as certainly as if we positively chose to disbelieve. It is as if a man should hesitate indefinitely to ask a certain woman to marry him because he was not perfectly sure that she would prove an angel after he brought her home. Would he not cut himself off from that particular angel-possibility as decisively as if he went and married some one else? Scepticism, then, is not avoidance of option; it is option of a certain particular kind of risk. *Better risk loss of truth than chance of error,—* that is your faith-vetoer's exact position. He is actively playing his stake as much as the believer is; he is backing the field against the religious hypothesis, just as the believer is backing the religious hypothesis against the field. To preach scepticism to us as a duty until "sufficient evidence" for religion be found, is tantamount therefore to telling us, when in presence of the religious hypothesis, that to yield to our fear of its being error is wiser and better than to yield to our hope that it may be true. It is not intellect against all passions, then; it is only intellect with one passion laying down its law. And by what, forsooth, is the supreme wisdom of this passion warranted? Dupery for dupery, what proof is there that dupery through hope is so much worse than dupery through fear? I, for one, can see no proof; and I simply refuse obedience to the scientist's command to imitate his kind of option, in a case where my own stake is important enough to give me the right to choose my own form of risk. If religion be true and the evidence for it be still insufficient, I do not wish, by putting your extinguisher upon my nature (which feels to me as if it had after all some business in this matter), to forfeit my sole chance in life of getting upon the winning side,—that chance depending, of course, on my willingness to run the risk of acting as if my passional need of taking the world religiously might be prophetic and right.

All this is on the supposition that it really may be prophetic and right, and that, even to us who are discussing the matter, religion is a live hypothesis which may be true. Now, to most of us religion comes in a still further way that makes a veto on our active faith even more illogical. The more perfect and more eternal aspect of the universe is represented in our religions as having personal form. The universe is no longer a mere *It* to us, but a *Thou,* if we are religious; and any relation that may be possible from person to person might be possible here. For instance, although in one sense we are passive portions of the universe, in another we show a curious autonomy, as if we were small active centres on our own account. We feel, too, as if the appeal of religion to us were made to our own active good-will, as if evidence might be forever withheld from us unless we met the hypothesis half-way. To take a trivial illustration: just as a man who in a company of gentlemen made no advances, asked a warrant for every concession, and believed no one's word without proof, would cut himself off by such churlishness from all the social rewards that a more trusting spirit would earn,—so here, one who should shut himself up in snarling logicality and try to make the gods extort his recognition willy-nilly, or not get it at all, might cut himself off forever from his only opportunity of making the gods' acquaintance. This feeling, forced on us we know not whence, that by obstinately believing that there are gods (although not to do so would be so easy both for our logic and our life) we are doing the universe the deepest service we can, seems part of the living essence of the religious hypothesis. If the hypothesis *were* true in all its parts, including this one, then pure intellectualism, with its veto on our making willing advances, would be an absurdity; and some participation of our sympathetic nature would be logically required. I, therefore, for one, cannot see my way to accepting the agnostic rules for truth-seeking, or wilfully agree to keep my willing nature out of the game. I cannot do so for this plain reason, that *a rule of thinking which would absolutely prevent me from acknowledging certain kinds of truth if those kinds of truth were really there, would be an irrational rule.* That for me is the long and short of the formal logic of the situation, no matter what the kinds of truth might materially be.

I confess I do not see how this logic can be escaped. But sad experience makes me fear that some of you may still shrink from radically saying with me, *in abstracto,* that we have the right to believe at our own risk any hypothesis that is live enough to tempt our will. I suspect, however, that if this is so, it is because you have got away from the abstract logical point of view altogether, and are thinking (perhaps without realizing it) of some particular religious hypothesis which for you is dead. The freedom to "believe what we will" you apply to the case of some patent superstition; and the faith you think of is the faith defined by the schoolboy when he said, "Faith is when you believe something that you know ain't true." I can only repeat that this is misapprehension. *In concreto,* the freedom to believe can only cover living options which the intellect of the individual cannot by itself resolve; and living options never seem absurdities to him who has them to consider. When I look at the religious question as it really puts itself to concrete men, and when I think of all the possibilities which both practically and theoretically it involves, then this command that we shall put a stopper on our heart, instincts, and courage, and *wait*—acting of course meanwhile more or less as if religion were *not* true[3]—till dooms-day, or till such time as our intellect and senses working together may have raked in evidence enough,—this command, I say, seems to me the queerest idol ever manufactured in the philosophic cave. Were we scholastic absolutists, there might be more excuse. If we had an infallible intellect with its objective certitudes, we might feel ourselves disloyal to such a perfect organ of knowledge in not trusting to it exclusively, in not waiting for its releasing word. But if we are empiricists, if we believe that no bell in us tolls to let us know for certain when truth is in our grasp, then it seems a piece of idle fantasticality to preach so solemnly our duty of waiting for the bell. Indeed we *may* wait if we will,—I hope you do so, we do so at our peril as much as if we believed. In either case we *act,* taking our life in our hands. No one of us ought to issue vetoes to the other, nor should we bandy words of abuse. We ought, on the contrary, delicately and profoundly to respect one another's mental freedom: then only shall we bring about the intellectual republic; then only shall we have that spirit of inner tolerance without which all our outer tolerance is soulless, and which is empiricism's glory; then only shall we live and let live, in specula-tive as well as in practical things. . . .

DISCUSSION QUESTIONS

1. Do you think Pascal's wager is an acceptable way to resolve the question of belief versus nonbelief? Why or why not?
2. Do you agree with James's claim that agnosticism is not a viable alternative? What are the reasons for your answer?
3. What are the conditions under which James thought it was appropriate to apply his decision procedure? Do you agree that, given these conditions, it is rationally acceptable to make a decision on the basis that James suggests? Give reasons for your answer.

[3]Since belief is measured by action, he who forbids us to believe religion to be true, necessarily also forbids us to act as we should if we did believe it to be true. The whole defence of religious faith hinges upon action. If the action required or inspired by the religious hypothesis is in no way different from that dictated by the naturalistic hypothesis, then religious faith is a pure superfluity, better pruned away, and con-troversy about its legitimacy is a piece of idle trifling, unworthy of serious minds. I myself believe, of course, that the religious hypothesis gives to the world an expres-sion which specifically determines our reactions, and makes them in a large part unlike what they might be on a purely naturalistic scheme of belief.

4. James obviously thought his approach to the question of faith was different from that of Pascal. Do you agree? Why or why not?

5. Do you think a person could have a satisfactory religious life if the person's initial faith commitment was made on the basis that James suggests?

6. Do you think that Kierkegaard and James would basically agree on the nature of faith? What evidence can you cite to support your answer?

Retrospective

We have looked at several different attitudes toward the relation between faith and reason. Antony Flew suggests that in the face of insufficient evidence, a person must give up the religious hypothesis. There is just too much about the world that seems to count against belief in a loving God, and if the believer persists in faith in spite of the preponderance of evidence by repeatedly qualifying the original belief, then it "dies the death of a thousand qualifications." Stubborn refusal to abandon a belief is evidence of a refusal to be rational about such matters.

C. S. Lewis rejected the view that the believer is irrational when stubbornly refusing to abandon belief. He showed the ambiguous meanings attached to the term "belief," and argued that there is nothing irrational in persisting in a belief in God once that belief arises. This is not so much an example of "doublethink" as it is a matter of loyalty demanded by the "logic of personal relations." If religious faith is a case of believing *in* rather than believing *that,* then the obstinacy of the believer is just as defensible as is loyalty to a friend under attack.

Kierkegaard took a stronger position: faith is essentially a risk and a leap. For Kierkegaard there is not even sufficient evidence to rationally justify belief in the first place, and as long as a person persists in believing, there is risk. "If I wish to preserve myself in faith," Kierkegaard said, "I must constantly be intent upon holding fast the objective uncertainty, so as to remain out upon the deep, over seventy thousand fathoms of water, still preserving my faith."

William James explored both the logical and psychological dimensions of faith and pointed out that faith in God, or denial of God's existence, is a forced option. This led him to reject the agnostic position of Huxley and Clifford as really atheism in disguise. James held that in matters of both faith and morals we have to make decisions without completely adequate evidence, and it is simply the nature of our human situation that in these cases our will guides us when reason cannot.

It should now be obvious to you that two different attitudes have emerged, reflecting the two poles of the reason-faith question. On the one hand is *rationalism,* the view that truth in religion (or in all matters) must be based on reason and not on faith. On the other hand is *fideism,* which is the view that truth in religion is based on faith rather than on reasoning and evidence. At the two extremes are Flew, on the side of rationalism, and Kierkegaard, on the side of fideism. What is interesting is that Flew and Kierkegaard would both agree that reason cannot provide the justification for believing in God, but this leads Flew to conclude that the believer is engaging in a sort of "doublethink"—a tendency to hold two contradictory beliefs at the same time—whereas it led Kierkegaard to counsel the leap of faith.

The force of James's analysis is to insist that we cannot avoid the issue of faith or unbelief, and that showing a skeptical attitude toward religious belief is no proof that one acts any more rationally than those who believe. "To preach scepticism to us as a duty until 'sufficient evidence' for religion be found," he observes, "is tantamount therefore to telling us that to yield to our fear of its being error is wiser and better than to yield to our hope that it may be true."

There are several additional questions raised by our study of the relation between faith and reason. The problem of evil is one of these, since it constitutes a major barrier to belief. Another is the difference faith makes in the life of the believer. Does the believer view life any differently than the unbeliever? Is life more meaningful for the believer? Kierkegaard thought so. Without faith, a person is without any sense of belonging in the world, and life appears without meaning and purpose. Kierkegaard called this experience of meaninglessness despair and saw it as a kind of sickness for which faith was the only cure. We will return to both the problem of evil and the issue of religion and life's meaning in subsequent sections.

Another problem raised by our study of faith and reason is the language of religion. This issue was addressed in the Flew-Hare-Mitchell discussion when Flew claimed that statements of religious belief are not really assertions at all but pseudoassertions, a kind of "doublethink" to which the ordinary standards of meaningfulness do not apply. So there is a cluster of concerns about language that have to be faced: Do we use language in the same way when speaking about God as when speaking of things in the world? If not, how is religious language different from ordinary language? Is religious language a kind of poetry? How do we distinguish meaningful religious statements from nonsense? These are just some of the issues that we will consider in the next section.

ADDITIONAL READING SUGGESTIONS
FOR PART THREE

The problem of both verification and falsification of religious statements is discussed in nontechnical terms in chapter six of John Hick, *Philosophy of Religion,* 2nd ed. Foundations of Philosophy Series (Englewood Cliffs: Prentice-Hall, 1973). Two other excellent sources also by Hick are his *Faith and Knowledge,* 2nd ed. (Ithaca: Cornell University Press, 1966) and the article on "Faith," *The Encyclopedia of Philosophy* (1967), 3, 165-69. There are many good books available on Kierkegaard, but two of the best are Louis Mackey, *Kierkegaard: A Kind of Poet* (Philadelphia: University of Pennsylvania Press, 1971) and Josiah Thompson, *The Lonely Labyrinth* (Carbondale: Southern Illinois University Press, 1967). Kierkegaard's understanding of faith is given contemporary expression by theistic existentialists. A readable and highly interesting confirmation of this can be found in chapter 9, "Faith and Enlightenment" in Karl Jaspers, *Way to Wisdom,* trans. Ralph Manheim (New Haven: Yale University Press, 1954).

part four

RELIGIOUS LANGUAGE

Religion
and
Language

Ordinary language is pretty messy, and philosophers are a breed of folks who want to tidy things up. The reason for this is not just a penchant for neatness, but the conviction that language is reason's tool, and the misuse of language can lead to faulty thinking. Considerable attention has been given by philosophers in the twentieth century to the study of language—its nature, its function, and its limitations. All this concern with language has had implications for the language of religion, for the question that has emerged is whether language functions in a special way when applied to religious matters, a way different from its ordinary function.

Just as our investigation of the arguments for the existence of God led to a consideration of the relation between faith and reason, the question of faith and reason leads to a consideration of the nature of religious language. The close relation between reason and language is seen even in the origin of the terms. In Greek—the language of the earliest Western philosophers—*logos* meant word, but was also extended to include the rational function of speech, embracing the rational element in thought. Hence the term *logos* came to mean both reason and word, and from this Greek root we get the English term *logic.* One of the important functions of philosophy is to investigate the structure of correct reasoning, and this leads to a study of the way language should function in order to reflect the logical modes of thought.

Why is there a problem of specifically *religious* language? We have already glimpsed something of the nature of the problem in Antony Flew's suggestion that statements of religious belief are not genuine assertions at all but a kind of "doublethink." Flew's views reflect a tradition going back to Immanuel Kant, who thought that such concepts as *cause, substance,* and *relation* function perfectly well when we are dealing with matters of sense experience, but that we have no justification for applying these concepts to transcendent realities. Kant concluded that when we use language that is not tied directly to sense experience, we are dealing only with a kind of speculative thought, most of which cannot be said to be meaningful. The question of the meaningfulness of religious language is raised squarely in the discussion between A. J. Ayer and F. C. Copleston, the first selection in this section. Ayer doubts the legitimacy of the language used in traditional metaphysical inquiry, and this includes all religious discourse as well. Copleston, in turn, attacks Ayer's conception of philosophy as being too narrow and defends the use of language referring to realities that lie beyond the bounds of sense.

Those who defend the meaningfulness of religious language recognize that there are problems to be resolved, for there are two separate, though related, issues that emerge from the consideration of religious language: First, is language used differently when it is used to make statements about God? Second, how are we to distinguish false statements about God from true ones? In a sense, the answer to the first question is both yes and no. Certainly we use the same language in speaking of religious matters that we use in referring to human experience, since it is the only language we have at our disposal. But it is also apparent that statements made about God, for example, do not use ordinary language in ordinary ways. The traditional affirmations claim that God is incorporeal, that is, God does not have a body or bodily form. To use the language of scripture, God is spirit. But biblical writers have also claimed that God is loving, that God is the source of knowledge and wisdom, and they have even spoken of God in terms of bodily functions—the "arm" of the Lord is sure, the "eye" of God is steadfast, and so forth. How can such language, when used in reference to a pure spirit, mean anything? Or if it does have meaning, what sort of meaning does this language have?

The term used to describe this function of language when applied beyond its literal meaning is *anthropomorphism,* from the Greek words *anthropos* (man), and *morphe* (form). In general, anthropomorphic language speaks in human terms of that which is not human. To speak of the "arm" of God, or the "finger" of God, or the "eye" of the Lord is to speak anthropomorphically, as is to speak of God's being jealous, angry, or possessing knowledge and wisdom. All these mental and physical characteristics are derived from human experience, and are applied to God in a nonliteral way. It is important to note that anthropomorphism is not limited to religious discourse, but is also present in the literature of imagination and fantasy. Part of the delight of Tolkien's Hobbit stories is the attractiveness of intelligent, talking animals with human form, as is also the case with C. S. Lewis's *Chronicles of Narnia.* And, of course, there would be no poetry if we were limited to merely the literal use of language, for the stock-in-trade of poets is simile, metaphor, symbol, and analogy, those special uses of language that enrich our discourse and enliven our sensibilities.

We might include all these nonliteral uses of language under the rubric "poetic function of language." This sort of language is the concern of literary critics and rhetoricians, but some philosophers, such as Aristotle, have held that all such nonliteral uses of language are merely ornaments, and that the *meaning* of poetic discourse could perfectly well be translated into ordinary language. This has also been argued by some twentieth-century thinkers, who view the symbolic and poetic aspects of language as simply a delight to the emotions which adds nothing to our understanding. Thus the line, "My love is like a red, red rose," literally means something like, "My love is pleasant to me as a beautiful flower is pleasing to me." You might test this theory yourself by taking your favorite poem and translating it into ordinary language, and then judging whether you have actually captured the meaning the poet had in mind.

Most philosophers who defend the meaningfulness of religious language have nonetheless concluded that language used to talk about God is different from language used literally. The other selections in this section explore three nonliteral ways language functions in religious discourse. Paul Tillich defends the special meaning inherent in symbols, H. P. Owen analyzes the analogical function of religious language, and Paul Ricoeur explores the role of metaphor as the creative edge of language.

If religious language is nonliteral use of language, can there be truth in religious discourse, and if so, how do we determine it? This is the second of our questions. If we are to be philosophical about this question, we cannot ignore the issue of the truth of language regardless of the context in which it is used. But how are we to determine the truth of nonliteral discourse? To put the question back into the context of poetry, can a poem be true or false? If so, how do we determine it? Or to state the matter even more boldly, who gives the "true" description of a rainbow, the poet who writes a poem about it, or the physicist who explains that the various colors, the wave lengths of which can be measured exactly, are due to the refraction of light caused by water particles in the air?

A simple answer to this question, and one that might at first appear attractive, is that the poet does not extend our knowledge at all but only appeals to our feelings, whereas the physicist extends our knowledge of physical reality. But is it really the case that poets do not expand our awareness, indeed our knowledge, of reality? It could be argued that a poet makes us aware of levels of reality of which we were previously unaware by calling our attention to things in a new and significant way. The physicist, to be sure, deals with reality too, but only in a limited and partial way with talk about observable and measurable quantities.

This is the constellation of questions around which the readings in this section revolve. The first reading is a discussion between F. C. Copleston, who defends the meaningfulness of religious language, and A. J. Ayer, who argues that religious language, while perhaps providing emotional satisfaction, cannot be cognitively meaningful. The next three readings take as their point of departure the assumption that religious language is meaningful and analyze how it is that religious language functions.

A. J. AYER AND F. C. COPLESTON

Discussion on Religious Language

In the Middle Ages philosophy was viewed as the "handmaiden of theology." Its principal function was thought to be the elucidation and examination of theological statements, and its usefulness was defended only insofar as it was applicable to theological concerns. Though our world view has changed since the Middle Ages, there are still philosophers who defend philosophy's handmaidenly role, no longer to theology but to science. Early in the twentieth century the view became prevalent that, insofar as it claims to deal with truth, philosophy has no independent method of its own distinct from that of the natural sciences. Philosophy's role was thought to be mainly that of analyzing various concepts in science and, if it had an independent contribution to make, it would be in the area of logic and logical analysis.

This view has its roots in the thought of the nineteenth-century philosopher August Comte, who suggested that in the development of thought there have been three discernible stages. The first he called the theological stage, in which explanations of natural occurrences were made in terms of divine or supernatural forces. The next stage is the metaphysical, in which abstract principles replaced divine forces as principles of explanation. The third and final stage Comte called the positive stage, and he felt that the modern age has squarely entered into it. Today the method of inquiry is that of science, and all natural occurrences are explained by observation, without appeal to either supernatural forces or abstract metaphysical principles. Adopting this Comtian language, the term *positivism* is applied to the view that rejects religion and metaphysics in favor of a scientific model of philosophy. Though there are different forms of positivism, all positivists reject religious language as being unscientific and having no place within philosophy.

In a book written when he was twenty-six, A. J. Ayer outlined a form of positivism which he called "logical positivism," intending by this label to include within the scope of his method the substantial advances made in the discipline of symbolic logic as a tool of analysis. Sometimes the philosophical approach Ayer represents is referred to as *logical empiricism*, which underscores the empiricist approach to truth. This book, *Language, Truth and Logic*, published in 1936, stressed as a central tenet the principle of verification. According to this principle, a statement is meaningful if and only if it is verifiable. As Ayer developed his view, it turned out that there are only two classes of statements that can be verified: logical truths, including mathematical statements; and empirical statements, sometimes called observation statements.

In the discussion that follows, the term *proposition* is used frequently, a term we previously encountered in the discussion of Flew's falsifiability principle. A proposition is an assertion that has truth value; that is, a statement asserts a proposition if it can be shown to be either true or false. The method for determining the truth value of a proposition, according to Ayer, is the principle of verification. The first class of propositions that can be verified are those which depend for their truth on the conventions of a logical system. Mathematical statements are of this kind. Statements in ordinary language, the truth of which can be determined solely by analysis of the meaning of the terms in the statement, also qualify as propositions. Examples are such statements as: "All bachelors are males," or "Every father is a parent," or "Triangles have three sides." In each of these statements, truth or falsity is determined solely by an analysis of the meaning of the terms. By now you have probably realized that you are encountering once again Kant's analytic type of statement whose truth or falsity can be known purely *a priori*. One more distinction in this short course in logic: If a logical statement is true, then it is called a *tautology;* if false, a *contradiction*. An added feature of logical statements is that they are either necessarily true or necessarily false.

Empirical statements, or observation statements, are the second class of verifiable statements. Empirical statements, unlike analytic statements, are contingently true or false, and the only way to discover their truth value is by means of observation. If someone says, "The temperature is 70° F in this room," the only way to determine whether the statement is true or false is to look at a reliable thermometer. If we say, "Caesar crossed the Rubicon," we cannot verify the truth of this statement directly, but by appealing to the records of antiquity, we can examine the observation statements of others. And since crossing a river is a perfectly ordinary human activity which does not defy the normal workings of nature, there is no added barrier to accepting the historical evidence supporting this statement. According to Ayer, these two classes of statements—analytic statements and empirically testable statements—exhaust the range of what is meaningful. If a statement cannot be shown to be of either type, it is meaningless.

The implication of the principle of verification for religious language is that, since the usual range of utterances in religion are not analytic or empirically testable, they must be dismissed as being without meaning. We can also see how Ayer's view differs from those of the traditional atheist or theist. Consider the statement, "God exists." The atheist would deny the truth of this statement and claim that it is false. The theist claims that it is true. Ayer's response to both would be that neither can prove the truth or falsity of the statement, since it deals with a reality beyond human experience. The statement, therefore, has no meaning at all. The agnostic's position is hardly any more defensible in Ayer's view than those of the theist and atheist. The agnostic errs in not simply rejecting the statement as having no meaning; to suspend judgment is to treat a religious statement as meaningful, which Ayer refuses to do.

There is a certain tidiness about Ayer's view. Immediately dismissed are all the metaphysical wrangles that have occurred in the history of philosophy. Also dismissed as meaningless is much of the language of ethics and esthetics. Philosophy would have a narrowed function—dealing principally with logical analysis—but at least a defensible function, and one that shares the respectable aura of science as well.

The following discussion makes evident that one of the main disagreements between the two participants is over the nature of philosophy, and philosophy is perhaps unique among human disciplines in that one of the central items of philosophical concern is its own nature. Copleston rejects Ayer's narrowed definition of philosophy and argues that philosophy should include metaphysical inquiry as well as logical analysis. The issue of metaphysical analysis pinpoints a fundamental difference between the two. Copleston understands "metaphysical reality" as referring to a "being which in principle (and not merely in fact) transcends the sphere of what can be sensibly experienced." Ayer, in contrast, defines metaphysics as "an attempt to gain knowledge about the world by non-scientific means." If we accept Ayer's definition of metaphysics, and if philosophy has no method different from that of the natural sciences, then obviously metaphysics is excluded from philosophical investigation. Copleston even suggests that the principle of verification "seems to have been formulated to rule out metaphysics." Ayer's response is that acceptance of his principle of verification rescues philosophical statements from becoming either meaningless or trivial.

As the discussion unfolds, you will be able to see clearly the difference between the two views of the nature of philosophy. But there are other issues that arise as well, such as the status of the principle of verification. Since proposed by Ayer in 1936, the principle itself has undergone considerable philosophical scrutiny and has been attacked by other philosophers as an inadequate criterion of meaningfulness.[1] Copleston mentions two of the usual sort of attacks made against the principle. The first has to do with a class of statements which are not verifiable under the criteria of the principle of verification but would be considered by most persons as meaningful. The example Copleston gives is the statement, "Atomic warfare will take place and it will blot out the entire human race." The statement seems to be perfectly meaningful, but it is not in principle verifiable, since were it true, there would be no one around to verify it. Ayer admits that this statement is not "practically" verifiable, although he insists that it describes "a possible situation." This response underscores a fundamental disagreement between Ayer and Copleston. Ayer assumes that unless something is capable of being experienced, it is meaningless to attempt to talk about it. This, of course, is precisely what Copleston denies. God, by

[1]For a rigorous critique of both the principle of verification and the principle of falsification, see Carl Hempel, "The Empiricist Criterion of Meaning," in *Classics of Analytic Philosophy*, ed. Robert Ammerman (New York: McGraw-Hill, 1965), pp. 218-221.

definition, is beyond the reach of our senses, and talk about God cannot even in principle be verified by means of the criteria used for verifying statements about the world of the senses.

The second criticism of the verification principle leveled by Copleston is the status of the principle itself. Let's take Ayer's formulation of the principle of verification: "to be significant a statement must be either on the one hand a formal statement. . . or on the other hand empirically testable." Is this statement verifiable by its own criteria? Let's see. Is it an analytic truth? Hardly. There is nothing in the meaning of the terms used in this statement that shows it to be necessarily true. Then, is it empirically testable? It is difficult to see just how it could be tested. Accordingly, Copleston charges that the principle of verification cannot be verified by its own criteria and therefore must be considered meaningless. Ayer does not attempt to verify the principle, insisting instead that it has the status of a "persuasive definition," but a person who sees philosophy's task as broader than does Ayer is not likely to be persuaded by it. By limiting the range of philosophical inquiry, the principle of verification makes philosophy's task less formidable, but for Copleston such a move eliminates many of philosophy's important concerns.

Copleston admits that logical analysis, in Ayer's sense of the term, is a valuable role for philosophy, but maintains that it is not philosophy's only task. Copleston would also admit that some metaphysical statements are meaningless, and add that if we are to talk meaningfully about God, we must begin with human experience—with the world—and argue from this to God as its cause. We will also be forced to use language analogically, and be prepared to defend the use of this kind of language with well-argued principles. All this seems too vague and sloppy for Ayer, and he rejects any kind of philosophical inquiry which cuts itself loose from logic and analysis of observation statements.

Few philosophers today would accept the title "logical positivist" with its principle of verification, for subsequent analysis of this criterion of meaningfulness has shown it to be inadequate.[2] On the other hand, the view persists among some philosophers that metaphysics in the sense that Copleston defends it is a suspect area of inquiry. Part of the reason for this may be due to the prestige of science and to the fact that many philosophers feel more comfortable devoting their attention to logical analysis than to traditional metaphysical speculation. Regardless of their views on the nature of philosophical inquiry, most philosophers would agree that an investigation into the nature and function of language is a fruitful, indeed a necessary, task if religious discourse is to be shown to be meaningful. It is for this reason that the other readings in this section will investigate the precise nature of religious discourse in an effort to understand better how it is that the language of religion functions.

[2]John Passmore gives an excellent summary of the background and present status of logical positivism in his article "Logical Positivism," *Encyclopedia of Philosophy* (1967), 5, 52-57.

Discussion Between Professor Ayer
and Father Copleston*

Ayer: Well, Father Copleston, you've asked me to summarize logical positivism for you, and it's not very easy. For one thing, as I understand it, logical positivism isn't a system of philosophy; it consists, rather, in a certain technique, a certain kind of attitude towards philosophical problems. Perhaps one thing which those of us who are called logical positivists tend to have in common is that we deny the possibility of philosophy as a speculative discipline. We should say that if philosophy was to be a branch of knowledge as distinct from the sciences it would have to consist in logic or in some form of analysis; and our reason for this would be somewhat as follows.

We maintain that you can divide propositions into two classes—formal and empirical. Formal propositions, like those of logic and mathematics, depend for their validity on the conventions of a symbol system. Empirical propositions, on the other hand, are statements of observation—actual or possible—or hypotheses from which such statements can be logically derived; and it is they that constitute science insofar as science isn't purely mathematical. Now our contention is that this exhausts the field of what we may call speculative knowledge. Consequently we reject metaphysics, if this be understood—and I think it commonly has been—as an attempt to gain knowledge about the world by non-scientific means. Inasmuch as metaphysical statements are not testable by observation, we hold they're not descriptive of anything; and from this we should conclude that if philosophy is to be a cognitive activity, it must be purely critical. It would take the form of trying to elucidate the concepts that were used in science or mathematics or in everyday language.

Copleston: Well, Professor Ayer, I can quite understand, of course, philosophers confining themselves to logical analysis if they wish to do so, and I shouldn't dream of denying or of belittling in any way its utility; I think it's obviously an extremely useful thing to do, to analyze and clarify the concepts used in science. In everyday life, too, there are many terms used that practically have taken on an emotional connotation—"progressive," or "reactionary," or "freedom," or "the modern mind." To make clear to people what's meant—or what *they* mean—by those terms, or the various possible meanings, is a very useful thing. But if the logical

*Source: This discussion was transcribed from a 1949 broadcast by the British Broadcasting Corporation and is used by permission of Professor Sir Alfred Ayer and Father Copleston, S. J.

positivist means that logical analysis is the *only* function of philosophy, that's the point at which I should disagree with him; and so would many other philosophers disagree, especially, I think, on the Continent.

Don't you think that by saying what philosophy is one presupposes a philosophy or takes up a position as a philosopher? For example, if one divides significant propositions into two classes—namely, purely formal propositions and statements of observation—one is adopting a philosophical position, one is claiming that there are no necessary propositions which are not purely formal. Moreover, to claim that metaphysical propositions to be significant should be verifiable as scientific hypotheses are verifiable is to claim that metaphysics—to be significant—should not be metaphysics.

Ayer: Oh, I agree that my position is philosophical, though not that it's metaphysical, as I hope to show later. To say what philosophy is is certainly a philosophical act, but this I mean is itself a question of philosophical analysis. We have to decide, among other things, what it is we're going to call philosophy—and I've given you my answer. It is not, perhaps, an obvious answer, but it at least has the merit that it rescues philosophical statements from becoming either meaningless or trivial. . . .

Copleston: . . . Well, perhaps we'd better attend to your principle of verifiability. You mentioned the principle of verification earlier. I thought possibly you'd state it. Professor, would you?

Ayer: Yes, I'll state it in a very loose form; namely, that to be significant a statement must be either on the one hand a formal statement—one that I should call analytic—or on the other hand empirically testable. I should try to derive this principle by an analysis of understanding. I should say that understanding a statement meant knowing what would be the case if it were true. Knowing what would be the case if it were true means knowing what observations would verify it. And this in turn means being disposed to accept some situations as warranting the acceptance or rejection of the statement in question. From which there are two corollaries. One—which we've been talking about to some extent—: The statements to which no situations are relevant one way or the other are ruled out as non-factual. And, secondly, the contents of the statement, the cash value, to use James's term, consists of a range of situations, experiences, that would substantiate or refute it.

Copleston: Thank you. Now I don't want to misinterpret your position, but it does seem to me that we're supposing a certain philosophical position. What I mean is this. If you say that any factual statement, in order to be meaningful, must be verifiable, and if you mean, by verifiable, verifiable by sense experience, then surely you are presupposing that all reality is given in sense experience. If you are presupposing this, you are presupposing that there can be no such thing as metaphysical reality, and if you presuppose this you are presupposing a philosophical position which cannot be demonstrated by the principle of verification. It seems to me that logical positivism claims to be what I might call a neutral technique, whereas in reality it presupposes the truth of positivism. And please pardon my saying so, but it looks to me as though the principle of verifiability was cogitated partly in order to exclude metaphysical propositions from the range of meaningful propositions.

Ayer: Even if that were so it doesn't prove anything, really. But to go back. I certainly shouldn't make any statement about all reality. That's precisely the kind of statement I use my principle in order not to make. Nor do I wish to restrict experience to sense experience. I shouldn't at all mind counting what might be called introspectable experiences or feelings; mystical experiences, if you like.

It would be true then that people who haven't had certain experiences won't understand propositions which refer to them, but that I don't mind either. I can quite well believe that your experience is different from mine. Let's assume, which is after all an empirical assumption, that you even have a sense difference from mine. I should then be in the position of a blind man, and I should admit that statements that are unintelligible to me might be meaningful to you. But I should then go on to say that the factual content of your statement was determined by your experiences—which contents are verifiers or falsifiers.

Copleston: Yes, you include introspection, and just assumed it, but my point is that you assumed that a factually informative statement is significant only if it is verifiable—at least in principle—by direct observation. Now obviously the existence of a metaphysical reality is not verifiable by direct observation unless you're willing to recognize a purely intellectual intuition as observation. I'm not very keen on appealing to intuition, though I see no compelling reason to rule it out from the beginning. However, if you mean, by verifiable, verifiable by direct sense observation, and/or by introspection, you seem to me to be ruling out metaphysics from the start. In other words, I suggest that acceptance of the principle of verification, as you appear to understand it, implies the acceptance of philosophical positivism. I think I should probably be prepared to accept the principle if it were understood in a very wide sense—that is, if verifiable by experience is understood as including intellectual intuition, and also as meaning simply that some experience, actual or conceivable, is relevant to the truth or falsity of the proposition concerned. But what I object to is any statement of the principle which tacitly assumes the validity of the definite philosophical position. Now you've made a distinction, I think, between the analytic statements, on the one hand, and the empirical statements, and the metaphysical and ethical statements on the other. Or at any rate the metaphysical statements—let's leave ethical out of it. You call the first group cognitive statements and the second emotive. Is that so?

Ayer: I think the word "emotive" isn't very happy, though I've used it in the past, and I suggest I make it "emotion," which isn't necessarily the case. But I accept what you say if you mean by emotive simply not cognitive.

Copleston: Very well, I accept, of course, your substitution of non-cognitive for emotive, but my objection still remains that by cognitive statements I presume that you mean statements which satisfy the criterion of meaning—that is to say, the principle of verifiability; and by non-cognitive statements I presume you mean statements which do not satisfy that criterion. If this is so, it seems to me that when you say that metaphysical statements are non-cognitive you are not saying much more than that statements which do not satisfy the principle of verification do not satisfy the principle of verification. In this case, however, no conclusion follows as to the significance or non-significance of metaphysical propositions, unless, indeed, one has previously accepted your philosophical position—that is to say, unless one has assumed that they are non-significant.

Ayer: It's not so simple as that. My procedure is this. I shall claim that the account I have given you of what understanding a statement is . . . does apply to ordinary common-sense statements and scientific statements. So I'd give a different account of how a mathematical statement functions, and a different account again of value judgment.

Copleston: Yes.

Ayer: I then say that statements which don't satisfy these conditions are not significant, not to be understood; and I think you can quite correctly object that by putting my definitions together all I come down to saying is that statements that are not scientific or common-sense statements are not scientific or common-sense statements. But then I want to go further and say that I totally fail to understand—and, again, I'm afraid I'm using my own sense of understanding; what else can I do?—I fail to understand what these other non-scientific statements and non-common-sense statements, which don't satisfy these criteria, propose to be. Someone may say he does understand them, in some sense of understanding other than the one I've defined. I reply: It's not clear to me what that sense of understanding is, nor, a fortiori, what it is he understands, nor how these statements function. But of course you may still say that in making it a question of how these statements function I'm presupposing my own criterion.

Copleston: Well, then, in your treatment of metaphysical propositions you are either applying the criterion of verifiablity or you are not. If you are, then the significance of metaphysical propositions would seem to be ruled out of court a priori, since the truth of the principle, as it seems to be understood by you, inevitably involves the non-significance of metaphysical propositions. In this case the application of the criterion to concrete metaphysical propositions constitutes a proof neither of the non-significance of metaphysical propositions nor of the truth of the principle. All that is shown, it seems to me, is that metaphysical propositions do not satisfy a definite assumed criterion of meaning. But it does not follow that one has to accept that criterion of meaning. You may legitimately say, if you like, "I will accept as significant factual statements only those statements which satisfy these particular demands or conditions." But it doesn't follow, does it, that I or anybody else has to make those particular demands before we are prepared to accept a statement as meaningful?

Ayer: What I do is to give a definition of certain related terms: "understanding," "meaningful," and so on. I can't possibly accept them, either. But I can perhaps make you unhappy about the consequences of not accepting them. What I should do is this. I should take any given proposition, and show how it functions. In the case of a scientific hypothesis, I would show that it had a certain function—namely, that, with other premises, you could deduce certain observational consequences from it. I should then say this is how this proposition works. This is what it does, this is what it amounts to. I then take mathematical propositions and play a slightly different game with them, and show that they function in a certain way, in a calculus, in a symbolic system. You then present me with these other statements, and I say: On the one hand, they have no observational consequences. On the other hand, they aren't statements of logic. All right. So you understand them. I have given a definition of understanding according to which they are not, in my usage of the term, capable of being understood. Nevertheless, you reject my definition; you are perfectly entitled to, because you can give understanding a different meaning if you like. I can't stop you. But now I say: Tell me more about them. In what sense are they understood? They are not understood in my sense. They aren't parts of a symbolic system. You can't do anything with them in the sense of deriving any observational consequences from them. What do you want to say about them? Well, you may just want to say they're facts or something of that sort. Then again I press you on your use of the word "facts."

Copleston: You seem to me to be demanding that in order for a factual statement to be significant, one must be able to deduce observational consequences from it. But I don't see why that should be so. If you mean directly observable consequences, you appear to me to be demanding too much. In any case, are there some propositions which are not verifiable, even in principle, but which would yet be considered by most people to have meaning and to be either true or false. Let me give an example. I don't want to assume the mantle of a prophet, and I hope the statement is quite false. But it is this. "Atomic warfare will take place and it will blot out the entire human race." Now, most people would think that this statement has meaning. It means what it says. But how could it possibly be verified empirically? Supposing it were fulfilled; the last man could not say with his last breath, "Copleston's prediction has been verified," because he would not be entitled to say this until he was dead— that is, until he was no longer in a position to verify the statement.

Ayer: It is certainly practically unverifiable. You can't be a man surviving all men. On the other hand, there's no doubt it describes a possible situation. Putting the observer outside the story, one knows quite well what it would be like to observe devastation and fail to observe any men. Now it wouldn't necessarily be the case that, in order to do that, one had to observe oneself. Just as, to take the case of the past, there were dinosaurs before there were men. Clearly, no man saw that, and clearly I, if I am the speaker, I can't myself verify it, but one knows what it would be like to have observed animals and not to have observed men.

Copleston: The two cases are different. In regard to the past, we have empirical evidence. For example, we have fossils of dinosaurs. But in the case of the prediction I mentioned, there would be nobody to observe the evidence and so to verify the proposition.

Ayer: In terms of the evidence, of course, it becomes very much easier for me. That would be too easy a way of getting out of our difficulty, because there is also evidence for the atomic thing.

Copleston: Yes, but there would be no evidence for the prediction that it will blot out the human race, even if one can imagine the state of affairs that would verify it. Thus by imagining it, one's imagining oneself into the . . .

Ayer: No, no.

Copleston: Yes, yes. One can imagine the evidence and one can imagine oneself verifying it; but in point of fact, if the prediction were fulfilled, there would be no one there to verify it. By importing yourself imaginatively into the picture, you are canceling out the condition of the fulfillment of the prediction. But let us drop the prediction. You have mentioned imagination. Now, what I should prefer to regard as the criterion of the truth or falsity of an existential proposition is simply the presence or absence of the asserted fact or facts, quite irrespective of whether I can know whether there are corresponding facts or not. If I can at least imagine or conceive the facts, the existence of which would verify the proposition, the proposition has significance for me. Whether I can or cannot know that the facts correspond is another matter.

Ayer: I don't at all object to your use of the word "facts" so long as you allow it to be observable facts. But take the contrary case. Suppose I say, "There's a drogulus over there." And you say, "What?" and I say, "Drogulus," and you say, "What's a drogulus?" "Well," I say, "I can't describe what a drogulus is because it's not the sort of thing you can see or touch; it has no physical effects of any kind; it's a disembodied being." And you say: "Well, how am I to tell if it's there or not?" And I say: "There's no way of telling. Everything's just the same if it's there or it's not there. But the fact is it's there. There's a drogulus there standing just behind you, spiritually behind you." Does that make sense?

Copleston: It seems to me to do so. I should say that a drogulus in the room or not is true or false, provided that you can—that you at any rate, I have some idea of what is meant by a drogulus, and if you can say to me it's a disembodied spirit, then I should say that the proposition is either true or false whether one can verify it or not. If you said to me: "By 'drogulus' I merely mean the word 'drogulus' and I attach no other significance to it whatsoever," then I should say that it isn't a proposition any more than if I said "piffle" was in the room.

Ayer: That's right. But what is "having some idea" of something? I want to say that having an idea of something is a matter of knowing how to recognize it. And you want to say that you can have ideas of things even though there's no possible situation in which you could recognize it because nothing would count as finding it. I would say that I understand the words "angel," "table," "clock," "drogulus" if I'm disposed to accept certain situations as verifying the presence or absence of what the word is supposed to stand for. But you want to admit these words without any reference to experience, whether the thing they are supposed to stand for exists, and everything is to go on just the same.

Copleston: No. I should say that you can have an idea of something if there's some experience that's relevant to the formation of the idea, not so much to its verification. I should say that I can form the idea of a drogulus or a disembodied spirit from the idea of body and the idea of mind. You may say that there's no mind and there's no spirit, but, at any rate, there is, as you'll admit, certain internal experience of thinking and so on which at any rate accounts for the formation of the idea. Therefore I can say I have an idea of a drogulus or whatever it is, even though I'm quite unable to know whether such a thing actually exists or not.

Ayer: You would certainly not have to know that it exists, but you would have to know what would count as its existing.

Copleston: Yes, well, if you mean by count as its existing that there must be some experience relevant to the formation of the idea, then I should agree.

Ayer: Not to the formation of the idea, but to the truth or falsity of the propositions in which it is contained.

Copleston: The word "metaphysics" and the phrase "metaphysical reality" can have more than one meaning, but when I refer to a "metaphysical reality" in our present discussion I mean a being which in principle (and not merely in fact) transcends the sphere of what can be sensibly experienced. Thus God is a metaphysical reality. Since God is, *ex hypothesi*, immaterial, he cannot, in principle, be apprehended by the senses.

May I add two remarks? My first remark is that I do not mean to imply that no sense experience is in any way relevant to establishing or discovering. I certainly do believe that metaphysics must be based on experience of some sort, but metaphysics involves intellectual reflection on experience. No amount of immediate sense experience will disclose the existence of a metaphysical reality. In other words, I should say, there is a halfway house between admitting only the immediate data of experience and, on the other hand, leaping to the affirmation of a metaphysical reality without any reference to experience at all. You yourself reflect on the data of experience. The metaphysician carries that reflection a stage further.

My second remark is this. Because one cannot have sense experience of a metaphysical reality it doesn't follow that one couldn't have another type of experience of it, and if anybody had such experience it does not seem to me that the metaphysical reality is deprived, as it were, of its metaphysical character and become non-metaphysical. I think that's an important point.

Ayer: Yes, but asking are there metaphysical realities isn't like asking are there still wolves in Asia, is it? It looks as if you've got a clear usage for metaphysical reality and then ask does it occur or not, does it exist or not, as if I'm arbitrarily denying that it exists. My difficulty is not in answering the question—are there or are there not metaphysical realities?—but in understanding what usage is being given to the expression "metaphysical reality." When am I to count a metaphysical reality? What would it be like to come upon a metaphysical reality? That's my problem. It isn't that I arbitrarily say there can't be such things, already admitting the use of the term, but that I'm puzzled about the use of the term. I don't know what people who say there are metaphysical realities mean by it.

Copleston: Well, that brings us back to the beginning—the function of philosophy, I think. I should say that one can't simply raise in the abstract the question: Are there metaphysical realities? Rather, one asks: Is the character of observable reality of such a kind that it leads one to postulate a metaphysical reality, a reality beyond the physical sphere? If one grants that it is, even then one can only speak about that metaphysical reality within the framework of human language. And language is, after all, primarily developed to express our immediate experience of surrounding things, and therefore there's bound, I fully admit, to be inadequacy in any statements about a metaphysical reality.

Ayer: But you're trying to have it both ways, you see. If it's something that you say doesn't have a meaning in my language, then I don't understand it. It's no good saying: "Oh, well, of course, it really has a meaning," because what meaning could it have except in the language in which it is used?

Copleston: Well, let's take a concrete example. If I say, for example, God is intelligent—well, you may very well say to me, "What meaning can you give to the word 'intelligent'?—because the only intelligence you have experienced is the human intelligence, and are you attributing that to God?" and I should have to say no, because I'm not. Therefore, if we agree to use the word "intelligent" simply to mean human intelligence, I should have to say God is not intelligent. But when I say that a stone is not intelligent I mean that a stone is less than intelligent; when I say God is intelligent I mean that God is more than intelligent, even though I can't give an adequate account of what that intelligence is in itself.

Ayer: Do you mean simply that he knows more than any given man knows? But to what are you ascribing this property? You haven't begun to make that clear.

Copleston: It's a point, of course. But what you are inviting me to do is to describe God in terms which will be as clear to you as the terms in which one might describe a familiar object of experience or an unfamiliar object which is yet so like familiar objects that it can be adequately described in terms of things which are really familiar to you. But God is *ex hypothesi* unique; and it's quite impossible to describe him adequately by using concepts which normally apply to all ordinary objects of experience. If it were possible, then God wouldn't be God. So I think you're really asking me to describe God in a manner possible only if he weren't God.

I freely admit that all human ideas on God are inadequate. I also affirm that this must be so, owing to the finitude of the human intellect and to the fact that we can come to a philosophical knowledge of God only through reflection on the things we experience. But it doesn't follow that we can have no knowledge of God. It does follow, though, that our philosophical knowledge of God cannot be more than analogical.

Ayer: Yes, but in the case of an ordinary analogy when you say that something is like something else you understand what both things are. But in this case, if you do say something is analogical I say: Analogical of what? And you don't tell me of what. You merely repeat the first term of analogy. Well, I get no analogy. It's like saying that something is "taller than," and I say, "Taller than?" and you repeat the first thing you say. Then I understand it's taller than itself, which is nonsense.

Copleston: I think that one must distinguish physical analogy and metaphysical analogy. If I say that God is intelligent, I don't say so simply because I want to call God intelligent, but either because I think that the world is such that it must be ascribed, in certain aspects at least, to a Being which can be described in human terms only as intelligent or because I am satisfied by some argument that there exists an absolute Being and then deduce that that Being must be described as intelligent. I am perfectly well aware that I have no adequate idea of what that intelligence is in itself. I am ascribing to God an attribute which, translated into human terms, must be called intelligence. After all, if you speak of your dog as intelligent, you are using the word in an analogous sense, and it has some meaning for you, even though you don't observe the dog's physical operations. Mathematicians who speak of multidimensional space have never observed, I suppose, such a space, but presumably they attach some meaning to the term. Or when we speak of "extrasensory perception" we are using the word "perception" analogously.

Ayer: Yes, but mathematical physicists do test their statements by observation, and I know what would count as a case of extrasensory perception. In the case of your statement I don't know what counts. Of course, you might give it an empirical meaning; you might say that by "God is 'intelligent' " you meant that the word had certain features. Then we'd inspect it to see if it had the features or not.

Copleston: Well, of course I do argue from the world to God. I must start from the world to God. I wouldn't wish to argue from God to the features of the world. But to keep within your terms of reference of empiricism, I should say that if God is personal then he's capable, for example, of entering into relationship with human beings. Then it's possible to find human beings who claim at any rate they have a personal intercourse with God.

Ayer: Then you've given your statement a perfectly good empirical meaning. But it would then be like a scientific theory, and you would be using it in exactly the same way as you might use a concept like "electron"—to account for, explain, predict a certain range of human experience—namely, that certain people did have these experiences which they described as "entering into communion with God." Then one would try to analyze it scientifically, find out in what conditions these things happened. Then you might put it up as a theory. What you'd done would be psychology.

Copleston: Well, as I said, I was entering into your terms of reference. I wouldn't admit that when I was saying God is personal I merely meant that God could enter into intercourse with human beings. But I should be prepared to say that he was personal even if I had no reason for supposing that he entered into intercourse with human beings.

Ayer: No, but it's only in that case one has anything one can control. The facts are that these human beings have these experiences. They describe these experiences in a way which implies more than that they're merely having them. But if one asks what more, then what answer does one get? Only, I'm afraid, repetition of the statement that was questioned in the first place.

Copleston: Well, let's come back to this religious experience. However you subsequently interpret the religious experience, you'd admit, then, that it was relevant to the truth or falsity of the proposition that God existed.

Ayer: Relevant only insofar as the proposition that God existed is taken as a prediction or description of the occurrence of their experiences. But not, of course, that one has any inference you might want to draw, such as that the world was created, or anything of that kind.

Copleston: No. We'll leave that out. What I'm trying to get at is that you'd admit the proposition "God exists" could be a meaningful form of metaphysical proposition.

Ayer: No, it wouldn't then be a meaningful metaphysical proposition. It'd be a perfectly good empirical proposition, like the proposition that the unconscious mind exists.

Copleston: The proposition that people have religious experience would be an empirical proposition, I quite agree. And the proposition that God exists would also be an empirical proposition, provided that all I meant by saying that God exists was that some people have a certain type of experience. But actually that's not all I mean by it. All I originally said was that if God is personal then one of the consequences would be that he could enter into communication with human beings. If he does so that doesn't make God an empirical reality in the sense of not being a metaphysical reality, but God can perfectly well be a metaphysical reality—that is, independent of physics or nature even if intelligent creatures have a non-sensible experience of him. However, if you wish to call metaphysical propositions empirical propositions, by all means do so. It then becomes a question of terminology, I think.

Ayer: Oh, no. I suggest that you're again trying to have it both ways. You see, you allow me to give these words, these shapes, or noises an empirical meaning. You allow me to say that the test . . . [of whether] what you call God exists or not is to be that certain people have certain experiences, just as the test whether the table exists or not is that certain people have experiences. Only the experiences are a different sort. Having got that admission, you then shift the meaning of the words "God exists"; you no longer make them refer simply to the possibility of having these experiences, and so argue that I have admitted a metaphysical proposition, but of course I haven't. All I've admitted is an empirical proposition, which you've chosen to express in the same words as you also want to use to express your metaphysical proposition.

Copleston: Pardon me. I didn't say that the test . . . [of whether] what I call God exists or not is that certain people have certain experiences. I said that if God exists one consequence would be that people could have certain experiences. However, even if I accept your requirements, it follows that in one case at least you are prepared to recognize the word "God" as meaningful.

Ayer: Of course I recognize it as meaningful if you give it an empirical meaning, but it doesn't follow there's any empirical evidence for the truth of your metaphysical proposition.

Copleston: But then I don't claim that metaphysical propositions are not in some way founded on reflection on experience. In a certain sense I should call myself an empiricist, but I think that your empiricism is too narrow.

Ayer: My quarrel with you is not that you take a wider view of experience than I do, but that you fail to supply any rules for the use of your expressions. Let me try to summarize. I'm not asking you for explicit definitions: All that I require is that some indication be given of the way in which the expression relates to some possible experience. It's only when a statement can't be interpreted as referring even indirectly to anything observable that I wish to dismiss it as metaphysical. It's not necessary that the observation should actually be made; there are cases, as you've pointed out, where for practical, or even for theoretical, reasons, the observation couldn't, in fact, be made, but one knows what it would be like to make it. The statements which refer to it would be said to be verifiable in principle, if not in fact. To put the point more simply, I understand a statement of fact, I know what to look for on the supposition that it's true. My knowing what to look for is itself a matter of my being able to interpret the statement as referring, at least, to some possible experience.

Now you may say—indeed, you have said—that this is all entirely arbitrary. The principle of verifiability is not itself a descriptive statement; its status is that of a persuasive definition. I am persuaded by it, but why should you be? Can I prove it? Yes—on the basis of other definitions. I have in fact tried to show you how it can be derived from an analysis of understanding. But if you're really obstinate you'll reject these other definitions, too, so it looks as if we reach a deadlock. . . . I claim for my method that it does yield valuable results in the way of analysis, and with this you seem disposed to agree. You don't deny the importance of the analytic method in philosophy, nor do you reject all the uses to which I put it; therefore you accept in the main the account that I give of empirical propositions. You have indeed objected to my treatment of the propositions of logic, but there I think that I'm in the right. At least I'm able to account for their validity, whereas on your view it is utterly mysterious.

The main difference between us is that *you* want to leave room for metaphysics. But now look at the result that you get. You put forward your metaphysical statements as ultimate explanations of fact, yet you admit that they're not explanations in any accepted sense of the term, and you can't say in what sense they *are* explanations. You can't show me how they're to be tested, and you seem to have no criterion for deciding whether they are true or false. This being so, I say they're unintelligible. You say no, you understand them; but for all the good they do you—I mean cognitively, not emotionally—you might just as well abandon them.

This is my case against your metaphysical statements. You may decline to be persuaded by it, but what sort of case can you make *for* them? I leave the last word to you.

Copleston: Well, I've enjoyed our discussion very much. I've contended that a metaphysical idea has meaning if some experience is relevant to the formation of that idea, and that a rational metaphysic is possible if there are—as I still think there are—principles which can express an intellectual apprehension and a nature of being. I think that one *can* have an intellectual experience—or intuition, if you like—of being. A metaphysical proposition is testable by rational discussion, but not by purely empirical means. When you say that metaphysical propositions are meaningless because they are unverifiable in your sense, I don't really think that this amounts to more than saying that metaphysics are not the same thing as empirical science.

In short, I consider that logical positivism, apart from its theory of analytic propositions, really embodies the notion of nineteenth-century positivism; that the terms "rational" and "scientific" have the same extension. This notion certainly corresponds to a popularly held prejudice, but I don't see any adequate reason for accepting it. I still find it difficult to understand the status of the principle of verification. It must be, I should have thought, either a proposition or not a proposition. If it is a proposition it must be, on your premises, either a tautology or an empirical hypothesis. If it's a tautology, then no conclusion follows as to metaphysics; if it's an empirical hypothesis, then the principle itself would require verification. But the principle of verification cannot itself be verified. If, however, the principle is not a proposition, it should be, on your premises, meaningless. In any case, if the meaning of an existential proposition consists, according to the principle, in its verifiability, it is impossible, I think, to escape an infinite regress, since the verification will itself need verification, and so on indefinitely; and if that is so, then all propositions, including scientific propositions, are meaningless.

DISCUSSION QUESTIONS

1. What is your own evaluation of the principle of verification as a criterion of the meaningfulness of statements? Give reasons for your answer.
2. Do you see any similarities between Ayer's principle of verification as a criterion for the meaningfulness of language and Flew's principle of falsification?
3. Do you find Ayer's or Copleston's view of the nature of religious language more acceptable? Why?
4. The positions espoused by Ayer and Copleston each presuppose a certain view of the nature of philosophy. What are these presuppositions, and which do you think is the more defensible view of the nature of philosophy?
5. In what ways do you think that religious language is different from other uses of language?

PAUL TILLICH

The Nature
of
Religious Language

We in the twentieth century do not have much use for symbols. They are just not our style. Being scientifically educated, trained to disregard the emotional as irrelevant, we find symbols to be merely ornamental, not at all adding to the meaning of things. In the reading that follows, Paul Tillich calls all these assumptions into question. He argues that symbols are an indispensable part of our language, and the only way we have of opening up to understanding new levels of reality and meaning. If we are to speak of God at all, our language must be symbolic through and through. All this is in marked contrast to the spirit of positivism represented by Ayer, which would like to dispense with everything but the literal meaning of words. We can therefore view Tillich's discussion of the nature of religious language as an alternative to logical positivism's theory of meaning. Like Copleston, Tillich would agree that logical analysis is a valuable role for philosophy, but if we confine ourselves to this task alone we will be poorer for it, in terms both of our understanding of reality and our understanding of ourselves. Since Tillich's discussion follows a five-step outline, we will follow this procedure in setting the context for the reading.

DISTINCTION BETWEEN SIGNS AND SYMBOLS

The first issue to be clarified is precisely what is meant by the term *symbol,* and the meaning of the term can best be seen in its distinction from the term *sign.* A sign is that which points beyond itself to something else. The red light at the corner intersection signifies the command "Stop." Many of the words in our language are signs, such as the words that name physical objects. "Desk" is an arbitrary sign that stands for the object named by this word. Symbols are also signs in that they point beyond themselves to something else which they signify. But symbols do more. They also participate in the reality they symbolize. The flag, for example, is literally nothing but a piece of cloth decorated with bright colors, but as a powerful symbol it shares in the power and glory of the nation. People fight for the flag. They die for it, not for the piece of cloth which is worth only a few dollars but for that which it symbolizes: freedom, homeland, the preservation of a way of life. The flag, as a symbol, shares in all those intangible realities that people associate with their country. There are other, more private kinds of symbols: an object that belonged to a deceased mother or father, wife or husband, which by its very presence summons back vividly the memory of the departed one. An engagement ring is not just a piece of metal worth a few dollars, it symbolizes a bond between two persons.

In ordinary language we also use the term symbol to refer to the notations of mathematics or symbolic logic. These are not symbols in the sense that Tillich uses the term. They are only signs pointing to a particular algebraic or mathematical function, a kind of shorthand intended to reduce the ambiguity present in natural language. Some philosophers have been fascinated with the clarity and precision of mathematical language and have attempted to model philosophy after mathematics. Descartes, Spinoza, and in our own time, Bertrand Russell, have all expressed this ideal. Rather than attempting to reduce language to mathematical precision, Tillich argues that symbols enrich language by giving expression to new meanings that cannot be formulated any other way.

THE FUNCTION OF SYMBOLS

Symbols are different from signs not only in their participation in that which they signify; symbols also open up new levels of reality. This new reality is understood by Tillich in a twofold sense. Symbols point to new levels of external reality, features of the world that would otherwise be closed to us, and to this corresponds new levels of what Tillich calls "internal reality," or levels of self-understanding. This is perhaps most evident in the arts: poetry, visual art, and music. The artist redescribes reality in symbolic form and thereby helps us see things in new and meaningful ways. We also can respond to this in terms of new levels of self-understanding and self-disclosure. When we are deeply moved by a painting, a symphonic composition, or a ballet, we experience reality in a different way than we would if we were confined merely to the literal meanings of words. A positivist might respond that all this is merely a veneer of emotion added to the substance of rationality. But are we not creatures of feeling as well as reason? By going beyond the level of literal meanings, do not symbols help us understand ourselves better in the fullness of our existential situation? Does not a great painting aid our self-understanding precisely because it does not appeal to us on a purely rational level? Here again we see the tension between the rational and nonrational approaches to religious that we surveyed in the first section.

A sign can be easily replaced. Since it is largely an arbitrary representation wherein one thing stands for another, a sign is a convention that is agreed to, but can also be changed by mutual consent. Symbols, in contrast, are not so easily manipulable. The great symbols of a culture are not invented by a single individual or even by a group. They arise as an expression of what Tillich refers to as a "group unconscious" or "collective unconscious" to give expression to an experience of new levels of reality. Symbols die when the situation that gave rise to them changes, as the virgin Mary ceased to be a vivid symbol for Protestant Christianity when mankind's relationship to God was understood in a new way.

THE NATURE OF RELIGIOUS SYMBOLS

Like all symbols, religious symbols open up a new level of reality. But in the case of religious symbols, the reality which they "open up" is the ultimate reality, God, or the dimension of the Holy (recall Otto's analysis of this term). In different cultures and at different times, a wide variety of things have been used to symbolize this ultimate dimension of reality. The proliferation of symbols is confusing to a person who studies the history of religions for the first time until one realizes the fact that some symbols are more appropriate to a particular group's "collective unconscious" than others. For example, in the Old Testament kingship is often used as a symbol for the sovereignty of God. In a society organized under a monarchy, kingship is an appropriate symbol for the ultimate reality, and this symbol has continued to be meaningful in societies with a monarchial structure. But what of this symbol's revealing power for democratic societies? Does it perhaps cease to have the power it once had for other societies at other times?

A student of the history and development of religions may at first be simply bewildered by the sheer variety of symbols that have been used to express the Holy. Even within a single religious tradition, such as the faith of ancient Israel, a variety of symbols were suggested as a way of speaking of God. One writer, who makes no claim for the completeness of this list, offers the following catalog of God-symbols from various books of the Old Testament, a list that is almost overwhelming in its variety: father, mother, husband, friend, shepherd, farmer, dairymaid, fuller (laundress), builder, potter, fisherman, tradesman, physician, teacher and scribe, nurse, metal worker, king, warrior, and judge.[1] What is significant in this list is the number of symbols that did thrive within the religion of Israel, and have since ceased to be prominent symbols for the expression of the nature of God. Tillich seems to suggest that each epoch discovers its own symbols, and perhaps one of the difficulties facing us today is that the older symbols no longer have the same revealing power for us that they once did, while we have few new symbols with which to replace them.

It is important to recognize that symbols only point to that which they symbolize; they are not identical with that reality. Idolatry results when the difference between symbols and that which is symbolized is erased. There is a certain conditionality to symbols: they are born, and they die. If ever a symbol is absolutized, it becomes instead an idol.

---

[1] Ian Ramsey, *Christian Empiricism* (Grand Rapids, Mich.: William B. Eerdmans Publishing Company, 1974), pp. 121ff.

THE LEVELS OF RELIGIOUS SYMBOLS

Symbolic language about God has attempted to speak of two levels of God's reality: the transcendent dimension, or God as more real than, and in some sense "beyond," physical reality; and the immanent dimension, which speaks of the experience of the reality of God within the world. How are we to express the transcendent dimension, that is, how are we to speak of God as the ultimate reality, or to use one of Tillich's favorite expressions, the "ground of being"? We could call God simply *being* itself, a favorite term for the philosophers of the Middle Ages, but it is difficult to see how we could relate to that which is described only as "ultimate being." Here the symbol of "person" seems appropriate, for person is the highest expression of what we ourselves are. The symbol of personhood is also a fertile symbol in that it allows us to express an understanding of God in terms of the highest qualities we experience in ourselves—love and mercy. At the immanent level, however, we speak of God as present within the world. Tillich points out that incarnations of the divine have been present in many religions, and Christianity is not unique in speaking of the divine becoming man. What Tillich does not point out, however, is that there was nothing in Judaism to support the idea of the incarnate manifestation of God; this was foreign to the religious experience of Israel. Although Christianity had its roots in Judaism, the Christian claim that Jesus was the divine become human was not acceptable to the Jewish religious sensibility.

Christianity not only speaks of the incarnation of God but also of the continued presence of God within the world. Tillich points out that the Christian sacraments are one of the symbolic modes of this expression. The Lord's Supper and baptism are symbolic, but to say this is not to imply that they are only signs pointing to past events but that they participate in the Holy which they symbolize.

THE TRUTH OF SYMBOLS

Finally, the question of the truth of symbols must be raised. Tillich claims that symbols are immune to empirical criticism, Such criticism would deal only with the literal meaning of terms, but the symbolic function of language goes beyond the literal meaning to a new level of self-understanding that can arise in no other way. Symbols are "true" when they adequately express this self-understanding, and Tillich has suggested that symbols are born out of a group's collective experience. Perhaps it would be better to speak of symbols as being either "adequate" or "inadequate" as a means of expressing the Holy or the Ultimate. A true symbol would then be one that succeeds in its role of opening up new levels of reality and corresponding levels of self-understanding.

We can hear echoes of Kierkegaard's view of truth as subjectivity. Symbols speak to the subjective thinker rather than the objective, and any criterion of meaning that would eliminate the religious use of language, which is thoroughly symbolic, would eliminate most other nonliteral uses of language as well. Tillich's analysis points up the irreplaceable function of symbols, for whenever we speak of the deepest levels of human understanding we must resort to symbols. To say that religious language is symbolic is therefore not to say that it is less meaningful than literal language, but rather more meaningful. Many of us, however, are so influenced by literal-minded prejudices that to say something is symbolic is tantamount to saying it is *merely* symbolic. But human beings seem to surround themselves with symbols in nonreligious as well as religious contexts. Poetry, art, music would be nonexistent if there were not a symbolic level of expression. We could reject symbolism as something to avoid, but the result of this would be a drastic narrowing of the range of meaningful expression. Rejecting symbolism would perhaps lessen the complexity of language, but at the same time it would close off other levels of meaning which can only be achieved through symbolic expression.

Religious Symbols*

The fact that there is so much discussion about the meaning of symbols going on in this country as well as in Europe is a symptom of something deeper, something both negative and positive in its import. It is a symptom of the fact that we are in a confusion of language in theology and philosophy and related subjects which has hardly been surpassed at any time in history. Words do not communicate to us any more what they originally did and what they were invented to communicate. This has something to do with the fact that our present culture has no clearing house such as medieval scholasticism was, Protestant scholasticism in the 17th century at least tried to be, and philosophers like Kant tried to renew. We have no such clearing house, and this is the one point at which we might be in sympathy with the present day so-called logical positivists or symbolic logicians or logicians generally. They at least try to produce a clearing house. The only criticism is that this clearing house is a very small room, perhaps only a corner of a house, and not a real house. It excludes most of life. But it could become useful if it increased in reach and acceptance of realities beyond the mere logical calculus.

The positive point is that we are in a process in which a very important thing is being rediscovered: namely, that there are levels of reality of great difference, and that these different levels demand different approaches and different languages; not everything in reality can be grasped by the language which is most adequate for mathematical sci-

*Source: Paul Tillich, "The Nature of Religious Language," *The Christian Scholar*, XXXVIII, 3, September, 1955. Used by permission.

ences. The insight into this situation is the most positive side of the fact that the problem of symbols is again taken seriously.

Let us proceed with the intention of clearing concepts as much as we are able, and let us take five steps, the first of which is the discussion of "symbols and signs." Symbols are similar to signs in one decisive respect: both symbols and signs point beyond themselves to something else. The typical sign, for instance the red light at the corner of the street, does not point to itself but it points to the necessity of cars stopping. And every symbol points beyond itself to a reality for which it stands. In this, symbols and signs have an essential identity—they point beyond themselves. And this is the reason that the confusion of language mentioned above has also conquered the discussion about symbols for centuries and has produced confusion between signs and symbols. The first step in any clearing up of the meaning of symbols is to distinguish it from the meaning of signs.

The difference, which is a fundamental difference between them is that signs do not participate in any way in the reality and power of that to which they point. Symbols, although they are not the same as that which they symbolize, participate in its meaning and power. The difference between symbol and sign is the participation in the symbolized reality which characterizes the symbols, and the non-participation in the "pointed-to" reality which characterizes a sign. For example, letters of the alphabet as they are written, an "A" or an "R" do not participate in the sound to which they point; on the other hand, the flag participates in the power of the king or the nation for which it stands and which it symbolizes. There has, therefore, been a fight since the days of William Tell as to how to behave in the presence of the flag. This would be meaningless if the flag did not participate as a symbol in the power of that which it symbolizes. The whole monarchic idea is itself entirely incomprehensible, if you do not understand that the king always is both: on the one hand, a symbol of the power of the group of which he is the king and on the other hand, he who exericses partly (never fully, of course) this power.

But something has happened which is very dangerous for all our attempts to find a clearing house for the concepts of symbols and signs. The mathematician has usurped the term "symbol" for mathematical "sign," and this makes a disentanglement of the confusion almost impossible. The only thing we can do is to distinguish different groups, signs which are called symbols, and genuine symbols. The mathematical signs are signs which are wrongly called symbols.

Language is a very good example of the difference between signs and symbols. Words in a language are signs for a meaning which they express. The word "desk" is a sign which points to something quite different—namely, the thing on which a paper is lying and at which we might be looking. This has nothing to do with the word "desk," with these four letters. But there are words in every language which are more than this, and in the moment in which they get connotations which go beyond something to which they point as signs, then they can become symbols; and this is a very important distinction for any speaker. He can speak almost completely in signs, reducing the meaning of his words almost to mathematical signs, and this is the absolute ideal of the logical positivist. The other pole of this is liturgical or poetic language where words have a power through centuries, or more than centuries. They have connotations in situations in which they appear so that they cannot be replaced. They have become not only signs pointing to a meaning which is defined, but also symbols standing for a reality in the power of which they participate.

Now we come to a second consideration dealing with the functions of symbols. The first function is implied in what has already been said—namely, the representative function. The symbol represents something which is not itself, for which it stands and in the power and meaning of which it participates. This is a basic function of every symbol, and therefore, if that word had not been used in so many other ways, one could perhaps even translate "symbolic" as "representative," but for some reason that is not possible. If the symbols stand for something which they are not, then the question is, "Why do we not have that for which they stand directly? Why do we need symbols at all?" And now we come to something which is perhaps the main function of the symbol—namely, the opening up of levels of reality which otherwise are hidden and cannot be grasped in any other way.

Every symbol opens up a level of reality for which nonsymbolic speaking is inadequate. Let us interpret this, or explain this, in terms of artistic symbols. The more we try to enter into the meaning of symbols, the more we become aware that it is a function of art to open up levels of reality; in poetry, in visual art, and in music, levels of reality are opened up which can be opened up in no other way. Now if this is the function of art, then certainly artistic creations have symbolic character. You can take that which a landscape of Rubens, for instance, mediates to you. You cannot have this experience in any other way than through this painting made by Rubens. This landscape has some heroic character; it has character of balance, of colors, of weights, of values, and so on. All this is very external. What this mediates to you cannot be expressed in any other way than through the painting itself. The same is true also in the relationship of poetry and philosophy. The temptation may often be to confuse the issue by bringing too many philosophical concepts into a poem. Now this is really the problem; one cannot do this. If one uses philosophical language or scientific language, it does not mediate the same thing which is mediated in the use of really poetic language without a mixture of any other language.

This example may show what is meant by the phrase "opening up of levels of reality." But in order to do this, something else must be opened up—namely, levels of the soul, levels of our interior reality. And they must correspond to the levels in exterior reality which are opened up by a symbol. So every symbol is two-edged. It opens up reality and it opens up the soul. There are, of course, people who are not opened up by music or who are not opened up by poetry, or more of them (especially in Protestant America) who are not opened up at all by visual arts. The "opening up" is a two-sided function—namely, reality in deeper levels and the human soul in special levels.

If this is the function of symbols then it is obvious that symbols cannot be replaced by other symbols. Every symbol has a special function which is just *it* and cannot be replaced by more or less adequate symbols. This is different from signs, for signs can always be replaced. If one finds that a green light is not so expedient as perhaps a blue light (this is not true, but could be true), then we simply put on a blue light, and nothing is changed. But a symbolic word (such as the word "God") cannot be replaced. No symbol can be replaced when used in its special function. So one asks rightly, "How do symbols arise, and how do they come to an end?" As different from signs, symbols are born and die. Signs are consciously invented and removed. This is a fundamental difference.

"Out of what womb are symbols born?" Out of the womb which is usually called today the "group unconscious" or "collective unconscious," or whatever you want to call it—out of a group which acknowledges, in this thing, this word, this flag, or whatever it may be, its own being. It is not invented intentionally; and even if somebody would try to invent a symbol, as sometimes happens, then it becomes a symbol only if the unconscious of a group says "yes" to it. It means that something is opened up by it in the sense which I have just described. Now this implies further that in the moment in which this inner situation of the human group to a symbol has ceased to exist, then the symbol dies. The symbol does not "say" anything any more. In this way, all of the polytheistic gods have died; the situation in which they were born, has changed or does not exist any more, and so the symbols died. But these are events which cannot be described in terms of intention and invention.

Now we come to a third consideration—namely, the nature of religious symbols. Religious symbols do exactly the same thing as all symbols do—namely, they open up a level of reality, which otherwise is not opened at all, which is hidden. We can call this the depth dimension of reality

itself, the dimension of reality which is the ground of every other dimension and every other depth, and which therefore, is not one level beside
the others but is the fundamental level, the level below all other levels, the
level of being itself, or the ultimate power of being. Religious symbols
open up the experience of the dimension of this depth in the human soul.
If a religious symbol has ceased to have this function, then it dies. And if
new symbols are born, they are born out of a changed relationship to the
ultimate ground of being, i.e., to the Holy.

The dimension of ultimate reality is the dimension of the Holy. And
so we can also say, religious symbols are symbols of the Holy. As such they
participate in the holiness of the Holy according to our basic definition of
a symbol. But participation is not identity; they are not themselves *the*
Holy. The wholly transcendent transcends every symbol of the Holy.
Religious symbols are taken from the infinity of material which the
experienced reality gives us. Everything in time and space has become at
some time in the history of religion a symbol for the Holy. And this is
naturally so, because everything that is in the world we encounter rests on
the ultimate ground of being. This is the key to the otherwise extremely
confusing history of religion. Those of you who have looked into this
seeming chaos of the history of religion in all periods of history from the
earliest primitives to the latest developments, will be extremely confused
about the chaotic character of this development. The key which makes
order out of this chaos is comparatively simple. It is that everything in
reality can impress itself as a symbol for a special relationship of the
human mind to its own ultimate ground and meaning. So in order to open
up the seemingly closed door to this chaos of religious symbols, one simply
has to ask, "What is the relationship to the ultimate which is symbolized in
these symbols?" And then they cease to be meaningless; and they become,
on the contrary, the most revealing creations of the human mind, the
most genuine ones, the most powerful ones, those who control the human
consciousness, and perhaps even more the unconsciousness, and have
therefore this tremendous tanacity which is characteristic of all religious
symbols in the history of religion.

Religion, as everything in life, stands under the law of ambiguity,
"ambiguity" meaning that it is creative and destructive at the same time.
Religion has its holiness and its unholiness, and the reason for this is
obvious from what has been said about religious symbolism. Religious
symbols point symbolically to that which transcends all of them. But since,
as symbols, they participate in that to which they point, they always have
the tendency (in the human mind, of course) to replace that to which they
are supposed to point, and to become ultimate in themselves. And in the
moment in which they do this, they become idols. All idolatry is nothing
else than the absolutizing of symbols of the Holy, and making them

identical with the Holy itself. In this way, for instance, holy persons can become a god. Ritual acts can take on unconditional validity, although they are only expressions of a special situation. In all sacramental activities of religion, in all holy objects, holy books, holy doctrines, holy rites, you find this danger which we will call "demonization." They become demonic at the moment in which they become elevated to the unconditional and ultimate character of the Holy itself.

Now we turn to a fourth consideration—namely, the levels of religious symbols. There are two fundamental levels in all religious symbols: the transcendent level, the level which goes *beyond* the empirical reality we encounter, and the immanent level, the level which we find *within* the encounter with reality. Let us look at the first level, the transcendent level. The basic symbol on the transcendent level would be God himself. But we cannot simply say that God is a symbol. We must always say two things about him: we must say that there is a non-symbolic element in our image of God—namely, that he is ultimate reality, being itself, ground of being, power of being; and the other, that he is the highest being in which everything that we have does exist in the most perfect way. If we say this we have in our mind the image of a highest being, a being with the characteristics of highest perfection. That means we have a symbol for that which is not symbolic in the idea of God—namely, "Being Itself."

It is important to distinguish these two elements in the idea of God. Thus all of these discussions going on about God being a person or not a person, God being similar to other beings or not similar, these discussions which have a great impact on the destruction of the religious experience through false interpretations of it, could be overcome if we would say, "Certainly the awareness of something unconditional is in itself what it is, is not symbolic." We can call it *"Being Itself," esse qua esse, esse ipsum,* as the scholastics did. But in our relationship to this ultimate we symbolize and must symbolize. We could not be in communication with God if he were only "ultimate being." But in our relationship to him we encounter him with the highest of what we ourselves are, *person.* And so in the symbolic form of speaking about him, we have both that which transcends infinitely our experience of ourselves as persons, and that which is so adequate to our being persons that we can say, "Thou" to God, and can pray to him. And these two elements must be preserved. If we preserve only the element of the unconditional, then no relationship to God is possible. If we preserve only the element of the ego-thou relationship, as it is called today, we lose the element of the divine—namely, the unconditional which transcends subject and object and all other polarities. This is the first point on the transcendent level.

The second is the qualities, the attributes of God, whatever you say about him: that he is love, that he is mercy, that he is power, that he is omniscient, that he is omnipresent, that he is almighty. These attributes of God are taken from experienced qualities we have ourselves. They cannot be applied to God in the literal sense. If this is done, it leads to an infinite amount of absurdities. This again is one of the reasons for the destruction of religion through wrong communicative interpretation of it. And again the symbolic character of these qualities must be maintained consistently. Otherwise, every speaking about the divine becomes absurd.

A third element on the transcendent level is the acts of God, for example, when we say, "He has created the world," "He has sent his son," "He will fulfill the world." In all these temporal, casual, and other expressions we speak symbolically of God. As an example, look at the one small sentence: *"God has sent his son."* Here we have in the word "has" temporality. But God is beyond *our* temporality, though not beyond every temporality. Here is space; "sending somebody" means moving him from one place to another place. This certainly is speaking symbolically, although spatiality is in God as an element in his creative ground. We say that he "has sent"—that means that he has caused something. In this way God is subject to the category of causality. And when we speak of him and his Son, we have two different substances and apply the category of substance to him. Now all this, if taken literally, is absurd. If it is taken symbolically, it is a profound expression, the ultimate Christian expression, of the relationship between God and man in the Christian experience. But to distinguish these two kinds of speech, the non-symbolic and the symbolic, in such a point is so important that if we are not able to make understandable to our contemporaries that we speak symbolically when we use such language, they will rightly turn away from us, as from people who still live in absurdities and superstitions.

Now consider the immanent level, the level of the appearances of the divine in time and space. Here we have first of all the incarnations of the divine, different beings in time and space, divine beings transmuted into animals or men or any kinds of other beings as they appear in time and space. This is often forgotten by those within Christianity who like to use in every second theological proposition the word "incarnation." They forget that this is not an especially Christian characteristic, because incarnation is something which happens in paganism all the time. The divine beings always incarnate in different forms. That is very easy in paganism. This is not the real distinction between Christianity and other religions.

Here we must say something about the relationships of the transcendent to the immanent level just in connection with the incarnation idea. Historically, one must say that preceding both of them was the situation in which the transcendent and immanent were not distinguished. In the Indonesian doctrine of "Mana," that divine mystical power which permeates all reality, we have some divine presence which is both immanent in everything as a hidden power, and at the same time transcendent, something which can be grasped only through very difficult ritual activities known to the priest.

Out of this identity of the immanent and the transcendent, the gods of the great mythologies have developed in Greece and in the Semitic nations and in India. There we find incarnations as the immanent element of the divine. The more transcendent the gods become, the more incarnations of personal or sacramental character are needed in order to overcome the remoteness of the divine which develops with the strengthening of the transcendent element.

And from this follows the second element in the immanent religious symbolism, namely, the sacramental. The sacramental is nothing else than some reality becoming the bearer of the Holy in a special way and under special circumstances. In this sense, the Lord's Supper, or better the materials in the Lord's Supper, are symbolic. Now you will ask perhaps, "only symbolic?" That sounds as if there were something more than symbolic, namely, "literal." But the literal is not more but less than symbolic. If we speak of those dimensions of reality which we cannot approach in any other way than by symbols, then symbols are not used in terms of "only" but in terms of that which is necessary, of that which we *must* apply. Sometimes, because of nothing more than the confusion of signs with symbols, the phrase "only a symbol" means "only a sign." And then the question is justified. "Only a sign?" "No." The sacrament is not only a sign. In the famous discussion between Luther and Zwingli, in Marburg in 1529, it was just this point on which the discussion was held. Luther wanted to maintain the genuinely symbolic character of the elements, but Zwingli said that the sacramental materials, bread and wine, are "only symbolic." Thus Zwingli meant that they are only signs pointing to a story of the past. Even in that period there was semantic confusion. And let us not be mislead by this. In the real sense of symbol, the sacramental materials are symbols. But if the symbol is used as *only* symbol (i.e., only signs), then of course the sacramental materials are more than this.

Then there is the third element on the immanent level. Many things—like special parts of the church building, like the candles, like the water at the entrance of the Roman Church, like the cross in all churches, especially Protestant churches—were originally only signs, but in use became symbols; call them sign-symbols, signs which have become symbols.

And now a last consideration—namely, the truth of religious symbols. Here we must distinguish a negative, a positive, and an absolute statement.First the negative statement. Symbols are independent of any empirical criticism. You cannot kill a symbol by criticism in terms of natural sciences or in terms of historical research. As was said, symbols can only die if the situation in which they have been created has passed. They are not on a level on which empirical criticism can dismiss them. Here are two examples, both connected with Mary, the mother of Jesus, as Holy Virgin. First of all you have here a symbol which has died in Protestantism by the changed situation of the relation to God. The special, direct, immediate relationship to God, makes any mediating power impossible. Another reason which has made this symbol disappear is the negation of the ascetic element which is implied in the glorification of virginity. And as long as the Protestant religious situation lasts it cannot be re-established. It has not died because Protestant scholars have said, "Now there is no empirical reason for saying all this about the Holy Virgin." There certainly is not, but this the Roman Church also knows. But the Roman Church sticks to it on the basis of its tremendous symbolic power which step by step brings her nearer to Trinity itself, especially in the development of the last decade. If this should ever be completed as is now discussed in groups of the Roman Church, Mary would become co-Saviour with Jesus. Then, whether this is admitted or not, she is actually taken into the divinity itself.

Another example is the story of the virginal birth of Jesus. This is from the point of view of historical research a most obviously legendary story, unknown to Paul and to John. It is a late creation, trying to make understandable the full possession of the divine Spirit of Jesus of Nazareth. But again its legendary character is not the reason why this symbol will die or has died in many groups of people, in even quite conservative groups within the Protestant churches. The reason is different. The reason is that it is theologically quasiheretical. It takes away one of the fundamental doctrines of Chalcedon, viz., the classical Christian doctrine that the full humanity of Jesus must be maintained beside his whole divinity. A human being who has no human father has no full humanity. This story then has to be criticized on inner-symbolic grounds, but not on historical grounds. This is the negative statement about the truth of religious symbols. Their truth is their adequacy to the religious situation in which they are created, and their inadequacy to another situation is their untruth. In the last sentence both the positive and the negative statement about symbols are contained.

Religion is ambiguous and every religious symbol may become idolatrous, may be demonized, may elevate itself to ultimate validity although nothing is ultimate but the ultimate itself; no religious doctrine and no religious ritual may be. If Christianity claims to have a truth superior to any other truth in its symbolism, then it is the symbol of the cross in which this is expressed, the cross of the Christ. He who himself embodies the fullness of the divine's presence sacrifices himself in order not to become an idol, another god beside God, a god into whom the disciples wanted to make him. And therefore the decisive story is the story in which he accepts the title "Christ" when Peter offers it to him. He accepts it under the one condition that he has to go to Jerusalem to suffer and to die, which means to deny the idolatrous tendency even with respect to himself. This is at the same time the criterion of all other symbols, and it is the criterion to which every Christian church should subject itself.

DISCUSSION QUESTIONS

1. Would you agree that most persons think that symbols do not provide additional insight but are merely ornamental? If so, to what would you attribute this prejudice against symbols?

2. Do you find the distinction between sign and symbol defensible? If so, can you give additional examples? If not, why not?

3. Using Tillich's analysis of the different levels of religious symbols, examine some of the religious symbols currently in use to determine to which level they point.

4. Which traditional religious symbols do you think no longer speak forcibly to contemporary persons? Using Tillich's analysis, how would you account for this?

5. Do you agree that to say that religious symbols can be born and can die implies that each generation must find symbols that work for it? Can you give some examples?

6. What is your reaction to the claim that religious symbols are more meaningful than the literal use of language?

H. P. OWEN

The Analogical Use
of
Language

In a marvelously inventive fable called *Flatland,* Edwin A. Abbott describes a country in which there are only two dimensions—length and breadth. Nothing in Flatland has height. Into this two-dimensional world comes a sphere from spaceland who tries to communicate to an inhabitant of Flatland that it is a solid having height. All this is too much for the Flatlander to understand, so the Spaceland sphere has to resort to analogy using the only thing within the Flatlander's experience that is appropriate: a circle. Although the sphere is not literally a circle, it must try to explain to the Flatlander what a sphere is using the notion of circle: "I am not a plane Figure, but a Solid. You call me a Circle; but in reality I am not a Circle, but an infinite number of Circles . . . your country of Two Dimensions is not spacious enough to represent me, a being of Three, but can only exhibit a slice or section of me, which is what you call a Circle."[1]

With respect to God, we are like the Flatlander. Limited as we are in intelligence, bound as we are to finite experience, we are unable to think or speak of God as God really is, and nothing we can say about God is literally true in the same sense as when applied to finite human experience. We are forced to use human language and images drawn from human experience when we talk about God. And like the Flatlander attempting to understand a sphere, we must resort to analogy when speaking of God.

No treatment of the topic of religious language would be complete without consideration of analogy, for one of the oldest defenses of the legitimacy of religious

---

[1] Edwin A. Abbot, *Flatland: A Romance of Many Dimensions,* 6th ed., (New York: Dover Publication, Inc., 1952), p. 73.

language is to analyze it in terms of the analogical function of language. The basic distinctions go all the way back to Aristotle, and the analogical use of language in religious discourse was thoroughly explored by St. Thomas Aquinas in the thirteenth century. The topic is no mere medieval curiosity, however, for as the following reading from the contemporary theologian H. P. Owen shows, the doctrine of analogy is still in the forefront of the current discussion of the nature of religious language. Discussions of analogy, as is the case with much of the discussion of the nature of language, frequently are quite technical. But a careful study of the issues raised by Owen will reveal some of the questions that currently are being raised in the discussion of analogy.[2]

The problem is basically this: how "can the concepts and images which we draw from our experience be applicable to God?" One response is to adopt the *via negativa* (the negative way) of theological discourse. Recognizing that nothing we can say of God means quite the same thing as it does when applied to objects within human experience, we should only refer to the divine attributes in terms of what God is *not:* God is *not* finite, God is *not* evil, God is *not* material, and so forth. Though the *via negativa* remains a valuable corrective to sloppily made statements about God, it by itself is not a sufficient mode of religious discourse. Among the objections Owen raises to the *via negativa,* two principal ones stand out. First, a negative utterance does not have the same connotation as does a positive one. If you were to say of a friend, "Susan is not untruthful," and someone asked, "Do you mean to say that Susan always tells the truth?" and you replied, "I didn't say that; I meant only that she is not untruthful," your response would be perceived as casting doubt on Susan's truthfulness. You did not mean to do this at all, yet your negative utterance had this connotation. The second objection to the *via negativa* is that it simply is not compatible with the language of scripture and devotion. Try to recast the Lord's Prayer into the language of the *via negativa* and see just how unsatisfactory this sort of language is. Additionally, it is difficult to be consistent in the use of the *via negativa,* for we want to speak positively of God, not just negatively.

We have inherited from the ancient Greek philosophers several basic distinctions in the way language functions, and one of these important distinctions is the difference between the univocal and equivocal use of language. A word is used *univocally* when it has more or less the same meaning when applied to different objects. We can speak of a beautiful day, a beautiful painting, a beautiful automobile, a beautiful person, and so forth, with generally the same meaning attached to the word "beautiful." There is some difference in meaning depending on the context, but there is no major shift of meaning in the various uses. When such a major shift of meaning occurs, a term is said to be used *equivocally,* and when words are used equivocally in an argument, the argument becomes invalid. Consider the following: John is poor (i.e., has no money) and is a student; thus John must be a poor (i.e., incompetent) student. There is no valid inference here, since "poor" has two different meanings in this sentence, and the shift in meaning from its first use to its second use renders the argument fallacious.

The problem for religious language emerges because neither the univocal nor

[2]Examples of the ongoing debate about analogical language are represented by the following books: Frederick Ferré, *Language, Logic and God* (New York: Harper & Row, 1961) and E. L. Mascall, *Existence and Analogy* (London: Longmans, Green, 1949).

equivocal use of language seems to allow us to speak positively about God. We cannot claim that positive statements about God are univocal, since the nature of God is such that no terms applied to God have the same meaning as when applied to us. Yet we would not want to say that language used of God is equivocal, that is, has totally different meanings than when applied to finite beings, for this would make theological utterances meaningless. We must find a third way of using language to speak of God, and this third way is analogy.

First, let's be clear about what an analogy is. An analogy is basically a comparison of two or more things in terms of their likeness, in a way that also recognizes their differences. Analogy does not ignore the differences between the things being compared, but instead focuses on their similarities. Analogies are frequently used in various kinds of achievement tests, and there the form is usually: "A is to B as C is to?," and the test taker is asked to supply the missing analogue. There is nothing strange about the analogical use of language, and we resort to it more frequently than you may at first think. For example, if you say that your cat is intelligent, you are speaking analogically. What you mean is that even though you are different from your cat, there is a resemblance between your nature and your intelligence and your cat's nature and its intelligence. The following diagram will illustrate these relations:

$$\frac{\text{Intelligence}}{\text{\textit{(fuller meaning)}}} \quad \overset{..}{..} \quad \frac{\text{Intelligence}}{\text{\textit{(limited meaning)}}}$$
$$\text{Your Nature} \qquad\qquad \text{Cat's Nature}$$

We can call this a downward analogy, since you are going from a fuller understanding of the term intelligence to a limited application of the term to your cat. The value of the analogical way of speaking is that it recognizes that human beings are different from cats, but also recognizes the similar meanings of *intelligence* when applied to different kinds of creatures. In this example human intelligence supplies the fuller meaning of the term, which is only partially applicable to feline intelligence.

Now reverse the process. We will begin with a limited sense of the term and apply it analogously to God in a fuller sense.

$$\frac{\text{Intelligence}}{\text{\textit{(limited meaning)}}} \quad \overset{..}{..} \quad \frac{\text{Intelligence}}{\text{\textit{(fuller meaning)}}}$$
$$\text{Your Nature} \qquad\qquad \text{God's Nature}$$

Since God's nature is so much greater than ours, God's intelligence is correspondingly greater than our own limited intelligence, the attribution of intelligence to God is an upward analogy in that human intelligence supplies only the partial, and limited, sense of the term.

TWO TYPES OF ANALOGY

Reflecting a medieval distinction, Owen points out that there are two different types of analogies, called the *Analogy of Attribution* and the *Analogy of Proportionality*. The Analogy of Attribution is sometimes called the *Analogy of Proportion,* but it is easy to confuse this with the second type of analogy, so we will always refer to the first type of analogy as the Analogy of Attribution.

The Analogy of Attribution

In this type of analogy, the predicate or quality attributed in the analogy properly belongs to only one of the things being compared. The classic example of this type of analogy (and the example used by Aristotle) is the use of the term "health." Health, properly speaking, is a quality that belongs to human beings, yet we can refer to nonhuman things as healthy in an analogous sense. If someone said, "Move to Florida because the climate of Florida is healthy," this could not be taken literally because a climate cannot possess the quality of health. But a statement of this kind is appropriate if understood as an analogical use of language, since to say that Florida's climate is "healthy" means that it is a cause of health or contributes to the health of human beings.

The analogy of attribution is not an effective mode of analogical predication when speaking of God for the following reason: the traditional view is that God is the cause of everything in nature. Therefore, according to the analogy of attribution, it would be proper to speak of God in terms of anything of which God is the cause. Since God caused everything, there would be no limit to what we could attribute to God. For example, we could say that God is material, since God created all material things. But this plainly won't do, since the usual affirmations about God are that God is not material but rather spiritual.

The Analogy of Proportionality

In this type of analogy, the quality or predicate is said to belong properly to both of the things being compared, although it belongs to them in different ways. The analogy previously given comparing human and feline intelligence was an analogy of proportionality. The intelligence attributed to the cat really belongs to the cat but is proportionate to the cat's nature, just as the intelligence attributed to a human being is proportionate to human nature. There is a major problem with this type of analogy. When we speak of cats being intelligent, we at least know something—in fact, quite a lot—about the nature of cats. But we do not know God's nature; that is we do not claim to understand the fullness of God's reality. We must say, therefore, only that we are claiming to say *that* God is wise, good, personal, and so forth, not *how* God possesses each of the attributes. Here the *via negativa* has a proper application, for each of the terms used to speak of God must be freed from its finite limitations before being applied to God.

FURTHER PROBLEMS WITH ANALOGY

In the concluding sections of the reading, Owen considers four additional objections to the analogical use of language. The first two are based on the mathematical analysis of analogy; the last two are more general in nature.

First Objection

Consider the following mathematical analogy: 3 is to 6 as 4 is to x. It is easy to solve a problem like this, since we know three terms of the analogy. But suppose the analogy were the following: 3 is to 6 as y is to x. We would be unable to solve this mathematical analogy, for y and x could be any number of different quantities. In the case of religious analogies, we know only two of the terms; we know nothing of God's nature, and therefore we are not entitled to speak analogously of any of God's attributes.

Owen replies that theistic analogies are not intended to be modeled strictly after mathematical analogies, and beyond this general response, he offers two additional replies. First, it is not the case that God is totally unknown to us. We have a limited and partial understanding of the nature of God and in terms of this can determine that some analogies are proper and others are not. Secondly, the doctrine of analogy does not commit us to the claim that we thoroughly understand the attributes we predicate of God; we can affirm *that* God is wise without also claiming that we understand *how* God is wise.

Second Objection

The second objection is more technical but is again based on what critics see as a faulty mathematical relationship. The traditional affirmations about God go beyond saying merely that God possesses goodness, for example, but say instead that God *is* good; that is, in God there is an identity of God's goodness and God's nature. But in the analogy we cannot say that human goodness is identical with human nature, for sometimes we are good, sometimes we are not, whereas God is always good. In a mathematical analogy it would be incorrect to say that two of the terms in the analogy are identical with each other but that the two other terms are not identical. Owen's response is that the criticism tries illegitimately to force onto theistic analogies the ratios of mathematical analogies. The whole point behind the use of religious analogy is to underscore both the likeness and the unlikeness of creator and creature. In the relationship of likeness we can compare divine goodness to human goodness. But it is precisely because of the unlikeness of human beings and God that we have to resort to the analogical use of language.

Third Objection

The third objection is similar to the second. A frequent objection to religious analogies is that there is really no identity between God and humankind; that being the case, there really is no basis for an analogy at all, and anything we say about God is equivocal. Owen again appeals to the principle of likeness and unlikeness. In some respects the creature is like the creator; in other respects the creature is totally unlike the creator. The use of analogy is intended to underscore the likeness without claiming an identity between the creator and the creature by simultaneously affirming the unlikeness of mankind and God.

Fourth Objection

If we believe that God's goodness is unknowable, then how can we claim that any analogy which compares human goodness to divine goodness is appropriate? Owen's response is to remind us that we begin with an understanding of what goodness means when applied to finite creatures. From this partial understanding of the meaning of the term we apply it to God, recognizing, however, that it is applied to God in a vaster sense than it has for finite beings. Again we must say that we can affirm a quality of God without claiming to exhaust the understanding of this term.

At every point we hedge when we make statements about God. But if we were to qualify language used about God completely, we would wind up saying nothing. Clearly the language of devotion requires that we be able to say something positive about God. The upshot of this is that we must admit that all language used to speak about God speaks of God only imperfectly and indirectly. We must also admit that nothing we say about God means quite the same thing as when applied to finite creatures (and this is an appropriate application of the *via negativa);* yet we can legitimately speak of God indirectly, using finite language based on finite human experience, Analogical language captures this sense of difference between human-kind and God but allows us to speak positively about God, though indirectly.

The Doctrine of Analogy*

The problem that faces the theist is this. God is infinite and incorporeal; but we, and all created things within this spatio-temporal universe, are finite and corporeal. How, then, can the concepts and images which we draw from our experience be applicable to God?

So far as *Christian* theism is concerned, the problem is crystallized in the affirmation of divine personality. God, we say, is personal. He has an intelligence and will that cohere in a subject-self; he is an "I" whom we address as "Thou" in prayer; he is the Love by which we are created and redeemed. Yet the only form of personality we know is our human one. How, then, can we apply terms taken from our finite and corporeal life to the life of the infinite and incorporeal Godhead?

Some theologians are reluctant to speak of God as personal. God, they say, is supra-personal. For the moment it is enough to reply that we are certainly to call God supra-personal if we are thinking of personality

*Source: H. P. Owen, *The Christian Knowledge of God* (London: University of London, The Athlone Press, 1969), pp. 207–14. © H. P. Owen 1969. Used by permission.

in its human form. But if we are theists (and especially if we are Christians) we cannot avoid speaking of God in terms drawn from our human form of personality. We cannot avoid it by calling him "spiritual" (instead of "personal"); for the only type of spirituality we know is the one with which we are acquainted in our personal existence.

In view of the difficulty involved in applying finite terms to God it is tempting to adopt the "negative way" *(via negativa)* in its undiluted form. According to this way, when we say that God is personal we are entitled to assert only that he is not impersonal. We should then take the same course when referring spiritual attributes to him. In calling him "wise" or "good" we should mean no more than that he is not foolish or wicked.

This purely negative approach is exposed to four unanswerable objections.

(a) It is not a reformulation, but an outright denial, of theism. The statement "God is not evil" is not equivalent to the statement "God is good." It may seem unnecessary to make so elementary a point. But exponents of the *via negativa* sometimes give the impression that they are conserving all that positive theology contains.

(b) The *via negativa,* if taken as a self-sufficient interpretation of theistic language, produces nonsense. What should we think of the following conversation between A and B on the subject of their mutual friend X? "I have always found that X never lies," says A. "You mean," B replies, "that X is always truthful." "Dear me, no," A answers. "I shouldn't go as far as that." Doubtless religious language functions in unique ways; but it cannot make any sense at all if it offends the first principles of reasoning.

(c) In fact every theist (however subtle he may be) is sooner or later bound to forsake the *via negativa.* He may be able to keep up an appearance of saying something that he considers meaningful when he speaks in a wholly negative way of the divine attributes. Yet if he were asked whether God transcends the world, could he seriously answer: "I don't know, but I'm sure he is not identical with it"?

(d) This use of the *via negativa* is incompatible with the language of the Bible and the requirements of worship. According to the Bible, God is *ultimately* personal; he is the Father in whose image every human person is created. Equally, worship implies that God, in his ultimate reality, is a personal being with whom we can commune.

Therefore, we cannot speak of God's personality in purely negative terms. The *via negativa* has its part to play (as I shall shortly show). But it must be based on the positive, or affirmative, way which I shall now examine.

There are three modes of positive predication: the univocal, the equivocal, and the analogical. We cannot predicate any terms of God univocally (that is, in the same senses that they have when applied to finite beings); for he is infinite. Also, we cannot predicate terms of him equivocally (that is, in totally different senses from the ones which they have when applied to finite beings); for our words would then be meaningless. Therefore, if we are to speak of him positively, we must do so by an analogical mode of predication.

It is necessary to distinguish between two types of analogy. In both types the same predicate (the analogue) is applied to different objects (the analogates); but they differ in their modes of application. According to the first (the analogy of attribution or proportion) the predicate actually (or formally) belongs to one (but not the other) of the objects. According to the second (the analogy of proportionality) both objects actually possess the predicate.

The concept of "health" is often used to illustrate the first type of analogy. Thus we can say both of a place that "it," and of a man that "he," is healthy. Yet health actually belongs to the man only. In calling the place healthy we mean merely that it is the cause of health in its inhabitants.

The concept of "life" illustrates the second type of analogy. When we say of a man that he, or of a plant that it, is living (or animate) we mean that life inheres in both of them (as it does not, for example, in a stone). But each possesses life in a manner that is proportionate to its nature. Thus we can construct the formula: "the life of a man is to the essence of a man as the life of a plant is to the essence of a plant."

Let us now apply these two types of analogy to personal theism. According to the first, when we say that God is personal we mean merely that he is the cause of personality in finite beings. But this is not all we mean. We mean exactly what we say—that God is personal "in himself." There is a further reason why the analogy of proportion cannot be theistically self-sufficient. We do not attribute to God's nature all the properties of which he is the cause. Thus we do not say that because he creates material bodies he himself is bodily.

Therefore we must resort to the analogy of proportionality. Personal attributes actually inhere in God; but they do so in a manner appropriate to his essence. Thus, though God is good, he is not good as we are good. His goodness corresponds to his self-existent being. He *is* goodness, just as he *is* all his attributes, in one eternal act.

Yet this at once raises a major problem. We do not know God's essence. Therefore we cannot understand the manner in which his attributes belong to him. In any comparison between God and man we understand the analogue only in the human analogate. Its mode of being in the divine analogate is permanently hidden from us in this life. Hence there is not a complete comparison between our use of analogy in the finite realm and our use of it in religion. When we interpret another person's character by analogy with our own we can (to some extent at least) imaginatively "enter into" his experience; for we are fellow-members of the human species. But we cannot enter into God's experience; for we cannot share his Godhood (or *aseitas*).[1]

Consequently, in our theistic use of the analogy of proportionality we must distinguish (as Aquinas did) between the object signified (*res significata*) and the mode of signification (*modus significandi*). Frederick Copleston expresses the distinction thus:

> None of the positive ideas by means of which we conceive the nature of God represent God perfectly. Our ideas of God represent God only in so far as these objects represent or mirror God, so that in as much as creatures represent God or mirror him only imperfectly, our ideas derived from our experience of the natural world, can themselves represent God only imperfectly. When we say that God is good or living, we mean that he contains, or rather is the perfection of, goodness or life, but in a manner which exceeds and excludes all the imperfections and limitations of creatures. As regards *what is predicated* (goodness, for example), the affirmative predicate which we predicate of God signifies a perfection without any defect; but as regards the *manner of predicating* it every such predicate involves a defect, for by the word (*nomen*) we express something in the way it is conceived by the intellect. It follows, then, that predicates of this kind may, as the Pseudo-Dionysius observed, be both affirmed and denied of God; affirmed *propter nominis rationem*, denied *propter significandi modum*.[2]

Hence, though we can predicate personality of God we cannot understand its mode of being. We know *that* God is personal; but *how* he is personal we do not know. The doctrine of analogy does not "explain" his nature in the sense of "making it plain" to our understanding. Rather it states a mystery which no human mind can pierce.

Therefore the positive way must be supplemented by the *via negativa*. In applying personal terms to God we must negate them. We must free them from their finite limitations before we can predicate them of infinite existence. I believe, and hope to show, that this activity of negation is not only a necessary, but also a rational, procedure.

The analogy of proportionality has been attacked on four main grounds. The first and second of these have recently been stated thus by G. E. M. Anscombe and P. T. Geach:

[1] Berkeley attenuates this difference in a manner that betrays the influence of his empiricism. In his *Alciphron* (4. 20) he adds (after a correct account of Cajetan) that God is an intelligent being "in the same sense with other spirits, though not in the same imperfect manner." As A. C. Fraser notes in his edition, Berkeley thus makes our knowledge of God and our knowledge of other, finite, spirits different only in degree.

[2] *A History of Philosophy*, Vol. 2 (London 1954, p. 351); cf. B. Mondin, *The Principle of Analogy* (The Hague 1963, pp. 93–102).

This is, of course, a mathematical metaphor—"x is to a as b is to c; required to find x"—and it is a thoroughly bad one. A rule-of-three sum can be worked only if three of the quantities involved are known; but God is not "known" in the relevant sense—i.e. something encountered as an item in the world. Moreover, since God's wisdom is supposedly identical with God, but not man's wisdom with man, the metaphor breaks down at once; for we cannot have in mathematics that x is to a as b is to c, and x=a, but not b=c.[3]

Both these objections rest on the assumption that theistic analogies are meant to be identical with mathematical ratios, and that if they are not so they are invalid. This assumption is groundless. The authors make it because of their pre-occupation with logic at the expense of metaphysics, and with the mathematical form of logic at the expense of other forms. But theists do not adopt the analogy of proportionality through a preference for a mathematical form of reasoning; they adopt it because it is the form which best expresses a metaphysical truth—the truth of the *ontological* relation that exists between God and his creatures.

Bearing these general considerations in mind, let us look at each objection. To the first of them two answers can be given. Firstly, God is not entirely unknown before the application of predicates; he is defined as self-existent being; and this definition determines the predicates' reference. Secondly, the theist obviously cannot "find" God's attributes; but he can *affirm* them—as the authors admit in the next paragraph when they state that we can "know that" God is wise and just although we cannot have "insight into" his wisdom or justice because his essence is incomprehensible. The second objection is weightier. It is, of course, true that on account of God's simplicity the analogy breaks down in the way the authors indicate; but (a) since we cannot conceive God's simplicity we are bound to consider his attributes and his nature separately (that is, from the standpoint of our own finite being), (b) from this standpoint the ratio holds, (c) the ratio does not specify the mode in which attributes inhere in God but merely asserts that they *do* inhere in a mode proportionate to his being.

In any case the important point is not the logical form of the analogy but its metaphysical content. Even if we discard the "ratio"-form we shall have to conserve its content if we wish (as Anscombe and Geach wish) to make straightforward statements concerning God which are neither equivocal nor univocal. If we want to say "God is wise" we can do so only by asserting (a) that there is both a likeness and an unlikeness between divine and human wisdom, (b) that the unlikeness is constituted by the difference between the self-existent and contingent modes in which the two

[3]*Three Philosophers* (Oxford 1961, p. 123).

forms of wisdom are exercised, and (c) that the likeness is constituted by the unique relation between the Creator and his spiritual creatures.

Thirdly, the doctrine of analogy has been found objectionable on the ground that, in order to avoid equivocality, it asserts an identity between God and man, but that "the supposition that any identity of characteristic can hold between God and man is incompatible with the fundamental theistic assumption that God is infinite."[4] But the doctrine does not assert a pure identity; it asserts an "identity in difference"; and it can specify the latter in terms of likeness and unlikeness. Thus divine love is like human love in so far as it is relational, it cares for the object loved, and it seeks to identify itself with the beloved; but it is unlike human love in so far as there is no human counterpart to the eternal relations of the Trinity, the universality and intensity of God's care, and God's self-identification with humanity in Christ.

The fourth objection to the analogy of proportionality is that we cannot meaningfully predicate an X of God when X is unknowable. In reply, it must be immediately admitted that the predication would be meaningless if X could never be given a meaning in terms of finite objects. But such a meaning can be given for every divine attribute. Moreover, although we cannot give the meaning (= positive content) of any attribute as it exists in God, we can (on the grounds that I have given) validly affirm that it exists in a mode appropriate to infinite being.

However, if we were to qualify our theistic analogues completely and in every case we should be condemned to complete agnosticism (in the literal sense of "ignorance"). Even if it is meaningful to affirm, and even if we have grounds for affirming, that God is infinitely personal we should be unable to give our belief any content that is both positive and true. God's personality would still be wholly inexpressible.

Although this agnosticism need not offend the speculative intellect it is bound to cause great difficulties in the sphere of devotion. In the normal life of prayer and worship the believer speaks of, and (yet more significantly) to, God as he might speak of and to a human friend. He recollects, or ought to recollect, God's majesty; and this recollection may be accompanied by a "sense of the numinous"; but he still thinks of God as a concrete person.

This view of God as a concrete, individual, person is present throughout the Bible. When Jesus spoke of God as Father he did not qualify his statements by the *via negativa*. Nor did he tell his disciples to do so. Being concerned with man's living relation to a living God he let the analogue stand in all its native strength. And the Church has taken him at

---

[4]Frederick Ferré in *Language, Logic and God* (London 1962, p. 76).

variety of uses of language. The twentieth-century philosopher Ludwig Wittgenstein suggested the analogy of games to describe this apparent chaotic situation in language. If you were to attempt to give a complete description of what constitutes the activity known as a "game," you would find a similar bewildering variety of activities. There are many different kinds of games—board games, ball games, card games, games that involve teams, games for single players, games with fixed rules, other games with flexible rules, and so forth. This variety of games can be grouped into classifications having certain "family resemblances," but some features of one family of games might be missing from a different family of games. Even though families of games share common characteristics with other families of games, these family resemblances are missing from other families. Something like this confronts us when we examine language: there are many different language games including the language of science, the language of art, the language of poetry and the language of religion. The error of logical positivism was the attempt to impose on all "language games," to use Wittgenstein's phrase, the criteria relevant only to the language of science. The selection from Paul Ricoeur showed that there are some common features among the language of religion, the languages of art and poetry, and scientific models. But this does not mean that any of these particular language games can be totally reduced to another.

In short, language seems to break all artificial boundaries that are set for it. And it is simply not convincing to say that certain kinds of discourse are not meaningful because they do not fit into a prescribed theory of meaningfulness. Not all areas of human investigation admit of the same degree of precision as one finds in natural science and mathematics, and it would be foolish to dismiss all language that does not fit a scientific model of language. Aristotle recognized this long ago when he said, "it is the mark of an educated man to look for precision in each class of things just so far as the nature of the subject admits; it is evidently equally foolish to accept probable reasoning from a mathematician and to demand from a rhetorician scientific proofs."[1]

If religious language constitutes a distinct "language game," to continue using Wittgenstein's phrase, it is also possible to distinguish within religious language many different forms of discourse. We have considered only three ways in which language functions to express religious matters: symbols, analogy, and metaphor. When we examine the many different religions that have existed during human history, we see many different types of religious language: legends, myths (narratives involving symbolic elements), poetry, chronicles, oracles, and so on. Even within the confines of Christian scripture, there is a rich variety of uses of language: parables, sayings, prayers, proverbs, pronouncements, hymnic material, and apocalyptic literature with its often exaggerated symbolism. Each of these distinct types of religious language raises its own questions for a theory of interpretation, and a great deal of attention is being given by contemporary philosophers and theologians to developing a theory of interpretation that does justice to the rich variety of religious linguistic materials. Our survey of some of the main problems in religious language must stop here, but the preceding has shown that a great deal of attention has been given to the questions arising from a study of the nature of religious language. It is also evident that there is still much work yet to be done.

[1]Aristotle, *Nicomachean Ethics* 1094b, 25, W. D. Ross translation.

ADDITIONAL READING SUGGESTIONS
FOR PART FOUR

Since much of the philosophy of the twentieth century has been devoted to an analysis of the nature and function of language, the amount of literature dealing with language and religion is enormous. A collection of essays spanning much of the diversity of this discussion is the volume edited by Ronald E. Santoni, *Religious Language and the Problem of Religious Knowledge* (Bloomington: Indiana University Press, 1968). A. J. Ayer advanced his views on the nature of religious statements in his *Language, Truth and Logic,* which was published in a second edition in 1946 (New York: Dover Publications). Copleston discusses Ayer in volume nine of his *History of Western Philosophy* (Garden City: Doubleday-Anchor, 1976). A defense of the meaningfulness of religious utterances and an analysis of their various forms can be found in Ian Ramsey, *Religious Language* (New York: Macmillan, 1963), and in a shortened form in part two, "The Meaning of God Talk" in his *Christian Empiricism,* ed. Jerry H. Gill (Grand Rapids: Eerdmans, 1974). An overall discussion of the many aspects of this topic, with a good bibliography, is William P. Alston, "Religious Language," *The Encyclopedia of Philosophy* (1967), 7, 168-74. A general discussion of some of the traditional affirmations about the function of religious language is included in chapters ten and eleven of C. S. Lewis, *Miracles* (London: Geoffrey Bles, 1947).

part five

THE PROBLEM
OF
EVIL

God and Evil

Either God cannot or he will not prevent evil. If God cannot prevent evil, then God is limited in power. If God will not prevent evil, then God is limited in benevolence. But if God is not limited in either power or benevolence, why is there evil in the world?

This paraphrase of the statement of the problem of evil made by the Greek philosopher Epicurus three centuries before the Christian era shows that the problem of evil is a concern not only for the Christian religion, but has arisen whenever human beings have attempted to reconcile the existence of evil with belief in a divine being of infinite power and goodness. We should neither underestimate the difficulty of the problem of evil nor think that there are easy solutions to it. The problem of evil is perhaps the most powerful objection ever raised against belief in God, and it cannot be dismissed lightly. For those who reject belief in an omnipotent and all-good God, it is probably the appalling depth and extent of human suffering and misery more than anything else that makes the assertion of a benevolent God seem so implausible.

An attempt to justify the goodness of God in spite of the presence of evil in the world is called a *theodicy,* from two Greek words meaning god and justice. Generating a theodicy is particularly difficult for the Judaeo-Christian tradition, because it has maintained three affirmations about God:

1. Evil exists
2. God is all-powerful
3. God is completely benevolent.

Since the problem of evil arises as a theological issue only when we insist on maintaining all three of these affirmations, we could obviously resolve the problem of evil by denying any one of them. Theodicies have been developed which address the problem of evil in this way, but since they would require giving up one of the three principal affirmations they have not found much acceptance within the Judaeo-Christian tradition.

That there is evil in the world is too obvious to be questioned. What may not be so obvious at first is that there is evil in the world because there are human beings in the world, for it would be fair to say that if there were no sentient creatures like us—beings capable of feeling pain, mental anguish, and the destruction of our fondest aspirations—then there would be no evil. Human beings are therefore the place where evil makes its appearance in the world. In an allied sense, evil arises because certain aspects of our worldly situation give rise to human suffering. The list of the sources of suffering is enormous and includes disease, war, famine, human cruelty to other human beings, psychological distress, and disappointment, to name only some. In attempting to sort out the various faces of evil, a distinction has frequently been made between natural evil and moral evil. *Natural evil* refers to those aspects of nature itself that produce pain and injury to human beings, such as natural disasters, disease, and death. *Moral evil* is suffering that is due to human perversity, and human beings are capable of causing great physical and psychological pain to their fellows with an ingenuity that is ample evidence of the enormity of the problem posed by moral evil.

These two kinds of evil raise different, thought related, questions for theism. Natural evil raises questions about the order of nature. Moral evil raises questions about human nature. In both cases the question for the theist is why God allows a world such as ours to exist. Why does the natural order produce human suffering? Could God have created the world in such a way that it would not produce events that caused human suffering? If so, why did God not? The question posed by moral evil is why God allows us to inflict misery and suffering on others. Could God have created free beings who nonetheless would not produce misery and suffering for their fellow human beings? These are some of the issues that will be addressed by the theodicies we will examine.

As a preliminary to further consideration of the problem of evil, ask yourself what amount of evil is attributable to natural causes, and what amount is attributable to human perversity. Would you say that the two kinds of evil are roughly equivalent? Or would you claim that sixty percent of the evil in the world could be classed as moral evil, with only forty percent attributable to natural evil? Or is the imbalance even higher—ninety percent moral evil and only ten percent natural? As you ponder this, consider that much of what we refer to as natural evil has indirect human causes. We could eliminate much of the starvation in the world if the world's resources were allocated differently. Many persons in the world still suffer from diseases for which there are known cures. And steps could be taken to alleviate many natural disasters, while for those that are unavoidable, human resources could be used to reduce much of the suffering caused by disasters. Considerations such as these have led thinkers to concentrate mainly on the problems of moral evil in their theodicies, since moral evil seems to constitute the major part of the problem.

THEMES IN THEODICIES

Before turning to a brief survey of themes that are found in various theodicies, one more point needs to be made. The problem of evil emerges only for those who believe in an all-powerful and all-good God. For the atheist the presence of evil in the world does not pose an intellectual difficulty; evil is just another fact of life—although a monstrous one. It is simply the case that there are features of the world that we find repugnant, and while this may give rise to the conclusion that the world is absurd, the atheist does not feel obliged to explain why there is evil in the world; that is just the way the world is. The existence of evil becomes a problem only for the theist who believes not only in God but in a certain kind of god, a God who is both all-powerful and completely benevolent. Even when the problem of evil does not arise as a theological difficulty, there can still be felt the enormous problem of suffering. Buddhism, which has no doctrine of a personal god, nevertheless considers salvation from suffering to be a central concern, and Buddhism has developed strategies for dealing with this feature of human experience. Even though Buddhism offers a profound sensitivity to the problem of suffering, it does not encounter the theological difficulties inherent in the Judaeo-Christian view.

Refer back to the three affirmations of the Judaeo-Christian tradition that give rise to the problem of evil. Since the problem of evil emerges when all three of these affirmations are held, several possible theodicies could result by simply denying one or more of these statements. But theodicies which would result from this tactic would sacrifice the traditional Judaeo-Christian beliefs about God and the world, and as a result such theodicies have not been found at the heart of Jewish or Christian attempts to defend the goodness of God in spite of the presence of evil in the world. The following themes indicate various approaches to explaining the presence of evil. Most theodicies will contain several of these themes, since no really satisfactory theodicy could be built on any one of them alone.

The Unreality of Evil

One approach to a theodicy results from denying the first of the three affirmations and claiming that evil is unreal. The most extreme form of this kind of theodicy claims that evil is an illusion; a less extreme form admits the reality of evil but denies that evil has any substantial reality.

Evil is an Illusion. Certain forms of Hinduism hold the view that evil, along with the whole of the visible world, is an illusion, or *maya*. Not only the experience of evil but all sense experiences are thus illusory. The view that evil is an illusion has never formed a part of the traditional views of either Judaism or Christianity, though something akin to this was suggested by Mary Baker Eddy as one of the doctrines of Christian Science. The Judaeo-Christian doctrine of creation affirms not only that the world is real, but that creation is basically good. It therefore finds unacceptable any view that suggests the unreality of the world.

Evil has no Substantial Reality. Given the belief that the created order is good and that God is the source of creation, St. Augustine developed a theodicy which held that evil has no independent, substantial reality. He rejected, as did orthodox Christianity, any theodicy which claimed that evil was due to the material aspects of the world. Matter is good; God created it as good, and everything that is created by God is good in its own proper way; things give rise to evil when that which is basically good has been perverted and corrupted. Augustine did not deny that evil is present in the world, but his concern was to explain the metaphysical status of evil, and he concluded that evil is a privation of that which is essentially good.

In other words, Augustine argued that evil is not a substance, a thing in the world, which has independent reality but appears only as a defect or privation in what is a basically good created order. Disease has no independent reality, for example, but appears as an absence of health. Sin occurs only in a will capable of choosing to do good which chooses evil instead. In short, evil is a kind of parasite on the good, a disorder in what would otherwise be a good creation. Augustine also accepted the Genesis story of the fall of Adam and Eve as an explanation for the origin of defective human nature. Whereas the Hindu doctrine of *maya* is a denial of the reality of evil, Augustine's view is not that evil is an illusion but only that it has no independent or substantial reality. This fundamental difference between the Augustinian notion of evil as privation of good and the Hindu doctrine of *maya* may call into question their being included in the same category. What they have in common, however, is their focus on the first of the three affirmations that give rise to the theological problem of evil. Augustine attempts to show that natural evil can be accounted for as a defect in what was designed by God as a good created order. Whereas this tactic sheds some light on the question of natural evil, it does not directly address the problem of moral evil. Therefore Augustine had to include elements of the free-will defense in his theodicy in order to address this latter concern.

A Limited God

Just as the view that evil is an illusion is a denial of the first of the affirmations that give rise to the problem of evil, the view that evil is due to God's limitation is a denial of the second affirmation. This denial has taken two forms: the view that God is limited by an equally powerful evil deity, and the view that God is either limited by the material of which the world is made, or that God is limited in ability.

Dualistic Theories. The view that there are two opposed but equally powerful deities, the one being the source of good, the other the source of evil, is a dualistic theodicy. Ancient Zoroastrian religion held this view, with *Ahura Mazdah* and *Angra Mainyu* being the opposed good and evil spirits. The good deity is simply incapable of preventing the other from producing evil in the world, and human beings are called upon to choose one of the sides of the struggle, with the outcome of the opposition between good and evil being very much undecided.

Properly speaking a dualism arises only when an explanation is offered in terms of two equal but opposed ultimate principles or realities, and neither Christianity nor Judaism finds a dualistic explanation acceptable. The devil cannot be interpreted as a being equal to but opposed to God, for the devil is a personification of an evil temporarily tolerated which will ultimately be destroyed.

A Finite God. Another form of a limited-God theodicy is offered in one of the readings in this section. John Stuart Mill argued that God is perhaps not all-powerful as traditional theistic belief held but is limited in power and maybe in intelligence. The evil in the world arises from this limitation. We will go into this view in more detail later, but we should recognize that while perhaps resolving the problem of evil, the view that God is finite would amount to a major alteration in the traditional Judaeo-Christian beliefs about God.

Denial of God's Benevolence

A denial of the third affirmation of the complete benevolence of God will likewise dispel the problem of evil but at the expense of our traditional concept of God. Though both Christianity and Judaism avow the goodness of God, not all religions have done so. Many of the ancient religions, such as those of Greece, had a polytheistic view in which some gods were good, and others were not. Since they were not committed to defending the total goodness of their deities, the Greeks did not face the theological difficulty of the problem of evil. They merely accepted that some gods were benevolent, and some were malevolent. In the reading from John Stuart Mill in this section it is suggested that perhaps God is not completely benevolent, as traditional theism has held. Mill argues that we simply have no basis in natural theology for assuming that God is completely just or that God wishes the happiness of creatures. The acceptance of either of these suggestions, of course, would result in a major change in the traditional views of the nature of God.

Karma Theories

The principle of *karma* is found in Indian religions, including both Buddhism and Hinduism, and is the view that the evils one suffers in this life, as well as the happiness that one enjoys, are the effects of deeds done in a previous life. The law of *karma* includes a principle of cause and effect since what happens to us is what we deserve because of deeds done in a previous incarnation. Christian theodicies do not appeal to the principle of *karma* since it is dependent on the doctrine of reincarnation, which has not been a part of traditional Jewish or Christian beliefs. The doctrine of *karma* can elicit a socially conservative response to suffering, since the belief that people suffer because they deserve to suffer removes some of the impetus toward the alleviation of suffering.

Even though Christianity and Judaism have no doctrine of reincarnation or of *karma,* many persons have assumed that when they suffer it is because of something they have done. To be sure, evil deeds do often cause suffering and distress for the person who commits them, but as a general explanation for evil this is unacceptable in the Judaeo-Christian view. In the Old Testament, the book of Job stands as a refutation of the view that persons suffer only in proportion to their misdeeds. Job's friends advised him to admit that he had done evil and to pray for forgiveness so that he might be freed from his suffering. Job stubbornly insisted on his innocence, and so represents the refusal of Hebrew religion to attempt to account for evil entirely as punishment for sins. The New Testament likewise rejects the view that people suffer in direct proportion to their misdeeds. In fact, the Christian affirmation is that people sometimes suffer precisely because they are innocent, and the centrality of the cross of Christ in Christian thought also is a repudiation of the view that suffering comes in proportion to what one might deserve.

Harmony Theories

Other theodicies have included the theme of universal harmony, a harmony that either is believed to exist now but is unknown to us because of our limited viewpoint, or one that will come into being sometime in the future. The Stoic poet Cleanthes gave expression to this viewpoint, even though he did not believe in God in the Jewish or Christian sense. He did believe that reality was ruled by a principle of reason and that everything that happened was part of the universal order of things. Because we are finite creatures, we cannot see the total harmony of the universe and therefore believe certain things to be evil. In the total view of things, however, evil as well as good is necessary to the total harmony. Another way of expressing this view is in terms of an analogy. In a painting there are dark areas as well as brighter hues. If we looked only at the dark areas we might think they were ugly, but seen in the context of the painting as a whole the dark areas contribute to the harmony and perfection of the entire painting, and are therefore as essential to the overall beauty of the painting as the more vibrant colors.

A variation of the harmony theodicy would be to admit that there is not a universal harmony at present, but maintain that there will be one sometime in the future, and the present distress is necessary in order to bring about this future harmony. Some Christian writers have argued for a theodicy with this feature in it, for basic to the Christian view of history is the affirmation that God at some future point will bring about a reordering of things so that the present evils of the world will be eliminated. A recurring objection to all harmony theories, whether they claim that there is presently a harmony or that there will be a future harmony, is the question of the morality of the intensity of our present suffering for the sake of some future harmony. Can we really believe that cancer is necessary to this harmony? Torture? Murder? Ivan Karamazov gives a powerful expression of this objection in *The Brothers Karamazov* when he insists that if the suffering of innocent children is necessary for the eternal harmony, he wants nothing to do with it and will gladly return his ticket to this adventure we call life. Others have objected to the harmony theodicy because it seems to call into question either the goodness or the power of God, or both. Could God not have brought about eternal harmony without our having to pay so high a price? If God could not, then why call God omnipotent. If God could have done this but chose not to, this would seem to call God's goodness into question. So we are back to where we started with the initial statement of the problem of evil.

Free-Will Theories

The most prevalent theme in theodicies is the emphasis on human free will. God chose to create beings having free will. We could not be truly free unless we were free to do evil; therefore the possibility of evil is inherent in our free will. We may not be able to explain why God created us with free will, or why God created anything for that matter. But if we believe that there is some ultimate value to be gained by our having the power of free choice, then we have one explanation for our capacity to do evil.

The free-will defense forms a part of the theodicies offered in this section by John Hick and C. S. Lewis, though neither could be classified solely as a free-will type of theodicy. Even if one accepts the free-will theodicy, there is still the fact of natural evil to be explained. St. Augustine held the view that the sin of the first man and woman resulted in a fall not only of humanity but of nature as well, so that after the original sin the order of nature itself was greatly changed. Neither Hick nor Lewis appeals to the Adam and Eve story as an explanation for natural evil, yet both offer intriguing suggestions on how the problems of natural evil and moral evil are related.

The above classification of themes in theodicies is not exhaustive, nor is this the only way to organize even the ones referred to. These are, however, the principal themes that have been used in theodicies by both Christian and non-Christian writers, and their enumeration of them here will serve to show some of the kinds of questions that will be raised in our readings.

JOHN HICK

The "Vale of Soul-Making" Theodicy

God created human beings in a state of perfection. God also placed the first parents of the race, Adam and Eve, in an idyllic situation in which every need was met, but the first human pair willfully rebelled against God and "fell" from their state of pristine purity. By this fall the course of human history was changed; the human race is still tainted by the original sin of Adam and Eve, and the entire natural order also reflects the fallenness of humankind.

This interpretation of the story found in the book of Genesis occupies a central place in the historical development of Christian theodicies and is represented by what Hick calls the "majority report" of St. Augustine, the fifth-century Christian theologian and bishop. Two assumptions are implicit in Augustine's theodicy:

1. Human free will plays a major role in accounting for the presence of evil in the world, and evil results from the willful rebellion of humanity against God.

2. The original situation of humanity was a state of perfection from which our first parents departed with dire consequences for the entire human race.

In the following selection from the contemporary philosopher John Hick, the first of the assumptions is accepted, but the second one is rejected in favor of what Hick refers to as the "minority" report represented by St. Irenaeus, a Christian writer of the second century.

Before turning to the details of Hick's theodicy, a word is in order about the Adam and Eve story. Such stories are referred to by contemporary scholars as "myths," the function of a myth being to provide in narrative form a comprehensive view of mankind and the world in terms of which human beings can understand the human situation. Myths are stories involving symbolic elements and accounting for deeds done "in those times" or "once upon a time"; that is, at a nondefinable time and place. The term "myth" connotes to many persons the sense of that which is false in contrast to that which is true, but this is not what the term means when applied to religious stories. The truth of a story such as this is found not in its literal meaning but what it says about the human situation. Like all significant religious stories, the Adam and Eve narrative offers a profound insight into the human condition; it loses most of its religious significance, however, if we try to take it as literal or historical fact. Note also the presence in the story of vivid symbols: the serpent in the garden, the forbidden fruit, the tree of knowledge, the tree of life, and the angel with the flaming sword. It is also important to know that the Hebrew term *Adam* means simply mankind, so the story can be understood to refer not just to a first human being but to Everyman, to each of us. Remember that in our study of religious language it was suggested that symbols open up new levels of self-understanding. If the Adam and Eve story is taken in its symbolic elements as pointing to a level of experience of reality which it opens up to us, the story means that we must recognize that we are in rebellion against God and that our actions have profound consequences.

There are several philosophical considerations which prevent an adequate theodicy from being based on the Adam and Eve story alone. First is the difficulty of making sense of the claim that a perfect being could willfully sin. If human beings were completely perfect in their original state, then how could they possess the imperfection indicated by willfully choosing to do evil? Second, there is the moral difficulty of explaining how God could hold all human beings responsible for what was done in antiquity by the first man and woman. Third, the nature of the punishment seems out of proportion to the original sin. The whole catalog of human suffering seems to be a morally intolerable penalty for the error of two persons who merely wanted to have forbidden knowledge. How can we morally defend a God who punishes us so severely for something over which we had no control?

Like all religious stories, what we make of the Adam and Eve narrative depends on which elements of the story we emphasize. If we take the story of Adam and Eve's "fall" as decisive for the rest of humanity, we confront the sort of problems just mentioned. But if we interpret the story as expressing the fact that each of us fails to live up to our noblest possibilities, then it says something profound about the human situation.[1] It says, among other things, that we are not in the perfected state God intends for us, but are in the process of being "formed into the finite likeness of God." A view similar to this was suggested by the contemporary Catholic theologian Teilhard de Chardin who viewed the evolutionary process as having reached the stage wherein we share in our spiritual evolution by developing moral qualities that reflect the nature of God.

Central to Hick's theodicy is the view that God's purpose is to lead us from mere biological life, which he refers to with the Greek term *bios,* to a qualitatively improved spiritual life, to which he gives another Greek term for life, *zoe.* Life as mere *bios* is our natural existence formed through the eons of evolution and

[1]For an insightful interpretation of the Adam and Eve story, see Paul Ricoeur, *The Symbolism of Evil,* trans. Emerson Buchanan (Boston: Beacon Press, 1969).

culminating in the emergence of the species *homo sapiens*. At this point we enter into the creative process as sort of co-creators with God. Life should therefore be viewed as an arena for the development of spiritual life and as the final stage in the evolutionary process for the directions of which we bear responsibility. The evil in the world is not to be seen as God's punishment for the sins of the first human beings, but as a necessary condition for the achievement of *zoe*, spiritual life which reflects the moral attributes of God. The world in which we find ourselves is the "vale of soul-making," to use a phrase of the poet John Keats. Such a world is not a perfect situation, and Hick charges that it is erroneous for antitheists to object to the nature of the world as not being an idyllic paradise. To expect this present world to be a hedonistic paradise in which every desire is gratified would be to think of human beings as pet animals. But clearly this is not what God intends for us. In the reading that follows, Hick says: "Men are not to be thought of on the analogy of animal pets, whose life is to be made as agreeable as possible, but rather on the analogy of human children, who are to grow to adulthood in an environment whose primary and overriding purpose is not immediate pleasure but the realizing of the most valuable potentialities of human personality."

For us to develop the fullness of our potential requires that we have freedom of choice. Freedom is only real when we are free to do good as well as to do evil, and the natural world provides an environment in which our choices have real consequences, either for good or ill. The human situation is one of struggle to achieve the highest potentialities of the human personality. Like Adam we find our situation to be one of defection from these possibilities, but the process of soul-making must continue in spite of our often and recurring failures. The natural order, with the natural evil that is part of its possibility, thus forms the backdrop for this transition from *bios* to *zoe*. Part of the attractiveness of Hick's theodicy is that it shows that the problems of moral evil and natural evil are interrelated concerns. By rejecting the second major assumption of the Augustinian theodicy, Hick affirms the view that human beings have not been victimized by a primeval "fall" of the race but that the Genesis story speaks to a view of humankind in the process of achieving the purposes which God wills for us.

Hick labels his view as both teleological and eschatological. It is teleological in the sense that human existence is seen to be purposive, to be directed toward the achievement of a goal. *Eschatology* refers to the doctrine of the events of the end-time or last days, and in this context refers to the biblical view that there will be a future and perfected state in which all those who have become "children of God" will share. Hick cites numerous biblical passages which give support to this interpretation of the Christian view of human history, such as the text which speaks of a "new heaven and a new earth." The perfected situation for human beings is thus not to be thought of as having existed in the distant past, but as something that will exist in a glorious future. It is toward this goal that all the drama of human existence is directed, and Hick insists that "our theodicy must find the meaning of evil in the part it is made to play in the eventual outworking of that purpose."

The following selection offers only the general outline of Hick's theodicy, which he works out in more detail in subsequent sections of the book from which the reading is taken. By tying it firmly to early Christian thought, and by fortifying it with

numerous biblical references, Hick shows that his "vale of soul-making" theodicy is
compatible with traditional Christian affirmations. An adequate theodicy, however,
must do more than this. It must also show that the goodness of God is not com-
promised by the presence of evil in the world. Hick addresses this issue by supporting the view that our present situation, with all the suffering this entails, is necessary
to achieve the perfected existence that is God's ultimate goal for humanity. It is the
good of this ultimate goal that eventually will justify the present experiences of
suffering and evil which are required to reach the goal. Referring to the themes
mentioned in the introduction, we can therefore classify Hick's theodicy as involving
elements of both the harmony type of theodicy and the free-will theodicy.

Evil and the God of Love*

Fortunately there is another and better way. As well as the "majority
report" of the Augustinian tradition, which has dominated Western
Christendom, both Catholic and Protestant, since the time of Augustine
himself, there is the "minority report" of the Irenaean tradition. This
latter is both older and newer than the other, for it goes back to St.
Irenaeus and others of the early Hellenistic Fathers of the Church in the
two centuries prior to St. Augustine, and it has flourished again in more
developed forms during the last hundred years.

Instead of regarding man as having been created by God in a
finished state, as a finitely perfect being fulfilling the divine intention for
our human level of existence, and then falling disastrously away from this,
the minority report sees man as still in process of creation. Irenaeus
himself expressed the point in terms of the (exegetically dubious) distinction between the "image" and the "likeness" of God referred to in Genesis
i. 26: "Then God said, Let us make man in our image, after our likeness."[1]
His view was that man as a personal and moral being already exists in the
image, but has not yet been formed into the finite likeness of God. By this
"likeness" Irenaeus means something more than personal existence as
such; he means a certain valuable quality of personal life which reflects
finitely the divine life. This represents the perfecting of man, the fulfilment of God's purpose for humanity, the "bringing of many sons to

*Source: From pp. 253–261 in *Evil and the God of Love*, Revised Edition by John Hick
Copyright © 1966, 1978 by John Hick. Reprinted by permission of Harper & Row,
Publishers, Inc. and John Hick.

[1]*A.H.* v. vi. 1. Cf. pp. 217 f. above.

glory,"[2] the creating of "children of God" who are "fellow heirs with Christ" of his glory.[3]

And so man, created as a personal being in the image of God, is only the raw material for a further and more difficult stage of God's creative work. This is the leading of men as relatively free and autonomous persons, through their own dealings with life in the world in which He has placed them, towards that quality of personal existence that is the finite likeness of God. The features of this likeness are revealed in the person of Christ, and the process of man's creation into it is the work of the Holy Spirit. In St. Paul's words, "And we all, with unveiled faces, beholding the glory of the Lord, are being changed into his likeness (εἰκών) from one degree of glory to another; for this comes from the Lord who is the Spirit";[4] or again, "For God knew his own before ever they were, and also ordained that they should be shaped to the likeness (εἰκών) of his Son."[5] In Johannine terms, the movement from the image to the likeness is a transition from one level of existence, that of animal life *(Bios)*, to another and higher level, that of eternal life *(Zoe)*, which includes but transcends the first. And the fall of man was seen by Irenaeus as a failure within the second phase of this creative process, a failure that has multiplied the perils and complicated the route of the journey in which God is seeking to lead mankind.

In the light of modern anthropological knowledge some form of two-stage conception of the creation of man has become an almost unavoidable Christian tenet. At the very least we must acknowledge as two distinguishable stages the fashioning of *homo sapiens* as a product of the long evolutionary process, and his sudden or gradual spiritualization as a child of God. But we may well extend the first stage to include the development of man as a rational and responsible person capable of personal relationship with the personal Infinite who has created him. This first stage of the creative process was, to our anthropomorphic imaginations, easy for divine omnipotence. By an exercise of creative power God caused the physical universe to exist, and in the course of countless ages to bring forth within it organic life, and finally to produce out of organic life personal life; and when man had thus emerged out of the evolution of the forms of organic life, a creature had been made who has the possibility of existing in conscious fellowship with God. But the second stage of the creative process is of a different kind altogether. It

[2]Hebrews ii. 10.

[3]Romans viii. 17.

[4]II Corinthians iii. 18.

[5]Romans viii. 29. Other New Testament passages expressing a view of man as undergoing a process of spiritual growth within God's purpose, are: Ephesians ii. 21; iii. 16; Colossians ii. 19; I John iii. 2; II Corinthians iv. 16.

cannot be performed by omnipotent power as such. For personal life is essentially free and self-directing. It cannot be perfected by divine fiat, but only through the uncompelled responses and willing co-operation of human individuals in their actions and reactions in the world in which God has placed them. Men may eventually become the perfected persons whom the New Testament calls "children of God," but they cannot be created ready-made as this.

The value-judgement that is implicitly being invoked here is that one who has attained to goodness by meeting and eventually mastering temptations, and thus by rightly making responsible choices in concrete situations, is good in a richer and more valuable sense than would be one created *ab initio* in a state either of innocence or of virtue. In the former case, which is that of the actual moral achievements of mankind, the individual's goodness has within it the strength of temptations overcome, a stability based upon an accumulation of right choices, and a positive and responsible character that comes from the investment of costly personal effort. I suggest, then, that it is an ethically reasonable judgement, even though in the nature of the case not one that is capable of demonstrative proof, that human goodness slowly built up through personal histories of moral effort has a value in the eyes of the Creator which justifies even the long travail of the soul-making process.

The picture with which we are working is thus developmental and teleological. Man is in process of becoming the perfected being whom God is seeking to create. However, this is not taking place—it is important to add—by a natural and inevitable evolution, but through a hazardous adventure in individual freedom. Because this is a pilgrimage within the life of each individual, rather than a racial evolution, the progressive fulfilment of God's purpose does not entail any corresponding progressive improvement in the moral state of the world. There is no doubt a development in man's ethical situation from generation to generation through the building of individual choices into public institutions, but this involves an accumulation of evil as well as of good.[6] It is thus probable that human life was lived on much the same moral plane two thousand years ago or four thousand years ago as it is today. But nevertheless during this period uncounted millions of souls have been through the experience of earthly life, and God's purpose has gradually moved towards its fulfilment within each one of them, rather than within a human aggregate composed of different units in different generations.

If, then, God's aim in making the world is "the bringing of many sons

[6]This fact is symbolized in early Christian literature both by the figure of the Antichrist, who continually opposes God's purposes in history, and by the expectation of cataclysmic calamity and strife in the last days before the end of the present world order.

to glory,"[7] that aim will naturally determine the kind of world that He has created. Antitheistic writers almost invariably assume a conception of the divine purpose which is contrary to the Christian conception. They assume that the purpose of a loving God must be to create a hedonistic paradise; and therefore to the extent that the world is other than this, it proves to them that God is either not loving enough or not powerful enough to create such a world. They think of God's relation to the earth on the model of a human being building a cage for a pet animal to dwell in. If he is humane he will naturally make his pet's quarters as pleasant and healthful as he can. Any respect in which the cage falls short of the veterinarian's ideal, and contains possibilities of accident or disease, is evidence of either limited benevolence or limited means, or both. Those who use the problem of evil as an argument against belief in God almost invariably think of the world in this kind of way. David Hume, for example, speaks of an architect who is trying to plan a house that is to be as comfortable and convenient as possible. If we find that "the windows, doors, fires, passages, stairs, and the whole economy of the building were the source of noise, confusion, fatigue, darkness, and the extremes of heat and cold" we should have no hesitation in blaming the architect. It would be in vain for him to prove that if this or that defect were corrected greater ills would result: "still you would assert in general, that, if the architect had had skill and good intentions, he might have formed such a plan of the whole, and might have adjusted the parts in such a manner, as would have remedied all or most of these inconveniences."[8]

But if we are right in supposing that God's purpose for man is to lead him from human *Bios,* or the biological life of man, to that quality of *Zoe,* or the personal life of eternal worth, which we see in Christ, then the question that we have to ask is not, Is this the kind of world that an all-powerful and infinitely loving being would create as an environment for his human pets? or, Is the architecture of the world the most pleasant and convenient possible? The question that we have to ask is rather, Is this the kind of world that God might make as an environment in which moral beings may be fashioned, through their own free insights and responses, into "children of God"?

Such critics as Hume are confusing what heaven ought to be, as an environment for perfected finite beings, with what this world ought to be, as an environment for beings who are in process of becoming perfected. For if our general conception of God's purpose is correct the world is not intended to be a paradise, but rather the scene of a history in which human personality may be formed towards the pattern of Christ. Men are

[7]Hebrews ii. 10.

[8]*Dialogues Concerning Natural Religion,* pt. xi. Kemp-Smith's ed. (Oxford: Clarendon Press, 1935), p. 251.

not to be thought of on the analogy of animal pets, whose life is to be made as agreeable as possible, but rather on the analogy of human children, who are to grow to adulthood in an environment whose primary and overriding purpose is not immediate pleasure but the realizing of the most valuable potentialities of human personality.

Needless to say, this characterization of God as the heavenly Father is not a merely random illustration but an analogy that lies at the heart of the Christian faith. Jesus treated the likeness between the attitude of God to man, and the attitude of human parents at their best towards their children, as providing the most adequate way for us to think about God. And so it is altogether relevant to a Christian understanding of this world to ask, How does the best parental love express itself in its influence upon the environment in which children are to grow up? I think it is clear that a parent who loves his children, and wants them to become the best human beings that they are capable of becoming, does not treat pleasure as the sole and supreme value. Certainly we seek pleasure for our children, and take great delight in obtaining it for them; but we do not desire for them unalloyed pleasure at the expense of their growth in such even greater values as moral integrity, unselfishness, compassion, courage, humour, reverence for the truth, and perhaps above all the capacity for love. We do not act on the premise that pleasure is the supreme end of life; and if the development of these other values sometimes clashes with the provision of pleasure, then we are willing to have our children miss a certain amount of this, rather than fail to come to possess and to be possessed by the finer and more precious qualities that are possible to the human personality. A child brought up on the principle that the only or the supreme value is pleasure would not be likely to become an ethically mature adult or an attractive or happy personality. And to most parents it seems more important to try to foster quality and strength of character in their children than to fill their lives at all times with the utmost possible degree of pleasure. If, then, there is any true analogy between God's purpose for his human creatures, and the purpose of loving and wise parents for their children, we have to recognize that the presence of pleasure and the absence of pain cannot be the supreme and overriding end for which the world exists. Rather, this world must be a place of soul-making. And its value is to be judged, not primarily by the quantity of pleasure and pain occurring in it at any particular moment, but by its fitness for its primary purpose, the purpose of soul-making.[9]

[9]The phrase "the vale of Soul-making" was coined by the poet John Keats in a letter written to his brother and sister in April 1819. He says, "The common cognomen of this world among the misguided and superstitious is 'a vale of tears' from which we are to be redeemed by a certain arbitrary interposition of God and taken to Heaven—What a little circumscribed straightened notion! Call the world if you Please

In all this we have been speaking about the nature of the world considered simply as the God-given environment of man's life. For it is mainly in this connection that the world has been regarded in Irenaean and in Protestant thought.[10] But such a way of thinking involves a danger of anthropocentrism from which the Augustinian and Catholic tradition has generally been protected by its sense of the relative insignificance of man within the totality of the created universe. Man was dwarfed within the medieval world-view by the innumerable hosts of angels and arch-angels above him—unfallen rational natures which rejoice in the im-mediate presence of God, reflecting His glory in the untarnished mirror of their worship. However, this higher creation has in our modern world lost its hold upon the imagination. Its place has been taken, as the minimizer of men, by the immensities of outer space and by the material universe's unlimited complexity transcending our present knowledge. As the spiritual environment envisaged by Western man has shrunk, his physical horizons have correspondingly expanded. Where the human creature was formerly seen as an insignificant appendage to the angelic world, he is now seen as an equally insignificant organic excrescence, enjoying a fleeting moment of consciousness on the surface of one of the planets of a minor star. Thus the truth that was symbolized for former ages by the existence of the angelic hosts is today impressed upon us by the vastness of the physical universe, countering the egoism of our species by making us feel that this immense prodigality of existence can hardly all exist for the sake of man—though, on the other hand, the very realiza-tion that it is not all for the sake of man may itself be salutary and beneficial to man!

However, instead of opposing man and nature as rival objects of God's interest, we should perhaps rather stress man's solidarity as an embodied being with the whole natural order in which he is embedded. For man is organic to the world; all his acts and thoughts and imaginations are conditioned by space and time; and in abstraction from nature he would cease to be human. We may, then, say that the beauties and sublimities and powers, the microscopic intricacies and macroscopic vastnesses, the wonders and the terrors of the natural world and of the life that pulses through it, are willed and valued by their Maker in a creative

---

'The vale of Soul-making.' " In this letter he sketches a teleological theodicy. "Do you not see," he asks, "how necessary World of Pains and troubles is to school an Intelligence and make it a Soul?" (*The Letters of John Keats*, ed. by M. B. Forman. London: Oxford University Press, 4th ed., 1952, pp. 334–5).

[10]Thus Irenaeus said that "the creation is suited to [the wants of] man; for man was not made for its sake, but creation for the sake of man" (*A.H.* v. xxix. 1), and Calvin said that "because we know that the universe was established especially for the sake of mankind, we ought to look for this purpose in his governance also" (*Inst.* 1. xvi. 6.).

act that embraces man together with nature. By means of matter and living flesh God both builds a path and weaves a veil between Himself and the creature made in His image. Nature thus has permanent significance; for God has set man in a creaturely environment, and the final fulfilment of our nature in relation to God will accordingly take the form of an embodied life within "a new heaven and a new earth."[11] And as in the present age man moves slowly towards that fulfilment through the pilgrimage of his earthly life, so also "the whole creation" is "groaning in travail," waiting for the time when it will be "set free from its bondage to decay."[12]

And yet however fully we thus acknowledge the permanent significance and value of the natural order, we must still insist upon man's special character as a personal creature made in the image of God; and our theodicy must still centre upon the soul-making process that we believe to be taking place within human life.

This, then, is the starting-point from which we propose to try to relate the realities of sin and suffering to the perfect love of an omnipotent Creator. And as will become increasingly apparent, a theodicy that starts in this way must be eschatological in its ultimate bearings. That is to say, instead of looking to the past for its clue to the mystery of evil, it looks to the future, and indeed to that ultimate future to which only faith can look. Given the conception of a divine intention working in and through human time towards a fulfilment that lies in its completeness beyond human time, our theodicy must find the meaning of evil in the part that it is made to play in the eventual outworking of that purpose; and must find the justification of the whole process in the magnitude of the good to which it leads. The good that outshines all ill is not a paradise long since lost but a kingdom which is yet to come in its full glory and permanence.

DISCUSSION QUESTIONS

1. Do you find the Augustinian or the Irenaean approach to a theodicy more adequate? Why?

2. Does the distinction between *bios* and *zoe* seem to you to capture a relevant distinction? What are the reasons for your answer?

3. Hick's theodicy may provide an answer to the problem of moral evil, but does it deal adequately with the problem of natural evil? Does Hick attempt to link these two kinds of evil?

4. Is the Adam and Eve narrative inimical to the type of theodicy suggested by Hick? If so, why? If not, why not?

[11]Revelation xxi. 1.
[12]Romans viii. 21–22.

5. Do you consider Hick's "Vale of Soul-making" approach an adequate theodicy? If so, what are your reasons? If not, why not?

6. How many of the themes of theodicies mentioned in the Introduction are appealed to in Hick's approach?

EDWARD H. MADDEN AND PETER HARE

In Opposition to Hick's "Vale of Soul-Making" Theodicy

Perhaps we are willing to admit that some degree of suffering in the world is necessary for the task of soul-making, and that any possible world in which there were free beings would contain some evil. But is the amount and intensity of the evil in the world required for the process of soul-making that is at the heart of Hick's theodicy? Might God not have been able to achieve this purpose without the massive misery that is present in the world? If God is omnipotent, as traditional belief claims, then why couldn't God have created a world in which moral progress was possible without wars, plagues, famines, and all the other terrible ills that characterize human existence?

These are the questions that form the crux of the counterattack to the Hick theodicy offered by Madden and Hare. In agreement with Hick, these philosophers also reject the notion that the most desirable world would be one in which human beings were like "pet animals" in a hedonistic paradise. But is a hedonistic paradise the only alternative to the present world with its superabundance of evil? Surely an omnipotent God could have created a world that is neither a hedonistic paradise nor a world containing the present amount of evil. Failure to see this point, they charge, is the central shortcoming of Hick's theodicy and constitutes one of three fallacies committed by Hick. Madden and Hare give the following names to these fallacies: "All or Nothing," "It Could Be Worse," and "Slippery Slope." Since Madden and Hare charge that Hick's theodicy founders because of these three fallacies, we will examine them a little more closely.

ALL OR NOTHING

This fallacy results from "the claim that something is desirable because its complete loss would be far worse than the evil its presence now causes." Let it be agreed that a hedonistic paradise would not accomplish the task of soul-building. Is this the only alternative God had to creating the present world? If so, it would be a strange kind of omnipotence that could only choose between two such extreme possibilities with no power to create a world with some evil—enough to accomplish the task of soul-building—but not so much as the present world has. It would be to claim that God was faced with what is called a "Hobson's choice," a take-it-or-leave-it alternative. Thomas Hobson was a seventeenth-century Englishman who rented horses, and insisted that his customers take the one nearest the door or none at all. That is hardly a good principle of business conduct, and much less is it the kind of choice we would feel comfortable attributing to an omnipotent and completely benevolent creator.

According to Madden and Hare, another indication of the "All or Nothing" fallacy is Hick's claim that our epistemic distance from God prevents our having much knowledge of God. *Epistemic* is derived from the Greek word for knowledge, and epistemic distance is a way of saying that the difference between us and God prevents our having complete knowledge of God. In our previous discussion of faith and reason we concluded that we could not have faith in God unless it were also the case that we do not have knowledge of God. But why should God have left human beings in complete ignorance; could God not have given humankind some limited knowledge of the divine purpose? Again, Madden and Hare charge, we find an example of the "All or Nothing" fallacy.

IT COULD BE WORSE

This fallacy results from "the claim that something is not really bad because it will be followed by all manner of desirable things." Applied to the problem of evil, this is a claim that the evils of the present will be overshadowed by the joy of future blessedness that awaits those who achieve their moral potentialities; therefore the present suffering is not as bad as it could be. It would be worse if there were no future joy to offset the present experience of evil, if we could not look forward to a future state in which the present suffering will be seen to have had a purpose. We can better illustrate the nature of the charge of fallacious reasoning by the following diagram: B represents bad things, that is, suffering and the experience of evil. G represents the absence of suffering and the enjoyment of happiness.

$$B \rightarrow G \text{ (Present Situation)}$$
$$B \rightarrow B \text{ (A Worse Situation)}$$

The fallacy arises in the assumption that $B \rightarrow B$ is the only alternative to $B \rightarrow G$. Madden and Hare insist that there is another alternative, one in which we would experience good things to be followed by further good things. We could diagram it as follows:

$$G \rightarrow G \text{ (A Better Situation)}$$

While it is true that suffering sometimes contributes to character building, in other instances it can lead to massive resentment, and we would have to admit that if the only justification for the presence of evil in the world is that it contributes to soul-building, we might have to pronounce God's experiment a failure. Frequently, perhaps more frequently than not, people are not ennobled by suffering but are embittered by it. Additionally, we have to recognize the presence of dysteleological suffering: suffering that does not seem to be productive of any good end. Teleological suffering is that which is necessary to achieve some particular goal, such as the agony endured by a long-distance runner in preparation for a race. Dysteleological suffering, on the other hand, has no apparent goal and is purely gratuitous and undeserved. Madden and Hare charge that the difficulty posed by dysteleological suffering leads Hick on to the "Slippery Slope" fallacy.

SLIPPERY SLOPE

This third fallacy results from the view that "if God once started eliminating evils of this world he would have no place to stop short of a 'perfect' world in which only robots and not men were possible." Even if God removed dysteleological suffering, for example, there would still be massive suffering in the world, so to completely meet the objection posed by the presence of evil in the world, Hick says that God would have to eliminate all evil. But Madden and Hare claim this is a fallacious inference, since an all-knowing and all-wise God could certainly improve the world without having to eliminate all evil entirely. In a sense this is a variant of the charge made in the "All or Nothing" fallacy: that the choice facing God was either the present world or one completely devoid of evil, a choice that Madden and Hare do not believe encompasses all the possibilities open to an omnipotent God.

FURTHER CONSIDERATIONS

If Hick is guilty of the three fallacies, then his "vale of soul-making" theodicy certainly seems to be undercut. But is Hick guilty as charged? This is the question you will have to decide for yourself as you read through the following selection. But as you analyze the arguments pro and con, these additional considerations may be helpful.

The counter arguments raised by the Madden-Hare attack on Hick's theodicy center on these statements:

1. God could possibly have created a world with no evil at all.
2. God could possibly have created a world with less evil than the present world exhibits.
3. God could possibly have created a world with a better balance of good and evil than the present world exhibits; that is, a world with as much good but less evil.

All parties to the debate agree that the first statement is true. There is no logical impossibility in the claim that God could have created a world in which there was no moral evil, but this would be at the expense of human freedom. Such a world would be analogous to the "pet animals in a cage" model that Madden and Hare, as well as Hick, reject as a desirable alternative.

The second statement is also true, since the first statement is true. If God could have created a world containing no moral evil, this clearly would have been a world with less evil than the present world exhibits. An omnipotent God could also have created a world in which there was no natural evil, but this would be a vastly different kind of world than the present one. The article by C.S. Lewis in this section explores some of the changes in the present world order that would result from the elimination of natural evil. Among other things, it would be a world in which the regularity and uniformity of nature—features necessary to natural science—would be lacking. But as has already been pointed out, Madden and Hare are not arguing for a world in which there is no evil, just a world in which there is less evil than the present world exhibits. The third statement, therefore, is the crucial one.

Could God have possibly created a world with a better balance of good and evil than the present world exhibits? This is what Madden and Hare claim.[1] Hick's point, however, is that once we start eliminating evil in the world, we would be logically compelled to eliminate all the evils in the world in order to meet the objection posed to the goodness of God by the presence of evil. This move is not the "All or Nothing" fallacy as Madden and Hare claim, but is required by the logic of the problem. Let's see how Hick might defend himself.

Suppose we could make a list of all the evils in the world—past, present, and future—and that we could rank them in order of evilness. At the top of the list would be the worst evil in the history of the world. Now suppose that we eliminated this evil. The next-worst evil on the list would then appear to be the worst, and the objection could still be made: Why is there this next-to-worse evil in the world? Couldn't God have made a better world if this evil were eliminated? So we strike out the next-worst evil. Then we are left with the next-to-the-next-worst evil. Again the same objection could be made, so we eliminate this evil. The process would continue until there was just one evil left on our list. At this point the same objection would arise: "The world would be better if this final evil were eliminated." When this final evil is eliminated, we are then left with a world totally without evil, a "hedonistic paradise," which all parties to the dispute agree would be less than desirable for soul-building. The Madden-Hare counter to this is that we do not have to eliminate all evil, just some of it. But where do we stop? If we stopped at any point where there was still some evil in the world, the logic of the Madden-Hare attack requires that this evil also be eliminated.

Considerations such as these are what lead Hick to conclude that the objection to God's goodness based on the presence of evil in the world can logically be addressed only by the complete and total elimination of evil, for the presence of any evil in the world still poses the same objection to the existence of a loving God. A completely perfect world, a "hedonistic paradise," however, is incompatible with both the existence of creatures having free will and with the goal of soul-making. The defense of Hick would claim that he had not committed either the "All or Nothing"

---

[1]Alvin Plantinga argues that it is not possible to prove that God could have created a world with as much moral good but less moral evil than the present world. See Alvin C. Plantinga, *God, Freedom, and Evil* (Grand Rapids, Mich.: William B. Eerdmans Publishing Company, 1977), p. 55–57.

fallacy or the "Slippery Slope" fallacy, but that the considerations he advances are required by the attack raised by the problem of evil itself.

At the heart of Hick's theodicy is the free-will defense, and this raises difficult questions in its own right. Why did God create beings with free will? Why is it that God chose to create beings capable of developing their moral and spiritual capabilities? Or why did God create anything at all?[2] These are the questions for which we simply have no answers, and Hick concludes that the problem of evil ultimately ends in mystery. The term mystery here does not refer to that for which we currently have no answer, but which we might know the answer to sometime in the future, but to that which is by its very nature unanswerable. Given our finitude and the inherent limitations of human knowledge, we cannot fathom the divine purpose. The believer, however, is committed to the view that the purposes of a loving God are just, and when Hick appeals to the future "magnitude of the good" of God's purposes, he is not appealing to a fallacious "It Could Be Worse" principle but rather restating the believer's commitment to the ultimate vindication of the goodness of God.

[2]The question Why is there something rather than nothing? is the fundamental philosophical mystery according to Martin Heidegger, *An Introduction to Metaphysics*, trans. Ralph Manheim (Garden City: Doubleday-Anchor, 1961).

Rejection of Hick's Theodicy*

The intellectual honesty of John Hick is impressive. Unlike the majority of Christian apologists he does not try to find safety in the number of solutions but instead searchingly criticizes and disowns many of the favorite solutions.[1] He concludes, nevertheless, that apologetics reduced to fighting trim is all the more effective. He believes that a sophisticated combination of the character-building and free-will solutions will serve. They show evil to serve God's purpose of "soul-making."

Earlier we pointed out the difficulties involved in the usual formulations of the character-building and free-will solutions. We shall consider here how successful Hick is in avoiding these difficulties.

According to Hick,

man, created as a personal being in the image of God, is only the raw material for a further and more difficult stage of God's creative work. This is the leading of men as relatively free and autonomous persons

*Source: Edward H. Madden and Peter H. Hare, *Evil and the Concept of God* (Springfield, Ill.: Charles C. Thomas, 1968), pp. 83–90, 102–3. © 1968 by Charles C. Thomas Publisher. Used by permission.

[1]John Hick: *Evil and the God of Love.* New York, Harper and Row, 1966, pp. 1–204.

through their own dealings with life in the world in which he has placed them, towards that quality of personal existence that is the finite likeness of God.[2]

The basic trouble, he says, with antitheistic writers is that "they assume that the purpose of a loving God must be to create a hedonistic paradise."[3] He concedes that evil is not serving any, even remote, hedonistic end, but insists that it is serving the end of the development of moral personalities in loving relation to God. It is logically impossible to do this either by forcing them to love him or by forcing them always to act rightly. A creature *forced* to love would not be genuinely loving and a creature *forced* to do the right would not be a moral personality. Only through freedom, suffering, and initial remoteness from God ("epistemic distance") can the sort of person God is looking for come about.

Before we discuss in detail the difficulties involved in Hick's position we will briefly describe three informal fallacies Hick adroitly uses in his solution. They are all fallacies which have been used in one form or another throughout the history of Christian apologetics, and we have had occasion to mention them in our discussion of other writers in the previous chapter. However, it will be convenient in discussing Hick's skillful and elaborate use of them to describe and label clearly these arguments: "All or nothing," "It could be worse," and "slippery slope."

All or nothing. This is the claim that something is desirable because its complete loss would be far worse than the evil its presence now causes. The erroneous assumption is that we must have this thing either in its present form and amount or not at all. But it is often the case that only *some* amount of the thing in *some* form is necessary to the achievement of a desirable end.

It could be worse. This is the claim that something is not really bad because it will be followed by all manner of desirable things. The erroneous assumption here is that showing that having these later desirable things is a great boon also shows that the original evil is a necessary and not gratuitous one. Actually it only shows that the situation would be still worse if the desirable things did not follow. To show that it could be worse does not show that it could not be better.

Slippery slope. This is the claim that if God once started eliminating evils of this world he would have no place to stop short of a "perfect" world in which only robots and not men were possible. The erroneous assumption is that God would have no criterion to indicate where on the slippery slope to stop and no ability to implement it effectively. The same argument is used in human affairs and the answer is equally clear. "Once we

[2]*Ibid.,* p. 290.
[3]*Ibid.,* p. 292.

venture, as we sometimes must, on a dangerous course which may lead to our salvation in a particular situation but which may also be the beginning of our path to perdition, the only answer we can give to the question 'Where will you stop?' is 'Wherever our intelligence tells us to stop!' "[4]

Hick's use of the free-will solution is an example of the "all or nothing" fallacy. He concedes that there is an appalling amount of moral evil in the world but insists that it would be logically impossible for God to achieve his purpose of soul-making by creating puppets who always acted rightly. This is a position we have criticized elsewhere and we must show here how the same criticism applies to Hick.

Hick says that the difficulty with criticisms of the free-will solution has been that they suppose God would have done better to create man as a "pet animal" in a cage, "as pleasant and healthful" as possible.[5] Undeniably critics of the free-will solution have often made this mistake, but it is a mistake easily avoided. We are prepared to grant that a better world would not have been created by making men as pet animals. However, the damaging question is whether God had only two alternatives: to create men with the unfortunate moral inclinations they have at present or to create men as pet animals. There are clearly other alternatives. There are, after all, many different ways for a parent to guide his child's moral growth while respecting his freedom.

Perhaps an analogy will be helpful. God, as Hick views him, might be described as headmaster to a vast progressive school where the absolute freedom of the students is sacred. He does not want to force any children to read textbooks because he, he feels, that will only produce students who are more motivated by fear of punishment than by love of knowledge for its own sake. Every student must be left to educate himself as much as possible. However, it is quite unconvincing to argue that because rigid regulation has horrible consequences, almost no regulation is ideal— there are dangers in either extreme. And it is just as much of a mistake to argue that because the possibility of God's creation of men as pet animals is ghastly to contemplate, God's creation of men with the sort of freedom they have now is the best possible choice.

One of Hick's more unfortunate uses of the "all or nothing" argument appears in his justification of man's "initial epistemic distance" from God. He suggests that God has deliberately refrained from giving much knowledge of himself to men for fear that it would jeopardize the development of "authentic fiduciary attitudes" in men. God is fearful (in our analogy) that "spoon-feeding" his creatures will prevent them from developing genuine intellectual curiosity. Because he thinks that constant

---

[4]Sidney Hook: *The Paradoxes of Freedom.* Berkeley, University of California Press, 1964, p. 48.

[5]Hick, *op. cit.*, p. 293.

and thorough spoon-feeding will ruin their intellects, he advocates contact between schoolboy and teacher only once a year.

But we are being too kind in our analogy. God does not even think it
wise to deliver a matriculation address to each student. Almost all students
must be content with meager historical records of a matriculation address
in the distant past and a hope of a commencement speech in the future. It
is no wonder there have been student riots. The countless generations
before Christ were especially destitute of faculty-student contact. And
even now the vast amount of humanity in non-Christian parts of the world
find it difficult to be admitted to the soul-making school at all.[6]

Sometimes Hick feels the weakness of the "all or nothing" argument
and accordingly shifts to the "it could be worse" strategy. "Christian
theodicy must point forward to that final blessedness, and claim that this
infinite future good will render worth while all the pain and travail and
wickedness that has occurred on the way to it."[7] To be sure, we should be
grateful to God for not tormenting us for an eternity, but the question
remains of why he is torturing us at all. However, this strategy is beside the
point. Hick must still show us how all the suffering in this world is the most
efficient way of achieving God's goal. Merely to assure the student who is
threatening riot that in his old age he will somehow come to regard the
indignities of his student days as rather unimportant is not to explain why
those indignities must be visited upon him at all.

Although Hick does not himself feel confident that in the Kingdom
of God all men will completely forget their earthly sufferings, he suggests
that, if such a loss of memory were to occur, it would help solve the
problem of evil.[8] However, we can concede complete heavenly amnesia
and this concession does not move us any closer to a solution. If a man
were to torture his wife, and afterwards somehow to remove completely
the memory of the torture from her mind so that she returned to her

---

[6]Some may protest that our use of a school analogy shows quite clearly that we have
mistakenly understood Hick to be talking about moral rather than theological evil
and about goodness rather than righteousness. However, this change in terminology
will not affect the argument in the slightest. We are not assuming a utilitarian or any
other theory of value; we are granting Hick any theory of value he likes. We may not
ourselves be excited by the prospect of souls being made or by people becoming
righteous, but we are granting this interest and then asking whether righteousness is
being produced in a way that we would expect in a world presided over by an
omnipotent, all-good God. We argue that it is not. It may be true that righteousness is
being *less* ineffectively produced than hedonistic values, but that hardly shows that
the former is being produced in a way compatible with theism. It would be foolish for
someone who has gone out of business to boast of his business success to another
person who has gone out of business on the grounds that he did not go out of business
so *soon*.

[7]*Ibid.*, p. 376.

[8]*Ibid.*, p. 386.

earlier love of him, this would certainly be better than retaining the painful memory, but it still would not explain the necessity of torturing her in the first place.

Hick, however, candidly admits to a feeling that neither of the two strategies discussed above is completely effective in the last analysis and realizes that he must face "excessive or dysteleological suffering."[9] Consequently he moves on to the "slippery slope" argument.

> Unless God eliminated all evils whatsoever there would always be relatively outstanding ones of which it would be said that He should have secretly prevented them. If, for example, divine providence had eliminated Hitler in his infancy, we might now point instead to Mussolini. . . . There would be nowhere to stop, short of divinely arranged paradise in which human freedom would be narrowly circumscribed.[10]

He claims, in other words, that there would be no way of eliminating some evils without removing all of them with the effect of returning us to the "all or nothing" situation.

This argument fails because the erroneous assumption is made that in the process of removing evils God would not be able precisely to calculate the effect of each removal and stop at exactly the point at which soul making was most efficiently achieved. Presumably at that point men would still suffer and complain about their suffering, but it would be possible to offer them an explanation of the necessity of this amount of suffering as a means to the end of soul making. In the analogy we used earlier, no matter how much is done to increase faculty-student contact there will still be some student complaints, but presumably it is possible to reach a point at which such students can be shown how the present amount of faculty-student contact is precisely the right amount to maximize creative intellectual activity.

Hick even comes to admit that this third strategy is no more effective than the first two.[11] He appears to be like a man flourishing toy weapons before an assailant, knowing that in the last analysis they cannot be effective, but hoping that the assailant will be scared off before he comes close enough to see that they are not genuine weapons. In the last analysis he must appeal to mystery. "I do not now have an alternative theory to offer that would explain in any rational or ethical way why men suffer as they do. The only appeal left is to mystery."[12]

Hick's use of mystery is not the usual appeal to mystical experience

[9]*Ibid.*, p. 363.
[10]*Ibid.*, p. 363.
[11]*Ibid.*, p. 369.
[12]*Ibid.*, pp. 369–70.

or commitment so often made by theists. He suggests that mystery, too, contributes to soul-making. Here again he uses the "all or nothing" argument and asks us to imagine a world which contained no unjust, excessive, or apparently unnecessary misery, a world in which suffering could always be seen to be either punishment justly deserved or a part of moral training.

> In such a world human misery would not evoke deep personal sympathy or call forth organized relief and sacrificial help or service. For it is presupposed in these compassionate reactions both that the suffering is not deserved and that it is *bad* for the sufferer.[13]

There are at least three ways of criticizing this strategy:

(a) It is quite possible to feel intense compassion for someone even though his suffering is understood to be an unavoidable means to an end, desirable both to the sufferer and to oneself. A husband may feel convinced that his wife's labor pains are a necessary means to a highly desirable end and at the same time feel great compassion. One can even feel compassion for the pain suffered by a criminal being punished in a way that one thinks is deserved.

(b) Even if some undeserved and unnecessary suffering is necessary to make possible compassion, it is obvious that a minute percentage of the present unnecessary suffering would do the job adequately.

(c) One must remember that while unjust suffering may increase compassion, it also creates massive resentment. This resentment often causes individuals indiscriminately to lash out at the world. The benefits of compassion are probably more than offset by the damage done by resentment.

However, Hick thinks that there is still one last justification for unjust suffering. He asks us to consider what would happen if all unjust suffering were eliminated. In such a world reward would be the predictable result of virtue and punishment the predictable outcome of wickedness. But in such a world doing right simply for its own sake—what Kant called the good will—would be impossible "for whilst the possibility of the good will by no means precludes that right action shall in fact eventually lead to happiness, and wrong action to misery, it does preclude this happening so certainly, instantly, and manifestly that virtue cannot be separate in experience and thought from its reward, or vice from its punishment."[14]

This solution, itself a sign that the end is near at hand, can be rejected with confidence for the following reasons.

(a) This effort to solve the problem of evil does not do justice to the

[13]*Ibid.*, p. 370.
[14]*Ibid.*, p. 371.

good sense God presumably would have were he to exist. God would certainly have sense enough to administer rewards and punishments in view of *motives* and not simply in view of what an agent *does*. It would already be an unjust response if God rewarded an agent for doing what is objectively right on prudential grounds alone.

(b) This effort misfires psychologically as well as theologically. If God usually rewarded men when they sincerely performed an act solely because it was right, this could only have a beneficial effect on human morality. If a parent regularly rewards the child who performs a good act only because he thinks it right more than he rewards a child performing the same act only to curry favor with the parent, this can only tend to reinforce the tendency to act virtuously.

(c) Even if completely regular rewarding of right-behavior would tend to undermine the good will, there is still every reason to believe that an enormous amount of the present unjust punishment could be eliminated without jeopardizing the possibility of acting from a sense of duty. The "all-or-nothing" fallacy is omnipresent in theistic arguments and its presence here at the end, after it had been supposedly rejected, comes as no surprise.

DISCUSSION QUESTIONS

1. Do you agree with Madden and Hare that Hick has committed the "All or Nothing" fallacy? Give reasons for your answer.

2. Madden and Hare also accuse Hick of the "It Could Be Worse" fallacy. Review the selection from Hick and see if you agree that he is guilty of this fallacy.

3. What is your own assessment of the possibility of Hick's avoiding the "Slippery Slope" fallacy?

4. Overall, do you think Madden and Hare give an accurate assessment of Hick's theodicy? Why or why not?

5. What counter moves would you suggest to Hick whereby he could defend his position from the Madden-Hare attack?

JOHN STUART MILL

A Limited God

Since the problem of evil arises when a person maintains the three affirmations that evil exists, God is omnipotent, and God is wholly benevolent, one way of dispelling the problem is to deny either the omnipotence or the benevolence of God. John Stuart Mill, a nineteenth-century philosopher, does both, and the result is a solution to the problem of evil at the expense of the traditional Christian view of God.

The view of God that Mill advances is so different from the traditional conception of God that it would seem a small step for Mill to deny the existence of God altogether. That he did not do so was due to the forces of natural theology in general, and the design argument in particular. Mill thought that natural theology provides some evidence for the existence of a creator, but as he analyzed this evidence Mill concluded that the creator pointed to by the design argument was vastly different from the traditional God of Jewish and Christian belief. Not only is Mill's analysis one possible response to the problem of evil, it also shows just how far natural theology can lead us in our attempt to find evidence for the existence of God of traditional theism.

DIVINE OMNIPOTENCE

The traditional view is that God is all-powerful, but not only does natural theology fail to provide evidence to support divine omnipotence, it even offers positive evidence against it. Mill gives two arguments to support this claim. The first argument is based on the existence in nature of numerous contrivances. By contrivances Mill seemed to mean some kind of device or mechanism for achieving a particular end and Mill probably had in mind such natural processes as evolution. Anytime a person has to resort to a contrivance to accomplish an end, this indicates a lack of power. For example, if you wanted to lift a one-thousand pound weight, a task clearly beyond the capability of most persons, you would have to rig up a block and tackle, which would be a contrivance to accomplish the task of lifting the weight. Such a contrivance would be an indication of your intelligence, but also an admission of the limits of your strength. The existence of multiple contrivances in nature, therefore, points to limitations in God's power. If God were truly omnipotent, God would not have had to fill nature with so many contrivances but could have accomplished the divine purpose—whatever that might be—directly and without the use of adaptations. Mill also suggests that perhaps the limitation in God's power was posed by the materials God had to work with in creating the universe, namely matter and energy, or matter and force as Mill refers to them. There is nothing in the design argument to support the claim that the creator of the cosmos created either matter or energy, and the most that the design argument can do is suggest that God took existing materials and fashioned a world out of them.

A second indication of a limitation in God's power, according to Mill, is our scanty knowledge of God. Natural theology points to the "traces" of God's creative activity in the cosmos, but these traces supply less than complete knowledge of God's purposes. So it could be argued, Mill suggests, that the limited knowledge God gave us of the divine activity is a further indication of God's limitation. A wholly powerful God could have given us more knowledge of the divine purpose. The view of God suggested by natural theology is that of a being with great, but perhaps limited power, who could only leave traces of divine creativity in the universe. This would make the God of natural theology more like *Demiurge* (or *Demiourgos,* to use Mill's older spelling) of ancient Greek religion. The term *Demiourgos* was the Greek word for workman, and referred to a kind of tinker or handyman who traveled about making and fixing things for people, using materials supplied by his customers. Plato applied the term *Demiurge* to his notion of a creator-god who fashioned a world out of existing materials; that is, Plato's creator-god merely shaped the world out of what was available. According to Mill this is the most that natural theology can give us, not the God of traditional Jewish and Christian thought who created the world *ex nihilo,* "out of nothing."

DIVINE OMNISCIENCE

That God is omniscient, or all-knowing, forms a part of the traditional view of God in Judaeo-Christian belief. What evidence can natural theology supply to support the existence of this divine attribute? Very little, Mill says. Mill admits that natural theology does not supply evidence that counts as strongly against omniscience as it does against divine omnipotence, but natural theology also offers no proof in support of this attribute. In other words, natural theology does not disprove or prove that God is omniscient. This consideration suggests that in addition to perhaps being limited by the available materials from which to create a world, God may also have been limited in intelligence. There are no grounds, Mill says, for supposing that the contrivances which form the natural order were the best possible or even the best of which divine creativity was possible. Likewise, there is no indication from natural theology that the creator could have forseen the bad side-effects that the created order would produce, side-effects that we experience as evil. Even if we accept the view that God fashioned the best world of which the divine intelligence was capable—and there is really no proof for this—there is no evidence that God foresaw the numerous problems that have cropped up in the world. The world may be thought of as a well-contrived machine which contained inherent defects that the designer had not foreseen, defects that only became apparent subsequently. The existence of evil, thought of in this way, may have simply been an unforeseen byproduct of the world created by God's limited intelligence.

DIVINE MORAL ATTRIBUTES

At the outset of his discussion of the moral attributes of God, Mill dismisses the problem—to him insuperable—of reconciling infinite power and infinite benevolence with the existence of evil in the world. He sets a more modest task for himself. If we grant that God was perhaps limited in power and in intelligence, then what can we say about God's moral attributes if we confine ourselves to what we can know from natural theology?

Mill answers that we can see some evidence for God's benevolence, but no proof for the view that God is wholly benevolent or completely just. There is certainly design in nature, but the apparent purpose of this design seems to be to provide for continuity of the created order for a certain period of time. Natural theology simply gives no evidence that God cares about us individually or that God has some final purpose to be achieved by creating human beings. It can be argued that God shows some concern for human happiness, but that is apparently not God's primary concern. As for divine justice, there is simply no evidence in nature at all that God's activity can be measured by the standards of human justice. Mill even goes so far as to suggest that justice is a human improvement in nature and that if we had conformed to the standards of the natural order we would never have achieved civilized society and its resulting justice.

Mill's conclusion is that natural theology gives us no evidence for the traditional God of Judaeo-Christian belief. All natural theology can offer is evidence of "a being of great but limited power . . . who desires, and pays some regard to, the happiness of his creatures, but who seems to have other motives of action which he cares more for, and who can hardly be supposed to have created the universe for that purpose alone."

Mill's approach does indeed "solve" the problem of evil, but is the deity that results of any religious significance? Many philosophers, including most of Mill's contemporaries, thought not. It would hardly seem appropriate to worship a being who is limited in power, perhaps also in intelligence, who simply muddled through and created the world out of existing materials doing the best that limited divine intelligence was capable of. Since Mill does not think that divine justice can be demonstrated through natural theology, the difficulty of reconciling divine justice with the fact of evil in the world likewise disappears. Therefore it would not be completely accurate to call Mill's view a theodicy; instead, it is a reinterpretation of the God of traditional theism, a God that would be compatible with "natural religion," to use Mill's phrase.

Mill's essay is important for showing the limits to natural theology, limits that we have already investigated in previous sections. But is his view of the world correct? That is, are we forced to interpret the presence of evil in the world as due to imperfections in the created order? If we accept something like Hick's theodicy, we might want to explore the possibility that any world containing truly free beings would be a world in which evil was possible. Even if we accept the traditional affirmation of divine omnipotence, could an all-powerful God have created a world in which free beings were capable of moral and spiritual development, without its also being a world where both natural and moral evils were possible? This is the question explored by C. S. Lewis in the next reading.

The Divine Attributes*

The question of the existence of a Deity, in its purely scientific aspect, standing as is shown in the First Part, it is next to be considered, given the indications of a Deity, what *sort* of a Deity do they point to? What attributes are we warranted, by the evidence which Nature affords of a creative mind, in assigning to that mind?

It needs no showing that the power if not the intelligence, must be so far superior to that of Man, as to surpass all human estimate. But from this to Omnipotence and Omniscience there is a wide interval. And the distinction is of immense practical importance.

It is not too much to say that every indication of Design in the Kosmos is so much evidence against the Omnipotence of the Designer. For what is meant by Design? Contrivance: the adaptation of means to an end. But the necessity for contrivance—the need of employing means—is a consequence of the limitation of power. Who would have recourse to means if to attain his end his mere word was sufficient? The very idea of means implies that the means have an efficacy which the direct action of the being who employs them has not. Otherwise they are not means, but an incumbrance. A man does not use machinery to move his arms. If he did, it could only be when paralysis had deprived him of the power of moving them by volition. But if the employment of contrivance is in itself a sign of limited power, how much more so is the careful and skilful choice

*Source: From John Stuart Mill, *Three Essays on Religion* (London: Longmans, Green & Co., 1875), pp. 176–90, 194.

of contrivances? Can any wisdom be shown in the selection of means, when the means have no efficacy but what is given them by the will of him who employs them, and when his will could have bestowed the same efficacy on any other means? Wisdom and contrivance are shown in overcoming difficulties, and there is no room for them in a Being for whom no difficulties exist. The evidences, therefore, of Natural Theology distinctly imply that the author of the Kosmos worked under limitations; that he was obliged to adapt himself to conditions independent of his will, and to attain his ends by such arrangements as those conditions admitted of.

And this hypothesis agrees with what we have seen to be the tendency of the evidences in another respect. We found that the appearances in Nature point indeed to an origin of the Kosmos, or order in Nature, and indicate that origin to be Design but do not point to any commencement, still less creation, of the two great elements of the Universe, the passive element and the active element, Matter and Force. There is in Nature no reason whatever to suppose that either Matter or Force, or any of their properties, were made by the Being who was the author of the collocations by which the world is adapted to what we consider as its purposes; or that he has power to alter any of those properties. It is only when we consent to entertain this negative supposition that there arises a need for wisdom and contrivance in the order of the universe. The Deity had on this hypothesis to work out his ends by combining materials of a given nature and properties. Out of these materials he had to construct a world in which his designs should be carried into effect through given properties of Matter and Force, working together and fitting into one another. This did require skill and contrivance, and the means by which it is effected are often such as justly excite our wonder and admiration: but exactly because it requires wisdom, it implies limitation of power, or rather the two phrases express different sides of the same fact.

If it be said, that an Omnipotent Creator, though under no necessity of employing contrivances such as man must use, thought fit to do so in order to leave traces by which man might recognize his creative hand, the answer is that this equally supposes a limit to his omnipotence. For if it was his will that men should know that they themselves and the world are his work, he, being omnipotent, had only to will that they should be aware of it. Ingenious men have sought for reasons why God might choose to leave his existence so far a matter of doubt that men should not be under an absolute necessity of knowing it, as they are of knowing that three and two make five. These imagined reasons are very unfortunate specimens of casuistry; but even did we admit their validity, they are of no avail on the supposition of omnipotence, since if it did not please God to implant in man a complete conviction of his existence, nothing hindered him from making the conviction fall short of completeness by any margin he chose to leave. It is usual to dispose of arguments of this description by the easy answer, that we do not know what wise reasons the Omniscient may have had for leaving undone things which he had the power to do. It is not perceived that this plea itself implies a limit to Omnipotence. When a thing is obviously good and obviously in accordance with what all the evidences of creation imply to have been the Creator's design, and we say we do not know what good reason he may have had for not doing it, we mean that we do not know to what other, still better object—to what object still more completely in the line of his purposes, he may have seen fit to postpone it. But the necessity of postponing one thing to another belongs only to limited power. Omnipotence could have made the objects compatible. Omnipotence does not need to weigh one consideration against another. If the Creator, like a human ruler, had to adapt himself to a set of conditions which he did not make, it is as unphilosophical as presumptuous in us to call him to account for any imperfections in his work; to complain that he left anything in it contrary to what, if the indications of design prove anything, he must have intended. He must at least know more than we know, and we cannot judge what greater good would have had to be sacrificed, or what greater evil incurred, if he had decided to remove this particular blot. Not so if he be omnipotent. If he be that, he must himself have willed that the two desirable objects should be incompatible; he must himself have willed that the obstacle to his supposed design should be insuperable. It cannot therefore *be* his design. It will not do to say that it was, but that he had other designs which interfered with it; for no one purpose imposes necessary limitations on another in the case of a Being not restricted by conditions of possibility.

Omnipotence, therefore, cannot be predicated of the Creator on grounds of natural theology. The fundamental principles of natural religion as deduced from the facts of the universe, negative his omnipotence. They do not, in the same manner, exclude omniscience: if we suppose limitation of power, there is nothing to contradict the supposition of perfect knowledge and absolute wisdom. But neither is there anything to prove it. The knowledge of the powers and properties of things necessary for planning and executing the arrangements of the Kosmos, is no doubt as much in excess of human knowledge as the power implied in creation is in excess of human power. And the skill, the subtlety of contrivance, the ingenuity as it would be called in the case of a human work, is often marvellous. But nothing obliges us to suppose that either the knowledge or the skill is infinite. We are not even compelled to suppose that the contrivances were always the best possible. If we venture to judge them as we judge the works of human artificers, we find abundant defects. The human body, for example, is one of the most striking instances of artful and ingenious contrivance which nature offers, but we may well ask whether so complicated a machine could not have been made to last longer, and not to get so easily and frequently out of order. We may ask why the human race should have been so constituted as to grovel in wretchedness and degradation for countless ages before a small portion of it was enabled to lift itself into the very imperfect state of intelligence, goodness and happiness which we enjoy. The divine power may not have been equal to doing more; the obstacles to a better arrangement of things may have been insuperable. But it is also possible that they were not. The skill of the Demiourgos was sufficient to produce what we see; but we cannot tell that this skill reached the extreme limit of perfection compatible with the material it employed and the forces it had to work with. I know not how we can even satisfy ourselves on grounds of natural theology, that the Creator foresees all the future; that he foreknows all the effects that will issue from his own contrivances. There may be great wisdom without the power of foreseeing and calculating everything: and human workmanship teaches us the possibility that the workman's knowledge of the properties of the things he works on may enable him to make arrangements admirably fitted to produce a given result, while he may have very little power of foreseeing the agencies of another kind which may modify or counteract the operation of the machinery he has made. . . .

We now pass to the moral attributes of the Deity, so far as indicated in the Creation; or (stating the problem in the broadest manner) to the question, what indications Nature gives of the purposes of its author. This question bears a very different aspect to us from what it bears to those teachers of Natural Theology who are incumbered with the necessity of admitting the omnipotence of the Creator. We have not to attempt the impossible problem of reconciling infinite benevolence and justice with infinite power in the Creator of such a world as this. The attempt to do so not only involves absolute contradiction in an intellectual point of view but exhibits to excess the revolting spectacle of a jesuitical defence of moral enormities.

On this topic I need not add to the illustrations given of this portion of the subject in my Essay on Nature. At the stage which our argument has reached there is none of this moral perplexity. Grant that creative power was limited by conditions the nature and extent of which are wholly unknown to us, and the goodness and justice of the Creator may be all that the most pious believe; and all in the work that conflicts with those moral attributes may be the fault of the conditions which left to the Creator only a choice of evils.

It is, however, one question whether any given conclusion is consistent with known facts, and another whether there is evidence to prove it:

and if we have no means for judging of the design but from the work actually produced, it is a somewhat hazardous speculation to suppose that the work designed was of a different quality from the result realized. Still, though the ground is unsafe we may, with due caution, journey a certain distance on it. Some parts of the order of nature give much more indication of contrivance than others; many, it is not too much to say, give no sign of it at all. The signs of contrivance are most conspicuous in the structure and processes of vegetable and animal life. But for these, it is probable that the appearances in nature would never have seemed to the thinking part of mankind to afford any proofs of a God. But when a God had been inferred from the organization of living beings, other parts of Nature, such as the structure of the solar system, seemed to afford evidences, more or less strong, in confirmation of the belief: granting, then, a design in Nature, we can best hope to be enlightened as to what that design was, by examining it in the parts of Nature in which its traces are the most conspicuous.

To what purpose, then, do the expedients in the construction of animals and vegetables, which excite the admiration of naturalists, appear to tend? There is no blinking the fact that they tend principally to no more exalted object than to make the structure remain in life and in working order for a certain time: the individual for a few years, the species or race for a longer but still a limited period. And the similar though less conspicuous marks of creation which are recognized in inorganic Nature, are generally of the same character. The adaptations, for instance, which appear in the solar system consist in placing it under conditions which enable the mutual action of its parts to maintain instead of destroying its stability, and even that only for a time, vast indeed if measured against our short span of animated existence, but which can be perceived even by us to be limited: for even the feeble means which we possess of exploring the past, are believed by those who have examined the subject by the most recent lights, to yield evidence that the solar system was once a vast sphere of nebula or vapour, and is going through a process which in the course of ages will reduce it to a single and not very large mass of solid matter frozen up with more than arctic cold. If the machinery of the system is adapted to keep itself at work only for a time, still less perfect is the adaptation of it for the abode of living beings since it is only adapted to them during the relatively short portion of its total duration which intervenes between the time when each planet was too hot and the time when it became or will become too cold to admit of life under the only conditions in which we have experience of its possibility. Or we should perhaps reverse the statement, and say that organization and life are only adapted to the conditions of the solar system during a relatively short portion of the system's existence.

The greater part, therefore, of the design of which there is indication in Nature, however wonderful its mechanism, is no evidence of any moral attributes, because the end to which it is directed, and its adaptation to which end is the evidence of its being directed to an end at all, is not a moral end: it is not the good of any sentient creature, it is but the qualified permanence, for a limited period, of the work itself, whether animate or inanimate. The only inference that can be drawn from most of it, respecting the character of the Creator, is that he does not wish his works to perish as soon as created; he wills them to have a certain duration. From this alone nothing can be justly inferred as to the manner in which he is affected towards his animate or rational creatures.

After deduction of the great number of adaptations which have no apparent object but to keep the machine going, there remain a certain number of provisions for giving pleasure to living beings, and a certain number of provisions for giving them pain. There is no positive certainty that the whole of these ought not to take their place among the contrivances for keeping the creature or its species in existence; for both the pleasures and the pains have a conservative tendency; the pleasures being generally so disposed as to attract to the things which maintain individual or collective existence, the pains so as to deter from such as would destroy it.

When all these things are considered it is evident that a vast deduction must be made from the evidences of a Creator before they can be counted as evidences of a benevolent purpose: so vast indeed that some may doubt whether after such a deduction there remains any balance. Yet endeavouring to look at the question without partiality or prejudice and without allowing wishes to have any influence over judgment, it does appear that granting the existence of design, there is a preponderance of evidence that the Creator desired the pleasure of his creatures. This is indicated by the fact that pleasure of one description or another is afforded by almost everything, the mere play of the faculties, physical and mental, being a never-ending source of pleasure, and even painful things giving pleasure by the satisfaction of curiosity and the agreeable sense of acquiring knowledge; and also that pleasure, when experienced, seems to result from the normal working of the machinery, while pain usually arises from some external interference with it, and resembles in each particular case the result of an accident. Even in cases when pain results, like pleasure, from the machinery itself, the appearances do not indicate that contrivance was brought into play purposely to produce pain: what is indicated is rather a clumsiness in the contrivance employed for some other purpose. The author of the machinery is no doubt accountable for having made it susceptible of pain; but this may have been a necessary condition of its susceptibility to pleasure; a supposition which avails nothing on the theory of an Omnipotent Creator but is an extremely probable one in the case of a contriver working under the limitation of inexorable laws and indestructible properties of matter. The susceptibility being conceded as a thing which did enter into design, the pain itself usually seems like a thing undesigned; a casual result of the collision of the organism with some outward force to which it was not intended to be exposed, and which, in many cases, provision is even made to hinder it from being exposed to. There is, therefore, much appearance that pleasure is agreeable to the Creator, while there is very little if any appearance that pain is so: and there is a certain amount of justification for inferring, on grounds of Natural Theology alone, that benevolence is one of the attributes of the Creator. But to jump from this to the inference that his sole or chief purposes are those of benevolence, and that the single end and aim of Creation was the happiness of his creatures, is not only not justified by any evidence but is a conclusion in opposition to such evidence as we have. If the motive of the Deity for creating sentient beings was the happiness of the beings he created, his purpose, in our corner of the universe at least, must be pronounced, taking past ages and all countries and races into account, to have been thus far an ignominious failure; and if God had no purpose but our happiness and that of other living creatures it is not credible that he would have called them into existence with the prospect of being so completely baffled. If man had not the power by the exercise of his own energies for the improvement both of himself and of his outward circumstances, to do for himself and other creatures vastly more than God had in the first instance, done, the Being who called him into existence would deserve something very different from thanks at his hands. Of course it may be said that this very capacity of improving himself and the world was given to him by God, and that the change which he will be thereby enabled ultimately to effect in human existence will be worth purchasing by the sufferings and wasted lives of entire geological periods. This may be so; but to suppose that God could not have given him these blessings at a less frightful cost, is to make a very strange supposition concerning the Deity. It is to suppose that God could not, in the first instance, create anything better than a Bosjesman or an Andaman islander, or something still lower; and yet was able to endow the Bosjesman or the Andaman islander with the power of raising himself into a Newton or a Fénelon. We certainly do not know the nature of the barriers which limit the divine omnipotence; but it is a very odd notion of them that they enable the Deity to confer on an almost bestial creature the power of producing by a succession of efforts what God himself had no other means of creating.

Such are the indications of Natural Religion in respect to the divine benevolence. If we look for any other of the moral attributes which a certain class of philosophers are accustomed to distinguish from benevolence, as for example Justice, we find a total blank. There is no evidence whatever in Nature for divine justice, whatever standard of justice our ethical opinions may lead us to recognize. There is no shadow of justice in the general arrangements of Nature; and what imperfect realization it obtains in any human society (a most imperfect realization as yet) is the work of man himself, struggling upwards against immense natural difficulties, into civilization, and making to himself a second nature, far better and more unselfish than he was created with. But on this point enough has been said in another Essay, already referred to, on Nature.

These, then, are the net results of Natural Theology on the question of the divine attributes. A Being of great but limited power, how or by what limited we cannot even conjecture; of great, and perhaps unlimited intelligence, but perhaps, also, more narrowly limited than his power: who desires, and pays some regard to, the happiness of his creatures, but who seems to have other motives of action which he cares more for, and who can hardly be supposed to have created the universe for that purpose alone. Such is the Deity whom Natural Religion points to. . . .

DISCUSSION QUESTIONS

1. Evaluate Mill's claim that natural theology fails to provide evidence in support of divine omnipotence. Do you agree with Mill? Why or why not?
2. Do you agree that a deity limited either in power or intelligence is not a proper object of worship? Give reasons for your answer.
3. Would you classify Mill's approach as a theodicy or merely a defense of theism?
4. Would you agree that Mill does not so much provide a response to the problem of evil as show the limits of natural theology? Explain and defend your answer.
5. What advantages, if any, does Mill's view have over an atheistic position?
6. What do you think of Mill's response to the problem of evil? What are your reasons?

C. S. LEWIS

Evil
and
the Power of God

The problem of evil arises in all its intensity because of the affirmation of divine omnipotence. If God is limited either in power or in intelligence, as John Stuart Mill suggested, then the problem of evil disappears. There would still be evil in the world, but it would no longer pose a problem since its presence could be explained as the result of conditions over which God had no control. Mill's view results in a vastly altered conception of God, who is no longer to be considered almighty or all-powerful but a being of great though limited power and intelligence. Mill "solved" the problem of evil by arguing for a limited God presumably because he could not reconcile the notion of divine omnipotence with the existence of a world—at least with the existence of *this* world. It is this presumption that C. S. Lewis calls into question.

Throughout our discussion of the problem of evil, the question has recurred of God's being able to create a world of free creatures which is also a world free from the possibility of evil. If we accept Mill's view that God is not omnipotent, it explains God's inability to create such a world. C. S. Lewis suggests, in contrast, that we can affirm both divine omnipotence and the claim that it is impossible for God to create a world containing free beings which would also not allow for the possibility of evil. The obvious retort to Lewis is the biblical claim that "with God all things are possible" (Matthew 19:26), which would seem to be a direct contradiction of the view that an omnipotent God would be unable to create a world free from evil and also inhabited by free beings.

CONDITIONAL AND INTRINSIC IMPOSSIBILITIES

The apparent conflict between divine omnipotence and the presence of evil in the world arises because of an equivocal use of the terms "impossible" and "almighty." We have already encountered the notion of the equivocal use of language in the section of religious language; a term is used equivocally when it is used in two different senses, and this is the case with the terms "possible" and "impossible." Lewis underscores this by analyzing the two senses in which we say that something is possible or impossible. Something can be relatively (or conditionally) impossible, which means that X is impossible unless . . . , the ellipsis here indicating the conditions which makes something an impossibility. Lewis gives the example of its being impossible to see the street from where we are now sitting unless we get up and move to the window. The phrase following the term *unless* gives the condition which makes the intended action impossible. We can multiply such examples almost endlessly: It is impossible to make good grades unless you study. It is impossible to win the race unless you apply yourself to physical training. It is impossible to start the automobile unless the battery has enough power. In all cases of the conditionally impossible, the impossibility arises from the set of conditions which make it impossible. Change the conditions and the impossibility vanishes.

The absolutely (or intrinsically) impossible is "impossible under all conditions and in all worlds and for all agents," as Lewis puts it. It is intrinsically impossible to make a square circle or a four-sided triangle. It is intrinsically impossible to create a free being who has no power of choice. Scripture says that "with God all things are possible"; Lewis responds that "intrinsic impossibilities are not things but nonentities." A square circle or a four-sided triangle is simply a meaningless combination of words. Even God cannot create a square circle, for this phrase is nonsense, and Lewis observes that "nonsense remains nonsense even when we talk it about God." Our previous study of religious language warned us about the unrestrained attribution to God of certain qualities, and here is another example of how our language can mislead us into talking nonsense about God. Therefore to say "with God all things are possible, so it must be possible for God to create a square circle" is not to utter a contradiction, but to equivocate on the meaning of the term "possible." Divine omnipotence implies that all things not *intrinsically* impossible are within God's power. The examples previously given of the conditionally impossible and the intrinsically impossible are straightforward and clear, but we probably cannot always tell whether something is intrinsically impossible or merely conditionally impossible. Lewis reminds us that the stock-in-trade of a good magician is the power to fool us into thinking that the impossible has taken place, so we must use caution in discriminating between the two kinds of impossibilities.

POSSIBLE AND IMPOSSIBLE WORLDS

We may be able to speak of possible worlds that God could have created but didn't, and we can also speak of impossible worlds—worlds that even an omnipotent God could not create. We have already encountered the suggestion that one possible world God could have created would be a world in which there was no evil. But it seems to be the case that such a world could not contain beings with freedom of choice. When we explore further the notion of a possible world containing free creatures, we are led to see that other features must also be present.

First, beings with freedom of choice would have to be presented with things to choose among; this means that any free beings must have an environment that is relatively stable and inflexible. This environment, or "field," is nature, and if we are to have any knowledge of nature, it must remain stable and independent of our will. Nature's being independent of us not only provides an environment in which we can make choices, it also means that a state of affairs agreeable to one person may not be agreeable to another person. The same rain that drenches the fields with needed moisture may bring a cold to someone caught in it without an umbrella.

Second, the kind of natural environment required for truly free choice must be one in which actions have predictable consequences. This means that of the actions we can choose among, some will have harmful effects on us or on other persons. Lewis argues that if nature adjusted itself to each of our actions so as to prevent harmful events from taking place, we would in effect lose the ability to exercise genuine free will. Imagine a world in which simple kinds of wrong actions would be impossible: if you picked up a stone to bash in the head of another person, it would turn to jelly. Perhaps your arms would even refuse to move so that the hurtful gesture itself could not be expressed. The molecules of air might refuse to carry the sound of accompanying hurtful remarks. Lewis suggests that "if the principle were carried out to its logical conclusion, evil thoughts would be impossible, for the cerebral matter which we use in thinking would refuse its task when we attempted to frame them." This is only a simple example of a harmful action; imagine how infinitely more variable nature would have to be in order to prevent wars, disease, poverty, economic depressions, and spiraling inflation. Additionally, in such a world natural science would be nonexistent, for science investigates the regularities and uniformity of natural processes. In a world that constantly rearranged and adjusted itself so as to prevent us from doing harmful things, there could be no regularity of nature to be investigated.

Third, any kind of human society also requires the existence of a neutral and fairly inflexible environment. We know each other through the mediation of a neutral nature that is distinct from us. We communicate by means of material resources, "so that what are acts of will and thought for you are noises and glances for me," as Lewis puts it. The same environment that allows communication and co-existence also makes possible harmful effects on each other. The same voice mechanism can be used both for praising and cursing, the same body for helping or hurting. It is interesting to note in this connection that in the thought of Judaism and early Christianity, to be human was to exist bodily. Neither Judaism nor early Christian thought divided human reality into body and spirit, as did the ancient Greeks. To be human is to be an embodied consciousness, and when early Christian writers reflected on human destiny they spoke of the resurrection of the body, not some kind of future existence as pure spirit. We will explore this more in the following section.

The upshot of Lewis's analysis is that the existence of free beings capable of genuine choice and of moral development demands the existence of a world in which evil can occur. Divine omnipotence is compatible with such a world, for to suggest that God could have created a world of free beings without providing a "relatively independent and 'inexorable' nature" would be like asking God to create a square circle. In other words, it would be intrinsically impossible for God to have created a world containing free beings which did not also admit of the potentiality of evil. There is therefore no contradiction between the existence of this world and the claim of divine omnipotence. Lewis's argument stands in direct opposition to Mill's suggestion of a limited God; God can still be thought of as all-powerful, but as incapable of doing the intrinsically impossible.

If the existence of free beings sheds some light on the reason for the presence of evil in the world, this still leaves us with the question—one that we have already encountered—of why God chose to create free beings, or why God chose to create anything at all. At this point, however, philosophical reflection must stop, for we simply have no way of answering this question. As Hick suggested we are left with mystery.

Divine Omnipotence*

Nothing which implies contradiction falls under the omnipotence of God.
THOMAS AQUINAS. *Summ. Theol.*, Iª Q XXV, Art. 4.

"If God were good, He would wish to make His creatures perfectly happy, and if God were almighty He would be able to do what He wished. But the creatures are not happy. Therefore God lacks either goodness, or power, or both." This is the problem of pain, in its simplest form. The possibility of answering it depends on showing that the terms "good" and "almighty," and perhaps also the term "happy" are equivocal: for it must be admitted from the outset that if the popular meanings attached to these words are the best, or the only possible, meanings, then the argument is unanswerable. In this chapter I shall make some comments on the idea of Omnipotence, and, in the following, some on the idea of Goodness.

Omnipotence means "power to do all, or everything."[1] And we are told in Scripture that "with God all things are possible." It is common enough, in argument with an unbeliever, to be told that God, if He existed and were good, would do this or that; and then, if we point out that the proposed action is impossible, to be met with the retort, "But I thought God was supposed to be able to do anything." This raises the whole question of impossibility.

*Source: C. S. Lewis, *The Problem of Pain* (London: Geoffrey Bles, 1940), pp. 14–24. Used by permission.

[1] The original meaning in Latin may have been "power *over* or *in* all." I give what I take to be current sense.

In ordinary usage the word *impossible* generally implies a suppressed clause beginning with the word *unless*. Thus it is impossible for me to see the street from where I sit writing at this moment; that is, it is impossible to see the street *unless* I go up to the top floor where I shall be high enough to overlook the intervening building. If I had broken my leg I should say "But it is impossible to go up to the top floor"—meaning, however, that it is impossible *unless* some friends turn up who will carry me. Now let us advance to a different plane of impossibility, by saying "It is, at any rate, impossible to see the street *so long as* I remain where I am and the intervening building remains where it is." Someone might add "unless the nature of space, or of vision, were different from what it is." I do not know what the best philosophers and scientists would say to this, but I should have to reply "I don't know whether space and vision *could possibly* have been of such a nature as you suggest." Now it is clear that the words *could possibly* here refer to some absolute kind of possibility or impossibility which is different from the relative possibilities and impossibilities we have been considering. I cannot say whether seeing round corners is, in this new sense, possible or not, because I do not know whether it is self-contradictory or not. But I know very well that if it is self-contradictory it is absolutely impossible. The absolutely impossible may also be called the intrinsically impossible because it carries its impossibility within itself, instead of borrowing it from other impossibilities which in their turn depend upon others. It has no *unless* clause attached to it. It is impossible under all conditions and in all worlds and for all agents.

"All agents" here includes God Himself. His Omnipotence means power to do all that is intrinsically possible, not to do the intrinsically impossible. You may attribute miracles to Him, but not nonsense. This is no limit to His power. If you choose to say "God can give a creature free-will and at the same time withhold free-will from it," you have not succeeded in saying *anything* about God: meaningless combinations of words do not suddenly acquire meaning simply because we prefix to them the two other words "God can." It remains true that all *things* are possible with God: the intrinsic impossibilities are not things but nonentities. It is no more possible for God than for the weakest of His creatures to carry out both of two mutually exclusive alternatives; not because His power meets an obstacle, but because nonsense remains nonsense even when we talk it about God.

It should, however, be remembered that human reasoners often make mistakes, either by arguing from false data or by inadvertence in the argument itself. We may thus come to think things possible which are really impossible, and *vice versâ*.[2] We ought, therefore, to use great cau-

---

[2] *E.g.*, every good conjuring trick does something which to the audience with their *data* and their power of reasoning, seems self-contradictory.

tion in defining those intrinsic impossibilities which even Omnipotence cannot perform. What follows is to be regarded less as an assertion of what they are than a sample of what they might be like.

The inexorable "laws of Nature" which operate in defiance of human suffering or desert, which are not turned aside by prayer, seem, at first sight to furnish a strong argument against the goodness and power of God. I am going to submit that not even Omnipotence could create a society of free souls without at the same time creating a relatively independent and "inexorable" Nature.

There is no reason to suppose that self-consciousness, the recognition of a creature by itself as a "self," can exist except in contrast with an "other," a something which is not the self. It is against an environment, and preferably a social environment, an environment of other selves, that the awareness of Myself stands out. This would raise a difficulty about the consciousness of God if we were mere theists: being Christians, we learn from the doctrine of the Blessed Trinity that something analogous to "society" exists within the Divine being from all eternity—that God is Love, not merely in the sense of being the Platonic form of love, but because, within Him, the concrete reciprocities of love exist before all worlds and are thence derived to the creatures.

Again, the freedom of a creature must mean freedom to choose: and choice implies the existence of things to choose between. A creature with no environment would have no choices to make: so that freedom, like self-consciouness (if they are not, indeed, the same thing) again demands the presence to the self of something other than the self.

The minimum condition of self-consciousness and freedom, then, would be that the creature should apprehend God and, therefore, itself as distinct from God. It is possible that such creatures exist, aware of God and themselves, but of no fellow-creatures. If so, their freedom is simply that of making a single naked choice—of loving God more than the self or the self more than God. But a life so reduced to essentials is not imaginable to us. As soon as we attempt to introduce the mutual knowledge of fellow-creatures we run up against the necessity of "Nature."

People often talk as if nothing were easier than for two naked minds to "meet" or become aware of each other. But I see no possibility of their doing so except in a common medium which forms their "external world" or environment. Even our vague attempt to imagine such a meeting between disembodied spirits usually slips in surreptitiously the idea of, at least, a common space and common time, to give the *co-* in *co-existence* a meaning: and space and time are already an environment. But more than this is required. If your thoughts and passions were directly present to me, like my own, without any mark of externality or otherness, how should I distinguish them from mine? And what thoughts or passions could we begin to have without objects to think and feel about? Nay, could I even begin to have the conception of "external" and "other" unless I had experience of an "external world"? You may reply, as a Christian, that God (and Satan) do, in fact, affect my consciousness in this direct way without signs of "externality." Yes: and the result is that most people remain ignorant of the existence of both. We may therefore suppose that if human souls affected one another directly and immaterially, it would be a rare triumph of faith and insight for any one of them to believe in the existence of the others. It would be harder for me to know my neighbour under such conditions than it now is for me to know God: for in recognising the impact of God upon me I am now helped by things that reach me through the external world, such as the tradition of the Church, Holy Scripture, and the conversation of religious friends. What we need for human society is exactly what we have—a neutral something, neither you nor I, which we can both manipulate so as to make signs to each other. I can talk to you because we can both set up sound-waves in the common air between us. Matter, which keeps souls apart, also brings them together. It enables each of us to have an "outside" as well as an "inside," so that what are acts of will and thought for you are noises and glances for me; you are enabled not only to *be,* but to *appear:* and hence I have the pleasure of making your acquaintance.

Society, then, implies a common field or "world" in which its members meet. If there is an angelic society, as Christians have usually believed, then the angels also must have such a world or field; something which is to them as "matter" (in the modern not the scholastic, sense) is to us.

But if matter is to serve as a neutral field it must have a fixed nature of its own. If a "world" or material system had only a single inhabitant it might conform at every moment to his wishes—"trees for his sake would crowd into a shade." But if you were introduced into a world which thus varied at my every whim, you would be quite unable to act in it and would thus lose the exercise of your free will. Nor is it clear that you could make your presence known to me—all the matter by which you attempted to make signs to me being already in my control and therefore not capable of being manipulated by you.

Again, if matter has a fixed nature and obeys constant laws, not all states of matter will be equally agreeable to the wishes of a given soul, nor all equally beneficial for that particular aggregate of matter which he calls his body. If fire comforts that body at a certain distance, it will destroy it when the distance is reduced. Hence, even in a perfect world, the necessity for those danger signals which the pain-fibres in our nerves are apparently designed to transmit. Does this mean an inevitable element of evil (in the form of pain) in any possible world? I think not: for while it may be true that the least sin is an incalculable evil, the evil of pain depends on degree, and pains below a certain intensity are not feared or resented at all. No one minds the process "warm—beautifully hot—too hot—it stings" which warns him to withdraw his hand from exposure to the fire: and, if I may trust my own feeling, a slight aching in the legs as we climb into bed after a good day's walking is, in fact, pleasurable.

Yet again, if the fixed nature of matter prevents it from being always, and in all its dispositions, equally agreeable even to a single soul, much less is it possible for the matter of the universe at any moment to be distributed so that it is equally convenient and pleasurable to each member of a society. If a man travelling in one direction is having a journey down hill, a man going in the opposite direction must be going up hill. If even a pebble lies where I want it to lie, it cannot, except by a coincidence, be where you want it to lie. And this is very far from being an evil: on the contrary, it furnishes occasion for all those acts of courtesy, respect, and unselfishness by which love and good humour and modesty express themselves. But it certainly leaves the way open to a great evil, that of competition and hostility. And if souls are free, they cannot be prevented from dealing with the problem by competition instead of by courtesy. And once they have advanced to actual hostility, they can then exploit the fixed nature of matter to hurt one another. The permanent nature of wood which enables us to use it as a beam also enables us to use it for hitting our neighbour on the head. The permanent nature of matter in general means that when human beings fight, the victory ordinarily goes to those who have superior weapons, skill, and numbers, even if their cause is unjust.

We can, perhaps, conceive of a world in which God corrected the results of this abuse of free-will by His creatures at every moment: so that a wooden beam became soft as grass when it was used as a weapon, and the air refused to obey me if I attempted to set up in it the sound waves that carry lies or insults. But such a world would be one in which wrong actions were impossible, and in which, therefore, freedom of the will would be void; nay, if the principle were carried out to its logical conclusion, evil thoughts would be impossible, for the cerebral matter which we use in thinking would refuse its task when we attempted to frame them. All matter in the neighbourhood of a wicked man would be liable to undergo unpredictable alterations. That God can and does, on occasions, modify the behaviour of matter and produce what we call miracles, is part of the Christian faith; but the very conception of a common, and therefore, stable, world, demands that these occasions should be extremely rare. In a game of chess you can make certain arbitrary concessions to your opponent, which stand to the ordinary rules of the game as miracles stand to the laws of nature. You can deprive yourself of a castle, or allow the other man sometimes to take back a move made inadvertently. But if you conceded everything that at any moment happened to suit him—if all his moves were revocable and if all your pieces disappeared whenever their position on the board was not to his liking—then you could not have a game at all. So it is with the life of souls in a world: fixed laws, consequences unfolding by causal necessity, the whole natural order, are at once the limits within which their common life is confined and also the sole condition under which any such life is possible. Try to exclude the possibility of suffering which the order of nature and the existence of free-wills involve, and you find that you have excluded life itself.

As I said before, this account of the intrinsic necessities of a world is meant merely as a specimen of what they might be. What they really are, only Omniscience has the data and the wisdom to see: but they are not likely to be *less* complicated than I have suggested. Needless to say, "complicated" here refers solely to the human understanding of them; we are not to think of God arguing, as we do, from an end (co-existence of free spirits) to the conditions involved in it, but rather of a single, utterly self-consistent act of creation which to us appears, at first sight, as the creation of many independent things, and then, as the creation of things mutually necessary. Even we can rise a little beyond the conception of mutual necessities as I have outlined it—can reduce matter as that which separates souls and matter as that which brings them together under the single concept of Plurality, whereof "separation" and "togetherness" are only two aspects. With every advance in our thought the unity of the creative act, and the impossibility of tinkering with the creation as though this or that element of it could have been removed, will become more apparent. Perhaps this is not the "best of all possible" universes, but the only possible one. Possible worlds can mean only "worlds that God could have made, but didn't." The idea of that which God "could have" done involves a too anthropomorphic conception of God's freedom. Whatever human freedom means, Divine freedom cannot mean indeterminacy between alternatives and choice of one of them. Perfect goodness can never debate about the end to be attained, and perfect wisdom cannot debate about the means most suited to achieve it. The freedom of God consists in the fact that no cause other than Himself produces His acts and no external obstacle impedes them—that His own goodness is the root from which they all grow and His own omnipotence the air in which they all flower.

And that brings us to our next subject—the Divine goodness. Nothing so far has been said of this, and no answer attempted to the objection that if the universe must, from the outset, admit the possibility of suffering, then absolute goodness would have left the universe uncreated. And I must warn the reader that I shall not attempt to prove that to create was better than not to create: I am aware of no human scales in which such a portentous question can be weighed. Some comparison between one state of being and another can be made, but the attempt to compare being and not being ends in mere words. "It would be better for me not to exist"—in what sense "for me"? How should I, if I did not exist, profit by not existing? Our design is a less formidable one: it is only to discover how, perceiving a suffering world, and being assured, on quite different grounds, that God is good, we are to conceive that goodness and that suffering without contradiction.

DISCUSSION QUESTIONS

1. Do you agree that the intrinsically impossible is not possible even for God?
2. Given the typology of themes in theodicies in the introduction to this section, to which of them does Lewis appeal in his article?
3. What is your evaluation of the implicit claim made by Lewis that natural science would be impossible in a world in which there was no possibility of evil?
4. Would a person be truly free if there was never an opportunity presented for doing evil? Why or why not?
5. What would be your response to someone who argued that human freedom and divine omnipotence are incompatible? That is, if we are really free, then even God could not prevent us from doing something we freely choose; but this would mean that God is not omnipotent.
6. Explain what you think Lewis meant by the following statement: "Perhaps this is not the 'best of all possible' universes, but the only possible one. Possible worlds can mean only 'worlds that God could have made, but didn't.' "
7. What is your evaluation of the theodicy suggested by Lewis?

Retrospective

The term mystery has appeared several times in this section, and before leaving the question of evil we should give additional attention to the relationship between evil and mystery. The contemporary philosopher who has done the most to raise mystery to the level of a philosophical category is the French thinker Gabriel Marcel. Echoing the difference between objective thinking and subjective thinking suggested by Kierkegaard, Marcel distinguishes between the notion of problem and mystery. A problem is a difficulty set before us from which we are detached and to which we respond with an increase in knowledge or technical skill. A solution to a problem may elude us, but we remain confident that more understanding, increased technical competence, or additional knowledge, will allow us to solve a problem. A mystery, in contrast, is that in which we participate and with which we are vitally involved. We cannot separate ourselves from a mystery as we can a problem, and no amount of increased knowledge or skill will dispel it. Mysteries are intrinsic to human existence and, according to Marcel, include life itself, faith, hope, love, death, and evil.

Given this distinction between problem and mystery, Marcel would not speak of the *problem* of evil at all, for evil remains a mystery impenetrable by rational analysis. Even if we could arrive at a perfect theodicy, one that absolutely accounted for the presence of evil in the world, this would in reality change nothing. We would still have to endure evil. It would still be a fact of the world. Whereas the point of solving a problem is to remove it, no increase in human knowledge or understanding will dispel evil. It remains an enigma, like life itself, and defies all attempts to resolve it. The mystery of evil, in effect, announces the defeat of philosophical analysis. None of the theodicies we have examined would remove the pain of a person suffering from terminal cancer or trying to reorder a life shattered by the loss of a loved one. Even a perfect theodicy would not make the experience of evil less intense.

One philosophical response to evil is simply to deny the affirmations that give rise to it as a theological difficulty. We have already seen that evil poses a difficulty to us only if we attempt to reconcile it with the existence of a loving and all-powerful God. But this approach would be a refusal to recognize evil as a problem, much less a mystery. For those who like their philosophy neat and tidy, this is the way to go. But if we believe that philosophy should be concerned with all areas of human existence, including those that seem to defy rational analysis, then we will inevitably run up against the limits to human reason posed by the question of evil.

To recognize the limits of human reason, however, is not an excuse to refuse to think through difficult topics such as the question of evil. We do encounter the domain of mystery in our analysis of evil, but we nevertheless benefit from the insights offered by philosophers who have wrestled with this difficult concern. The three affirmations that give rise to the problem of evil—evil exists, God is all-powerful, God is completely benevolent—have been examined by readings in this section. St. Augustine's suggestion that evil is not a thing in nature but a deprivation of the basically good status of created order, sheds light on the nature of evil itself. Lewis offered a further analysis of those features in the natural order that we find objectionable, and pointed out that in order for there to be a world at all—at least a world containing free beings—there must be an independent and inexorable nature that inevitably will also give rise to unpleasant circumstances.

The second affirmation, the omnipotence of God, was also subjected to rigorous analysis by Lewis, and his conclusion was that it makes no sense to attribute mutually contradictory activities to God. God cannot make a square circle, and not even divine omnipotence can create a world of free beings in which evil is not also possible.

The third affirmation concerning the benevolence of God was likewise subjected to scrutiny by John Hick. If we assume that the notion of benevolence only includes God's desire for the short-term happiness of human beings, then of course we are faced with a difficult problem of reconciling this with the presence of evil in the world. But if we believe that God's ultimate purpose is to bring into being spiritual creatures who have freely chosen the good over the evil, then the kind of world in which we find ourselves can be understood as the "vale of soul-making."

Even if we acknowledge the realm of mystery encountered in dealing with the problem of evil, there is still room for critical evaluation of suggested theodicies and analysis of the affirmations that give rise to the theological difficulty. One of the roles for rational analysis is to ferret out the nonsense that has been written on all sides of the issue. We should neither be content to let nonsense be affirmed of God nor should we be happy with nonsense affirmed of an antitheistic position. Even after we have done this and discover that there still is a score of difficult issues the complete analysis of which still seems to elude us, we should not despair. Philosophy has always focused on those issues that raise major intellectual difficulties, and whenever an issue is completely resolved, it is no longer of philosophic interest. That philosophy continues to deal with issues that defy full analysis is what makes philosophy so interesting . . . and also so important.

ADDITIONAL READING SUGGESTIONS
FOR PART FIVE

Various types of theodicies are discussed in highly readable terms in chapter nine of Ed. L. Miller, *God and Reason* (New York: The Macmillan Company, 1972). A defense of the theistic position is offered by Alvin Plantinga, *God, Freedom and Evil* (New York: Harper & Row, 1974; paperback edition, Grand Rapids, Mich.: Eerdmans, 1978) in a book that is important but in places difficult. A specifically Christian response to the problem of evil is J. S. Whale, *The Christian Answer to the Problem of Evil* (London: SCM Press, 1957), which is a small book based on a broadcast talk for the British Broadcasting Company. As always, John Hick is an excellent guide to the many dimensions of the problem in his book *Evil and the God of Love,* rev. ed. (New York: Harper & Row, 1977). Hick also offers an overview of the history of the discussion of the problem, and an extensive bibliography, in his article "Evil, the Problem of," *The Encyclopedia of Philosophy* (1967), 4, 136–41.

part six

DEATH
AND
HUMAN DESTINY

INTRODUCTION

Religion
and
Death

That everybody dies is a fact confirmed by experience. But is death the end of everything for an individual? At death the body decays and returns to dust, but what of the *soul,* the *ego,* the *self?* Does the consciousness of the individual survive the dissolution of the body? If so, how?

This constellation of questions represents an ancient concern of humankind. The reflections of the earliest Greek philosophers included a concern with death and the proper human attitude toward this inevitable fact. Human beings seem to be unique among the earth's creatures in that we not only die but are fully aware of the inevitably of death; coupled with this awareness seems to be a refusal to believe that death is the end. Among peoples both ancient and modern can be found the stubborn conviction that there is some kind of future existence in store for us, and this is a belief that seems to span all cultures and all time periods. The belief in some kind of future life seems to have been present even in the Neanderthal age. Archaeologists have discovered that prehistoric graves were filled with food and implements, presumably intended to be used by the deceased in a future life—a testimony to the belief in some kind of afterlife among our earliest ancestors.

Attitudes toward death are conditioned by other viewpoints, particularly our attitude toward the nature of human reality. If we think that human beings are something special and unique in nature, this would seem to reinforce the conviction that human beings are in some sense immune to the inevitable destruction and decay that are an intrinsic part of nature. If, on the other hand, we accept the naturalistic view that human beings are just another part of nature, a chance byproduct of an impersonal cosmos, then human destiny would appear to be to live for sixty or seventy years and then cease to exist totally and completely. Both of these viewpoints have appeared whenever human beings began to reflect on death, and neither of them can be characterized as a particularly modern view.

The startling thing about us is that we try to avoid thinking about death at all. We are perhaps more removed from death than any previous people. Unlike former peoples who confronted death almost constantly, many of us have never seen a person die. We segregate our dying and place them in sterile surroundings to pass away out of the sight of friends and loved ones. We treat death as a kind of obscenity not to be mentioned in polite company, and all the skills of the contemporary funeral industry are calculated to shield us from the brutal fact of death. We do not even refer to the dead directly but instead speak of the "deceased," the "departed," or the "loved one." All the skills of the cosmetic arts are employed to make a corpse appear "natural" as it lies in an expensive hardwood casket, cushioned in layers of velvet and satin. If some future archaeologists were to attempt to reconstruct our attitudes toward death from our burial practices, they would probably conclude that our primary interest was in disguising death.

THREE ATTITUDES TOWARD DEATH

The fact of death presents philosophy with a strange paradox. On the one hand, empirical evidence tells us that everyone dies. But we know so little of death, that it is at once the most obvious and the least well known fact of human existence. For a philosophy wedded to stubborn empirical facts, death is a closed topic; yet the anticipation of death, even the fear of death, are also empirical facts that must be taken into account in any serious philosophical reflection on the nature of human existence. Though there are variations in these views, there are basically three attitudes toward death and human destiny that have appeared in the history of philosophy and are also represented in various religious traditions.

The first view is that the soul is immortal by nature and will survive the dissolution of the body. This was Plato's view, and it was based on a distinction between the body and the soul which inhabited the body. At death the body decays but the soul escapes the imprisonment of the body to live on. This view of the soul's natural immortality was incorporated into Christian thought in the Middle Ages but in fact was not present in the earliest Christian reflections about human destiny.

The second view, in some sense the opposite of the first, is that there is no separate soul substance but that the soul or "life" of the body is merely a function of the material nature of the body. When the body dies, the activity we refer to as life or consciousness ceases, and there is no continued consciousness after death. This view was held by the ancient Greek materialists and is represented by the selection from Russell in this section.

The third view is that the "soul" or "life" of the individual is not immortal by nature, but through the sovereign love and power of God the life of the individual can be re-created beyond death in terms of a new bodily existence. This belief in resurrection was the view of early Christianity and is reflected in the writings of St. Paul included in this section.

SOME CENTRAL QUESTIONS

As we explore these different attitudes toward death, we will see that three principal philosophical concerns stand out and will form the focal point of our discussion:

1. What is the evidence to support the belief that death is not the cessation of consciousness?
2. What is the proper attitude toward death, fear or calm acceptance?
3. Is life made more meaningful by the view that death is the cessation of consciousness or by the view that there is a continuation of life after death?

The first question is central to all the readings in this section. The article by Bertrand Russell takes the view that there is no evidence at all to support the belief that death is not the cessation of consciousness, and that all the weight of scientific investigation argues against the view that we survive death. In the selection from 1 Corinthians, St. Paul gives expression to the Christian hope for resurrection from the dead, and the evidence he provides to support this belief is the resurrection of Jesus, which was attested by the hundreds of eyewitnesses, including St. Paul himself. John Hick next explores the evidence offered by those who claim to have communicated with the dead to determine if such claims can stand up under the probing of careful analysis. Finally there is the selection from Raymond Moody's book *Life After Life* which offers both a summary and an analysis of the reports of those who have clinically died but been brought back to life to tell of their experiences.

The second question—the proper attitude toward death—has a venerable place in the history of philosophy. The ancient Greek philosopher Epicurus held the view that fear of death stems from the belief in a life after death, a life that is fearful because of the unknown terrors that it presents to us. Epicurus accepted the materialistic metaphysics of the Greek atomists, who held that all reality could be explained in terms of arrangements of material atoms. If human beings, like all reality, are made of atoms, at death the matter that constitutes them simply dissipates, and all consciousness ceases. This is also the view put forward in a more sophisticated form by Bertrand Russell. If we accept the view that death is the cessation of consciousness, then there is nothing to fear. The Greek Stoic philosophers likewise held that death is not to be feared, but they thought that the fear of death can be banished only through the recognition that human beings are an integral part of nature, and that it is in the nature of human existence to die. The calm acceptance of this will remove any fear that death may pose to us.

The third question will call for your own philosophical analysis. Do you find life more meaningful on the supposition of continued existence after death, or does the possibility of death as the cessation of all consciousness make this present life more meaningful? We will return to this question in the retrospective to this Part. It is interesting to notice the response to this question from those who have clinically died, or undergone so-called near-death experiences as reported by Raymond Moody. There is the near-unanimous agreement among these persons that their experiences have not only removed the fear of dying, but have filled them with a renewed sense of the worth and significance of life itself. This, of course, is not the only possible response to the question, and Bertrand Russell gives a totally different one. It is to his views that we will first turn.

BERTRAND RUSSELL

The Finality
of
Death

Although Bertrand Russell was a twentieth-century philosopher and the views he expressed are fortified by reference to contemporary natural science, there is nothing particularly modern about his claim that we do not survive death. Russell's views would have seemed perfectly reasonable to Democritus and his contemporary, Leucippus. These two Greek philosophers of the fifth century B.C. are credited with developing the view known as atomism, and as was mentioned in the introduction, the metaphysical views of atomism left no place for any doctrine of personal immortality. According to the atomist view of reality, all things are composed of atoms—small, indivisible bits of matter—which differ from each other only in size and shape. In the process of decay and corruption, the combination of atoms that forms a particular thing is broken up, with the atoms finding new arrangements and new combinations. The atoms are used over and over again, but objects composed of atoms are only temporary and transitory. When a human being dies, the atoms that composed that person's body will be reused in some other reality. The human soul, according to the atomists, was also composed of extremely small atoms, and when a person dies the soul-atoms dissipate into the upper atmosphere.

The atomistic theory of Democritus and Leucippus provided an explanation for a prevalent view shared by the Greeks: only the gods are immortal, and the suggestion that human beings survive death would be an act of gross impiety. It was only later that belief in the doctrine of the soul's immortality became widespread; when Plato argued for this view it was perceived by many of his contemporaries as a new and startling doctrine, as evidenced by Glaucon's incredulous response to it in the tenth book of Plato's *Republic* (608D). The reason for this detour through the thought of the ancient Greeks is to show that Russell's view is not particularly a modern one. That Russell picks up on an ancient Greek tradition counts neither for or against his view point, of course, but we sometimes have the mistaken view that only ancient and less enlightened peoples were capable of believing in a future life, whereas we who are the heirs of the scientific approach have outgrown such superstitions. This, is certainly an incorrect reading of history, for whenever human beings have reflected on human destiny and death, both views have cropped up: the view that we survive death, and the opposing view that death is the cessation of all consciousness.

At the outset of his essay, Russell refers to the difficult problem of personal identity. What is it that enables you to say that you are the same person today you were fifteen years ago? There probably is not much physical similarity, particularly if fifteen years ago you were a young child. In addition, we are led to believe that the physical body is constantly building new cells and that older cells are dying, so that every seven years or so the matter that constitutes your body has been completely replaced (though some of us may sometimes feel that we missed the last overhaul).

Much serious philosophy has been devoted in recent years to the problem of personal identity, for it constitutes an interesting puzzle in its own right independent of the question of personal survival of death. Russell is in agreement with the general direction of contemporary thought when he suggests that the principle of identity is found in the continuity of habits and memory. You can say that you are the same person you were fifteen years ago because there is a continuity of experiences and memories with those of the person you were fifteen years earlier. You can perhaps recollect memories of that time, and perhaps you still have habits that you developed at that earlier period. All of your inherited characteristics and acquired traits are present through time, and provide a structure that you identify as yourself. This structure of activity, memory, habits, and acquired traits depends on the physical body; when the body dies and decays all the activities that are associated with the body likewise cease. Although Russell does not use the term, he is suggesting that all conscious activity is an epiphenomenon dependent on the physical body. An *epiphenomenon* is a phenomenon appearing with something else which is referred to as its cause. For example, the computing activity of a computer is an epiphenomenon dependent on its physical mechanism, and if the machine is destroyed, all computational activity will cease. The same is true of human reality, Russell says. When the body decays, all activities dependent on the body—feeling, thought and memory—also cease. Russell's view is summed up by the statement in his essay "What I Believe" when he wrote, "when I die, I shall rot, and nothing of my ego will survive."[1]

What, then, makes us think that we will survive death? Not rational arguments, Russell says, but emotions. The most significant of these emotions is the fear of death itself. This fear is a useful thing, Russell insists, for a real fear of death might prevent us from doing foolish things. Overcoming the fear of death is beneficial for the military, and as a case in point Russell refers to the existence during the Crusades of a secret Moslem sect called the Assassins (from the word *hashashin,*

---

[1]Bertrand Russell, "What I Believe," in *The Basic Writings of Bertrand Russell,* eds. Robert E. Egner and Lester E. Denonn (New York: Simon and Schuster, 1961), p. 370.

a reference to the fact that they committed their acts while under the influence of hashish). The Assassins were promised a hedonistic paradise in the next life, complete with dancing girls and sensuous delights, if they carried through their acts of murder and revenge. In a somewhat cynical vein, Russell suggests that apart from adding to the natural ferocity of human beings, overcoming the fear of death is not a desirable goal.

A counter response might be that to view human beings as perishing completely at death does not add much to the dignity of humanity. If the universe is a product of intelligent design, it would not seem very intelligent to let human beings utterly perish at death. To this Russell has two responses. First, nature appears to be indifferent to our values and our hopes; second, the sense of good and evil developed by human beings is relative and conditioned by our struggle for existence. For every example of human compassion there is a counter example of human cruelty. How can we say much in support of human goodness at a time when the major nations of the world spend half of their revenues on perfecting the means of killing each other? If the activity of human beings is a testimony to intelligent design, Russell says, then the purpose of the designer must have "been that of a fiend." For Russell it is preferable to believe that the universe, including human reality, is a mere accident, and perhaps not a very fortuitous one at that.

Russell's brief essay shows that the question of human destiny is linked directly to some of the other questions we have investigated. In the background of the article is the ominous problem posed by the presence of moral evil in the world. The usual arguments for the existence of God are rejected by Russell, and perhaps you will agree with Russell that human beings are an accidental aspect of the cosmic order, perhaps even a mistake in the evolutionary process. If so, you should be aware that there are startling points of agreement between Russell and St. Paul. Christian thought also finds human beings to be prone to error, trapped in sin, to use a theological term, and not capable of much good if left to their own devices. The monstrous presence of moral evil is never downplayed either in Jewish or Christian scripture, and St. Paul would also accept the view that the human personality is not naturally immortal. But the difference between St. Paul and Lord Russell is that St. Paul believed that the power of God brought new possibilities to humanity. Through the power of God working in the lives of individuals, good can be brought about. And it is likewise through the power of God that human beings have hope for a future life, a life that will be a recreation of the personality in a new spiritual body and in a new order of existence. We will return to these themes in the introductory section to the next reading.

Do We Survive Death?*

Before we can profitably discuss whether we shall continue to exist after death, it is well to be clear as to the sense in which a man is the same person as he was yesterday. Philosophers used to think that there were definite substances, the soul and the body, that each lasted on from day to day, that a soul, once created, continued to exist throughout all future time, whereas a body ceased temporarily from death till the resurrection of the body.

The part of this doctrine which concerns the present life is pretty certainly false. The matter of the body is continually changing by processes of nutriment and wastage. Even if it were not, atoms in physics are no longer supposed to have continuous existence; there is no sense in saying: this is the same atom as the one that existed a few minutes ago. The continuity of a human body is a matter of appearance and behavior, not of substance.

The same thing applies to the mind. We think and feel and act, but there is not, in addition to thoughts and feelings and actions, a bare entity, the mind or the soul, which does or suffers these occurrences. The mental continuity of a person is a continuity of habit and memory: there was yesterday one person whose feelings I can remember, and that person I regard as myself of yesterday; but, in fact, myself of yesterday was only certain mental occurrences which are now remembered and are regarded as part of the person who now recollects them. All that constitutes a person is a series of experiences connected by memory and by certain similarities of the sort we call habit.

If, therefore, we are to believe that a person survives death, we must believe that the memories and habits which constitute the person will continue to be exhibited in a new set of occurrences.

No one can prove that this will not happen. But it is easy to see that it is very unlikely. Our memories and habits are bound up with the structure of the brain, in much the same way in which a river is connected with the riverbed. The water in the river is always changing, but it keeps to the same course because previous rains have worn a channel. In like manner, previous events have worn a channel in the brain, and our thoughts flow along this channel. This is the cause of memory and mental habits. But the brain, as a structure, is dissolved at death, and memory therefore may be expected to be also dissolved. There is no more reason to think otherwise

*Source: Bertrand Russell, "Do We Survive Death?" in *Why I Am Not a Christian* (London: George Allen & Unwin, Ltd., 1957), pp. 88–93. Copyright © 1957 by Allen & Unwin. Reprinted by permission of Simon & Schuster, a Division of Gulf & Western Corporation, and Allen & Unwin.

than to expect a river to persist in its old course after an earthquake has raised a mountain where a valley used to be.

All memory, and therefore (one may say) all minds, depend upon a property which is very noticeable in certain kinds of material structures but exists little if at all in other kinds. This is the property of forming habits as a result of frequent similar occurrences. For example: a bright light makes the pupils of the eyes contract; and if you repeatedly flash a light in a man's eyes and beat a gong at the same time, the gong alone will, in the end, cause his pupils to contract. This is a fact about the brain and nervous system—that is to say, about a certain material structure. It will be found that exactly similar facts explain our response to language and our use of it, our memories and the emotions they arouse, our moral or immoral habits of behavior, and indeed everything that constitutes our mental personality, except the part determined by heredity. The part determined by heredity is handed on to our posterity but cannot, in the individual, survive the disintegration of the body. Thus both the hereditary and the acquired parts of a personality are, so far as our experience goes, bound up with the characteristics of certain bodily structures. We all know that memory may be obliterated by an injury to the brain, that a virtuous person may be rendered vicious by encephalitis lethargica, and, that a clever child can be turned into an idiot by lack of iodine. In view of such familiar facts, it seems scarcely probable that the mind survives the total destruction of brain structure which occurs at death.

It is not rational arguments but emotions that cause belief in a future life.

The most important of these emotions is fear of death, which is instinctive and biologically useful. If we genuinely and wholeheartedly believed in the future life, we should cease completely to fear death. The effects would be curious, and probably such as most of us would deplore. But our human and subhuman ancestors have fought and exterminated their enemies throughout many geological ages and have profited by courage; it is therefore an advantage to the victors in the struggle for life to be able, on occasion, to overcome the natural fear of death. Among animals and savages, instinctive pugnacity suffices for this purpose; but at a certain stage of development, as the Mohammedans first proved, belief in Paradise has considerable military value as reinforcing natural pugnacity. We should therefore admit that militarists are wise in encouraging the belief in immortality, always supposing that this belief does not become so profound as to produce indifference to the affairs of the world.

Another emotion which encourages the belief in survival is admiration of the excellence of man. As the Bishop of Birmingham says, "His mind is a far finer instrument than anything that had appeared earlier— he knows right and wrong. He can build Westminster Abbey. He can make an airplane. He can calculate the distance of the sun. . . . Shall, then, man at death perish utterly? Does that incomparable instrument, his mind, vanish when life ceases?"

The Bishop proceeds to argue that "the universe has been shaped and is governed by an intelligent purpose," and that it would have been unintelligent, having made man, to let him perish.

To this argument there are many answers. In the first place, it has been found, in the scientific investigation of nature, that the intrusion of moral or aesthetic values has always been an obstacle to discovery. It used to be thought that the heavenly bodies must move in circles because the circle is the most perfect curve, that species must be immutable because God would only create what was perfect and what therefore stood in no need of improvement, that it was useless to combat epidemics except by repentance because they were sent as a punishment for sin, and so on. It has been found, however, that, so far as we can discover, nature is indifferent to our values and can only be understood by ignoring our notions of good and bad. The Universe may have a purpose, but nothing that we know suggests that, if so, this purpose has any similarity to ours.

Nor is there in this anything surprising. Dr. Barnes tells us that man "knows right and wrong." But, in fact, as anthropology shows, men's views of right and wrong have varied to such an extent that no single item has been permanent. We cannot say, therefore, that man knows right and wrong, but only that some men do. Which men? Nietzsche argued in favor of an ethic profoundly different from Christ's, and some powerful governments have accepted his teaching. If knowledge of right and wrong is to be an argument for immortality, we must first settle whether to believe Christ or Nietzsche, and then argue that Christians are immortal, but Hitler and Mussolini are not, or vice versa. The decision will obviously be made on the battlefield, not in the study. Those who have the best poison gas will have the ethic of the future and will therefore be the immortal ones.

Our feelings and beliefs on the subject of good and evil are, like everything else about us, natural facts, developed in the struggle for existence and not having any divine or supernatural origin. In one of Aesop's fables, a lion is shown pictures of huntsmen catching lions and remarks that, if he had painted them, they would have shown lions catching huntsmen. Man, says Dr. Barnes, is a fine fellow because he can make airplanes. A little while ago there was a popular song about the cleverness of flies in walking upside down on the ceiling, with the chorus: "Could Lloyd George do it? Could Mr. Baldwin do it? Could Ramsay Mac do it? Why, NO." On this basis a very telling argument could be constructed by a theologically-minded fly, which no doubt the other flies would find most convincing.

Moreover, it is only when we think abstractly that we have such a high opinion of man. Of men in the concrete, most of us think the vast majority very bad. Civilized states spend more than half their revenue on killing each other's citizens. Consider the long history of the activities inspired by moral fervor: human sacrifices, persecutions of heretics, witch-hunts, pogroms leading up to wholesale extermination by poison gases, which one at least of Dr. Barnes's episcopal colleagues must be supposed to favor, since he holds pacifism to be un-Christian. Are these abominations, and the ethical doctrines by which they are prompted, really evidence of an intelligent Creator? And can we really wish that the men who practiced them should live forever? The world in which we live can be understood as a result of muddle and accident; but if it is the outcome of deliberate purpose, the purpose must have been that of a fiend. For my part, I find accident a less painful and more plausible hypothesis.

DISCUSSION QUESTIONS

1. Explain what Russell meant by saying, "The continuity of a human body is a matter of appearance and behavior, not of substance." Do you agree? Why or why not?

2. Discuss the difference between proving that life after death is possible and proving that life after death is not impossible. Are Russell's arguments directed against both endeavors? Give reasons for your answer.

3. What evidence can you cite to demonstrate that consciousness is or is not an epiphenomenon?

4. Do you agree with Russell that overcoming the fear of death is not a desirable goal?

5. How is the question of personal identity related to the issue of life after death?

6. Do you consider Russell's attitude toward death an optimistic or pessimistic one? Why?

ST. PAUL

The Resurrection
of
the Body

When the idea of an existence after death arose among the ancient Greeks, it was scarcely a hopeful doctrine. According to views that can be traced back to Homer, the dead inhabit a realm known as *Hades* (which means the unseen) where the shades of people dwell in a shadowy existence that could not even be called consciousness. Professor John Burnet suggests that "the traditional Athenian beliefs about the soul were cheerless enough, and we cannot wonder at the popularity of the Eleusinian Mysteries, which promised a better lot of some sort to the initiated after death."[1] The Eleusinian Mysteries Burnet refers to was one of a host of secret societies that promised their members a better lot in the next world. These mystery religions were uncommonly successful in keeping their secret rites secret, so not much is known about them, but they were extremely popular during the early years of Christianity. As was previously mentioned, there were other Greek views that denied completely any doctrine of the survival of death. Then, as now, radically different views of human destiny were held.

Four centuries before the birth of Jesus, the Greek philosopher Plato attempted to give philosophical support to the doctrine of the immortality of the soul. But when Plato spoke of the soul's immortality, he meant not only that the soul survives the dissolution of the body, but that the soul also existed before its birth into a body. By suggesting a radical distinction between soul and body, Plato placed the emphasis on the importance of purifying the soul through the pursuit of wisdom and

[1]John Burnet, "The Socratic Doctrine of the Soul," *Proceedings of the British Academy, 1915–16* (London: Published for the British Academy by Humphrey Milford, Oxford University Press, 1916), p. 248.

virtue. The body *(soma)* was the prison of the soul *(psyche),* and the goal of life was to be freed from the entrapment of the body. The body belongs to the sensible world and shares its corruptible nature, whereas the soul is related to the unchanging and imperishable realm of eternal reality. Wisdom is therefore the pursuit of the eternal, and in this pursuit of wisdom the body is only a hindrance to the soul. In Plato's view the entire life of a philosopher should be a turning away from the body and toward the eternal. This is the pursuit of wisdom, and philosophy is a love of wisdom. The soul of a philosopher at death is freed from the cycle of death and rebirth, and will not have to be reborn into another body. But a soul which has not been purified during life by the pursuit of wisdom will be reborn into another body and can achieve release from the cycle of death and rebirth only if it devotes itself to the pursuit of wisdom in some subsequent incarnation. For Plato, philosophy was more than a pursuit of truth, it was also a way to salvation. There are echoes here of themes from Indian thought with its doctrines of *karma* and reincarnation. In such books as the *Phaedo* and the *Republic,* Plato advanced arguments for the soul's immortality and attempted to demonstrate that the pursuit of virtue and the purification of the soul is life's most important task. In short, he argued that the lover of wisdom must be a stranger to this life and must try to live aloof from the body and cleanse the soul through the study of philosophy. In Plato's view, the true philosopher cares nothing for this life, for the body is an evil.

The other source for our views of death and future life is the religion of Israel. For most of its pre-Christian period, Judaism did not possess any view of an afterlife, focusing instead on the ethical obligations of living in covenant relationship with God. Like the Greeks, the ancient Hebrews had a vague notion that the soul *(nephesh)* of a person went at death into the shadowy world of *Sheol,* a place comparable to the Greek *Hades.* Sheol was a land of forgetfulness where nothing was totally real. Occasionally, but very rarely, do Jewish scriptures suggest that a shade from *Sheol* can be called back to earth—as the shade of the prophet Samuel was called back to speak to King Saul at the request of the witch of Endor.[2] But this occurrence is rare in Jewish thought, and had no enduring religious significance.

It was only in the late books of the Old Testament—Job, Daniel, and the latter parts of Isaiah—that a different possibility for human destiny was recognized. This was not conceived, in the Greek fashion, as the immortality of the soul; the Jews had a much too unitary view of the human personality to conceive of a disembodied soul existing apart from a body. What developed, rather, was the view that at the Day of the Lord (a phrase used to refer to a time of both blessing and judgment), some of the righteous dead would come back to earth in bodily form and as real persons. In Job we find this raised only as a tentative possibility: "If a man die, shall he live again?"[3] In Daniel, however, the possibility is more vivid: "And many of those who sleep in the dust of the earth shall awake, some to everlasting life, and some to shame and everlasting contempt."[4] The doctrine of the resurrection of the dead was still highly controversial in Judaism during the emergence of Christianity. We can see this reflected in the New Testament Gospels as one of the ongoing quarrels

[2] 1 Samuel 28:8–20
[3] Job 14:14
[4] Daniel 12:2

between the Pharisees and Sadducees. The Pharisees supported the doctrine of resurrection whereas the Sadducees, defenders of the "old-time religion," rejected it as a modernistic innovation.

The differences between the Greek and Hebrew views of human destiny are significant. For Plato, human beings are incarnated souls. In Jewish thought, human beings are animated bodies. It is not surprising that, with its roots in Judaism, the Christian view of human destiny reflects more the Jewish idea of resurrection than the Greek view of the soul's natural immortality. The following selection from 1 Corinthians is thought by many scholars to be the earliest literary reference to the resurrection of Jesus. What is significant in this statement is that St. Paul does not propose any philosophical arguments to support a doctrine of the immortality of the soul. Indeed, the trouble with such doctrines is that they assume the soul is by nature immortal. For Paul, in contrast, the Christian hope for resurrection is not based on some inherent quality of the human soul, but centers wholly in the power of God to bring new life to our mortal bodies.

Though the New Testament was written in Greek, and Paul was doubtless familiar with Greek attitudes toward the doctrine of the immortality of the soul (he quotes the Greek playwright Menander in verse 33), he follows a different course in the following selection. The Christian hope is for resurrection of the body, and the support St. Paul gives for this is not a set of philosophical arguments but the claim that Jesus was risen from the dead. The resurrection of Jesus is not only the basis for the Christian hope for individual resurrection, it also formed the heart of early Christian preaching. The evidence cited in support of the resurrection of Jesus is the many persons who saw Jesus after his resurrection, and the list given includes the "more than five hundred of his followers" mentioned in verse 6. In the Gospels reference is made to the empty tomb of Jesus as evidence for his resurrection, but Paul does not include that here, focusing instead on the eyewitness accounts.

A great deal hinges on the resurrection of Jesus. For Paul, this validated all the struggles that he and others were enduring, including his controversy with his opponents at Ephesus, referred to as "wild beasts" in verse 32. Conversely, "if Christ has not been raised from death, then we have nothing to preach and you have nothing to believe" (verse 14). What was ironic about the attitude of the Corinthian Christians to whom Paul was writing is that they apparently did not believe in the resurrection of the dead, but nevertheless continued to practice baptism, including the bizarre practice of being baptized for departed friends—a practice that seems to have been unique to Corinth, and did not reflect universal Christian practice. Since baptism, in Paul's view, was symbolic of the death and resurrection of Christ,[5] it would make no sense to practice it if one denied that the resurrection of the dead is assured by Christ's resurrection.

Paul did not stop with the proclamation of the Christian hope of resurrection; he also offered an analogy for conceiving of what this means. Reflecting the Jewish view that to exist is to have a body, Paul suggested that the resurrected state will be a bodily state. He gave the analogy of a seed which, when planted, dies in order to give rise to a full-grown plant. This metaphor taken from the processes of nature points to the resurrection body being as different from our present body as the plant

[5]Romans 6:3–5

is from the seed. But despite all its differences, the resurrection body will be a body; a "spiritual body," as St. Paul puts it, not a disembodied spirit as was conceived of in Greek thought. The transformation from the earthly to the spiritual body would occur through the power of God, and even those who are alive when Jesus returns again would experience such a transformation. Paul's comments in verses 51–52 indicate that he shared a view widely held by early Christians that the return of Jesus would occur during their lifetime. Even though they were wrong about this, it does not affect Paul's doctrine of resurrection, for the doctrine did not hinge upon the mistaken belief in the imminent return of Jesus.

Whereas the distinction between the Greek view of the soul's natural immortality and the Christian doctrine of bodily resurrection is very clear in the following passage, the difference between the two views was successively blurred over time. By the time of St. Thomas Aquinas in the thirteenth century the two doctrines had merged, and arguments in the Greek fashion were used by Christian writers. But for St. Paul, the evidence supporting the Christian hope for resurrection from the dead is not philosophical argument but the resurrection of Christ, which was attested to by hundreds of eyewitnesses. Take away this, says St. Paul, and there is little left.

Hope for Bodily Resurrection*

THE RESURRECTION OF CHRIST

And now I want to remind you, my brothers, of the Good News which I preached to you, which you received, and on which your faith stands firm. That is the gospel, the message that I preached to you. You are saved by the gospel if you hold firmly to it—unless it was for nothing that you believed.

I passed on to you what I received, which is of the greatest importance: that Christ died for our sins, as written in the Scriptures; that he was buried and that he was raised to life three days later, as written in the Scriptures; that he appeared to Peter and then to all twelve apostles. Then he appeared to more than five hundred of his followers at once, most of whom are still alive, although some have died. Then he appeared to James, and afterward to all the apostles.

Last of all he appeared also to me—even though I am like someone whose birth was abnormal.[1] For I am the least of all the apostles—I do not

---

*Source: From the *Good News Bible—New Testament:* Copyright © American Bible Society, 1966, 1971, 1976, 1 Corinthians 15. Used by permission.

[1]whose birth was abnormal; *or* who was born at the wrong time.

even deserve to be called an apostle, because I persecuted God's church. But by God's grace I am what I am, and the grace that he gave me was not without effect. On the contrary, I have worked harder than any of the other apostles, although it was not really my own doing, but God's grace working with me. So then, whether it came from me or from them, this is what we all preach, and this is what you believe.

OUR RESURRECTION

Now, since our message is that Christ has been raised from death, how can some of you say that the dead will not be raised to life? If that is true, it means that Christ was not raised; and if Christ has not been raised from death, then we have nothing to preach and you have nothing to believe. More than that, we are shown to be lying about God, because we said that he raised Christ from death—but if it is true that the dead are not raised to life, then he did not raise Christ. For if the dead are not raised, neither has Christ been raised. And if Christ has not been raised, then your faith is a delusion and you are still lost in your sins. It would also mean that the believers in Christ who have died are lost. If our hope in Christ is good for this life only and no more,[2] then we deserve more pity than anyone else in all the world.

But the truth is that Christ has been raised from death, as the guarantee that those who sleep in death will also be raised. For just as death came by means of a man, in the same way the rising from death comes by means of a man. For just as all people die because of their union with Adam, in the same way all will be raised to life because of their union with Christ. But each one will be raised in his proper order: Christ, first of all; then, at the time of his coming, those who belong to him. Then the end will come; Christ will overcome all spiritual rulers, authorities, and powers, and will hand over the Kingdom to God the Father. For Christ must rule until God defeats all enemies and puts them under his feet. The last enemy to be defeated will be death. For the scripture says, "God put *all* things under his feet." It is clear, of course, that the words "all things" do not include God himself, who puts all things under Christ.

But when all things have been placed under Christ's rule, then he himself, the Son, will place himself under God, who placed all things under him; and God will rule completely over all.

Now, what about those people who are baptized for the dead? What do they hope to accomplish? If it is true, as some claim, that the dead are not raised to life, why are those people being baptized for the dead?

[2] If our hope in Christ is good for this life only and no more; *or* If all we have in this life is our hope in Christ.

And as for us—why would we run the risk of danger every hour? My brothers, I face death every day! The pride I have in you, in our life in union with Christ Jesus our Lord, makes me declare this. If I have, as it were, fought "wild beasts" here in Ephesus simply from human motives, what have I gained? But if the dead are not raised to life, then, as the saying goes, "Let us eat and drink, for tomorrow we will die."

Do not be fooled. "Bad companions ruin good character." Come back to your right senses and stop your sinful ways. I declare to your shame that some of you do not know God.

THE RESURRECTION BODY

Someone will ask, "How can the dead be raised to life? What kind of body will they have?" You fool! When you plant a seed in the ground, it does not sprout to life unless it dies. And what you plant is a bare seed, perhaps a grain of wheat or some other grain, not the full-bodied plant that will later grow up. God provides that seed with the body he wishes; he gives each seed its own proper body.

And the flesh of living beings is not all the same kind of flesh; human beings have one kind of flesh, animals another, birds another, and fish another.

And there are heavenly bodies and earthly bodies; the beauty that belongs to heavenly bodies is different from the beauty that belongs to earthly bodies. The sun has its own beauty, the moon another beauty, and the stars a different beauty; and even among stars there are different kinds of beauty.

This is how it will be when the dead are raised to life. When the body is buried, it is mortal; when raised, it will be immortal. When buried, it is ugly and weak; when raised, it will be beautiful and strong. When buried, it is a physical body; when raised, it will be a spiritual body. There is, of course, a physical body, so there has to be a spiritual body. For the scripture says, "The first man, Adam, was created a living being"; but the last Adam is the life-giving Spirit. It is not the spiritual that comes first, but the physical, and then the spiritual.

The first Adam, made of earth, came from the earth; the second Adam came from heaven. Those who belong to the earth are like the one who was made of earth; those who are of heaven are like the one who came from heaven. Just as we wear the likeness of the man made of earth, so we will wear[3] the likeness of the man from heaven.

What I mean, brothers, is that what is made of flesh and blood

[3]we will wear; *some manuscripts have* let us wear.

cannot share in God's Kingdom, and what is mortal cannot possess immortality.

Listen to this secret truth: we shall not all die, but when the last trumpet sounds, we shall all be changed in an instant, as quickly as the blinking of an eye. For when the trumpet sounds, the dead will be raised, never to die again, and we shall all be changed. For what is mortal must be changed into what is immortal; what will die must be changed into what cannot die. So when this takes place, and the mortal has been changed into the immortal, then the scripture will come true: "Death is destroyed; victory is complete!"

> "Where, Death, is your victory?
> Where, Death, is your power to hurt?"

Death gets it power to hurt from sin, and sin gets its power from the Law. But thanks be to God who gives us the victory through our Lord Jesus Christ!

So then, my dear brothers, stand firm and steady. Keep busy always in your work for the Lord, since you know that nothing you do in the Lord's service is ever useless.

DISCUSSION QUESTIONS

1. Are the doctrines of bodily resurrection and immortality of the soul mutually exclusive? Give reasons for your answer.
2. Of the evidence cited by St. Paul in support of the resurrection of the body, which do you find most convincing?
3. Explain the differences between the Greek and Hebrew views of human destiny.
4. Examine the metaphors Paul used to describe the resurrection body. With the previous discussion of religious language in mind, discuss the significance of these metaphors.
5. How is the significance of the resurrection of Jesus reflected in early Christian attitudes toward baptism?

JOHN HICK

Immortality and Resurrection

Both the Greek idea of the soul's natural immortality and the Christian notion of bodily resurrection pose conceptual difficulties in attempting to make sense of what it could possibly mean to say that the "same person" who previously lived in an earthly body exists after death. The belief in bodily resurrection raises, in a particularly pointed way, the problem of the identification of a resurrected individual with that individual's previous manifestation.

This conceptual puzzle is addressed by Hick in several "thought experiments" in the selection that follows. Hick's analysis shows that the problem is not insurmountable. If it makes sense to find the principle of identity in the continuity of memory and habits, as Russell suggested, then the re-creation of a person with the same memories and habits and with the same physical appearance in another time and space would, in effect, be the re-creation of the same person. In Hick's model, and he suggests it only as one possible model, a resurrected John Smith who was identical in every respect with the pre-resurrection John Smith could be said to be the same person. This, of course, reduces the difficulty of the problem of identity to a minimum. A more interesting thought experiment might be to attempt to determine how different the resurrected John Smith could be with respect to the pre-resurrection John Smith and still be the same person. As Russell pointed out, we claim an identity today with the person we were several years ago even though the matter that composes our bodies is different, and our bodies may not even look the same now as they did then. Neither would it be the case that a resurrected John Smith would have to retain all the memories and habits of the pre-resurrection John Smith. Memories fade through the years, and habits change, yet we claim continuity with the person we used to be. In the case of a person with a total loss of memory, we still allow the claim of continuity with that person's past. In general, it would seem safe to conclude that a great deal of change in the pre-resurrection John Smith and the resurrected John Smith could be allowed without sacrificing the claim that he is the same person.

A more basic question, however, concerns the kind of evidence that might be available to support the view that we survive death. The Christian doctrine of resurrection is tied directly to the conviction that it is through the power of God that the individual can hope for re-creation after death. In contrast to the Greek doctrine of immortality in which the soul was thought immortal by nature, the Christian doctrine of resurrection stresses God's activity in re-creating the individual as a spiritual body. The only evidence St. Paul gives for this doctrine is the resurrection of Jesus, which was attested to by eyewitnesses including Paul himself. But we have to admit that as evidence this is less than infallible. We would have to accept the veracity of St. Paul's claim and the dependability of the witnesses before this could be said to constitute proof for us. In the final analysis it all comes down to confidence in the power of God that was at work in Jesus Christ. This is even borne out by the language of the New Testament which always speaks of God as the power behind the resurrection. When referring to Christ's resurrection, New Testament writers are always careful to say that he was "raised up" or that "God raised him up," not that Jesus raised himself from the dead. The emphasis is on God's action, and we are once again confronted with the necessity of faith in God as the ultimate basis for belief in the resurrection.

After the introductory sections, which provide an excellent summary and review of some of the themes we have already examined, Hick turns his attention to another possible avenue of proof for the view that we survive death. The spiritualist movement, with its claims of being able to communicate with the dead, appears to offer additional support for the belief that individual consciousness survives the dissolution of the physical body. If there were incontrovertible evidence that mediums and other sensitive persons could in fact communicate with those who have died, this would offer persuasive evidence that we might survive death. All such claims, however, are clouded by the trickery and fraud known to abound in attempts to communicate with the dead. An effort to rule out trickery by applying the controls offered by scientific standards of research has been made by the discipline known as parapsychology, which is dedicated to the investigation of such phenomena as telepathy, clairvoyance, thought transfer, and the claims of those who say that they can communicate with departed spirits.

Hick's probing analysis of the evidence offered to support the claims of spirit communication points out the restraint that should be applied in evaluating such claims. He further suggests that there may be some basis for explaining the activities of certain mediums by appealing to extrasensory perception. Evidence from the findings of parapsychological investigations seem to point to the ability of some individuals to be affected by the thoughts of a second person about a third person. Since the alleged communication with the dead always occurs in the presence of a living person who knew the dead person, the medium may be able to determine from the thoughts of the person present during a seance the characteristics of the "departed spirit" with whom the medium is attempting to communicate.

Even in those cases where all trickery has been ruled out, the alleged communication with the dead could be plausibly explained by means of telepathy. And extrasensory perception is a phenomenon that has been well documented, though not satisfactorily explained. Hick's conclusion is that it may be "that genuine mediums are simply persons of exceptional telepathic sensitiveness who unconsciously derive the 'spirits' from the clients' minds."

Hick's writing style is straightforward and clear, and needs no further amplifcation here. His conclusion that parapsychological research does not offer any real evidence of the survival of death seems to be justified. But beyond this, we can also conclude that even if there were solid evidence that the spirits of those who have died survived in some form and were able to communicate with those still living, this in itself would not enhance the Christian doctrine of resurrection. It would, in fact, be irrelevant to it, since the doctrine of resurrection does not envision a "ghostly" future existence, but rather the total re-creation of the person. Nor would incontrovertible evidence of the survival of death by an individual consciousness support the view that the soul is immortal. There is nothing in the claim of communication with the dead, even if such communication were genuine, to prove that the souls of the dead survive forever, which is what the doctrine of the immortality of the soul claims. All it would prove is that an individual consciouness can survive the death of the body for a time—perhaps a year, ten years, or whatever—not that it survives forever.

Since the philosophical concern with these issues must focus on the questions of evidence and argument, we must conclude with Hick that parapsychology offers little in the way of support for the belief that we survive death. Although spiritualism is a religious movement dedicated to this belief and the corollary belief in the ability of communicating with the dead, these claims do not stand up well to philosophical scrutiny.

Human Destiny:
Immortality and Resurrection*

THE IMMORTALITY OF THE SOUL

Some kind of distinction between physical body and immaterial or semimaterial soul seems to be as old as human culture; the existence of such a distinction has been indicated by the manner of burial of the earliest human skeletons yet discovered. Anthropologists offer various conjectures about the origin of the distinction: perhaps it was first suggested by memories of dead persons; by dreams of them; by the sight of reflections of oneself in water and on other bright surfaces; or by meditation upon the significance of religious rites which grew up spontaneously in face of the fact of death.

*Source: John Hick, *Philosophy of Religion,* 2nd edition, ©1973, pp. 97–106. Reprinted by permission of Prentice-Hall, Inc.

It was Plato (428/7–348/7 B.C.), the philosopher who has most deeply and lastingly influenced Western culture, who systematically developed the body-mind dichotomy and first attempted to prove the immortality of the soul.[1]

Plato argues that although the body belongs to the sensible world,[2] and shares its changing and impermanent nature, the intellect is related to the unchanging realities of which we are aware when we think not of particular good things but of Goodness itself, not of specific just acts but of Justice itself, and of the other "universals" or eternal Ideas in virtue of which physical things and events have their own specific characteristics. Being related to this higher and abiding realm, rather than to the evanescent world of sense, reason or the soul is immortal. Hence, one who devotes his life to the contemplation of eternal realities rather than to the gratification of the fleeting desires of the body will find at death that whereas his body turns to dust, his soul gravitates to the realm of the unchanging, there to live forever. Plato painted an awe-inspiring picture, of haunting beauty and persuasiveness, which has moved and elevated the minds of men in many different centuries and lands. Nevertheless, it is not today (as it was during the first centuries of the Christian era) the common philosophy of the West; and a demonstration of immortality which presupposes Plato's metaphysical system cannot claim to constitute a proof for the twentieth-century disbeliever.

Plato used the further argument that the only things that can suffer destruction are those that are composite, since to destroy something means to disintegrate it into its constituent parts. All material bodies are composite; the soul, however, is simple and therefore imperishable. This argument was adopted by Aquinas and has become standard in Roman Catholic theology, as in the following passage from the modern Catholic philosopher, Jacques Maritain:

> A spiritual soul cannot be corrupted, since it possesses no matter; it cannot be disintegrated, since it has no substantial parts; it cannot lose its individual unity, since it is self-subsisting, nor its internal energy, since it contains within itself all the sources of its energies. The human soul cannot die. Once it exists, it cannot disappear; it will necessarily exist for ever, endure without end. Thus, philosophic reason, put to work by a great metaphysician like Thomas Aquinas, is able to prove the immortality of the human soul in a demonstrative manner.[3]

This type of reasoning has been criticized on several grounds. Kant pointed out that although it is true that a simple substance cannot disin-

---

[1]*Phaedo.*

[2]The world known to us through our physical senses.

[3]Jacques Maritain, *The Range of Reason* (London: Geoffrey Bles Ltd. and New York: Charles Scribner's Sons, 1953), p. 60.

tegrate, consciousness may nevertheless cease to exist through the diminution of its intensity to zero.[4] Modern psychology has also questioned the basic premise that the mind is a simple entity. It seems instead to be a structure of only relative unity, normally fairly stable and tightly integrated but capable under stress of various degrees of division and dissolution. This comment from psychology makes it clear that the assumption that the soul is a simple substance is not an empirical observation but a metaphysical theory. As such, it cannot provide the basis for a general proof of immortality.

The body–soul distinction, first formulated as a philosophical doctrine in ancient Greece, was baptized into Christianity, ran through the medieval period, and entered the modern world with the public status of a self-evident truth when it was redefined in the seventeenth century by Descartes. Since World War II, however, the Cartesian mind–matter dualism, having been taken for granted for many centuries, has been strongly criticized by philosophers of the contemporary analytical school.[5] It is argued that the words that describe mental characteristics and operations—such as "intelligent," "thoughtful," "carefree," "happy," "calculating" and the like—apply in practice to types of human behavior and to behavioral dispositions. They refer to the empirical individual, the observable human being who is born and grows and acts and feels and dies, and not to the shadowy proceedings of a mysterious "ghost in the machine." Man is thus very much what he appears to be—a creature of flesh and blood, who behaves and is capable of behaving in a characteristic range of ways—rather than a nonphysical soul incomprehensibly interacting with a physical body.

As a result of this development much mid-twentieth-century philosophy has come to see man in the way he is seen in the biblical writings, not as an eternal soul temporarily attached to a mortal body, but as a form of finite, mortal, psychophysical life. Thus, the Old Testament scholar, J. Pedersen, says of the Hebrews that for them ". . . the body is the soul in its outward form."[6] This way of thinking has led to quite a different conception of death from that found in Plato and the neo-Platonic strand in European thought.

THE RE-CREATION OF THE PSYCHOPHYSICAL PERSON

Only toward the end of the Old Testament period did after-life beliefs come to have any real importance in Judaism. Previously, Hebrew

[4]Kant, *Critique of Pure Reason, Transcendental Dialectic*, "Refutation of Mendelssohn's Proof of the Permanence of the Soul."
[5]Gilbert Ryle's *The Concept of Mind* (London: Hutchinson & Co., Ltd., 1949) is a classic statement of this critique.
[6]*Israel* (London: Oxford University Press, 1926), I, 170.

religious insight had focused so fully upon God's covenant with the nation, as an organism that continued through the centuries while successive generations lived and died, that the thought of a divine purpose for the individual, a purpose that transcended this present life, developed only when the breakdown of the nation as a political entity threw into prominence the individual and the problem of his personal destiny.

When a positive conviction arose of God's purpose holding the individual in being beyond the crisis of death, this conviction took the non-Platonic form of belief in the resurrection of the body. By the turn of the eras, this had become an article of faith for one Jewish sect, the Pharisees, although it was still rejected as an innovation by the more conservative Sadducees.

The religious difference between the Platonic belief in the immortality of the soul, and the Judaic-Christian belief in the resurrection of the body is that the latter postulates a special divine act of re-creation. This produces a sense of utter dependence upon God in the hour of death, a feeling that is in accordance with the biblical understanding of man as having been formed out of "the dust of the earth,"[7] a product (as we say today) of the slow evolution of life from its lowly beginnings in the primeval slime. Hence, in the Jewish and Christian conception, death is something real and fearful. It is not thought to be like walking from one room to another, or taking off an old coat and putting on a new one. It means sheer unqualified extinction—passing out from the lighted circle of life into "death's dateless night." Only through the sovereign creative love of God can there be a new existence beyond the grave.

What does "the resurrection of the dead" mean? Saint Paul's discussion provides the basic Christian answer to this question.[8] His conception of the general resurrection (distinguished from the unique resurrection of Jesus) has nothing to do with the resuscitation of corpses in a cemetery. It concerns God's re-creation or reconstitution of the human psychophysical individual, not as the organism that has died but as a *soma pneumatikon*, a "spiritual body," inhabiting a spiritual world as the physical body inhabits our present physical world.

A major problem confronting any such doctrine is that of providing criteria of personal identity to link the earthly life and the resurrection life. Paul does not specifically consider this question, but one may, perhaps, develop his thought along lines such as the following.[9]

Suppose, first, that someone—John Smith—living in the USA were suddenly and inexplicably to disappear from before the eyes of his

[7]Genesis, 2:7; Psalm 103:14.

[8]I Corinthians 15.

[9]The following paragraphs are adapted, with permission, from a section of my article, "Theology and Verification," published in *Theology Today* (April, 1960) and reprinted in *The Existence of God* (New York: The Macmillan Company, 1964).

friends, and that at the same moment an exact replica of him were inexplicably to appear in India. The person who appears in India is exactly similar in both physical and mental characteristics to the person who disappeared in America. There is continuity of memory, complete similarity of bodily features including fingerprints, hair and eye coloration, and stomach contents, and also of beliefs, habits, emotions, and mental dispositions. Further, the "John Smith" replica thinks of himself as being the John Smith who disappeared in the USA. After all possible tests have been made and have proved positive, the factors leading his friends to accept "John Smith" as John Smith would surely prevail and would cause them to overlook even his mysterious transference from one continent to another, rather than treat "John Smith," with all John Smith's memories and other characteristics, as someone other than John Smith.

Suppose, second, that our John Smith, instead of inexplicably disappearing, dies, but that at the moment of his death a "John Smith" replica, again complete with memories and all other characteristics, appears in India. Even with the corpse on our hands we would, I think, still have to accept this "John Smith" as the John Smith who died. We would have to say that he had been miraculously re-created in another place.

Now suppose, third, that on John Smith's death the "John Smith" replica appears, not in India, but as a resurrection replica in a different world altogether, a resurrection world inhabited only by resurrected persons. This world occupies its own space distinct from that with which we are now familiar. That is to say, an object in the resurrection world is not situated at any distance or in any direction from the objects in our present world, although each object in either world is spatially related to every other object in the same world.

This supposition provides a model by which one may conceive of the divine re-creation of the embodied human personality. In this model, the element of the strange and the mysterious has been reduced to a minimum by following the view of some of the early Church Fathers that the resurrection body has the same shape as the physical body,[10] and ignoring Paul's own hint that it may be as unlike the physical body as a full grain of wheat differs from the wheat seed.[11]

What is the basis for this Judaic-Christian belief in the divine re-creation or reconstitution of the human personality after death? There is, of course, an argument from authority, in that life after death is taught throughout the New Testament (although very rarely in the Old Testament). But, more basically, belief in the resurrection arises as a corollary of faith in the sovereign purpose of God, which is not restricted by death

[10]For example, Irenaeus, *Against Heresies*, Book II, Chap. 34, para. 1.
[11]I Corinthians, 15:37.

and which holds man in being beyond his natural mortality. In the words of Martin Luther, "Anyone with whom God speaks, whether in wrath or in mercy, the same is certainly immortal. The Person of God who speaks, and the Word, show that we are creatures with whom God wills to speak, right into eternity, and in an immortal manner."[12] In a similar vein it is argued that if it be God's plan to create finite persons to exist in fellowship with himself, then it contradicts both his own intention and his love for the creatures made in his image if he allows men to pass out of existence when his purpose for them remains largely unfulfilled.

It is this promised fulfillment of God's purpose for man, in which the full possibilities of human nature will be realized, that constitutes the "heaven" symbolized in the New Testament as a joyous banquet in which all and sundry rejoice together. As we saw when discussing the problem of evil, no theodicy can succeed without drawing into itself this eschatological[13] faith in an eternal, and therefore infinite, good which thus outweighs all the pains and sorrows that have been endured on the way to it.

Balancing the idea of heaven in Christian tradition is the idea of hell. This, too, is relevant to the problem of theodicy. For just as the reconciling of God's goodness and power with the fact of evil requires that out of the travail of history there shall come in the end an eternal good for man, so likewise it would seem to preclude man's eternal misery. The only kind of evil that is finally incompatible with God's unlimited power and love would be utterly pointless and wasted suffering, pain which is never redeemed and worked into the fulfilling of God's good purpose. Unending torment would constitute precisely such suffering; for being eternal, it could never lead to a good end beyond itself. Thus, hell as conceived by its enthusiasts, such as Augustine or Calvin, is a major part of the problem of evil! If hell is construed as eternal torment, the theological motive behind the idea is directly at variance with the urge to seek a theodicy. However, it is by no means clear that the doctrine of eternal punishment can claim a secure New Testament basis.[14] If, on the other hand, "hell" means a continuation of the purgatorial suffering often experienced in this life, and leading eventually to the high good of heaven, it no longer stands in conflict with the needs of theodicy. Again, the idea of hell may be de-literalized and valued as a *mythos,* as a powerful and pregnant symbol of the grave responsibility inherent in man's freedom in relation to his Maker.

---

[12]Quoted by Emil Brunner, *Dogmatics,* II, 69.

[13]From the Greek *eschaton,* end.

[14]The Greek word *aionios,* which is used in the New Testament and which is usually translated as "eternal" or "everlasting," can bear either this meaning or the more limited meaning of "for the aeon, or age."

DOES PARAPSYCHOLOGY HELP?

The spiritualist movement claims that life after death has been proved by well-attested cases of communication between the living and the "dead." During the closing quarter of the nineteenth century and the decades of the present century this claim has been made the subject of careful and prolonged study by a number of responsible and competent persons.[15] This work, which may be approximately dated from the founding in London of the Society for Psychical Research in 1882, is known either by the name adopted by that society or in the United States by the name parapsychology.

Approaching the subject from the standpoint of our interest in this chapter, we may initially divide the phenomena studied by the parapsychologist into two groups. There are those phenomena that involve no reference to the idea of a life after death, chief among these being psychokinesis and extrasensory perception (ESP) in its various forms (such as telepathy, clairvoyance, and precognition). And there are those phenomena that raise the question of personal survival after death, such as the apparitions and other sensory manifestations of dead persons and the "spirit messages" received through mediums. This division is, however, only of preliminary use, for ESP has emerged as a clue to the understanding of much that occurs in the second group. We shall begin with a brief outline of the reasons that have induced the majority of workers in this field to be willing to postulate so strange an occurrence as telepathy.

Telepathy is a name for the mysterious fact that sometimes a thought in the mind of one person apparently causes a similar thought to occur to someone else when there are no normal means of communication between them, and under circumstances such that mere coincidence seems to be excluded.

For example, one person may draw a series of pictures or diagrams on paper and somehow transmit an impression of these to someone else in another room who then draws recognizable reproductions of them. This might well be a coincidence in the case of a single successful reproduction; but can a series consist entirely of coincidences?

Experiments have been devised to measure the probability of chance coincidence in supposed cases of telepathy. In the simplest of

[15]The list of past presidents of the Society for Psychical Research includes the philosophers Henri Bergson, William James, Hans Driesch, Henry Sidgwick, F. C. S. Schiller, C. D. Broad, and H. H. Price; the psychologists William McDougall, Gardner Murphy, Franklin Prince, and R. H. Thouless; the physicists Sir William Crookes, Sir Oliver Lodge, Sir William Barrett, and Lord Rayleigh; and the classicist Gilbert Murray.

these, cards printed in turn with five different symbols are used. A pack of fifty, consisting of ten bearing each symbol, is then thoroughly shuffled, and the sender concentrates on the cards one at a time while the receiver (who of course can see neither sender nor cards) tries to write down the correct order of symbols. This procedure is repeated, with constant reshuffling, hundreds or thousands of times. Since there are only five different symbols, a random guess would stand one chance in five of being correct. Consequently, on the assumption that only "chance" is operating, the receiver should be right in about 20 per cent of his tries, and wrong in about 80 per cent; and the longer the series, the closer should be the approach to this proportion. However, good telepathic subjects are right in a far larger number of cases than can be reconciled with random guessing. The deviation from chance expectation can be converted mathematically into "odds against chance" (increasing as the proportion of hits is maintained over a longer and longer series of tries). In this way, odds of over a million to one have been recorded. J. B. Rhine (Duke University) has reported results showing "antichance" values ranging from seven (which equals odds against chance of 100,000 to one) to eighty-two (which converts the odds against chance to billions).[16] S.G. Soal (London University) has reported positive results for precognitive telepathy with odds against chance of $10^{35} \times 5$, or of billions to one.[17] Other researchers have also recorded confirming results.[18] In the light of these reports, it is difficult to deny that some positive factor, and not merely "chance," is operating. "Telepathy" is simply a name for this unknown positive factor.

How does telepathy operate? Only negative conclusions seem to be justified to date. It can, for example, be said with reasonable certainty that telepathy does not consist in any kind of physical radiation, analogous to radio waves. For, first, telepathy is not delayed or weakened in proportion to distance, as are all known forms of radiation; and, second, there is no organ in the brain or elsewhere that can plausibly be regarded as its

[16]J. B. Rhine, *Extrasensory Perception* (Boston: Society for Psychical Research, 1935), Table XLIII, p. 162. See also Rhine, *New Frontiers of the Mind* (New York: Farrar and Rinehart, Inc., 1937), pp. 69f.

[17]S. G. Soal, *Proceedings of the Society for Psychical Research*, XLVI, 152–98 and XLVII, 21–150. See also S. G. Soal's *The Experimental Situation in Psychical Research* (London: The Society for Psychical Research, 1947).

[18]For surveys of the experimental work, see Whately Carrington, *Telepathy* (London: Methuen & Co. Ltd., 1945); G. N. M. Tyrrell, *The Personality of Man* (London: Penguin Books Ltd., 1946); S. G. Soal and F. Bateman, *Modern Experiments in Telepathy* (London: Faber & Faber Ltd. and New Haven, Conn.: Yale University Press, 1954); and for important Russian work, L. L. Vasiliev, *Experiments in Mental Suggestion*, 1962 (Church Crookham: Institute for the Study of Mental Images, 1963—English translation).

sending or receiving center. Telepathy appears to be a purely mental occurrence.

It is not, however, a matter of transferring or transporting a thought out of one mind into another—if, indeed, such an idea makes sense at all. The telepathized thought does not leave the sender's consciousness in order to enter that of the receiver. What happens would be better described by saying that the sender's thought gives rise to a mental "echo" in the mind of the receiver. This "echo" occurs at the unconscious level, and consequently the version of it that rises into the receiver's consciousness may be only fragmentary and may be distorted or symbolized in various ways, as in dreams.

According to one theory that has been tentatively suggested to explain telepathy, our minds are separate and mutually insulated only at the conscious (and preconscious) level. But at the deepest level of the unconscious, we are constantly influencing one another, and it is at this level that telepathy takes place.[19]

How is a telepathized thought directed to one particular receiver among so many? Apparently the thoughts are directed by some link of emotion or common interest. For example, two friends are sometimes telepathically aware of any grave crisis or shock experienced by the other, even though they are at opposite ends of the earth.

We shall turn now to the other branch of parapsychology, which has more obvious bearing upon our subject. The *Proceedings of the Society for Psychical Research* contains a large number of carefully recorded and satisfactorily attested cases of the appearance of the figure of someone who has recently died to living people (in rare instances to more than one at a time) who were, in many cases, at a distance and unaware of the death. The S.P.R. reports also establish beyond reasonable doubt that the minds that operate in the mediumistic trance, purporting to be spirits of the departed, sometimes give personal information the medium could not have acquired by normal means and at times even give information, later verified, which had not been known to any living person.

On the other hand, physical happenings, such as the "materializations" of spirit forms in a visible and tangible form, are much more doubtful. But even if we discount the entire range of physical phenomena, it remains true that the best cases of trance utterance are impressive and puzzling, and taken at face value are indicative of survival and communication after death. If, through a medium, one talks with an intelligence that gives a coherent impression of being an intimately known friend who has died and establishes identity by a wealth of private information and indefinable personal characteristics—as has occasionally

[19]Whately Carrington, *Telepathy* (London: Methuen & Co. Ltd., 1945), Chaps. 6–8.

happened—then we cannot dismiss without careful trial the theory that what is taking place is the return of a consciousness from the spirit world.

However, the advance of knowledge in the other branch of parapsychology, centering upon the study of extrasensory perception, has thrown unexpected light upon this apparent commerce with the departed. For it suggests that unconscious telepathic contact between the medium and his or her client is an important and possibly a sufficient explanatory factor. This was vividly illustrated by the experience of two women who decided to test the spirits by taking into their minds, over a period of weeks, the personality and atmosphere of an entirely imaginary character in an unpublished novel written by one of the women. After thus filling their minds with the characteristics of this fictitious person, they went to a reputable medium, who proceeded to describe accurately their imaginary friend as a visitant from beyond the grave and to deliver appropriate messages from him.

An even more striking case is that of the "direct voice" medium (i.e., a medium in whose séances the voice of the communicating "spirit" is heard apparently speaking out of the air) who produced the spirit of one "Gordon Davis" who spoke in his own recognizable voice, displayed considerable knowledge about Gordon Davis, and remembered his death. This was extremely impressive until it was discovered that Gordon Davis was still alive; he was, of all ghostly occupations, a real-estate agent, and had been trying to sell a house at the time when the séance took place![20]

Such cases suggest that genuine mediums are simply persons of exceptional telepathic sensitiveness who unconsciously derive the "spirits" from their clients' minds.

In connection with "ghosts," in the sense of apparitions of the dead, it has been established that there can be "meaningful hallucinations," the source of which is almost certainly telepathic. To quote a classic and somewhat dramatic example: a woman sitting by a lake sees the figure of a man running toward the lake and throwing himself in. A few days later a man commits suicide by throwing himself into this same lake. Presumably, the explanation of the vision is that the man's thought while he was contemplating suicide had been telepathically projected onto the scene via the woman's mind.[21]

In many of the cases recorded there is delayed action. The telepathically projected thought lingers in the recipient's unconscious mind until a suitable state of inattention to the outside world enables it to appear to his

[20]S. G. Soal, "A Report of Some Communications Received through Mrs. Blanche Cooper," Sec. 4, *Proceedings of the Society for Psychical Research*, XXXV, 560–89.

[21]F. W. H. Myers, *Human Personality and Its Survival of Bodily Death* (London: Longmans, Green, & Co., 1903), I, 270–71.

conscious mind in a dramatized form—for example, by a hallucinatory voice or vision—by means of the same mechanism that operates in dreams.

If phantoms of the living can be created by previously experienced thoughts and emotions of the person whom they represent, the parallel possibility arises that phantoms of the dead are caused by thoughts and emotions that were experienced by the person represented when he was alive. In other words, ghosts may be "psychic footprints," a kind of mental trace left behind by the dead, but not involving the presence or even the continued existence of those whom they represent.

These considerations tend away from the hopeful view that parapsychology will open a window onto another world. However, it is too early for a final verdict; and in the meantime one should be careful not to confuse absence of knowledge with knowledge of absence.[22]

DISCUSSION QUESTIONS

1. Which of the alleged evidences for survival after death offered by psychical research do you find most convincing? Least convincing?

2. Do you agree that even if there were undeniable evidence from psychical research that individual consciousnesses survived death, this would not prove the immortality of the soul? Why or why not?

3. Explain what Hick meant when he said that "ghosts may be 'psychic footprints,' a kind of mental trace, left behind by the dead." Do you agree with this?

4. Do you agree with Hick that "one should be careful not to confuse absence of knowledge with knowledge of absence"? What are your reasons?

5 Given our readings thus far, what do you consider to be the best argument in support of the claim that we survive death?

---

[22] Perhaps the most thorough philosophical discussion of the subject is C. D. Broad's *Lectures on Psychical Research* (London: Routledge & Kegan Paul Ltd., and New York: Humanities Press, Inc., 1962).

RAYMOND A. MOODY, JR.

Near-Death
Experiences

Death remains a puzzle to us in spite of the fact that it is a universal human experience, because no one has ever returned from death to tell us about it. Therefore our view of death will be in large part a function of our scientific, metaphysical, and religious views. We began this section with an examination of the views of Bertrand Russell who argued, on the basis of scientific presuppositions, that hopes for an afterlife are unfounded. Russell admits that there is no proof that we do not survive death, though he thinks this is highly unlikely given the nature of consciousness as an epiphenomenon, a function of the physical body. His conclusion is that when the physical body ceases to function, all its allied functions, including conscious activity, likewise cease.

While certainly plausible, Russell's view is not universally accepted. It is not surprising that there was an eager audience waiting for alternative testimony such as is offered in Raymond A. Moody's book *Life After Life*. Listed on the best-seller charts for months, this book contains reports from those who have "died" in a technical, clinical sense, but who through modern medical techniques were resuscitated. Moody has doctorates in both philosophy and medicine and is therefore in a unique position to gather and evaluate the reports of those who have had this experience. What intrigued Moody in his conversations with these persons was the uniformity of their reports. It is also significant that the individuals who had undergone these experiences were reluctant to talk about them until prodded by a sympathetic and eager investigator.

The hypothesis is a bold one: though death is the experience from which no one has returned to give a report, the new possibilities offered by modern medicine

331

allows persons who have "died" in a clinical sense but have been revived to report their experiences, and perhaps from these reports we can gain additional insight into the nature of death. Moody's book is filled with numerous interviews with patients who have undergone the experience of clinical death, and from these reports he has compiled a composite experience which is included in the following selection from his book. This composite does not reflect the experience of any single individual, but it contains elements that were reported repeatedly in interviews. Additionally, not everyone who was pronounced dead but was later revived reported these experiences; some individuals remember nothing of the period during which they were clinically dead.

What is interesting about these accounts is that they do not seem to differ for believers in God and nonbelievers, although the reports of believers show distinctively religious elements, such as the identification of the "being of light" with a divine figure. It is also interesting that these reports contain elements also found in some ancient accounts of the fate of the dead, such as the stories from the Orphic religion which Plato relates, or the Tibetan Book of the Dead.

What can we, philosophically, make of these reports?

First, it would be a mistake to take these experiences as in any way offering unassailable proof that we survive death. Being philosophically astute, Moody is careful not to do so. In his book he offers alternative explanations which might satisfactorily account for these experiences: wish fulfillment, neurological causes, or some other psychological basis for these experiences which cannot be ruled out *a priori*. Moody suggests that at this point in the development of our knowledge we are not in the possession of sufficient data to allow us to generalize from these experiences. It also might be the case that adjustments in our scientific assumptions will be required for us to understand these experiences fully. At any rate, the reports of those who have clinically died should not be simply dismissed out of hand.

Second, the parallels between these reports and certain themes in ancient writings are intriguing, but it would be an error to take them as confirmation of ancient stories of the fate of the dead, such as are found in the Tibetan Book of the Dead or in Orphic literature. Moody's research does provide one possible explanation for the origin of these ancient religious traditions about death. Although cases of survival of near-death experiences are more numerous today as a result of the advancement of medical science, we must not assume that there were never similar cases in antiquity. When persons today are resuscitated from clinical death, they give credit to the extraordinary accomplishments of medicine. But in ancient times if a person had such an experience and was revived, it is easy to understand how that person might have interpreted the experience as a revelation of the mysteries of death, which would perhaps be interpreted as a deep religious insight that should become a part of the teachings of a religious tradition.

Third, even if we accept the reports of those who have undergone near-death experiences as providing dependable information concerning what happens when a person dies, they do not confirm the view that we survive death for an extended period. Some kind of conscious activity might survive the death of the physical body . . . for an hour, a day, or who knows how long? Nothing in these accounts supports belief in immortality, such as the Greeks conceived it, nor do these reports offer confirmation of the doctrine of resurrection as St. Paul thought of it.

Fourth, an objection to these reports as not really dealing with death at all can be made on the basis of the logic of the term itself. One could argue that a person who has "died" according to the clinical definition but has been resuscitated has not in fact died at all. If by "death" we mean the cessation of all vital signs, the absence of all conscious activity, and the beginnings of the body's decomposition, then the logical implication is that none of the persons interviewed by Moody had in fact died. We then would be dealing with not an experience of dying, but a near-death experience, which is quite a different thing.

Finally, there is the question of how such near-death experiences affect the hopes and beliefs of religious faith. There is no question but that religious faith in the minds of many persons is directly tied to hope for life after death. There are, however, religions without any doctrine of a personal afterlife, such as Buddhism and Confucianism, which are principally concerned with the ethical obligations of this present life. But it is still the case that a vital element in most religions is that they offer some hope for the future in spite of death. The Greek mystery religions, which have already been referred to, were obsessed with the question of the survival of death. And as the selection from St. Paul showed, the hope for resurrection is at the heart of Christian belief. One might then expect to find churchmen eagerly embracing the reports of Moody and others as confirmations of the truth of the Christian doctrine of an afterlife; in fact, such has not been the case. Some Christian spokespersons have rejected these reports as offers of "cheap grace," which undermine the motivation for right living by a soothing assurance that death holds only pleasantness regardless of the kind of life one leads here and now. This kind of reaction points directly to the question of the relationship between religion and ethics that we will explore further in the next section.

After the initial excitement dies down, we will probably conclude that near-death experiences are neither confirmations of the religious hope for a future life nor threats to it. But what are we to conclude about these experiences at the present moment? Moody puts it well when he observes, "I am left, not with conclusions or evidence or proofs, but with something much less definite—feelings, questions, analogies, puzzling facts to be explained."

Life After Life?*

Despite the wide variation in the circumstances surrounding close calls with death and in the types of persons undergoing them, it remains true that there is a striking similarity among the accounts of the experiences themselves. In fact, the similarities among various reports are so

*Source: Raymond A. Moody, Jr. *Life After Life* (New York: Bantam Books, 1976), pp. 21–25, 181–84. ©1975 by Raymond A. Moody, Jr. Used by permission.

great that one can easily pick out about fifteen separate elements which recur again and again in the mass of narratives that I have collected. On the basis of these points of likeness, let me now construct a brief, theoretically "ideal" or "complete" experience which embodies all of the common elements, in the order in which it is typical for them to occur.

A man is dying and, as he reaches the point of greatest physical distress, he hears himself pronounced dead by his doctor. He begins to hear an uncomfortable noise, a loud ringing or buzzing, and at the same time feels himself moving very rapidly through a long dark tunnel. After this, he suddenly finds himself outside of his own physical body, but still in the immediate physical environment, and he sees his own body from a distance, as though he is a spectator. He watches the resuscitation attempt from this unusual vantage point and is in a state of emotional upheaval.

After a while, he collects himself and becomes more accustomed to his odd condition. He notices that he still has a "body," but one of a very different nature and with very different powers from the physical body he has left behind. Soon other things begin to happen. Others come to meet and to help him. He glimpses the spirits of relatives and friends who have already died, and a loving, warm spirit of a kind he has never encountered before—a being of light—appears before him. This being asks him a question, nonverbally, to make him evaluate his life and helps him along by showing him a panoramic, instantaneous playback of the major events of his life. At some point he finds himself approaching some sort of barrier or border, apparently representing the limit between earthly life and the next life. Yet, he finds that he must go back to the earth, that the time for his death has not yet come. At this point he resists, for by now he is taken up with his experiences in the afterlife and does not want to return. He is overwhelmed by intense feelings of joy, love, and peace. Despite his attitude, though, he somehow reunites with his physical body and lives.

Later he tries to tell others, but he has trouble doing so. In the first place, he can find no human words adequate to describe these unearthly episodes. He also finds that others scoff, so he stops telling other people. Still, the experience affects his life profoundly, especially his views about death and its relationship to life.

It is important to bear in mind that the above narrative is not meant to be a representation of any one person's experience. Rather, it is a "model," a composite of the common elements found in very many stories. I introduce it here only to give a preliminary, general idea of what a person who is dying may experience. Since it is an abstraction rather than an actual account, in the present chapter I will discuss in detail each common element, giving many examples.

Before doing that, however, a few facts need to be set out in order to put the remainder of my exposition of the experience of dying into the proper framework.

1. Despite the striking similarities among various accounts, no two of them are precisely identical (though a few come remarkably close to it).

2. I have found no one person who reports every single component of the composite experience. Very many have reported most of them (that is, eight or more of the fifteen or so) and a few have reported up to twelve.

3. There is no one element of the composite experience which every single person has reported to me, which crops up in every narrative. Nonetheless, a few of these elements come fairly close to being universal.

4. There is not one component of my abstract model which has appeared in only one account. Each element has shown up in many separate stories.

5. The order in which a dying person goes through the various stages briefly delineated above may vary from that given in my "theoretical model." To give one example, various persons have reported seeing the "being of light" before, or at the same time, they left their physical bodies, and not as in the "model," some time afterward. However, the order in which the stages occur in the model is a very typical order, and wide variations are unusual.

6. How far into the hypothetical complete experience a dying person gets seems to depend on whether or not the person actually underwent an apparent clinical death, and if so, on how long he was in this state. In general, persons who were "dead" seem to report more florid, complete experiences than those who only came close to death, and those who were "dead" for a longer period go deeper than those who were "dead" for a shorter time.

7. I have talked to a few people who were pronounced dead, resuscitated, and came back reporting none of these common elements. Indeed, they say that they don't remember anything at all about their "deaths." Interestingly enough, I have talked with several persons who were actually adjudged clinically dead on separate occasions years apart, and reported experiencing nothing on one of the occasions, but having had quite involved experiences on the other.

8. It must be emphasized that I am writing primarily about reports, accounts, or narratives, which other persons have given to me verbally during interviews. Thus, when I remark that a given element of the abstract, "complete" experience does not occur in a given account, I do not mean necessarily to imply that it did not happen to the person involved. I only mean that this person did not tell me that it did occur, or that it does not definitely come out in his account that he experienced it. . . .

In writing this book I have been acutely conscious that my purpose and perspectives might very easily be misunderstood. In particular, I would like to say to scientifically-minded readers that I am fully aware that what I have done here does not constitute a scientific study. And to my fellow philosophers I would insist that I am not under the delusion that I have "proven" there is life after death. To deal with these matters thoroughly would involve the discussion of technical details which lie beyond the scope of this book, so I shall limit myself to the following brief remarks.

In such specialized studies as logic, law, and science the words "conclusion," "evidence," and "proof" are technical terms and have more sophisticated meanings than they do in common usage. In everyday language these same words are used very loosely. A glance at any of the more sensational popular magazines will enable one to see that almost any unlikely tale will be given as "proof" of some improbable claim.

In logic what can and cannot be said to follow from a given set of premises is not at all a casual matter. It is very vigorously and precisely defined by rules, conventions, and laws. When one says that one has drawn a certain "conclusion," one is implicitly making the claim that anyone who begins from the same premises must arrive at the same conclusion, unless he has made a mistake in logic.

These remarks indicate why I refuse to draw any "conclusions" from my study and why I say that I am not trying to construct a proof of the ancient doctrine of the survival of bodily death. Yet I think that these reports of near-death experiences are very significant. What I want to do is find some middle way of interpreting them—a way which neither rejects these experiences on the basis that they do not constitute scientific or logical proof nor sensationalizes them by resorting to vague emotional claims that they "prove" that there is life after death.

At the same time, it seems to me to be an open possibility that our present inability to construct a "proof" may not represent a limitation imposed by the nature of the near-death experiences themselves. Perhaps it is instead a limitation of the currently accepted modes of scientific and logical thought. It may be that the perspective of scientists and logicians of the future will be very different. (One must remember that historically logic and scientific methodology have not been fixed and static systems but growing, dynamic processes.)

So I am left, not with conclusions or evidence or proofs, but with something much less definite—feelings, questions, analogies, puzzling facts to be explained. In fact, it might be more appropriate to ask, not what conclusions I have drawn on the basis of my study, but rather how the study has affected me personally. In response I can only say: There is something very persuasive about seeing a person describe his experience which cannot easily be conveyed in writing. Their near-death experiences were very real events to these people, and through my association with them the experiences have become real events to me.

I realize, however, that this is a psychological consideration and not a logical one. Logic is a public matter, and psychological considerations are not public in the same way. One person may be affected or changed in one way and another person in a different way by the same set of circumstances. It is a matter of disposition and temperament, and I do not wish to imply that my own reaction to this study should be a law for the thinking of everyone else. In view of this, some might ask, "If the interpretation of these experiences is ultimately such a subjective matter, why study them?" I can think of no other way to answer this than to point again to the universal human concern with the nature of death. I believe that any light whatever which can be shed on the nature of death is to the good.

Enlightenment on this subject is needed by members of many professions and academic fields. It is needed by the physician who has to deal with the fears and hopes of the dying patient and by the minister helping others to face death. It is needed also by psychologists and psychiatrists, because in order to devise a workable and reliable method for the therapy of emotional disturbances they need to know what the mind *is* and whether it can exist apart from the body. If it cannot, then the emphasis of psychological therapy would shift ultimately toward physical methods—drugs, electric shock therapy, brain surgery, and the like. On the other hand, if there are indications that the mind can exist apart from the body and that it is something in its own right, then therapy for mental disorders must finally be something very different.

However, more than academic and professional issues are involved. It involves deeply personal issues, for what we learn about death may make an important difference in the way we live our lives. If experiences of the type which I have discussed are real, they have very profound implications for what every one of us is doing with his life. For, then it would be true that we cannot fully understand this life until we catch a glimpse of what lies beyond it.

DISCUSSION QUESTIONS

1. What do you think the near-death experience recorded by Moody can tell us about death?

2. Do you agree with Moody's conclusion that near-death experiences do not provide us with a proof of the doctrine of the survival of bodily death? Why or why not?

3. What is your evaluation of the interpretation that sees the kind of experience described by Moody as not an experience of dying at all but only a near-death experience? What are your reasons?

4. Do you think Moody's research is a confirmation or refutation of St. Paul's view of bodily resurrection? Give reasons for your answer.

5. Does reading Moody's work in any way alter your view of death? If so, how? If not, why not?

Retrospective

We began this section with three questions. The first one dealt with the kind of evidence that is available to support the belief that death is not the cessation of consciousness, and this question was addressed directly by all the selections in this section. Bertrand Russell suggested that all the evidence of scientific investigation seems to be against the view that individual consciousness survives the dissolution of the body. For him, any hope for a future life is futile and not supported by the evidence, though he admits that the emotional reinforcement for this belief is strong. A distinctively religious alternative was offered by St. Paul's claim that the resurrection of Jesus provides assurance for belief in a future resurrection, and the evidence he cites for the resurrection of Jesus is the eyewitness reports of those who had seen the risen Christ.

The evidence for survival of death offered by psychic research is open to serious reservations. Hick's analysis shows that alleged communication with the dead can be explained in other ways, notably through extrasensory perception, which has received enough experimental validation to be taken seriously. The availability of an alternative explanation for these phenomena reduces their usefulness as evidence for an after life. Likewise, the reports of the experiences of those who have clinically died and been resuscitated raise many interesting issues, but they cannot be offered as proof of life after death. These experiences offer a fruitful field for further investigation by professionals in many fields, as Moody points out, but they do not leave us with anything that can be called proof.

Like other issues that we have examined in the philosophy of religion, the question of death and human destiny does not seem to be one that can be completely resolved one way or the other. But precisely because the evidence is ambiguous, the question of the survival of death remains an open one for religion. Even Russell, who thinks that the weight of scientific evidence counts against any doctrine of survival, acknowledges that there is no decisive proof against it. St. Paul was certainly aware of the fact that people in his own time refused to believe in the resurrection of Jesus, and the eyewitness testimony remains inconclusive to many persons today. We have also seen that the other sorts of evidence offered to support the view of survival of death are likewise open to question. The upshot of all this is that philosophical analysis can allow us to clarify the issues raised by this topic, but not completely resolve them.

The second question raises the issue of the proper attitude toward death, an issue addressed indirectly by several readings in this section. Russell's views would seem to be in agreement with those of the ancient Greek atomists who thought that viewing death as the complete cessation of consciousness removed all fear of death. St. Paul, in contrast, offers the doctrine of resurrection as an alternative to what he perceives as the dismal view that death ends all. This question leads directly to the third one: Is life made more meaningful by the view that death is the cessation of consciousness, or by the view that there is a continuation of consciousness after death? There is little doubt that our attitude toward death has profound implications for our attitude toward life, and in his interviews Moody reports that those who had near-death experiences sense a renewed meaning of the importance of life. Not only did they feel a reordered sense of priorities, they no longer feared death and were not obsessed by it in the course of their lives. It does not get our attention when a philosopher like Martin Heidegger tells us that all human existence is "being towards death," and the refusal to recognize this inevitable fact results in a kind of inauthenticity in our daily lives. Perhaps the immediate value of Moody's work is that it does in fact get our attention, and it may be in this aspect of his book that his most important contribution has been made.

Some persons have argued that if we consider this life the only life that we will have, we will view it as more meaningful than if we see it merely as the preparation for an afterlife. This view would seem to be compatible with Russell's suggestion that human destiny is to live for a few years and then cease to live altogether. An opposite conclusion is reached by Gabriel Marcel, who argues that the view that death ends all results in a debasing of life.

> Here we must stress a paradox to which we cannot, I think, direct our attention too closely; theoretically one might have imagined—and this indeed was what many people did in the nineteenth century—that as soon as the majority of men in a given society ceased to believe in an afterlife, life in this world would be more and more lovingly taken care of and would become the object of an increased regard. *What has happened is something quite different, the very opposite in fact: this cannot, I think, be overemphasized.* Life in this world has become more and more widely looked upon as a sort of worthless phenomenon, devoid of any intrinsic justification, and as thereby subject to countless interferences which in a different metaphysical context would have been considered sacrilegious.[1]

This way of posing the alternative views of death and human destiny relates directly to the question of religion and human conduct, which is the concern of the next section in this book. But before leaving the topic of death and the individual's hope for the future, one final observation must be made. Although a completely impregnable argument for life after death does not seem to be available, there is likewise no unassailable proof of the impossibility of another existence. Here again we encounter uncertainty, which leaves room for a faith commitment. Seen from the viewpoint of faith, death need not be viewed as the final chapter in the story of human destiny. This point is well made by the distinguished American philosopher Geddes MacGregor:

> If I can see this life as the gift of God I shall be so thankful for each moment of it that to complain of death would be as churlish as to call a benefactor parsimonious who for fifty years had inexplicably given me an annuity and then as inexplicably let the flow of the cornucopia stop. In the face of such a record of generosity, moreover, I should be included to interpret the cessation as, rather, auguring a new and even larger beneficence.[2]

[1]Gabriel Marcel, *The Mystery of Being* (Chicago: Henry Regnery Company, Gateway Edition, 1960), 2, 165–66.

[2]Geddes MacGregor, *Philosophical Issues in Religious Thought* (Boston: Houghton Mifflin Company, 1973), p. 296.

ADDITIONAL READING SUGGESTIONS
FOR PART SIX

A good bibliography and historical survey of attitudes toward death is Robert G. Olson, "Death," *The Encyclopedia of Philosophy* (1967), 2, 307–9. John Hick provides a thorough and readable analysis of the various dimensions of the topic in his massive *Death and Eternal Life* (New York: Harper & Row, 1976). A debate of sorts on the topic of death is constituted by the two articles on "Death" by D. M. Mackinnon and Antony Flew in *New Essays in Philosophical Theology,* ed. Antony Flew and Alasdair MacIntyre (London: SCM Press, 1955). Additional considerations of his research into near-death experiences is offered by Raymond A. Moody, *Reflections on Life After Life* (New York: Bantam Books, 1977).

part seven

RELIGION
AND
ETHICS

The Relation of Ethics to Religion

Religion and ethics are two terms that are frequently used together, yet an on-going philosophical debate concerns the precise relation between the two. Ethics, or the inquiry into the principles regulating human conduct, is a discipline that has been a part of philosophy's concern since its origins with the Greeks, and as a philosophical discipline ethics has often been regarded as independent of any religious commitments. When we examine the attitudes of Christianity and Judaism toward ethics, however, we discover that ethical concerns are intimately enmeshed in both traditions. This indicates that we cannot do justice to either without seeing the close relation they affirm between religious faith and ethical values.

TWO ERRONEOUS VIEWS

Leaving the Judaeo-Christian tradition for a moment, let us look at two views of the relation between religion and ethics that are clearly erroneous. The first view is the claim that there can be no ethical thinking separate from and independent of religion. This claim can be shown to be false both on historical and philosophical grounds. The history of philosophy presents us with numerous ethical systems which are not tied to any religious tradition. The *Nicomachean Ethics* of Aristotle, for example, espouses principles of conduct that most Jewish and Christian moralists would find generally acceptable, yet it is an ethical system completely divorced from religion. Indeed, Aristotle's metaphysical views include no personal God in either a Christian or Jewish sense, yet some of Aristotle's ethical principles are highly compatible with both of these religions. Stoic ethics, the ethics of Epicureanism, and, closer to our own time, the ethics of utilitarianism were all developed independently of religions. As a philosophical inquiry, ethics must be autonomous from religion, else it ceases to be a philosophical inquiry and becomes theology instead. Of course, one might choose to argue that no genuine ethical insight can be gained apart from religion, but this would be to take a philosophical position that would require some kind of supporting argument, and if it could be established it would entail the reduction of ethics to religion. That many ethical systems claim autonomy from religion shows that this claim is at least subject to dispute.

Whereas the first erroneous claim is that there can be no morality without religion, the second erroneous claim is that there can be no religion without morality, since religion necessarily has moral content. Again, there is solid historical evidence against this view. Many primitive religions had no moral concern at all; the term "primitive" here is not intended to be pejorative, but simply to indicate a less-developed religion. Many of the ancient Greek religions, for example, were concerned only with placating the gods and thereby avoiding divine wrath. Professor Nowell-Smith puts it well when he says that "In none of the earliest cultures were the gods endowed with high moral attributes; nor were they thought to concern themselves much with the behavior of human beings as long as the latter performed their religious duties punctiliously. Religion seems to have been concerned with averting of disasters and with salvation in the life after death, and both were to be achieved by means of ritual."[1]

Although religion and ethics can be separate areas of concern, one reason we tend to see them as inter-related is because of their close connection in both Judaism and Christianity. In the more developed religions, and this certainly includes both Judaism and Christianity, moral demands for upright living are at the heart of religious obligation. The Hebrew prophets of the eighth century B.C. emphasized, in a highly developed way, the moral implications of faith in the living God: "And what does the Lord require of you but to do justice, and to love kindness, and to walk humbly with your God?" (Micah 6:8). The New Testament also echoes this: "We love, because he first loved us. If any one says, 'I love God,' and hates his brother, he is a liar; for he who does not love his brother whom he has seen, cannot love God whom he has not seen" (1 John 4:19, 20). Even religions with no personal God, such as Buddhism and Confucianism, place a priority on ethics, so much so that Confucianism is virtually an ethical system. But not all religions can claim the higher degree of ethical content that these religions have.

THE AUTONOMY OF ETHICS

There seems, then, to be grounds for believing in the independence of morality from religion. Although the preponderance of the philosophical tradition is on the side of the autonomy of ethics, there has been wide disagreement as to the source of our knowledge of ethics. Some philosophical traditions have argued for

---

[1]Patrick H. Nowell-Smith, "Religion and Morality," *The Encyclopedia of Philosophy* (1967), 7, 155.

the existence of a special moral sense; others have found the source of ethics to be in the power of reason. Philosophers have also disagreed whether the rightness of an action is a function of the motives of the agent or of the consequences of the action. It is an intriguing characteristic of these philosophical debates that although philosophers of different schools have often agreed on *what* is right, they do not always agree on *why* it is right.

One ethical system that was generated in antiquity and has had a profound effect on Christian moral philosophy was the ethical system of the Stoics. Believing that rational beings can discover the principles of right action through the power of reason, they claimed that correct conduct is that which conforms to the *Lex Naturale* or Natural Law. The view that there is a Natural Law independent of individual whim and fancy had a profound effect on the development of Roman civil law, which directly influenced the formation of our own legal system. Natural Law also provided a metaphysical foundation for ethics through much of the Middle Ages. Christian philosophers of the Middle Ages viewed the Natural Law doctrine as also being the Law of God. That we are aware of the Natural Law provided medieval Christian philosophers with evidence for the existence of God. But when they explored further the question of the status of the Natural Law, they confronted a dilemma. Is the Natural Law our duty merely because God says it is, or does God give us rational insight into the Natural Law because it is good in itself? If we say that something is our duty merely because God commanded it, and God could have commanded the exact opposite which would likewise have been good, this makes morality conventional and arbitrary. But if we say that goodness is independent of God, this would seem to make God subservient to an independent morality, which would be in conflict with the divine attributes of omniscience and omnipotence. The solution to this dilemma was to suggest a third alternative: It is God's nature to be good; therefore God wills only the good for us, since God cannot act contrary to his nature. This view of God as ultimate in reality, in truth, and goodness, established an unbreakable connection between religion and morality in the minds of the philosophers of the Middle Ages.

By the eighteenth century, however, there was a different mood in ethics. Too many wars had been fought in the name of God (invoked by persons on both sides) for philosophers to be content to allow morality to be defined by religious zealots. So attempts were made to determine a rational basis for morality independent of any religious context. No philosopher better represented this spirit of the Enlightenment, as the age was called, better than Kant. Kant argued for the view that an action was morally significant only if it was done for the sake of duty. Compulsion, fear of punishment, the command of an authority, even concern for desirable consequences, all would remove the moral significance of an act. The only reason for ascribing moral worth to an action is that it is done by a person of good will out of a sense of duty. At one level we would probably want to agree with Kant. If someone refuses to tell a lie because of the fear of punishment, that person is not acting out of a sense of duty to tell the truth but from fear of consequences. In contrast, if someone tells the truth, even though the consequences might be unpleasant, there is more moral significance to this action than there would be if the person were telling the truth only out of a fear of punishment.

Not only did Kant think that ethics was autonomous, he went further to suggest that religion is subordinate to ethics. True religion, according to Kant, is the recognition of ethical duties as divine commands.[2] The implication of Kant's view is that we should judge the claims of religion by the principles of morality, and be willing to analyze ethical problems independently of religious presuppositions and commitments.

FOUR VIEWS OF RELIGION AND ETHICS

Even if we allow for the automony of ethics, there are still substantive issues to be discussed concerning the relation of morality and religion. The readings in this section do not exhaust the possibilities, but they give expression to four attitudes toward the question.

The first reading expresses the most extreme view of all. Nietzsche not only sees ethics as independent of religion, he supports the view that ethics can only prosper when it is completely divorced from religion inasmuch as he advocates the rejection of all traditional Judaeo-Christian values in what he refers to as a transvaluation of all existing values. Needless to say, the ethics which Nietzsche arrives at are quite different than those supported by Kant, Mill, or most other ethical philosophers.

A less extreme view of the autonomy of ethics is suggested by Kai Nielsen, who argues that without religious support ethics will not disintegrate into nihilism as some critics have charged. A coherent and adequate ethics, compatible with the traditional values of the Judaeo-Christian tradition, can be established, he thinks, quite apart from religious commitments.

Paul Tillich moves closer to the integration of religion and ethics when he suggests that moral systems, which he calls moralisms, remain only rule-bound formulas until they are accompanied by a renewed orientation in the life of the individual, an orientation that can only be accomplished by a religious attitude toward one's being. Finally, we will examine the views of Reinhold Niebuhr, who suggests that ethics can only provide the framework for a meaningful life if it is energized by the creative power of love which comes through divine grace. Both Tillich and Niebuhr might agree that ethics has a certain autonomy from religion, but they both insist that ethics receives its power through a vision of human reality and its relation to the world that, in the final analysis, is religious.

[2] Immanuel Kant, *Religion Within the Limits of Reason Alone*, trans. Theodore M. Greene and Hoyt H. Hudson (New York: Harper & Row, 1960), p. 142.

FRIEDRICH NIETZSCHE

Ethics
Against
Religion

No more complete separation between religion and ethics has ever been articulated than in the writings of Friedrich Nietzsche, a nineteenth-century German philosopher and professor of classics. Not only did Nietzsche think that ethics should be independent of religion, he was convinced that the entire ethical system of the Judaeo-Christian religious tradition must be abandoned if Western civilization were to be saved.

These are bold claims, but Nietzsche saw himself as the prophet of the end of an era. Central to Nietzsche's vision was the conviction that God was no longer a motive force in European civilization. Whereas for centuries belief in God had provided the foundation for Western morality and culture, he believed that this was no longer the case. God was a relic of a defunct metaphysics, a remnant of primitive superstitions; in short, Nietzsche proclaimed that "God is dead." This striking phrase was intended to say something different than merely that there is no God. To announce that God is dead implies that at one time God was alive, at least in the sense that God and the resulting theistic values provided cohesion for society. Although people no longer believe in God as the source of meaning and value, they continue to follow the ethical principles derived from the Judaeo-Christian view of God and the world. Belief in God was a metaphysical prop for an entire value system in Western culture. People no longer find God necessary, so the prop is gone; yet allegiance is still given to the values derived from theism. Nietzsche was convinced that this value system would topple like a house of cards, and unless something was there to take its place, European culture would sink into an era of nihilism.

What are we to do when the basis for our value system is gone? Who can take

God's place? Nietzsche's answer is that we must become God; that is, we ourselves must become the source of meaning and value. Life will have no other meaning than that which we give to it. Not all of us are capable of carrying such a burden. In fact, only a noble few will have the courage to face up to the new realities and be willing to provide a new ethics. Nietzsche referred to the individual who is willing to do this as the *Ubermensch,* which can be translated as either superman or overman. However it is translated, it includes persons of both sexes. *Mensch* in German embraces both men and women, though Nietzsche had a particularly jaded view of women ("Thou goest to woman? Do not forget thy whip"[1]), which might be partially explained by the fact that he was reared in an all-female household consisting of his mother, sister, grandmother, and two maiden aunts.

The first two parables in the following selection emphasize the crisis of the age that Nietzsche felt was upon us. Without the security offered by belief in God, we are like a ship that has left the safety of the land and embarked on a wild and terrifying sea: "Times will come when thou wilt feel that it is infinite, and that there is nothing more frightful than infinity." The second parable of the madman in the marketplace is even more forcible. The madman, with a lighted lamp, rushes into the marketplace at mid-day to announce the death of God. The announcement is met with bemused responses from the audience. So the madman concludes, "I come too early . . . this prodigious event is still on its way. . . ." Though the madman's hearers did not really believe in God, they had not realized the full magnitude of the implication of the death of God. The meaning of this was yet to be understood by them. "How shall we console ourselves?" the madman asks. "Shall we not ourselves have to become Gods, merely to seem worthy of it?"

Nietzsche was convinced that when the full implications of the death of God were realized, the breakdown of the existing morality would lead to an era of nihilism which could only be surmounted by the development of a new morality. Being a philosopher of culture, Nietzsche was convinced that such a cycle had occurred before. Whenever there is an absence of value, the resulting chaos is overcome only when great individuals emerge as the creators of meaning and value. These noble persons determine what is good and what is bad on the basis of their own preference, and if they are truly noble they are also persons of courage and creativity. They do not view suffering and hardship as bad, for suffering may be good if it leads to great accomplishments. Courage is a virtue when it results in the overcoming of obstacles and the generation of noble standards of conduct. A society is great only when it gives rise to great individuals—creative artists, powerful warriors, great writers and creative geniuses in all areas of endeavor. This is the manifestation of what Nietzsche called master morality, with its emphasis on creativity, respect among those who are truly equals, and strength of will as a supreme virtue.

Every society also contains numerous persons not capable of great accomplishments, whom Nietzsche describes as "the cowardly, the timid, the insignificant, and those thinking merely of narrow utility." For such persons the master morality is impossible; they cannot achieve greatness. So in their weakness they console themselves with a slave morality in which resentment against the creative

---

[1]*Thus Spake Zarathustra,* trans. Thomas Common, section 18, in *The Complete Works of Nietzsche,* ed. Oscar Levy (Edinburgh & London: T. N. Foulis, 1910), vol. 11, p. 77.

and powerful is central. Slave morality exalts as virtuous all those dispositions that make existence for the unfit a little more endurable: "It is here that sympathy, the kind, helping hand, the warm heart, patience, diligence, humility, and friendliness attain to honour. . . ." There is thus a great reversal of values between the master morality and the slave morality. What the master morality considers evil, the slave morality exalts as virtue. And what slave morality considers despicable, master morality honors as good. If it were just a matter of three moralities co-existing, then perhaps we could overlook the consolation that slave morality gives to the weak and to the misfits. But the two cannot be reconciled, Nietzsche thought. Slave morality, when it becomes ascendent, drags down the noble ones and results in a general stagnation in society.

The ethical standards of Judaism and Christianity represent for Nietzsche the slave morality par excellence. Even when God was still alive as the foundation of these values, the resulting morality was antithetical to the creation of greatness in a society. It is thus not to the Hebrew prophets nor to the teachings of Jesus that Nietzsche looked for the standards of value, but to the Greek sense of aristocracy and to the heroes of German and Scandinavian legends. Nietzsche was convinced that now that the God of the Judaeo-Christian religious tradition was dead in the hearts and minds of people, the only alternative to chaos was the emergence of a new aristocracy with its master morality. Democracy with its fallacious proclamation that all persons are equal was but a political manifestation of slave morality, likewise to be rejected. Elsewhere in Beyond Good and Evil, Nietzsche says that in the past the world has been ruled by the "misfits, the physiologically botched, the cunning and revengeful." The masses, by elevating the ethics of weakness to the status of virtue, have been able to subjugate the strong. All this, Nietzsche says, must change. The theistic prop for European slave morality is gone, though perhaps we have not yet realized it.

Nietzsche died in the first year of the twentieth century and did not live to see the two world wars that broke out in Europe in the first half of the century. Whereas the dominant mood of nineteenth-century philosophy was a commitment to progress with its promise of inevitable achievements, Nietzsche stood somewhat alone as the prophet of an impending crisis. In one sense, Nietzsche was right. All was not well with European culture, and it is significant that the two world wars, with the greatest devastation ever witnessed in human history, began not in the most backward nations of the world but in the most civilized and technologically advanced. It may be significant that the central figure in the parable of the person announcing the death of God is a madman; not a scholar, not a philosopher, not a theologian, but an insane person. Was Nietzsche saying that European society contained within itself the seeds of its own destruction, and that the Western world was on the brink of going through a period of insane barbarism? Perhaps. Did he also mean to imply that experiencing the death of God and attempting to become God will drive us to madness? Again perhaps. Nietzsche's writing is enigmatic and often generative of more meanings than maybe even he realized. But even if we agree that Nietzsche was a prophetic figure who correctly sensed the spirit of the times more accurately than his contemporaries, we must also note that his ethical alternative has remained a decidedly minority report in the history of philosophy.

Not only are Nietzsche's views in direct opposition to the major ethical systems of the philosophic tradition, there is also his startling claim that we all must become gods, that is, each of us will have to become the center of meaning and value for our lives. Not only is this a heavy burden, it is not at all clear that human beings are capable of assuming such an awesome responsibility without a major distortion of their personalities. The Old Testament begins with a story of how human beings desired to become God, an attempt that has been called the original sin. Perhaps it is simply the case that religion's greatest contribution to ethics will be the constant reminder it provides that humanly generated values are provisional and imperfect, and that lasting values must be rooted in a transcendent source. When human beings no longer accept the reality of such a transcendent source, a crisis will result, and maybe it was Nietzsche's genius to see this earlier than his contemporaries. But Nietzsche's claim that the only alternative to this crisis was his own transvalued values remains just as debatable now as it was when he first announced it.

Master and Slave Morality*

In the Horizon of the Infinite.—We have left the land and have gone aboard ship! We have broken down the bridge behind us,—nay, more, the land behind us! Well, little ship! look out! Beside thee is the ocean; it is true it does not always roar, and sometimes it spreads out like silk and gold and a gentle reverie. But times will come when thou wilt feel that it is infinite, and that there is nothing more frightful than infinity. Oh, the poor bird that felt itself free, and now strikes against the walls of this cage! Alas, if homesickness for the land should attack thee, as if there had been more *freedom* there,—and there is no "land" any longer!

The Madman.—Have you ever heard of the madman who on a bright morning lighted a lantern and ran to the market-place calling out unceasingly: "I seek God! I seek God!"—As there were many people standing about who did not believe in God, he caused a great deal of amusement. Why! is he lost? said one. Has he strayed away like a child? said another. Or does he keep himself hidden? Is he afraid of us? Has he taken a sea-voyage? Has he emigrated?—the people cried out laughingly, all in a hubbub. The insane man jumped into their midst and transfixed them with his glances. "Where is God gone?" he called out. "I mean to tell you!

*Source: Friedrich Nietzsche, *The Joyful Wisdom,* trans. Thomas Common, sections 124–25; *Beyond Good and Evil,* trans. Helen Zimmern, section 260. In *The Complete Works of Nietzsche,* ed. Oscar Levy, vols. 10 and 11 (Edinburgh & London: T. N. Foulis, 1910, 1911).

We have killed him,—you and I! We are all his murderers! But how have we done it? How were we able to drink up the sea? Who gave us the sponge to wipe away the whole horizon? What did we do when we loosened this earth from its sun? Whither does it now move? Whither do we move? Away from all suns? Do we not dash on unceasingly? Backwards, sideways, forewards, in all directions? Is there still an above and below? Do we not stray, as through infinite nothingness? Does not empty space breathe upon us? Has it not become colder? Does not night come on continually, darker and darker? Shall we not have to light lanterns in the morning? Do we not hear the noise of the grave-diggers who are burying God? Do we not smell the divine putrefaction?—for even Gods putrefy! God is dead! God remains dead! And we have killed him! How shall we console ourselves, the most murderous of all murderers? The holiest and the mightiest that the world has hitherto possessed, has bled to death under our knife,—who will wipe the blood from us? With what water could we cleanse ourselves? What lustrums, what sacred games shall we have to devise? Is not the magnitude of this deed too great for us? Shall we not ourselves have to become Gods, merely to seem worthy of it? There never was a greater event,—and on account of it, all who are born after us belong to a higher history than any history hitherto!"—Here the madman was silent and looked again at his hearers; they also were silent and looked at him in surprise. At last he threw his lantern on the ground, so that it broke in pieces and was extinguished. "I come too early," he then said, "I am not yet at the right time. This prodigious event is still on its way, and is travelling,—it has not yet reached men's ears. Lightning and thunder need time, the light of the stars needs time, deeds need time, even after they are done, to be seen and heard. This deed is as yet further from them than the furthest star,—*and yet they have done it!*"—It is further stated that the madman made his way into different churches on the same day, and there intoned his *Requiem aeternam deo.* When led out and called to account, he always gave the reply: "What are these churches now, if they are not the tombs and monuments of God?"—. . .

In a tour through the many finer and coarser moralities which have hitherto prevailed or still prevail on the earth, I found certain traits recurring regularly together and connected with one another, until finally two primary types revealed themselves to me, and a radical distinction was brought to light. There is *master-morality* and *slave-morality;*—I would at once add, however, that in all higher and mixed civilisations, there are also attempts at the reconciliation of the two moralities; but one finds still oftener the confusion and mutual misunderstanding of them, indeed, sometimes their close juxtaposition—even in the same man, within one soul. The distinctions of moral values have either originated in a ruling caste, pleasantly conscious of being different from the ruled—or among the ruled class, the slaves and dependents of all sorts. In the first case, when it is the rulers who determined the conception "good," it is the exalted, proud disposition which is regarded as the distinguishing feature, and that which determines the order of rank. The noble type of man separates from himself the beings in whom the opposite of this exalted, proud disposition displays itself: he despises them. Let it at once be noted that in this first kind of morality the antithesis "good" and "bad" means practically the same as "noble" and "despicable";—the antithesis "good" and "*evil*" is of a different origin. The cowardly, the timid, the insignificant, and those thinking merely of narrow utility are despised; moreover, also, the distrustful, with their constrained glances, the self-abasing, the dog-like kind of men who let themselves be abused, the mendicant flatterers, and above all the liars:—it is a fundamental belief of all aristocrats that the common people are untruthful. "We truthful ones"—the nobility in ancient Greece called themselves. It is obvious that everywhere the designations of moral value were at first applied to *men,* and were only derivatively and at a later period applied to *actions;* it is a gross mistake, therefore, when historians of morals start with questions like, "Why have sympathetic actions been praised?" The noble type of man regards *himself* as a determiner of values; he does not require to be approved of; he passes the judgment: "What is injurious to me is injurious in itself"; he knows that it is he himself only who confers honour on things; he is a *creator of values.* He honours whatever he recognises in himself: such morality is self-glorification. In the foreground there is the feeling of plenitude, of power, which seeks to overflow, the happiness of high tension, the consciousness of a wealth which would fain give and bestow:—the noble man also helps the unfortunate, but not—or scarcely—out of pity, but rather from an impulse generated by the super-abundance of power. The noble man honours in himself the powerful one, him also who has power over himself, who knows how to speak and how to keep silence, who takes pleasure in subjecting himself to severity and hardness, and has reverence for all that is severe and hard. "Wotan placed a hard heart in my breast," says an old Scandinavian Saga: it is thus rightly expressed from the soul of a proud Viking. Such a type of man is even proud of *not* being made for sympathy; the hero of the Saga therefore adds warningly: "He who has not a hard heart when young, will never have one." The noble and brave who think thus are the furthest removed from the morality which sees precisely in sympathy, or in acting for the good of others, or in *désintéressement,* the characteristic of the moral; faith in oneself, pride in oneself, a radical enmity and irony towards "selflessness," belong as definitely to noble morality, as do a careless scorn and precaution in presence of sympathy and the "warm heart."—It is the powerful who *know*

how to honour, it is their art, their domain for invention. The profound
reverence for age and for tradition—all law rests on this double
reverence,—the belief and prejudice in favour of ancestors and unfavourable to newcomers, is typical in the morality of the powerful; and if,
reversely, men of "modern ideas" believe almost instinctively in "progress" and the "future," and are more and more lacking in respect for old
age, the ignoble origin of these "ideas" has complacently betrayed itself
thereby. A morality of the ruling class, however, is more especially foreign
and irritating to present-day taste in the sternness of its principle that one
has duties only to one's equals; that one may act towards beings of a lower
rank, towards all that is foreign, just as seems good to one, or "as the heart
desires," and in any case "beyond good and evil": it is here that sympathy
and similar sentiments can have a place. The ability and obligation to
exercise prolonged gratitude and prolonged revenge—both only within
the circle of equals,—artfulness in retaliation, *raffinement* of the idea in
friendship, a certain necessity to have enemies (as outlets for the emotions
of envy, quarrelsomeness, arrogance—in fact, in order to be a good
friend): all these are typical characteristics of the noble morality, which, as
has been pointed out, is not the morality of "modern ideas," and is
therefore at present difficult to realise, and also to unearth and
disclose.—It is otherwise with the second type of morality, *slave-morality.*
Supposing that the abused, the oppressed, the suffering, the unemanci-
pated, the weary, and those uncertain of themselves, should moralise,
what will be the common element in their moral estimates? Probably a
pessimistic suspicion with regard to the entire situation of man will find
expression, perhaps a condemnation of man, together with his situation.
The slave has an unfavourable eye for the virtues of the powerful; he has a
scepticism and distrust, a *refinement* of distrust of everything "good" that is
there honoured—he would fain persuade himself that the very happiness
there is not genuine. On the other hand, *those* qualities which serve to
alleviate the existence of sufferers are brought into prominence and
flooded with light; it is here that sympathy, the kind, helping hand, the
warm heart, patience, diligence, humility, and friendliness attain to honour; for here these are the most useful qualities, and almost the only
means of supporting the burden of existence. Slave-morality is essentially
the morality of utility. Here is the seat of the origin of the famous
antithesis "good" and *"evil":*—power and dangerousness are assumed to
reside in the evil, a certain dreadfulness, subtlety, and strength, which do
not admit of being despised. According to slave-morality, therefore, the
"evil" man arouses fear; according to master-morality, it is precisely the
"good" man who arouses fear and seeks to arouse it, while the bad man is
regarded as the despicable being. The contrast attains its maximum when,
in accordance with the logical consequences of slave-morality, a shade of

depreciation—it may be slight and well-intentioned—at last attaches itself even to the "good" man of this morality; because, according to the servile mode of thought, the good man must in any case be the *safe* man: he is good-natured, easily deceived, perhaps a little stupid, *un bonhomme.* Everywhere that slave-morality gains the ascendency, language shows a tendency to approximate the significations of the words "good" and "stupid."—A last fundamental difference: the desire for *freedom,* the instinct for happiness and the refinements of the feeling of liberty belong as necessarily to slave-morals and morality, as artifice and enthusiasm in reverence and devotion are the regular symptoms of an aristocratic mode of thinking and estimating.—Hence we can understand without further detail why love *as a passion*—it is our European specialty—must absolutely be of noble origin; as is well known, its invention is due to the Provençal poet-cavaliers, those brilliant ingenious men of the *"gai saber,"* to whom Europe owes so much, and almost owes itself.

DISCUSSION QUESTIONS

1. Do you accept the view that ethics is autonomous, that is, independent of religion? Why or why not?

2. Do you think Nietzsche is correct in his claim that Western civilization no longer accepts the religious basis for ethics but nonetheless persists in advocating the values that were derived from the Judaeo-Christian tradition? What reasons could you advance to support your answer?

3. Why did Nietzsche equate slave morality with a morality derived from religious principles? Do you think it was legitimate for him to do this?

4. Explain what Nietzsche meant when he suggested a morality that would be "beyond good and evil."

5. Evaluate Nietzsche's claim that democracy is an instance of slave morality and is derived from Judaeo-Christian values.

6. What aspects of Nietzsche's point of view do you find most convincing? Least convincing? Why?

KAI NIELSEN

A Religionless Ethics

Those who think there can be no ethics without religion charge that when the religious basis for ethics is removed, the results are disastrous. At best, ethics then becomes a matter of convention involving only the "tribal" customs of a society which have no real basis except the mutual agreement of a group. At worst, ethical skepticism abounds and nihilism—the total rejection of established rules and institutions—becomes pervasive. Without the religious view of life, according to the religious moralist, there is no one central meaning which gives significance to life. All the little meanings which we human beings create for ourselves will eventually fail us, and we will be left only with meaninglessness and despair over the insignificance of human existence.

Kai Nielsen argues that things are not as bad as all this. Without a religious basis for ethics, we need not sink into either conventionalism or nihilism. Nor does Nielsen see the alternative to be the creation of a master morality à la Nietzsche with its transvaluation of the present meanings of good and evil. Nothing so drastic as that is needed. To be sure, the announcement that "God is dead" will be a profound shock to Jewish and Christian believers, for whom much is dependent on God. But Nielsen argues that if the believer "can keep his nerve, think the matter over, and thoroughly take it to heart, life can still be meaningful and morality yet have an objective rationale." In fact, the morality we will be left with will not be all that different from the traditional standards of conduct of the great religions.

A SECULAR MORALITY

The term *secular* is derived from the Latin word for world and so secular ethics refers to a morality that is derived from and directed toward this world. A theistic ethics is one that is dependent upon a supernatural view of things. Even with a secular view of life, Nielsen says, we would continue to find many things worth striving for, and ethics would be a rational response to achieving these goals. Echoing the views of Aristotle, Nielsen suggests that the goal of life, the thing most worth striving for, is happiness. We might not be able to define completely what we mean by happiness, but there are a lot of words which we use in meaningful ways that we cannot exhaustively define, so this state of affairs should not disturb us. We can, however, point to some of the things that contribute to happiness: freedom from pain and want, enjoyment, security and emotional peace, human companionship and love, meaningful work, art, music, and dance. The list of things contributing to happiness could include the desire to alleviate suffering and to contribute to the well-being of others. Compassion is a virtue not limited to a religion-based morality.

But what happens when our interests clash, when your desire for happiness runs counter to someone else's? We need ethical rules to help us sort out conflicting goals. Central to such a moral system is the principle of justice, which says that everybody should be treated fairly and given equal consideration. Here the defender of a religious morality might argue that any appeal to justice implies respect for other persons, and this principle is derived from the religious view that human beings, as creatures of God, are worthy of infinite respect. In other words, even though the secular moralist accepts the principle of respect for other persons, the religious moralist might argue that this principle is really derived from a religious view and is being "bootlegged" into secular morality. Nielsen's response is that the origin of a principle is quite irrelevant to its validity. If an insane person tells us that we should leave the building because it is on fire, we would be wise to consider the message quite apart from its source. Even if the principle of respect for other persons originated in a religion-based ethics, this does not mean that it can only be justified by a religious view of things. At least the religious moralist would have to argue that this is the case, and this has not been done. In fact, Kant argued quite independently of religion for the principle of respect for persons as a precept known and justified by human reason alone.

Nielsen suggests that one difference between a secular morality and a religion-based morality might be found in the number of ethical principles required for each. A perfectly acceptable secular morality can be derived from two principles, according to Nielsen, and we can recognize the first of these as Aristotelian and the second as Kantian. Let's call them S^1 and S^2.

> S^1: Happiness is good
>
> S^2: Treat every man as an end and never as a means only

Both of these principles have been argued for independently of religion, and can be justified as rational principles quite apart from religious considerations. In contrast the religious moralist could argue that only one principle is required for a religion-based morality. Let's call it R^1.

R^1: We ought to do what God wills

As we examine these two different approaches, it might seem that religious morality is simpler than secular morality since it needs only one principle, R^1, whereas secular morality needs S^1 and S^2. Nielsen argues that things are more complicated than that, for the religious moralist also subscribes to the claim that human beings are creatures of God and are therefore of infinite value. Nielsen finds this claim terribly obscure, whereas the two principles of secular morality do not suffer from the intellectual obfuscation which he feels is inherent in the religious view of ethics. He asks, "And if we are prepared simply to commit ourselves to one principle, why not to two principles, neither of which involves any appeal to conceptions whose very intelligibility is seriously in question?"

THE CHALLENGE OF EGOISM

The religious moralist has another line of attack open. If we remove the religious foundation from ethics, what is to prevent ethics from disintegrating into complete egoism? Baldly put, egoism is the view that we should do what is best for us, and the interests of others be damned. There are different kinds of egoism, and philosophers have distinguished two principal types: *psychological egoism* is the claim that as a matter of fact people do act only out of self-interest; *ethical egoism* is the claim that people should act out of self-interest. As an empirical claim about human behavior, psychological egoism is simply false. People do not always act in their own best interests. Not only are there cases of unselfish and altruistic behavior, there are also examples of self-destructive behavior, neither of which would occur if psychological egoism were operative. Ethical egoism, in contrast, is not a claim about how people do in fact behave but about how they should behave, and as an ethical theory it looks simple and easy to justify, though further examination reveals that it is more complicated than it first appears.

Suppose you are a dedicated ethical egoist, concerned only with your own self-interest. First of all, you will have to decide whether it is your short-term or long-term interest that is primary. If in the long run an action brings more pain and unhappiness than it brings pleasure in the short run, and if you are rational, you would have to conclude that you should restrain your short-term self-interest. A case in point is found in the importance of living in society. Human beings, as far as we can determine, are social creatures who require a culture and a community. But living in society requires that everybody restrain their selfish interests, for if everyone acted only out of self-interest, we would find that human society is impossible and would exist in a war-like state where each person is threatened by every other person. We would have to conclude that our own self-interest must include concern for the welfare of others. Moreover, it would be reasonable to infer that we must all band together into a society in which we restrain our selfish impulses so that, in the long run, our individual needs will better be met. The more we analyze ethical egoism, the more difficult it becomes to support it as a coherent and rational ethical theory. This is not the place for a thorough-going critique of ethical egoism, for Nielsen's point is that even a cursory analysis gives evidence that "even if men were thorough egoists, we would still have rational grounds for subscribing to a principle of respect for persons."

It is possible, however, to imagine a person so wealthy, powerful, and highly placed that such an individual can simply ignore the rights of others. What are we to say about such a person? Nielsen answers that each of us, at some point, must decide what sort of person he or she will be, that is, whether we will be moral or not. Our highly placed egoist who disdains completely the welfare of others has simply chosen not to be a moral person. But this situation, Nielsen says, is no different for the secular moralist or the religious moralist. At some point each must decide whether or not to be moral, and the only difference is whether that decision is made in favor of the principles of secular morality or religious morality. Nielsen thinks that the former are preferable since they do not require "buying into" a religious view which he feels is incoherent.

On the grounds staked out by Nielsen, he appears to have justified his claim that ethics is possible without religion, and the ethics he defends includes those perennial values that Nietzsche rejected in favor of a redefined sense of good and evil. But the question remains whether Nielsen has adequately characterized all of religion's possible contributions to ethics. It is the exploration of other possible ties between religion and ethics that will be the theme of the last two readings of this section.

Ethics Without Religion*

There certainly are fundamental difficulties and perhaps even elements of incoherence in Christian ethics, but what can a secular moralist offer in its stead? Religious morality—and Christian morality in particular—may have its difficulties, but secular morality, religious apologists argue, has still greater difficulties. It leads they claim, to ethical scepticism, nihilism, or, at best, to a pure conventionalism. Such apologists could point out that if we look at morality with the cold eye of an anthropologist we will—assuming we are clearheaded—find morality to be nothing more than the often conflicting *mores* of the various tribes spread around the globe. If we eschew the kind of insight that religion can give us, we will have no Archimedean point in accordance with which we can decide how it is that we ought to live and die. If we look at ethics from such a purely secular point of view, we will discover that it is constituted by tribal conventions, conventions which we are free to reject if we are

*Source: Kai Nielsen, "Ethics Without Religion," *The Ohio University Review* VI (1964):48–51; 57–62. Copyright Ohio University 1965. Reprinted by permission of *The Ohio Review,* Ohio University, Athens, Ohio 45701.

sufficiently free from ethnocentrism. We can continue to act in accordance with them or we can reject them and adopt a different set of conventions; but whether we act in accordance with the old conventions or forge "new tablets," we are still acting in accordance with certain conventions. Relative to them certain acts are right or wrong, reasonable or unreasonable, but we cannot justify these fundamental moral conventions themselves or the ways of life which they partially codify.

When these points are conceded, theologians are in a position to press home a powerful apologetic point. When we become keenly aware, they argue, of the true nature of such conventionalism and when we become aware that there is no overarching purpose that men were destined to fulfill, the myriad purposes, the aims and goals humans create for themselves, will be seen not to be enough. When we realize that life does not have a meaning—that is, a significance—which is there to be found, but that we human beings must by our deliberate decisions give it whatever meaning it has, we will (as Sartre so well understood) undergo estrangement and despair. We will drain our cup to its last bitter drop and feel our alienation to the full. Perhaps there are human purposes, purposes to be found *in* life, and we can and do have them even in a Godless world, but without God there can be no one overarching purpose, no one basic scheme of human existence, in virtue of which we could find a meaning for our grubby lives. It is this overall sense of meaning that man so ardently strives for, but it is not to be found in a purely secular worldview. You secularists, a new Pascal might argue, must realize, if you really want to be clear-headed, that no purely human purposes are ultimately worth striving for. What you humanists can give us by way of a scheme of human existence will always be a poor second-best and not what the human heart most ardently longs for.

The considerations for and against an ethics not rooted in a religion are complex and involuted; a fruitful discussion of them is difficult, for in considering the matter our passions, our anxieties, our (if you will) ultimate concerns are involved, and they tend to blur our vision, enfeeble our understanding, of what exactly is at stake. But we must not forget that what is at stake here is just what kind of ultimate commitments or obligations a man could have without evading any issue, without self-deception or without delusion. I shall be concerned to display and assess, to make plain but also to weigh, some of the most crucial considerations for and against a purely secular ethic. While I shall in an objective fashion try to make clear what the central issues are, I shall also give voice to my reflective convictions on this matter. I shall try to make evident my reasons for believing that we do not need God or any religious conception to support our moral convictions. I shall do this, as I think one should in philosophy, by making apparent the dialectic of the problem (by bringing to the fore the conflicting and evolving considerations for and against) and by arguing for what I take to be their proper resolution.

I am aware that Crisis Theologians would claim that I am being naive, but I do not see why purposes of purely human devising are not ultimately worth striving for. There is much that we humans prize and would continue to prize even in a Godless world. Many things would remain to give our lives meaning and point even after "the death of God."

Take a simple example. All of us *want* to be happy. But in certain bitter or sceptical moods we question what happiness is or we despairingly ask ourselves whether anyone can really be happy. Is this, however, a sober, sane view of the situation? I do not think that it is. Indeed we cannot adequately define "happiness" in the way that we can "bachelor," but neither can we in that way define "chair," "wind," "pain," and the vast majority of words in everyday discourse. For words like "bachelor," "triangle," or "father" we can specify a consistent set of properties that all the things and only the things denoted by these words have, but we cannot do this for "happiness," "chair," "pain," and the like. In fact, we cannot do it for the great majority of our words. Yet there is no greater loss here. Modern philosophical analysis has taught us that such an essentially Platonic conception of definition is unrealistic and unnecessary.[1] I may not be able to define "chair" in the way that I can define "bachelor," but I understand the meaning of "chair" perfectly well. In normal circumstances, at least, I know what to sit on when someone tells me to take a chair. I may not be able to define "pain," but I know what it is like to be in pain, and sometimes I can know when others are in pain. Similarly, though I cannot define "happiness" in the same way that I can define "bachelor," I know what it is like to be happy, and I sometimes can judge with considerable reliability whether others are happy or sad. "Happiness" is a slippery word, but it is not so slippery that we are justified in saying that nobody knows what happiness is.

A man could be said to have lived a happy life if he had found lasting sources of satisfaction in his life and if he had been able to find certain goals worthwhile and to achieve at least some of them. He could indeed have suffered some pain and anxiety, but his life must, for the most part, have been free from pain, estrangement, and despair, and must, on balance, have been a life which he has liked and found worthwhile. But surely we have no good grounds for saying that no one achieves such a balance or that no one is ever happy even for a time. We all have some idea

---

[1]This is convincingly argued in Michael Scriven's essay "Definitions, Explanations, and Theories" in *Minnesota Studies in the Philosophy of Science,* III, ed. Herbert Feigl, Michael Scriven, and Grover Maxwell (Minneapolis, 1958), pp. 99–195.

of what would make us happy and of what would make us unhappy; many people, at least, can remain happy even after "the death of God." At any rate, we need not strike Pascalian attitudes, for even in a purely secular world there are permanent sources of human happiness for anyone to avail himself of.

What are they? What are these relatively permanent sources of human happiness that we all want or need? What is it which, if we have it, will give us the basis for a life that could properly be said to be happy? We all desire to be free from pain and want. Even masochists do not seek pain for its own sake; they endure pain because this is the only psychologically acceptable way of achieving something else (usually sexual satisfaction) that is so gratifying to them that they will put up with the pain to achieve it. We all want a life in which sometimes we can enjoy ourselves in which we can attain our fair share of some of the simple pleasures that we all desire. They are not everything in life, but they are important, and our lives would be impoverished without them.

We also need security and emotional peace. We need and want a life in which we will not be constantly threatened with physical or emotional harassment. Again this is not the only thing worth seeking, but it is an essential ingredient in any adequate picture of the good life.

Human love and companionship are also central to a significant or happy life. We prize them, and a life which is without them is most surely an impoverished life, a life that no man, if he would take the matter to heart, would desire. But I would most emphatically assert that human love and companionship are quite possible in a Godless world, and the fact that life will some day inexorably come to an end and cut off love and companionship altogether enhances rather than diminishes their present value.

Furthermore, we all need some sort of creative employment or meaningful work to give our lives point, to save them from boredom, drudgery, and futility. A man who can find no way to use the talents he has or a man who can find no work which is meaningful to him will indeed be a miserable man. But again there is work—whether it be as a surgeon, a farmer, or a fisherman—that has a rationale even in a world without God. And poetry, music, and art retain their beauty and enrich our lives even in the complete absence of God or the gods.

We want and need art, music, and the dance. We find pleasure in travel and conversation and in a rich variety of experiences. The sources of human enjoyment are obviously too numerous to detail. But all of them are achievable in a Godless universe. If some can be ours, we can attain a reasonable measure of happiness. Only a Steppenwolfish personality beguiled by impossible expectations and warped by irrational guilts and fears can fail to find happiness in the realization of such ends. But to be free of impossible expectations people must clearly recognize that there is no "one big thing" or, for that matter, "small thing" which would make them permanently happy; almost anything permanently and exclusively pursued will lead to that nausea that Sartre has so forcefully brought to our attention. But we can, if we are not too sick and if our situation is not too precarious, find lasting sources of human happiness in a purely secular world.

It is not only happiness for ourselves that can give us something of value, but there is the need to do what we can to diminish the awful sum of human misery in the world. I have never understood those who say that they find contemporary life meaningless because they find nothing worthy of devoting their energies to. Throughout the world there is an immense amount of human suffering, suffering that can, through a variety of human efforts, be partially alleviated. Why can we not find a meaningful life in devoting ourselves, as did Doctor Rieux in Albert Camus's *The Plague,* to relieving somewhat the sum total of human suffering? Why cannot this give our lives point, and for that matter an over-all rationale? It is childish to think that by human effort we will someday totally rid the world of suffering and hate, of deprivation and sadness. This is a permanent part of the human condition. But specific bits of human suffering can be alleviated. The plague is always potentially with us, but we can destroy the Nazis and we can fight for racial and social equality throughout the world. And as isolated people, as individuals in a mass society, we find people turning to us in dire need, in suffering and in emotional deprivation, and we can as individuals respond to those people and alleviate or at least acknowledge that suffering and deprivation. A man who says, "If God is dead, nothing matters," is a spoilt child who has never looked at his fellow men with compassion.

Yet, it might be objected, if we abandon a Judaeo-Christian *Weltanschauung,* there can, in a secular world, be no "one big thing" to give our lives an overall rationale. We will not be able to see written in the stars the final significance of human effort. There will be no architectonic purpose to give our lives such a rationale. Like Tolstoy's Pierre in *War and Peace,* we desire *somehow* to gather the sorry scheme of things entire into one intelligible explanation so that we can finally crack the riddle of human destiny. We long to understand why it is that men suffer and die. If it is a factual answer that is wanted when such a question is asked, it is plain enough. Ask any physician. But clearly this is not what people who seek such answers are after. They want some *justification* for suffering; they want some way of showing that suffering is after all for a good purpose. It can, of course, be argued that suffering sometimes is a good thing, for it occasionally gives us insight and at times even brings about in the man who suffers a capacity to love and to be kind. But there is plainly an excessive amount of human suffering—the suffering of children in children's hospitals, the suffering of people devoured by cancer, and the sufferings of millions of Jews under the Nazis—for which there simply is no justification. Neither the religious man nor the secularist can explain, that is justify, such suffering and find some overall "scheme of life" in which it has some place, but only the religious man needs to do so. The secularist understands that suffering is not something to be justified but simply to be struggled against with courage and dignity. And in this fight, even the man who has been deprived of that which could give him some measure of happiness can still find or make for himself a meaningful human existence. . . .

The dialectic of our problem has not ended. The religious moralist might acknowledge that human happiness is indeed plainly a good thing while contending that secular morality, where it is consistent and reflective, will inevitably lead to some variety of egoism. An individual who recognized the value of happiness and self-consciousness might, if he were free of religious restraints, ask himself why he should be concerned with the happiness and self-awareness of *others*, except where their happiness and self-awareness would contribute to his own good. We must face the fact that sometimes, as the world goes, people's interests clash. Sometimes the common good is served only at the expense of some individual's interests. An individual must therefore, in such a circumstance, sacrifice what will make him happy for the common good. Morality requires this sacrifice of us, *when it is necessary* for the common good; morality, any morality, exists in part at least to adjudicate between the conflicting interests and demands of people. It is plainly evident that everyone cannot be happy all the time and that sometimes one person's happiness or the happiness of a group is at the expense of another person's happiness. Morality requires that we attempt to distribute happiness as evenly as possible. We must be fair: each person is to count for one and none is to count for more than one. Whether we like a person or not, whether he is useful to his society or not, his interests, and what will make him happy, must also be considered in any final decision as to what ought to be done. The requirements of justice make it necessary that each person be given equal consideration. I cannot justify my neglect of another person in some matter of morality simply on the grounds that I do not like him, that he is *not* a member of my set, or that he is *not* a productive member of society. The religious apologist will argue that behind these requirements of justice as fairness there lurks the ancient religious principle that men are creatures of God, each with an infinite worth, and thus men are never to be treated only as means but as persons deserving of respect in their own right. They have an infinite worth simply as persons.

My religious critic, following out the dialectic of the problem, should query: why should you respect someone, why should you treat all people equally, if doing this is not in your interest or not in the interests of your group? No purely secular justification can be given for so behaving. My critic now serves his *coup de grâce:* the secularist, as well as the "knight of faith," acknowledges that the principle of respect for persons is a precious one—a principle that he is unequivocally committed to, but the religious man alone can *justify* adherence to this principle. The secularist is surreptitiously drawing on Christian inspiration when he insists that all men should be considered equal and that people's rights must be respected. For a secular morality to say all it wants and needs to say, it must, at this crucial point, be parasitical upon a God-centered morality. Without such a dependence on religion, secular morality collapses into egoism.

It may well be the case that, as a historical fact, our moral concern for persons came from our religious conceptions, but it is a well known principle of logic that the validity of a belief is independent of its origin. What the religious moralist must do is to show that only on religous grounds could such a principle of respect for persons be justifiably asserted. But he has not shown that this is so; and there are good reasons for thinking that it is not so. Even if the secularist must simply subscribe to the Kantian principle, "Treat every man as an end and never as a means only," as he must subscribe to the claim, "Happiness is good," it does not follow that he is on worse ground than the religious moralist, for the religious moralist too, as we have seen, must simply subscribe to his ultimate moral principle, "Always do what God wills." *In a way,* the religious moralist's position here is simpler than the secularist's, for he needs only the fundamental moral principle that he ought to do what God wills. The secularist appears to need at least two fundamental principles. But in another and more important way the religious moralist's position is more complex, for he must subscribe to the extraordinarily obscure notion that man is a creature of God and as such has infinite worth. The Kantian principle may in the last analysis simply require subscription, but it is not inherently mysterious. To accept it does not require a crucifixion of the intellect. And if we are prepared simply to commit ourselves to one principle, why not to two principles, neither of which involves any appeal to conceptions whose very intelligibility is seriously in question?

The above argument is enough to destroy the believer's case here. But need we even make those concessions? I do not think so. There is a purely secular rationale for treating people fairly, for regarding them as persons. Let me show how this is so. We have no evidence that men ever lived in a pre-social state of nature. Man, as we know him, is an animal with a culture; he is part of a community, and the very *concept* of community implies binding principles and regulations—duties, obligations and rights. Yet, by an exercise in imagination, we could conceive, in broad outline at any rate, what it would be like to live in such a pre-social state. In such a state no one would have any laws or principles to direct his behaviour. In that sense man would be completely free. But such a life, as Hobbes graphically depicted, would be a clash of rival egoisms. Life in that state of nature would, in his celebrated phrase, "be nasty, brutish and short." Now if men were in such a state and if they were perfectly rational egoists, what kind of community life would they choose, given the fact that they were, very roughly speaking, nearly equal in strength and ability? (That in communities as we find them men are not so nearly equal in power is beside the point, for our *hypothetical* situation.) Given that they all start from scratch and have roughly equal abilities, it seems to me that it would be most reasonable, even for rational egoists, to band together into a community where each man's interests were given equal consideration, where each person was treated as deserving of respect.[2] Each rational egoist would want others to treat him with respect, for his very happiness is contingent upon that; and he would recognize, if he were rational, that he could attain the fullest cooperation of others only if other rational egoists knew or had good grounds for believing that their interests and their persons would also be respected. Such cooperation is essential for each egoist if all are to have the type of community life which would give them the best chance of satisfying their own interests to the fullest degree. Thus, even if men were thorough egoists, we would still have rational grounds for subscribing to a principle of respect for persons. That men are not thoroughly rational, do not live in a state of nature, and are not thorough egoists, does not gainsay the fact that we have rational grounds for regarding social life, organized in accordance with such a principle, as being objectively better than a social life which ignored this principle. The point here is that even rational egoists could see that this is the best possible social organization where men are nearly equal in ability.

Yet what about the world we live in—a world in which, given certain extant social relationships, men are not equal or even nearly equal in power and opportunity? What reason is there for an egoist who is powerfully placed to respect the rights of others, when they cannot hurt him? We can say that his position, no matter how strong, might change and he

---

[2]Some of the very complicated considerations relevant here have been subtly brought out by John Rawls in his "Justice as Fairness," *The Philosophical Review*, LXVII (1958), 164–194. I think it could be reasonably maintained that my argument is more vulnerable here than at any other point. I would not, of course, use it if I did not think that it could be sustained, but if anyone should find the argument as presented here unconvincing I would beg him to consider the argument that precedes it and the one that immediately follows it. They alone are sufficient to establish my general case. Since this essay was first prepared for publication, George von Wright's powerful book *THE VARIETIES OF GOODNESS* (London, 1963) has come into my hands. The point made above is argued for convincingly and in detail in Chapter X of that book.

might be in a position where he would need his rights protected, but this is surely not a strong enough reason for respecting those rights. To be moral involves respecting those rights, but our rational egoist may not proposed to be moral. In considering such questions we reach a point in reasoning at which we must simply *decide* what sort of person we shall strive to become. But, as I have said, the religious moralist reaches the same point. He too must make a decision of principle, but the principle he adopts is a fundamentally incoherent one. He not only must decide, but his decision must involve the acceptance of an absurdity.

It is sometimes argued by religious apologists that only if there is a God who can punish men will we be assured that naturally selfish men will be fair and considerate of others. Without this punitive sanction or threat men would go wild. Men will respect the rights of others only if they fear a wrathful and angry God. Yet it hardly seems to be the case that Christians, with their fear of hell, have been any better at respecting the rights of others than non-Christians. A study of the Middle Ages or the conquest of the non-Christian world makes this plain enough. And even if it were true (as it is not) that Christians were better in this respect than non-Christians, it would not show that they had a superior moral reason for their behavior, for in so acting and in so reasoning, they are not giving a morally relevant reason at all but are simply acting out of fear for their own hides. Yet Christian morality supposedly takes us beyond the clash of the rival egoisms of secular life.

In short, Christian ethics has not been able to give us a sounder ground for respecting persons than we have with a purely secular morality. The Kantian principle of respect for persons is actually bound up in the very idea of morality, either secular or religious, and there are good reasons, of a perfectly mundane sort, why we should have the institution of morality as we now have it, namely, that our individual welfare is dependent on having a device which equitably resolves social and individual conflicts. Morality has an objective rationale in complete independence of religion. Even if God is dead, it doesn't really matter.

It is in just this last thrust, it might be objected, that you reveal your true colors and show your own inability to face a patent social reality. At this point the heart of your rationalism is very irrational. For millions of people "the death of God" means very much. It really does matter. In your somewhat technical sense, the concept of God may be chaotic or unintelligible, but this concept, embedded in our languages—embedded in "the stream of life"—has an enormous social significance for many people. Jews and Christians, if they take their religion to heart, could not but feel a great rift in their lives with the loss of God, for they have indeed organized a good bit of their lives around their religion. Their very life-ideals have grown out of these, if you will, myth-eaten concepts. What should have been said is that if "God is dead" it matters a lot, but we should stand up like men and face this loss and learn to live in the Post-Christian era. As Nietzsche so well knew, to do this involves a basic reorientation of one's life and not just an intellectual dissent to a few statements of doctrine.

There is truth in this and a kind of "empiricism about man" that philosophers are prone to neglect. Of course it does matter when one recognizes that one's religion is illusory. For a devout Jew or Christian to give up his God most certainly is important and does take him into the abyss of a spiritual crisis. But in saying that it doesn't *really* matter I was implying what I have argued for in this essay, namely, that if a believer loses his God but can keep his nerve, think the matter over, and thoroughly take it to heart, life can still be meaningful and morality yet have an objective rationale. Surely, for good psychological reasons, the believer is prone to doubt this argument, but if he will only "hold on to his brains" and keep his courage, he will come to see that it is so. In this crucial sense it remains true that if "God is dead" it doesn't really matter.

DISCUSSION QUESTIONS

1. What reasons does Nielsen give to support his claim that an autonomous ethics need not sink into either conventionalism or nihilism? Do you agree?

2. Do you agree that one difference between a secular morality and a religion-based morality is the number of ethical principles required for each? Why or why not?

3. A principle that is central to Nielsen's secular ethics is respect for persons. Do you agree that this principle can be justified apart from a religious view of reality?

4. Religion for many people provides one, overall meaning for life, but Nielsen argues that life can nonetheless be meaningful without an overall meaning, provided we have some success in realizing the goals we set for ourselves and find other sources of satisfaction. Do you agree? Why or why not?

5. Has Nielsen's article changed in any way your view of the relation between religion and ethics? Give reasons for your answer.

PAUL TILLICH

Morality Versus Moralisms

Christianity did not claim to be distinctive because it offered a new morality, nor did early Christian writers suggest that non-Christians are ignorant of the demands of moral living. The problem as they saw it is not that people don't know their duties, but that in spite of knowing what is good they still do not do it. What Christian faith offers to individuals, they thought, was not another set of moral principles but a new orientation in life and a renewal of one's being which would bring about a style of conduct consistent with the life of faith.

If all that religion had to offer us was a set of moral principles, then the difference between religious morality and secular morality would be negligible, and we would probably have to agree with Professor Nielsen's claim that we do not really need a religious basis for ethics. If, however, religion offers something other than merely a set of moral principles, then we will have to reconsider the critique of religious morality that Nielsen offered. Tillich suggests that religion does indeed offer something different than mere moral codes, or moralisms, as he calls them.

MORALITY UNCONDITIONAL; MORALISMS CONDITIONAL

A key term in Tillich's discussion of the difference between morality and moralisms is *unconditional*. That morality is an unconditional demand was defended at great length by Immanuel Kant, and Tillich's rather casual reference to this Kantian motif indicates that he thinks his readers will be familiar with the outlines of

Kant's approach. To repeat all of Kant's analysis here would take us too far away from our present concern, but the following example may shed some light on the reasons Kant argued that morality was unconditional.

Suppose there is a fund-raising drive in your community to build a childrens' wing on the local hospital. The new wing will cost five million dollars, and five individuals each give one million dollars to the fund. For the sake of our example, we will assume that we know the motives behind these gifts (though in real-life we seldom know the motives behind actions), and knowing the motives we can judge the moral significance of the gifts.

Giver	Motive
1. Local Businessperson	Tax write-off and favorable publicity
2. Mayor	Political advantage; this gift will make him popular
3. Contractor (the same one who built the hospital)	Guilt for using cheap and substandard materials in building the hospital
4. Local Philanthropist	Enjoyment of public acclaim
5. Anonymous Donor	Moral obligation to relieve suffering

According to Kant, only the gift given out of a sense of moral obligation to relieve suffering had genuine moral significance, and only the gift of person No. 5 is unconditional. The other four gifts are conditioned by prudential concerns, desire for public approval, guilt, or reasons of self-interest. Kant would argue that a moral action must be unconditional, that is done only out of a respect for duty and because it is the right thing to do. In other words, to be moral is to recognize that we ought to do our duty.

Now what our duty really is may be difficult to determine. But whatever our duty is, we ought to do it; that is the unconditional demand of morality. The specific content of our moral duty is not unconditional but is in fact conditioned by such factors as our cultural situation, our understanding of the world, even the opportunities open to us. The systems of rules that are originated to serve as guides to action Tillich calls moralisms.

The distinction between morality and moralism was made by medieval philosophers in their distinction between Natural Law and Positive Law. Natural Law is our moral duty; Positive Law is the set of conventional arrangements that we make in order to live together in human society. Ideally Positive Law should conform to Natural Law, but Positive Law is concerned with specific issues, not general principles. There is, for example, nothing in the Natural Law to tell us precisely what sort of highway code we should have or whether we should have a bicameral legislature or a monarchy; no-fault auto insurance or no insurance laws at all; whether a young person should be allowed to purchase liquor at age 16, 18, or 21. All these Positive Laws are subject to a great deal of variation and are highly relative; just to confirm this, contrast the liquor laws of half a dozen states; all are designed to protect the moral integrity of their citizens, but the laws of the states are all different. Tillich's point is that the content of moralisms, or Positive Law, is relative whereas our moral duty is not.

ESSENTIAL AND ACTUAL BEING

All of us recognize that there are lots of things we ought to do but do not do; in short, we recognize that we do not live up to our duty. When we think of all the things we ought to do, we are thinking of an ideal or essential self, a self we ought to be. Morality is what relates to our essential being, that person we ought to be. But our actual being, what we are, is different from our essential being. We can put this in more traditional language by saying that there is a difference between the *Is* and the *Ought*.

A significant factor emerges when we recognize the difference between the Is and the Ought, and to illustrate this let's put the distinctions in graphic form:

Our Essential Being	**Our Actual Being**
(What we Ought to be)	(What we actually are)
Morality ———————	——————— Moralism

There is a gulf between our essential and actual being; the significance of this is that we recognize a moral obligation which we do not fulfill due to this split between our essential and actual being. If we were our essential being, we would be moral and would feel no sense of duty, for duty arises when we recognize that we are not what we ought to be. But at the same time, if in our actual being we were not aware of the essential being which we are not, we would likewise feel no sense of moral obligation. Moral obligation appears to us in our actual being as a legal demand, as a set of rules to be followed.

Here is where the difficulty comes in. Moral rules, or moralisms, cannot make us moral. In case you missed it, let me repeat it: Moral rules cannot make us moral. In fact, moralisms make matters worse, for the appearance of moralisms widens the gulf between our essential being and our actual being. The better we recognize what we ought to be, the greater the estrangement between our essential self and our actual self. A truly moral self would be one which acted in accordance with a good will, that is, we would be truly moral only if the estrangement between our essential being and our actual being were overcome. Moralisms cannot overcome this estrangement; in fact, they only make it worse. So we are tempted to do one of two things: either we claim that we have kept all the moral rules, and this results in hypocrisy; or we despair over ever being able to keep all the moral rules, and this results in cynicism.

Let's try to illustrate this with a nonreligious example. Suppose you have decided that you need more friends. You discover a paperback entitled *How To Have More Friends*. Surely this holds the key to enlarging your circle of friends, you think. As you pore over the book you discover that the author has given a set of rules for making friends. You faithfully memorize the rules and then try to put them into practice. No matter how hard you try, you still are not making new friends. Somehow it is all hollow; the rules don't help. In fact, they seem to be driving off what few friends you have. All your posturing, all your pretending of interest in other people comes through as insincere, phony, and pretentious. Word gets around that you have become strange in your behavior. Even some of your casual acquaintances begin to avoid you. All the rules for making friends, instead of producing more friends, have done the exact opposite. So you burn your book and forget about all the rules. Then you discover a genuine friendship and realize that friendships are possible only if you are really a friend, and that rules don't help. Genuine friendship is beyond rules and regulations. Once you have established a relationship of friendship with someone else, you no longer need the rules.

FORGIVENESS AND REGENERATION

The same dynamics are found in morality. Moral rules do not make us moral. If we were moral, we would not need moral rules. It is a kind of moral "catch 22"; if we were moral we would not need rules (moralisms), but the fact that we need moralisms indicates that we are not moral.

How do we break out of this cycle? Tillich pinpoints two elements in religion that are all important: forgiveness and regeneration. Forgiveness is being accepted, even though we may not be very acceptable; this acceptance also includes self-acceptance. Regeneration means overcoming the split between what we are and what we ought to be; in short, it is the development of a new being.

The difference between morality and moralisms is also pinpointed by two different kinds of justice. Justice, as the goal of moralisms, can be the unity and harmony of the entire system, as it was for the Greeks, or the quality of God that makes God the Lord of the Universe, as it was in the Old Testament, or it could have other orientations depending on the moralisms that give it expression. For morality, however, justice is transformed into justification; as Tillich puts it, "Justification by grace is the highest form of divine justice." This brief sentence contains theological terms filled with meaning which cannot be adequately discussed here. But in Tillich's context the significance of the term justification is that divine power makes us just; divine justification does not condemn but rather transforms, and this transformation, which is at the basis of all morality, is the power of love.

All this might be clearer if there were another word we could use instead of love; love is used to cover so many different meanings that it is difficult to use the term and pinpoint its religious significance. In this context it does not refer primarily to an emotion, but to the power of regeneration. Love is the power to overcome separation and estrangement, especially estrangement in our own being. We can overcome the separation from our essential being through the power of love, and this means that first of all love must be directed to oneself. This is not selfishness; selfish love would be directed only to our actual self. It is rather a matter of self-affirmation and self-acceptance which helps overcome the split between our actual and essential being.

The significant fact about all this is that love cannot be forced. No set of moral rules will ever enable a person to be loving. And if love is missing from a person's orientation, there will be a continued split between that person's actual self and essential self. Only if there is the reintegrated being in one's own personality brought about by the power of love is there then the regenerated being that makes possible the living of a moral life.

Love, the key to morality, removes the need for moralisms. This is the reason that Tillich says that "Love participates, and participation overcomes authority." If you really love another person, the relationship does not need to be defined by rules. Love is both the acceptance of self and the acceptance of the other, and neither partner in the relationship is destroyed.

Moralisms and Morality: Theonomous Ethics*

MORALISMS CONDITIONED, MORALITY UNCONDITIONAL

People today are afraid of the term "unconditional." This is understandable if one considers the way in which many rather conditioned ideas and methods have been imposed on individuals and groups in the name of an unconditional truth, authoritatively and through suppression. The destructive consequences of such a demonic absolutism have produced a reaction even against the term unconditional. The mere word provokes passionate resistance. But not everything which is psychologically understandable is for this reason true. Even the most outspoken relativists cannot avoid something absolute. They acknowledge the unconditional quest to follow logical rules in their reasoning, and to act according to the law of scientific honesty in their thinking and speaking. Their character as scientific personalities is dependent on the unconditional acceptance of these principles.

This leads us to a more general understanding of the unconditional character of the moral imperative. What Immanuel Kant has called the "categorical imperative" is nothing more than the unconditional character of the "ought-to-be," the moral commandment. Whatever its content may be, its form is unconditional. One can rightly criticize Kant because he establishes a system of ethical forms without ethical contents. But just this limitation is his greatness. It makes as sharp as possible the distinction between morality which is unconditional, and moralisms which are valid only conditionally and within limits. If this is understood, the relativity of all concrete ethics (moralisms) is accepted and emphasized. The material

*Source: Reprinted from *Ministry and Medicine in Human Relations,* ed. Iago Galdston. By permission of International Universities Press, Inc. Copyright 1955 by International Universities Press, Inc.

cited by the sociologist, anthropologist, and psychologist showing the endless differences of ethical ideals is no argument against the unconditional validity of the moral imperative. If we disregard this distinction, we either fall into an absolute skepticism which, in the long run, undermines morality as such, or we fall into an absolutism which attributes unconditional validity to one of the many possible moralisms. Since, however, each of these moralisms has to maintain itself against others, it becomes fanatical, for fanaticism is the attempt to repress elements of one's own being for the sake of others. If the fanatic encounters these elements in somebody else, he fights against them passionately, because they endanger the success of his own repression.

The reason for the unconditional character of the moral imperative is that it puts our essential being as a demand against us. The moral imperative is not a strange law, imposed on us, but it is the law of our own being. In the moral imperative we ourselves, in our essential being, are put against ourselves, in our actual being. No outside command can be unconditional, whether it comes from a state, or a person, or God—if God is thought of as an outside power, establishing a law for our behavior. A stranger, even if his name were God, who imposes commands upon us must be resisted or, as Nietzsche has expressed it in his symbol of the "ugliest man," he must be killed because nobody can stand him. We cannot be obedient to the commands of a stranger even if he is God. Nor can we take unconditionally the content of the moral imperative from human authorities like traditions, conventions, political or religious authorities. There is no ultimate authority in them. One is largely dependent on them, but none of them is unconditionally valid.

The moral command is unconditional because it is we ourselves commanding ourselves. Morality is the self-affirmation of our essential being. This makes it unconditional, whatever its content may be. This is quite different from an affirmation of one's self in terms of one's desires and fears. Such a self-affirmation has no unconditional character; ethics based on it are ethics of calculation, describing the best way of getting fulfillment of desires and protection against fears. There is nothing absolute in technical calculation. But morality as the self-affirmation of one's essential being is unconditional.

The contents, however, of the moral self-affirmation are conditioned, relative, dependent on the social and psychological constellation. While morality as the pure form of essential self-affirmation is absolute, the concrete systems of moral imperatives, the "moralisms" are relative. This is not relativism (which as a philosophical attitude is self-contradictory), but it is the acknowledgment of man's finitude and his dependence on the contingencies of time and space. No conflict between the ethicist, theological or philosophical, and the anthropologist or sociologist is necessary. No theologian should deny the relativity of the moral contents; no ethnologist should deny the absolute character of the ethical demand. . . .

MORALISMS OF LAW AND MORALITY OF GRACE

Because the moral imperative puts our essential against our actual being, it appears to us as law. A being which lives out of its essential nature is law to itself. It follows its natural structure. But this is not the human situation. Man is estranged from his essential being and, therefore, the moral imperative appears as law to him: Moralism is legalism!

The law is first of all "natural law." In the Stoic tradition this term does not mean the physical laws but the natural laws which constitute our essential nature. These laws are the background of all positive laws in states and other groups. They are also the background of the moral law, which is our problem today. The moral law is more oppressive than the severest positive law, just because it is internalized. It creates conscience and the feeling of guilt.

So we must ask: What is the power inducing us to fulfill the law? The power behind the positive laws is rewards and punishments. What is the power behind the moral law? One could say: the reward of the good and the punishment of the uneasy conscience, often projected as heavenly rewards and punishments in purgatory or hell. (Cf. Hamlet's words about the conscience, which makes cowards of us.) But this answer is not sufficient. It does not explain the insuperable resistance the law provokes against itself, in spite of punishments and rewards. The law is not able to create its own fulfillment.

The reason for this is visible when we consider the words of Jesus, Paul, and Luther saying that the law is only fulfilled if it is fulfilled with joy, and not with resentment and hate. But joy cannot be commanded. The law brings us into a paradoxical situation: It commands, which means that it stands against us. But it commands something which can be done only if it does *not* stand against us, if we are united with what it commands. This is the point where the moral imperative drives towards something which is not command but reality. Only the "good tree" brings "good fruits." Only if being precedes that which ought-to-be, can the ought-to-be be fulfilled. Morality can be maintained only through that which is given and not through that which is demanded; in religious terms, through grace and not through law. Without the reunion of man with his own essential nature no perfect moral act is possible. Legalism drives either to self-complacency (I have kept *all* commandments) or to despair (I cannot keep *any* commandment). Moralism of law makes pharisees or cynics, or it produces in the majority of people an indifference which lowers the moral imperative to conventional behavior. Moralism necessarily ends in the quest for grace.

Grace unites two elements: the overcoming of guilt and the overcoming of estrangement. The first element appears in theology as the "forgiveness of sins," or in more recent terminology, as "accepting acceptance though being unacceptable." The second element appears in theology as "regeneration" or in more recent terminology, as the "entering into the new being" which is above the split between what we are and what we ought to be. Every religion, even if seemingly moralistic, has a doctrine of salvation in which these two elements are present.

And psychotherapy is involved in the same problems. Psychotherapy is definitely antimoralistic. It avoids commandments because it knows that neurotics cannot be healed by moral judgments and moral demands. The only help is to accept him who is unacceptable, to create a communion with him, a sphere of participation in a new reality. Psychotherapy must be a therapy of grace or it cannot be therapy at all. There are striking analogies between the recent methods of mental healing and the traditional ways of personal salvation. But there is also one basic difference. Psychotherapy can liberate one from a special difficulty. Religion shows to him who is liberated, and has to decide about the meaning and aim of his existence, a final way. This difference is decisive for the independence as well as for the co-operation of religion and psychotherapy.

MORALISMS OF JUSTICE AND MORALITY OF LOVE

The moral imperative expresses itself in laws which are supposed to be just. Justice, in Greek thinking, is the unity of the whole system of morals. Justice, in the Old Testament, is that quality of God which makes Him the Lord of the Universe. In Islam, morality and law are not distinguished, and in the philosophy of Hegel, ethics are treated as a section of the philosophy of law (*Recht*). Every system of moral commandments is, at the same time, the basis for a system of laws. In all moralisms the moral imperative has the tendency to become a legal principle. Justice, in Aristotle, is determined by proportionality. Everybody gets what he deserves according to quantitative measurements. This is not the Christian point of view. Justice, in the Old Testament, is the activity of God toward the fulfillment of His promises. And justice, in the New Testament, is the unity of judgment and forgiveness. Justification by grace is the highest form of divine justice. This means that proportional justice is not the answer to the moral problem. Not proportional, but transforming justice has divine character. In other words: Justice is fulfilled in love. The moralisms of justice drive toward the morality of love.

Love, in the sense of this statement, is not an emotion, but a principle of life. If love were primarily emotion it would inescapably conflict with justice, it would add something to justice which is not justice. But love does not add something strange to justice. Rather it is the ground, the power, and the aim of justice. Love is the life which separates itself from itself and drives toward reunion with itself. The norm of justice is reunion of the estranged. Creative justice—justice, creative as love—is the union of love and justice and the ultimate principle of morality.

From this it follows that there is a just self-love, namely the desire of reunion of oneself with oneself. One can be loveless toward oneself. But if this is the case, one is not only without love but also without justice toward oneself—and toward others. One must accept oneself just as one is accepted in spite of being unacceptable. And in doing so one has what is called the right self-love, the opposite of the wrong self-love. In order to avoid many confusions one should replace the word self-love completely. One may call the right self-love self-acceptance, the wrong self-love self-ishness, and the natural self-love self-affirmation. In all cases the word "self," as such, has no negative connotations. It is the structure of the most developed form of reality, the most individualized and the most universal being. Self is good, self-affirmation is good, self-acceptance is good, but selfishness is bad because it prevents both self-affirmation and self-acceptance.

Love is the answer to the problem of moralisms and morality. It answers the questions implied in all four confrontations of moralism and morality. Love is unconditional. There is nothing which could condition it by a higher principle. There is nothing above love. And love conditions itself. It enters every concrete situation and works for the reunion of the separated in a unique way.

Love transforms the moralisms of authority into a morality of risk. Love is creative and creativity includes risk. Love does not destroy factual authority but it liberates from the authority of a special place, from an irrational hypostatized authority. Love participates, and participation overcomes authority.

Love is the source of grace. Love accepts that which is unacceptable and love renews the old being so that it becomes a new being. Medieval theology almost identified love and grace, and rightly so, for that which makes one graceful is love. But grace is, at the same time, the love which forgives and accepts.

Nevertheless, love includes justice. Love without justice is a body without a backbone. The justice of love includes that no partner in this relation is asked to annihilate himself. The self which enters a love relation is preserved in its independence. Love includes justice to others and to oneself. Love is the solution of the problem: moralisms and morality.

DISCUSSION QUESTIONS

1. Do you find convincing the distinction Tillich suggests between morality and moralisms? What are your reasons?
2. Tillich accepts Kant's claim that the only truly moral action is unconditioned. Do you agree?
3. Show how the difference between what Tillich calls our essential being and our actual being is related to the difference between the "is" and the "ought."
4. Do you agree that moral rules cannot make us moral? What evidence can you give from your own experience of the truth of your answer?
5. What is your evaluation of Tillich's claim that religion's contribution to morality consists of forgiveness and regeneration?
6. What did Tillich mean by saying, "Love transforms the moralisms of authority into a morality of risk"?

REINHOLD NIEBUHR

The Need of Ethics
for
Religion

If, as Tillich suggested, love is the key to understanding the relation between religion and ethics, we should not be surprised to find a great deal said about the importance of love in the scriptures of both Judaism and Christianity. The Law of Moses commanded its adherents to "love your neighbor as yourself" (Leviticus 19:18). This injunction is cited by Jesus as one of the two great commandments, the other being to love God with one's whole being (Deuteronomy 6:5; cf. Matthew 22:36–40). The golden rule, "And as you wish that men would do to you, do so to them" (Luke 6:31) is but another way of stating for others this principle of love that is deeply rooted in the religious faith of Israel. Jesus also told his disciples that they would be known as his disciples by their love, and that they should love others as he had loved them (John 15:12, 17). The later books of the New Testament also state that God *is* love and that the motivation for loving one another is that God first loved us (1 John 4:16, 19).

Love, as the moral ideal of the Judaeo-Christian religious tradition, is basic to understanding the relation between religion and ethics, but as Niebuhr analyzes this relation he points up the obvious fact that this ideal is not exemplified in practice. Every human community seems to be marred by selfishness, the tendency to exploitation, perhaps even greed. If the past history of the human race is any indication, we are not likely to realize in any human society or humanly devised order the ideal of love that stands at the center of the religious orientation toward ethics. This state of affairs poses a problem for a philosophical concern with ethics: Of what value is a moral ideal that seems to be impossible to practice? Is it not the rational thing to simply give up all attempts to achieve an impossible moral ideal and be content with the closest approximation to this that we can achieve? This is precisely the conclusion that many persons will reach when faced with the difficulty of achieving the ideal of love in personal relationships, but if we go this route, Niebuhr says, we will sink into either fanaticism or despair. Fanaticism results when we elevate as the supreme principle of morality one qualified aspect of morality, and despair results when we recognize that we do not seem to be able to live up to the highest standards of moral life.

THE JUDGE AND GROUND OF MORALITY

Niebuhr argues that we can avoid the twin dangers of fanaticism and despair by affirming a moral ideal that is rooted in what is essentially a religious view of life. Central to the religious view of morality is the reality of God "who is both the ground and the ultimate fulfillment of existence, who is both the creator and the judge of the world. . . ." The importance of God and divine love as both the judge and ground of morality is crucial for understanding Niebuhr's analysis, so we will turn to each of these notions for further discussion.

Rooted in the nature of God as love, the moral ideal of love serves as a judgment on all provisional human societies. What this means, in practice, is that the lofty ideal of divine love serves as a critique of all human attempts to achieve this quality in society. Whenever we might be tempted to identify a given human social or political order as the ultimate type of human society, we can judge that order by the principle of love found in the "prophetic faith" and discover that this social order does not measure up to the high standards of the moral ideal. In other words, the moral ideal of love serves as a warning against thinking that any particular human society is completely moral. If we recognize that all human societies are imperfect and do not deserve our ultimate allegiance, we will be less likely to give any nation or the state our unqualified allegiance. Whenever people give their ultimate loyalty to the nation or the state, they are driven to fanaticism, as the political history of the twentieth century vividly illustrates.

The political corollary of the ethical ideal of love is the political ideal of equality. Though this may be our political goal, we will have to admit that no completely egalitarian society exists, and indeed no such society may ever exist. Yet the principle of equality, though not perfectly realized, is necessary as a critique of all entrenched privileges and inequities. The moral ideal, translated into a political ideal, is a standard that serves as a judgment of all human attempts to approximate it in human society. As Niebuhr puts it, the ideal of equality "remains, nevertheless, a principle of criticism under which every scheme of justice stands and a symbol of the principle of love involved in all moral judgments."

Even if we admit that love, and its political equivalent equality, are ethical ideals that stand in judgment on all attempts to realize them in practice, how is love a ground for morality? To put the question differently, why can't we achieve love without religion; and if we can, why do we need to talk about love in a religious context at all? Niebuhr's answer to this question also shows in what sense he considers divine love the ground of morality. First we must recognize that love is not just an emotion or an act of the will. If it were, then love as the ideal of all ethical values could be achieved apart from a religious orientation. To show the connection between love and religious faith we must fully take into consideration the fact that religious persons have not always achieved the moral ideal; in fact, the history of Christianity has its share of failures to exemplify the ideal of love. Nonetheless, there are notable examples of compassion, altruism, and concern for others that are directly attributable to the religious impulse. Of course, we must be willing to judge the actions of persons claiming to be motivated by religious principles by the standard of the ethical ideal; in short, any claim to be acting from religious principles must be judged by the "moral fruits" of those principles. But if love is not just a result of an act of the will, how do we account for it?

Here Niebuhr reflects a theme from Tillich's discussion of the difference between morality and moralism. Moralisms are commands to accomplish moral goals, and as commands they threaten us because they also condemn us for not achieving the moral ideal. When we do achieve an act of love, it is something that we have willed, but our will does not accomplish this because of a command. It is rather the case that our will gives expression to that which we are. In the language of traditional theology, love is both a fruit of grace and a fruit of faith. To speak of love as the product of grace means that its source is ultimately God. To speak of love as a fruit of faith means that it flows from a religious orientation toward life.

CONTRITION AND GRATITUDE

Central to the religious orientation toward life are the twin attitudes of gratitude and contrition, which Niebuhr terms the fruits of a prophetic faith. Contrition is the attitude that results from a recognition that every moral achievement is less than the essential goodness which is the ideal of moral life. To recognize that we are not what we ought to be results in contrition, yet the attitude of gratitude prevents our falling into despair over failure to live up to the demands of the moral imperative. As Niebuhr puts it, "Gratitude for what life is in its essence creates a propulsive power to affirm in existence what is truly essential, the harmony of life with life." Gratitude enables us to see life as more than a mere biological fact; as a spiritual reality given by God. Consequently, each of us, given this religious orientation, will view others under the aura of a transcendent perspective. Again to quote Niebuhr: "Awed by the majesty and goodness of God, something of the pretense of our pretentious self is destroyed and the natural cruelty of our self-righteousness is mitigated by emotions of pity and forgiveness."

To recapitulate, Niebuhr argues that moral rules cannot make us moral. Moral rules can command and condemn, but they cannot motivate. What we need is a source of motivation which enables us to act on moral principles not out of obedience to a set of rules, but out of a reorientation in our attitude toward life. In short, we are truly moral when our life gives expression to a love which flows from our own being. And Niebuhr suggests that we can develop this orientation toward life most fully if we have a religious view of reality.

The Relevance of an Impossible Moral Ideal*

Moral life is possible at all only in a meaningful existence. Obligation
can be felt only to some system of coherence and some ordering will. Thus
moral obligation is always an obligation to promote harmony and to
overcome chaos. But every conceivable order in the historical world
contains an element of anarchy. Its world rests upon contingency and
caprice. The obligation to support and enhance it can therefore only arise
and maintain itself upon the basis of a faith that it is the partial fruit of a
deeper unity and the promise of a more perfect harmony than is revealed
in any immediate situation. If a lesser faith than this prompts moral
action, it results in precisely those types of moral fanaticism which impart
unqualified worth to qualified values and thereby destroy even their
qualified worth. The prophetic faith in a God who is both the ground and
the ultimate fulfillment of existence, who is both the creator and the judge
of the world, is thus involved in every moral situation. Without it the
world is seen either as being meaningless or as revealing unqualifiedly
good and simple meanings. In either case the nerve of moral action is
ultimately destroyed. The dominant attitudes of prophetic faith are
gratitude and contrition; gratitude for Creation and contrition before
Judgment; or, in other words, confidence that life is good in spite of its
evil and that it is evil in spite of its good. In such a faith both sentimentality
and despair are avoided. The meaningfulness of life does not tempt to
premature complacency, and the chaos which always threatens the world
of meaning does not destroy the tension of faith and hope in which all
moral action is grounded.

The prophetic faith, that the meaningfulness of life and existence
implies a source and end beyond itself, produces a morality which implies
that every moral value and standard is grounded in and points toward an
ultimate perfection of unity and harmony, not realizable in any historic
situation. An analysis of the social history of mankind validates this
interpretation.

In spite of the relativity of morals every conceivable moral code and
every philosophy of morals enjoins concern for the life and welfare of the
other and seeks to restrain the unqualified assertion of the interests of the
self against the other. There is thus a fairly universal agreement in all
moral systems that it is wrong to take the life or the property of the
neighbor, though it must be admitted that the specific applications of

*Source: Abridged from pp. 105–9, 214–15, 218–20 in *An Interpretation of Christian
Ethics* by Reinhold Niebuhr. Copyright 1935 by Harper & Row, Publishers, Inc.
Reprinted by permission of Harper & Row, Publishers, Inc.

these general principles vary greatly according to time and place. This minimal standard of moral conduct is grounded in the law of love and points toward it as ultimate fulfillment. The obligation to affirm and protect the life of others can arise at all only if it is assumed that life is related to life in some unity and harmony of existence. In any given instance motives of the most calculating prudence rather than a high sense of obligation may enforce the standard. Men may defend the life of the neighbor merely to preserve those processes of mutuality by which their own life is protected. But that only means that they have discovered the inter-relatedness of life through concern for themselves rather than by an analysis of the total situation. This purely prudential approach will not prompt the most consistent social conduct, but it will nevertheless implicitly affirm what it ostensibly denies—that the law of life is love.

Perhaps the clearest proof, that the law of love is involved as a basis of even the most minimal social standards, is found in the fact that every elaboration of minimal standards into higher standards makes the implicit relation more explicit. Prohibitions of murder and theft are negative. They seek to prevent one life from destroying or taking advantage of another. No society is content with these merely negative prohibitions. Its legal codes do not go much beyond negatives because only minimal standards can be legally enforced. But the moral codes and ideals of every advanced society demand more than mere prohibition of theft and murder. Higher conceptions of justice are developed. It is recognized that the right to live implies the right to secure the goods which sustain life. This right immediately involves more than mere prohibition of theft. Some obligation is felt, however dimly, to organize the common life so that the neighbor will have fair opportunities to maintain his life. The various schemes of justice and equity which grow out of this obligation, consciously or unconsciously imply an ideal of equality beyond themselves. Equality is always the regulative principle of justice; and in the ideal of equality there is an echo of the law of love, "Thou shalt love thy neighbor AS THYSELF." If the question is raised to what degree the neighbor has a right to support his life through the privileges and opportunities of the common life, no satisfactory, rational answer can be given to it, short of one implying equalitarian principles: He has just as much right as yourself.

This does not mean that any society will ever achieve perfect equality. Equality, being a rational, political version of the law of love, shares with it the quality of transcendence. It ought to be, but it never will be fully realized. Social prudence will qualify it. The most equalitarian society will probably not be able to dispense with special rewards as inducements to diligence. Some differentials in privilege will be necessary to make the performance of certain social functions possible. While a rigorous equalitarian society can prevent such privileges from being perpetuated from one generation to another without regard to social function, it cannot eliminate privileges completely. Nor is there any political technique which would be a perfect guarantee against abuses of socially sanctioned privileges. Significant social functions are endowed by their very nature with a certain degree of social power. Those who possess power, however socially restrained, always have the opportunity of deciding that the function which they perform is entitled to more privilege than any ideal scheme of justice would allow. The ideal of equality is thus qualified in any possible society by the necessities of social cohesion and corrupted by the sinfulness of men. It remains, nevertheless, a principle of criticism under which every scheme of justice stands and a symbol of the principle of love involved in all moral judgments. . . .

The Christian doctrine of love is thus the most adequate metaphysical and psychological framework for the approximation of the ideal of love in human life. It is able to appropriate all the resources of human nature which tend toward the harmony of life with life, without resting in the resources of "natural man." It is able to set moral goals transcending nature without being lost in other-worldliness. The degree of approximation depends upon the extent to which the Christian faith is not merely a theory, but a living and vital presupposition of life and conduct. The long history of Christianity is, in spite of its many failures, not wanting in constant and perennial proofs that love is the fruit of its spirit. Martyrs and saints, missionaries and prophets, apostles and teachers of the faith, have showed forth in their lives the pity and tenderness toward their fellow men which is the crown of the Christian life. Nor has Christianity failed to impart to the ordinary human relations of ordinary men the virtues of tenderness and consideration.

While every religion, as indeed every human world view, must finally justify itself in terms of its moral fruits it must be understood that the moral fruits of religion are not the consequence of a conscious effort to achieve them. The love commandment is a demand upon the will, but the human will is not enabled to conform to it because moralistic appeals are made to obey the commandment. Moralistic appeals are in fact indications of the dissipation of primary religious vitality. Men cannot, by taking thought, strengthen their will. If the will is the total organized personality of the moment, moving against recalcitrant impulse, the strength of the will depends upon the strength of the factors which enter into its organization. Consequently, the acts and attitudes of love in which the ordinary resources of nature are supplemented are partly the consequence of historic and traditional disciplines which have become a part of the socio-spiritual inheritance of the individual and partly the result of concatenations of circumstance in which the pressure of events endows the individual with powers not ordinarily his own. . . .

But love is not only a fruit of grace, but also a fruit of faith; which is to say that the total spiritual attitude which informs a life determines to what height a moral action may rise in a given moment. Deeds of love are not the consequence of specific acts of the will. They are the consequence of a religio-moral tension in life which is possible only if the individual consciously lives in the total dimension of life. The real motives of love, according to the Christian gospel, are gratitude and contrition. Gratitude and contrition are the fruits of a prophetic faith which knows life in its heights and in its depths. To believe in God is to know life in its essence and not only in its momentary existence. Thus to know it means that what is dark, arbitrary, and contingent in momentary existence can neither be accepted complacently nor tempt to despair.

To understand life in its total dimension means contrition because every moral achievement stands under the criticism of a more essential goodness. If fully analyzed the moral achievement is not only convicted of imperfection, but of sin. It is not only wanting in perfect goodness, but there is something of the perversity of evil in it. Such contrition does not destroy selfishness in the human heart. But there is a difference between the man who understands something of the mystery of evil in his own soul and one who complacently accepts human egoism as a force which must be skillfully balanced with altruism in order that moral unity may be achieved.

To understand life in its total dimension means to accept it with grateful reverence as good. It is good in its ultimate essence even when it seems evil and chaotic in its contingent and momentary reality. Faith in its essence is not an arbitrary faith. Once held, actual historic existence verifies it; for there are in life as we know it in history and nature innumerable symbols of its ultimate and essential nature. Grateful reverence toward the goodness of life is a motive force of love in more than one sense. Gratitude for what life is in its essence creates a propulsive power to affirm in existence what is truly essential, the harmony of life with life. Furthermore, under the insights of such a faith, the fellow man becomes something more than the creature of time and place, separated from us by the contingencies of nature and geography and set against us by the necessities of animal existence. His life is seen under the aura of the divine and he participates in the glory, dignity and beauty of existence. We do not love him because he is "divine." If that pantheistic note creeps into prophetic faith it leads to disillusion. He is no more divine that we are. We are all imbedded in the contingent and arbitrary life of animal existence and we have corrupted the harmless imperfections of nature with the corruptions of sin. Yet we are truly "children of God" and something of the transcendent unity, in which we are one in God, shines through both the evil of nature and the evil in man. Our heart goes out to our fellow man, when seen through the eyes of faith, not only because we see him thus under a transcendent perspective but because we see ourselves under it and know that we are sinners just as he is. Awed by the majesty and goodness of God, something of the pretense of our pretentious self is destroyed and the natural cruelty of our self-righteousness is mitigated by emotions of pity and forgiveness.

The moral effectiveness of the religious life thus depends upon deeper resources than moral demands upon the will. Whenever the modern pulpit contends itself with the presentation of these demands, however urgent and fervent, it reveals its enslavement to the rationalistic presuppositions of our era. The law of love is not obeyed simply by being known. Whenever it is obeyed at all, it is because life in its beauty and terror has been more fully revealed to man. The love that cannot be willed may nevertheless grow as a natural fruit upon a tree which has roots deep enough to be nurtured by springs of life beneath the surface and branches reaching up to heaven.

DISCUSSION QUESTIONS

1. Niebuhr claims that fanaticism and despair are twin dangers that confront us when we are content with merely an approximation of the moral ideal. Explain what Niebuhr might have meant by that.

2. Do you agree with Niebuhr's claim that we cannot truly realize love without religion? Why or why not?

3. Is there anything in your own experience either to verify or falsify Niebuhr's claim that moral rules can command and condemn but not motivate?

4. Evaluate the following statement made by Niebuhr: "The Christian doctrine of love is thus the most adequate metaphysical and psychological framework for the approximation of the ideal of love in human life." Do you agree?

5. Upon the basis of the readings in this section, what is your own answer to the question of the relation between religion and ethics?

Retrospective

The views of the relationship between religion and ethics that we have examined have ranged from Nietzsche's radical separation between them to Niebuhr's close identification of the two. Given the breadth of viewpoints, what are we to conclude about the proper relationship between these two important human concerns?

First we would have to agree with Nietzsche that theistically based values have been the dominant force in ethics in Western culture for the past fifteen hundred years. We might, however, want to disagree with Nietzsche's assessment that we have come to an end of the era when such values continue to be possible. It is certainly possible to question Nietzsche's ethics as the only viable alternative to the nihilism he thought would follow in the wake of the announcement of the death of God. To be sure, many persons no longer look to God or theistic commitments to provide the ethical basis for their lives, yet the alternative is not the complete transvaluation of values that Nietzsche proposed.

Second, we should note that nowhere does Nietzsche present a reasoned case for adopting his ethical orientation. What he offers is a proposal for a radical departure from traditional values as a way of preserving Western culture from an era of barbarism. Even if Nietzsche's proposals were widely adopted, this would not be an assurance that the threatened nihilism would not still descend upon us. Some interpreters of Nietzsche have even thought that his philosophy might lead to and support a different kind of barbarism.

Third, Professor Nielsen makes a persuasive case for the possibility of constructing an ethical system on a purely secular basis that would be consistent with the traditional values of Western culture. Even if we accept Nietzsche's announcement of the death of God, we can still find a humanistic basis for ethics that would not produce the dislocation in our value system that Nietzsche seemed to think was called for.

If it is possible, as seems to be the case, to arrive at a moral system embodying a set of moral principles apart from a religious basis, what does religion have to contribute to ethics? Both Tillich and Niebuhr agree that religion's contribution to our moral life does not consist in offering us a superior set of moral rules. Both thinkers, in fact, insist that moral rules by themselves do not really contribute to moral development. What religion offers to ethics, and certainly this is the case with the Christian religious tradition, is the possibility of a regenerated life. As Tillich would put it, religion offers the possibility of a new being from which moral actions flow as the indication of a reoriented life. Moral rules condemn us when we fail to live up to them, and Christianity diagnoses the human problem as not that human beings are ignorant of moral obligation but that, knowing their obligation, they have nonetheless failed to live up to it. The Christian religion's response is that only if we have a renewed being will we find that morality flows from our acts of will as the fruit of a regenerated being.

It has often been the case that religious spokespersons have held out the hope of promised rewards and the threats of future punishment as motivation for correct living. And, it is said, only a religious view of reality can provide the framework in which future rewards and punishments are possible. Yet it must be admitted that rewards and punishments do not seem to affect our behavior all that much, and the fear of punishment does not seem to be sufficient to sustain us through a lifetime of moral development. Interpreters of the Christian faith have, at their best, emphasized the significance of the life of faith as motivation for moral development rather than the fear of punishment; and central to the life of faith is the importance of love.

It is in his analysis of love as a moral ideal that Reinhold Niebuhr argues for the greatest contribution of religion to morality. All human attempts at realizing the moral ideal of love will fail, but the ideal itself remains important as the basis for a critique of all human societies. This ideal announces that we should not give any human social order our ultimate loyalty, and that we should not identify any nation or state as the perfect fulfillment of the moral order. To do so would be to risk giving our ultimate loyalty to that which is not ultimate, which would result in fanaticism.

Both Tillich and Niebuhr suggest that religion's main function is to provide a new orientation in life, and out of this new orientation a motivation for moral development follows. It is for this reason that both thinkers find a close association between religion and ethics, for their view is that all the values in life are enhanced by a religious view of reality. Central to this view is the importance of a transcendent reality which assures that the meaning of life is not dependent upon human effort alone.

ADDITIONAL READING SUGGESTIONS
FOR PART SEVEN

Two excellent collections of essays on the relation between religion and ethics are the volumes edited by Gene Outka and John P. Reeder, Jr., *Religion and Morality* (Garden City: Doubleday-Anchor, 1973) and Ian Ramsey, *Christian Ethics and Contemporary Philosophy* (London: SCM Press, 1966). If you are unfamiliar with recent philosophical work in ethics, a good source for an overview is Mary Warnock, *Ethics Since 1900* (London: Oxford University Press, 1960). Another good source for a summary and bibliography is Patrick H. Nowell-Smith, "Religion and Morality," *The Encyclopedia of Philosophy* (1967), 7, 150–58. A sympathetic treatment of Nietzsche's philosophy is Walter Kaufmann, *Nietzsche,* 3rd ed. (Princeton: Princeton University Press, 1968). The attempt of Kant to base religion solely on a moral foundation is discussed by Allen W. Wood, *Kant's Moral Religion* (Ithaca: Cornell University Press, 1970).

Biographical Summaries

AYER, A. J. (1910–): Wykeham Professor of Logic, Oxford, and Fellow of the British Academy. Among his many books are *Language, Truth, and Logic; The Problem of Knowledge;* and *The Concept of a Person.*

BERGER, PETER (1929–): Professor of Sociology at Rutgers and author of many works exploring the relation between sociology and religion, among which are *The Sacred Canopy, Pyramids of Sacrifice,* and *Facing Up to Modernity.* He is former president of the Society for the Scientific Study of Religion.

BUBER, MARTIN (1878–1965): Viennese-born philosopher who was professor of the Philosophy of Jewish Religion and Ethics at Frankfurt-am-Main University from 1924–33; in 1938 he emigrated to Palestine where he was professor of the Sociology of Religion in the Hebrew University. In addition to *I and Thou* he wrote *Between Man and Man, The Phophetic Faith,* and *The Eclipse of God.*

COPLESTON, F. C. (1907–): Philosopher and Fellow of the British Academy. A noted Jesuit who has taught at Oxford, the University of London, and the Gregorian University in Rome, Copleston has also held visiting professorships at the University of Santa Clara and the University of Hawaii. His *History of Philosophy* is now in its ninth volume. Other works include *Philosophers and Philosophies* and *Contemporary Philosophy.*

DESCARTES, RENÉ (1596–1650): French philosopher and mathematician who is regarded by many as the thinker who signalled the end of medieval philosophy and the rise of modern philosophical themes. His works *Discourse on Method* and *Meditations on First Philosophy* address many of the problems that have become the concern of modern philosophy.

EWING, A. C. (1899–): British philosopher; Lecturer in Moral Science at Cambridge from 1931 until 1954 when he was named Reader in Philosophy, a position he held until his retirement in 1966. He was a Fellow of the British Academy and the author of *The Definition of Good, The State and World Government,* and *The Morality of Punishment.*

FLEW, ANTONY (1923–): British philosopher who is professor and chairman of the Department of Philosophy at the University of Reading. Among his many books are *God and Philosophy, Thinking Straight,* and *The Presumption of Atheism.*

HARE, PETER (1935–): Professor of philosophy at the State University of New

York at Buffalo and co-author with Edward Madden of *Evil and the Concept of God* and *Causing, Perceiving and Believing: An Examination of the Philosophy of C. J. Ducasse.*

HARE, R. M. (1919–): British philosopher who is White's Professor of Moral Philosophy and Fellow of Corpus Christi College, Oxford. He is a Fellow of the British Academy and has lectured at numerous American universities. His books include *The Language of Morals, Freedom and Reason,* and *Applications of Moral Philosophy.*

HICK, JOHN (1922–): H. G. Wood Professor of Theology at Birmingham University. He has taught in the United States at Cornell and Princeton and is the author of many books on the philosophy of religion, including *Faith and Knowledge, Evil and the God of Love,* and *Death and Eternal Life.*

JAMES, WILLIAM (1842–1910): American philosopher and psychologist. He received a medical education at Harvard and began his teaching career as a medical professor; he began teaching psychology and philosophy in 1879. In philosophy he is perhaps best known for his philosophical method which he called pragmatism and explained in a work entitled *Pragmatism: A New Name for Some Old Ways of Thinking.* His two-volume *Principles of Psychology* was the standard work in the field for years, and his *Varieties of Religious Experience* is still a classic on the topic.

KIERKEGAARD, SØREN (1813–1855): Danish philosopher and major precursor of existential philosophy. His works, many of which were written under pseudonyms, all stress the importance of becoming an individual. Among his most widely read works are *Either/Or* (2 vols.), *Fear and Trembling;* and *The Sickness Unto Death.*

LEWIS, C. S. (1898–1963): British philosopher, theologian, and literary critic. From 1925–54 Lewis was Fellow at Magdalene College, Oxford, and during the last eight years of his life he held the chair of Medieval and Renaissance English at Magdalene College, Cambridge. Though his appointment was in literature, his works on theology are perhaps more widely read than his literary works. *The Screwtape Letters, The Problem of Pain,* and *Miracles* provide a clear picture of his religious views. Lewis is also the author of *The Chronicles of Narnia.*

MADDEN, EDWARD H. (1925–): Professor of Philosophy at the State University of New York at Buffalo. His books include *Problems of Psychology; The Structure of Scientific Thought;* and *Causing, Perceiving and Believing.*

MILL, JOHN STUART (1806–1873): English philosopher, economist, and social critic. Mill was one of the leaders in the social movement known as utilitarianism and was an early advocate of women's equality, as well as a staunch supporter of individual liberty. His works include *System of Logic* (2 vols.), *Principles of Political Economy* (2 vols.), and *Utilitarianism.*

MITCHELL, BASIL (1917–): Nolloth Professor of the Philosophy of the Christian Religion, Oxford, and Fellow of Oriel College. His works dealing with religion include *Faith and Logic, Religion in a Secular Society,* and *The Justification of Religious Beliefs.*

MOODY, RAYMOND A., JR. (1944–): Physician and author; received his doctorate in philosophy from the University of Virginia and his medical degree from the Medical College of Georgia. His doctoral dissertation in philosophy was *The Meaning of Proper Names,* and he was a resident in psychiatry at the University of Virginia Medical School.

NIEBUHR, REINHOLD (1892–1971): American theologian who began his career as a parish pastor in a working class section of Detroit. From 1928–1960 he was a professor at Union Theological Seminary. His books include *Moral Man and Immoral Society, An Interpretation of Christian Ethics,* and *Beyond Tragedy: Essays on the Christian Interpretation of History.*

NIELSEN, KAI (1926–): Professor of Philosophy at the University of Calgary. Author of numerous articles on religion and ethics; his books include *Reason and Practice, Scepticism,* and *Ethics Without God.*

NIETZSCHE, FRIEDRICH (1844–1900): German philosopher and social historian. Nietzsche was appointed to a professorship of Greek literature and philosophy at Basel when he was only 24. His numerous works include *Thus Spoke Zarathustra, The Genealogy of Morals,* and *The Will to Power.*

OTTO, RUDOLF (1869–1937): German theologican and philosopher of religion. Otto held positions at Göttingen, Breslau, and Marburg, where he taught from 1917 until his death. In addition to *The Idea of the Holy,* he wrote *Naturalism and Religion,* and *Mysticism, East and West.*

OWEN, H. P. (1926–): Professor of Christian Doctrine, King's College, University of London. He is the author of *Revelation and Existence; The Moral Argument for Christian Theism;* and *Concepts of Deity.*

PAUL (died c. 64 A.D.): Disciple of Jesus and a leading figure in the expansion of Christianity. Originally a persecutor of Christians, he became, as he put it, an apostle to the Gentiles. As many as thirteen of the twenty-seven books of the New Testament have been attributed to him. Books which clearly show his understanding of Christianity are Romans and Galatians. An ancient tradition says that he was killed by the Roman emperor Nero.

RICOEUR, PAUL (1913–): French philosopher who is currently professor at the University of Paris (Nanterre) and the University of Chicago. Among his many books are *The Symbolism of Evil, Freud and Philosophy,* and *The Rule of Metaphor.*

RUSSELL, BERTRAND (1872–1970): British philosopher and mathematician. He was awarded the Order of Merit by the British government in 1949 and received the Nobel Prize for literature in 1950. With Alfred North Whitehead he wrote *Principia Mathematica,* which had a major influence on the development of modern symbolic logic. Russell probably wrote more books than any other philosopher of modern times. Among his most widely read books, and a good place for someone unacquainted with his work to begin, are *The Problems of Philosophy* and *My Philosophical Development.*

TAYLOR, RICHARD (1919–): Professor of Philosophy at the University of Rochester and author of *Good and Evil; Freedom, Anarchy and the Law;* and *With Heart and Mind.*

TILLICH, PAUL (1886–1965): German theologian who fled Hitler's regime in 1933. He was professor of Systematic Theology and Philosophy of Religion at Union Theological Seminary in New York until 1956. From 1956 until his death he held chairs at both Harvard and the University of Chicago. His *Systematic Theology* (3 vols.) is the most complete expression of his views; his shorter works include *The Courage to Be* and *The Dynamics of Faith.*

Glossary

Agnosticism: The view that it is not possible to attain certain kinds of knowledge. As originated by Thomas Huxley, the term refers to his view that we cannot know whether God does or does not exist. That being the case, Huxley urged the complete suspension of belief.

Analytic: A statement is analytic if its truth or falsity can be determined by analysis of the terms in the statement alone. Statements that are analytically true are said to be either true by definition or logically true. Examples are: "All bachelors are males" and "A rose is a rose."

Anthropomorphism: The use of human characteristics to describe nonhuman realities. In religion any description of the divine in terms of human characteristics is an example of anthropomorphism; for example, the "mind of God."

A Posteriori: Literally means following after and refers to that kind of knowledge which follows upon and is dependent upon sense experience, as opposed to that kind of knowledge that human reason can know independently of the senses.

A Priori: Knowledge that is derived solely from reason independently of the senses. The truth of *a priori* knowledge is claimed to be both necessary and universal.

Aseity: That which has no other source than itself and depends upon nothing else than itself; completely independent. God according to the traditional view is said to possess the quality of aseity.

Blik: A term coined by R. M. Hare to refer to any unverifiable, unfalsifiable assumption or set of assumptions in terms of which we view the world. It is in the nature of a *blik* to determine what kinds of evidence count against it. Hare thought that we all have *bliks*, though some are sane, others are insane.

Category Mistake: A term used by Gilbert Ryle to refer to those cases when words are taken to belong to a different category than their true one.

Contingent: Dependent, not having the characteristic of necessity.

Contradiction: A statement that is internally inconsistent so that on any interpretation it comes out false. Contradictions are false on logical grounds.

Cosmological: A term derived from the Greek word meaning order and used to refer to the natural order as an ordered system. Applied to a type of argument for the existence of God, it refers to that kind of reasoning which proceeds from the apparent order and regularity of the world to God as the best explanation for this order.

Demiurge: Derived from a Greek word for handyman or "tinkerer" who fashioned articles out of materials supplied by customers. When applied to the notion of a creator-god, it refers to the view that the creator fashioned a cosmos out of available materials but did not create those materials. This kind of creator was suggested by the ancient Greek philosopher Plato and by John Stuart Mill in the nineteenth century.

Dualism: Any explanation offered in terms of two equal but opposed powers, principles, or beings. A religious view is dualistic when it suggests that there are two equal but opposed deities, one evil and one good. Such a view is found in Zoroastrian religion.

Egoism: The ethical view that self-interest is the rule of conduct. There are two types of egoism: **psychological egoism,** which is the claim that as a matter of fact people do act only out of self-interest, and **ethical egoism,** which is the claim that people ought to act only out of self-interest.

Epiphenomenon: That which accompanies and is dependent upon another phenomenon which is referred to as its cause. Bertrand Russell suggests that consciousness is an epiphenomenon which is dependent upon the physical body.

Epistemology: The theory of knowledge; an inquiry into the origin, validity, and limits of knowledge.

Equivocal: The use of language in which a term has two or more different meanings. When language is used equivocally in an argument, the fallacy of equivocation results.

Eschatological: Literally the doctrine of last things; in religious thought the events surrounding the end of things. Sometimes in a religious context it refers only to doctrines concerning future occurrences.

Esthetics: Sometimes spelled aesthetics; the philosophy of art and beauty; the philosophical inquiry into the nature and status of art.

Ethics: The philosophical investigation of the principles governing human actions in terms of their goodness, badness, rightness, and wrongness.

Falsifiability: A principle appealed to by Antony Flew which says that in order to be a genuine assertion, a statement must in principle be capable of being proved false, or falsified. If nothing will count against the statement to falsify it, then according to Flew it is not a genuine assertion.

Fideism: Derived from the Latin word for faith, fideism is the view that truth in religion is based solely on faith rather than on reasoning and evidence. Fideism is the opposite of rationalism.

Hermeneutics: The principles for interpreting a written text. The term has in recent years been extended to include more than written texts and has been used to refer to the principles for interpreting any human action in order to proceed with rigorous philosophical analysis of that action.

Heuristic: From the Greek word for discovery; refers to that which stimulates interest in and furthers investigation of a topic.

Holy: Originally meant that which is separate and wholly other; gradually the term took on the sense of moral perfection. The word is used by Rudolf Otto in its original sense to refer to the Wholly Other, the *Mysterium Tremendum.* See **Numinous.**

Karma: In Hindu and Buddhist thought, a law of cause and effect in terms of which one's future existence is affected by the ethical nature of one's present actions; and conversely, one's present situation is the result of deeds done in a previous existence.

Lex Naturale: See **Natural Law.**

Logical Positivism: The view that philosophy has no method independent of that of science and that philosophy's only task is logical analysis. According to the principle of verifiability, which was defended by logical positivists as a way of distinguishing meaningful statements from nonsense, a statement is meaningful if and only if it is analytic or can be verified empirically.

Maya: A term in Hinduism meaning illusion. According to this Hindu doctrine, the physical, visible world has no real existence but is illusion or maya.

Metaphysics: The philosophical inquiry into the nature of ultimate reality. The term can also refer to the analysis of fundamental principles used in philosophical analysis.

Moral Evil: Suffering in the world caused by human perversity, not by the natural processes of nature.

Mores: A term used by anthropologists to refer to the customs or folkways of a people which have taken on moral significance and have the force of law.

Mysticism: An experience is mystical if it is characterized by a sense of unity and oneness with the divine in which the individual loses all sense of individuality and is transported beyond time and space into an experience that is ineffable in the extreme. Two types of mysticism are extrovertive, or outward-looking, in which one experiences a oneness with nature; and introvertive, or inward-looking, in which there is an experience of complete withdrawal from nature.

Natural Evil: That suffering in the world due to the processes of nature, in contrast to suffering caused by human perversity. Floods, hurricanes, earthquakes, and disease are examples of natural evil.

Natural Law: The universally valid principles of conduct known by reason alone and therefore accessible to all people, as opposed to the "Positive Law" of a state or society. Originated in ancient Greek philosophy, Natural Law theories were used by philosophers of the Middle Ages as another proof of the existence of God, who was thought to be the author of the Natural Law.

Natural Theology: That which can be known about God purely by the power of human reason unaided by revelation. Natural theology claims to be able to provide proofs of God's existence either completely *a priori,* and therefore independent of the senses, or *a posteriori,* that is, based on certain facts about the natural order.

Naturalism: The view that nature is the totality of reality and needs no supernatural cause or explanation.

Nihilism: In ethics the view that there are no principles of morality. The term can also refer to a situation in which there is a complete breakdown of all previous ethical systems and the collapse of moral principles.

Numinous: A term coined by Rudolf Otto and derived from the Latin term *numen,* meaning divine power. It refers to that which is experienced as the "wholly other" or as the *Mysterium Tremendum.* Otto also referred to the numinous as the holy. See **holy.**

Omnipotence: Having all power; a characteristic attributed to the traditional Judaeo-Christian God.

Omniscience: Having knowledge of all things, or perfect knowledge; a characteristic traditionally attributed to God.

Ontological: Derived from the Greek word for being, the term relates to the question of being. The ontological argument is an argument for God's existence based solely on an analysis of the concept of the being of God. Ontology is the metaphysical inquiry into the nature of being in general.

Objectivism: In ethics the view that ethical statements can be true or false independently of a person's feelings about them.

Parapsychology: A discipline concerned with investigating such phenomenon as clairvoyance, telepathy, thought transfer, and all forms of extrasensory perception.

Positivism: In general a view which rejects the possibility of metaphysics. August Comte suggested that the history of thought has proceeded through three stages, the religious, metaphysical, and positive. The latter stage is characterized by a rejection of all religious and metaphysical thinking. See **logical positivism.**

Proposition: A proposition is expressed by a sentence that has a truth value; that is, it can either be true or false. The sentence "The book is blue" expresses a proposition. The sentence "Close the door" does not express a proposition. To express a proposition, a statement must have propositional content, which means that it refers to something and predicates a quality of it.

Rationalism: In religion it is the view that truth must be based on reason and not on faith; the opposite of fideism.

Semantics: The systematic investigation of the development and changes in the meaning and form of language.

Subjectivism: In ethics the view that ethical statements are descriptions of the way people feel about certain actions. According to subjectivism, there are no moral standards independent of human feelings.

Sufficient Reason, Principle of: The principle that holds that things do not happen without a cause or without some reason sufficient to explain their happening. The principle of sufficient reason cannot be proved but has been suggested as a basic presupposition of all thought.

Synthetic: Refers to those kinds of statements in which the predicate adds something not already contained in the subject. The truth or falsity of synthetic statements is determined by observation and sense experience.

Tautology: A statement that is necessarily true or logically true.

Teleological: From the Greek word for end or purpose; refers to that which is purposive. The teleological argument for God's existence is based on the alleged claim that the world exhibits order and purpose, which can best be explained with reference to God.

Tetragrammaton: The four Hebrew letters, transliterated as YHWH, which were thought by ancient Jews to be the name of God. Probably derived from the verb *to be*, the term was taken for this reason by medieval Christian interpreters to mean that God's name was "Being." The term was treated with something akin to superstitious reverence by ancient Jews and was never pronounced, though had it been pronounced it probably would be as Yahweh.

Theodicy: An attempt to justify the goodness of God in spite of the presence of evil in the world.

Theophany: A manifestation or appearance of the divine at a definite time and a definite place. Moses' experience of the burning bush was an example of a theophany.

Transcendent: Literally means that which goes beyond; in religion the transcendent refers to that which lies beyond the physical or natural order. The traditional Judaeo-Christian view of God is that God is a transcendent being.

Univocal: The use of language in which a term has one and only one meaning, or at least one central meaning in terms of which its various usages can be understood.

Verification Principle: A principle suggested by A. J. Ayer by means of which to distinguish meaningful statements from nonsense. According to the verification principle, a statement is meaningful if and only if it is analytic or can in principle be verified empirically.

Weltanschauung: The German term for worldview.

Index